D0897956

DA
390.1   194306
.H4
K67
1989

Msgr. Wm. Barry Memorial Library
Barry University
Miami, FL   33161

KOPPERMAN

SIR ROBERT HEATH...

ROYAL HISTORICAL SOCIETY

STUDIES IN HISTORY 56

SIR ROBERT HEATH 1575 – 1649

Sir Robert Heath by Wenceslaus Hollar
Photograph courtesy of University of London Library

SIR ROBERT HEATH
1575 – 1649

WINDOW ON AN AGE

Paul E. Kopperman

THE ROYAL HISTORICAL SOCIETY
THE BOYDELL PRESS

© Paul E. Kopperman 1989

First published 1989

A Royal Historical Society publication
Published by The Boydell Press
an imprint of Boydell & Brewer Ltd
PO Box 9   Woodbridge   Suffolk IP12 3DF
and of Boydell & Brewer Inc.
Wolfeboro   New Hampshire 03894-2069   USA

ISBN 0 86193 213 7

ISSN 0269-2244

British Library Cataloguing in Publication Data
Kopperman, Paul E., 1945-
    Sir Robert Heath 1575 – 1649 : window on an age — (Royal
    Historical Society studies in history; 56)
    1. England. Heath, Sir Robert, 1575 – 1649
    I. Title II. Series
    942.06'1'0924
    ISBN 0-86193-213-7

Library of Congress Cataloging-in-Publication Data
Kopperman, Paul E.
    Sir Robert Heath, 1575 – 1649 : window on an age / Paul E.
    Kopperman.
        p. cm. — (Royal Historical Society studies in history,
    ISSN 0269 – 2244 ; 56)
    Bibliography: p.
    Includes index.
    ISBN 0-86193-213-7 (alk. paper)
    1. Heath, Robert, Sir, 1575 – 1649. 2. Great Britain—
History—Early Stuarts, 1603 – 1649—Biography. 3.
Legislators—Great Britain—Biography. 4. Judges—Great
Britain—Biography. 5. Great Britain—Biography. I. Title. II.
Series: Royal Historical Society studies in history ; no. 56.
DA390.1.H4K67   1989
941.06'092'4—dc19
[B]   88-38052
                                                             CIP

⊙   The paper used in this publication meets the minimum
requirements of American National Standard for Information
Sciences — Permanence of Paper for Printed Library Materials,
ANSI Z39.48-1984.

Printed in Great Britain by
St Edmundsbury Press, Bury St Edmunds, Suffolk

Contents

The Society records its gratitude to the following whose generosity made possible the initiation of this series: The British Academy; The Pilgrim Trust; The Twenty-Seven Foundation; The United States Embassy's Bicentennial funds; The Wolfson Trust; several private donors.

Acknowledgements

The debts of gratitude that one incurs in researching and writing a study such as this are many. That this book represents, although in greatly revised form, an earlier project, my doctoral dissertation, means that some debts are of long standing. In preparing my dissertation, I was buoyed up by the support provided by Dr Frank Foster, my advisor, and by Professor Walter L. Arnstein, both of the University of Illinois. As I revised the text for publication, I looked to colleagues in both Britain and the United States to provide critiques, and their cooperation and care were admirable. A number of scholars were kind enough to comment on all or part of my typescript: Dr John Morrill, Selwyn College, Cambridge; Professor Barry Supple, Christ's College, Cambridge; Dr Joan Thirsk, Indian Institute, Oxford; Professor J. H. Baker, St Catharine's College, Cambridge; Miss Betty R. Masters, Corporation of London Records Office; Professor Robert G. Lang, University of Oregon; Dr William B. Bidwell, The Yale Center for Parliamentary History; Mr Stephen F. Black, Washington, D.C.; and Professor L. D. Neal, University of Illinois. Their comments were of inestimable value to me, and my gratitude to them is in due proportion. It is impossible to give sufficient credit to, or even to name, all of the librarians and archivists who helped me along the way. I will make special note of Mrs Mary Ceibert and Mr Fred Nash, both of the Rare Book Room, University of Illinois, and hope that these two names may stand for the many. For necessary help of a different sort, I wish to express my gratitude to my wife, Diane, for her encouragement, and to our daughter, Melissa, who, as I entered the last phase of my work, page-proofing, spurred me on with the special authority that only a four-year-old can muster. Finally, I acknowledge the greatest debt of all: to my late father, Abraham, and to my mother, Elsa Lehman Kopperman. Their constant encouragement has helped to direct me toward the completion of this project, as it has directed me in so many endeavours.

To all of those noted here, as to many others whose names could not be included within this framework, I offer profound thanks.

The portrait of Sir Robert Heath by Wenceslaus Hollar, from William Dugdale, *Origines Juridiciales* (London, 1666) is reproduced by permission of the University of London Library. Other representations of Heath are discussed in chapter 9, p. 302 n82.

Paul E. Kopperman

Abbreviations

Archives

BL	British Library, London
BOD	Bodleian Library, Oxford
CLRO	Corporation of London Records Office
ITL	Inner Temple Library, London
PRO	Public Record Office (Chancery Lane or Kew)
SBT	Shakespeare's Birthplace Trust, Stratford upon Avon
SG	Society of Genealogists, London ('Top. Mss.' is the abbreviation for the SG collection of Topographical Manuscripts, which is arranged by county and locality — parish, town, or manor. 'Unbd. Mss.' refers to the Society's Unbound Manuscripts collection, which is arranged by surname.)
U. of I.	University of Illinois Library (Urbana), Rare Book Room
YCPH	Yale Center for Parliamentary History, New Haven

Printed sources

(For complete citations see bibliography)

'Anniversarium'	(Sir) Robert Heath, 'Anniversarium'
APC	Acts of the Privy Council of England
CD 1621	Notestein, Relf, and Simpson (eds.), Commons Debates 1621

Introduction

Traditionally, the subjects of biography have been men and women whose lives appear to mirror an age. The giants of history, the Cromwells and the Churchills, have known dozens of studies. This bias toward 'great men' has shaped the historical mentality, as demonstrated in the need felt by many biographers to defend their subjects — no matter how little known — in terms of impact, to argue that they had some profound, even if previously undetected, influence on the political, military, or cultural history of their period.

According to these criteria, Sir Robert Heath could not be considered a promising subject for a full-length study, although a case might be made for him by concentrating on those aspects of his career where he was most influential. Certainly, he knew success. During a lengthy career in royal service, he played a major role in several events that are of undoubted historical importance. Few historians would deny the significance of the Five Knights' Case of 1627 — the trigger of the Petition of Right — or of the government campaign against the parliamentary radicals, notably Sir John Eliot, during the late 1620s. Against the knights and against Eliot, it was Heath who, as attorney-general, upheld the king's cause. His part in these matters has, more than any other aspect of his career, won him the attention — not, by any means, uniformly favourable — of historians. So has his career in the Commons during the years 1621–5, for he was an active parliamentarian, at once a noteworthy reformer and an able defender of the crown. So has his dismissal, in 1634, as chief justice of the Common Pleas. So has his involvement in colonial affairs, particularly in the Carolinas, where he was the first proprietor. But his achievements are not the stuff of which historical heroes are made. Rather, they seem to leave him, as he always has been, a footnote to early Stuart history.

1

In this biography, however, Heath's importance will not be measured in traditional terms. It is not for his impact on his times that he will be studied, but as a window on an age. While his evident influence on early Stuart England is surpassed by that of a number of his contemporaries, few of them can equal his ability to elucidate the period. His term as recorder of London says much about City politics. His career as law officer tells us much about the inner workings of Stuart government. Through the medium of Heath, major aspects of parliamentary history during the 1620s become more comprehensible. His career as a protégé says much about the patronage system, as does his dismissal from the bench. His philosophy, that of a high-prerogative lawyer, sheds light on an influential group of crown servants which, although widely condemned, has been little studied. No less revealing is his private life, as family man and businessman.

During the past two decades, as historians have moved on to ask new questions, and have sought answers through new methodologies, biography has come under increasing criticism. Indeed, some scholars today question whether it is a branch of history at all. Their attitude derives partly from a desire to concentrate on social history, on the group rather than the individual, and also from the perceived — and too often real — tendency of biographers to isolate their subjects from the wider historical context. While rejecting extreme derogation of biography, it is wise to concede that the biographical medium has not met the needs of the new history as well as it might. Nevertheless, there can be a 'new biography' as an integral part of the new history. Indeed, there have been a number of works that have extended the bounds of traditional biography, such as the fine study of Ralph Josselin, by Alan MacFarlane.

It is hoped that this biography of Sir Robert Heath can serve contemporary historical scholarship. I shall attempt whenever possible to answer, through Heath, the questions that historians in various fields are today asking of the early Stuart period. In the text, Heath will be linked to the broader history of his period, while the notes will reflect the ways in which his life, career, and philosophy exemplify or extend the generalisations that historians have made concerning his age.

The tendency of contemporary historians to emphasise large groups is to be commended. So, too, is their drive to use the group as a basis for theory on the nature and direction of society. But historical theories on the nature of the mass must finally stand or fall as they apply to individuals. It is for this reason that Sir Robert Heath, a man who may be better known than the vast majority of his contemporaries, is worthy of detailed examination.

1

The Road to Court

In the world of the Elizabethans, 'family' was all-important. It was in terms of family, first and foremost, that one found identity, purpose, security and direction. More than any other institution, family shaped the world of Sir Robert Heath.

By 1575, the year of his birth, Heath connections were to be found almost throughout England. In Durham were the Heaths of Kepier, a branch that had gained sudden wealth when one of its members, John Heath, warden of the Fleet, had in the wake of the Northern Rising of 1569 managed to secure large tracts of forfeited land. Nicholas Heath, archbishop of York and lord chancellor to Mary Tudor, was the product of a line that was in the sixteenth century primarily associated with Tamworth, although it could have been identified with any of several centres from Staffordshire to Surrey. Both the Heaths of Kepier and the Heaths of Tamworth valued education, the former favouring Cambridge, the latter Oxford. Education had its practical end, most often leading to a career in law.[1]

---

[1] Robert Surtees, *The History and Antiquities of the County Palatine of Durham* (Durham, 1816), I, 65–71; Owen Manning and William Bray, *The History and Antiquities of the County of Surrey* (London, 1814), III, 47n; John Le Neve, *Pedigrees of the Knights made by King Charles II, King James II, King William III and Queen Mary, King William alone, and Queen Anne*, ed. G. W. Marshall, Harleian Society, *Publications*, 8 (1873), 408; John and J. A. Venn (comps.), *Alumni Cantabrigienses* (Cambridge, 1922), part I, vol. II, 347–8 (see under 'Heath'; Bartholemew, Edward, John, Nicholas, Thomas); Joseph Foster (comp.), *Alumni Oxonienses: The Members of the University of Oxford, 1500–1714* (Oxford, 1891), II, 686–7 (see under 'Heath'; Nicholas, Richard, Thomas). Roger and Sir Richard Heath, members of the Tamworth (later, Hatchlands) line, were both benchers of the Inner Temple, and as such they figure prominently in *ITR*, vols. II–III; note also the article on Sir Richard in the *DNB*. John Heath, of Kepier, entered Gray's Inn on 8 Aug. 1620: Joseph Foster (ed.), *The Register of Admissions to Gray's Inn* (London, 1889), p. 161.

As an adult, Sir Robert was at least moderately close to members of both branches.[2] Perhaps he was in his youth, as well, but in all probability his main contacts were with family from his neighbourhood. His line, together with several others, was centred in eastern Surrey and western Kent, most notably in the environs of Limpsfield, Edenbridge, and Brasted. The Heaths of this area generally fell into the broad category of yeomanry and lesser gentry. Most lived on the land, but a number of men from the family — in Heath's own line, the better part — entered the business world of London as merchants or craftsmen, embarked on a professional career, usually in law, or sought employment in crown service.[3]

Sir Robert's people were lesser gentry. That they had fair status may, however, be deduced from the fact that Heath's aunt, Joan, numbered among her three husbands two note-worthy London Drapers: Sir Martin Calthorp, lord mayor 1588 – 9, and Edward Boys, a member of the influential Kentish family that was centred at Bonnington.[4] Her success in marriage may have reflected not only the prestige of her line, but also its connections. In an age that regularly saw in-laws link families, marriage had tied the Heaths of Limpsfield to several other gentry families in Surrey and Kent, notably the Titchbournes of

---

[2] Roger and later Sir Richard Heath figure prominently in the correspondence of Sir Robert Heath and his sons, particularly after 1640. During the late 1620s, Sir Robert joined a relative from Kepier in a salting venture; see p. 265.

[3] W. B. Bannerman (ed.), *The Visitations of the County of Sussex Made and Taken in the Years 1530 . . . and 1633 – 4*, Harleian Society, Publications, 53 (1905), 133 – 4; Robert Hovenden (ed.), *The Visitation of Kent, Taken in the Years 1619 – 1621*, Harleian Society, Publications, 52 (1898), 184; 'Liber E. H.', 156 – 57; J. B. Whitmore and A. W. H. Clarke (eds.), *London Visitation Pedigrees, 1664*, Harleian Society, Publications, 92 (1940), 75 – 6. R. I. Woodhouse (ed.), *Registers of Merstham*, (London, 1902), *passim*.

[4] Manning and Bray, III, 47n; Edward Hasted, *The History and Topographical Survey of the County of Kent* (London, 1778), I, 379n. On Calthorp, see John Stow, *A Survey of the History of London*, ed. John Strype (London, 1720), I, 138; Francis Blomefield, *An Essay towards a Topographical History of the County of Norfolk* (London, 1851), IX, 305. Calthorp left his widow £800, one-third of his estate: PRO, PCC wills, 37 Cobham, 48 Leicester. In 1573 he sold Robert Heath the elder a manor, their only known business dealing: W. A. Copinger, *The Manors of Suffolk* (London, 1905), III, 337.

Edenbridge and the Seliards of Brasted.[5] Allied families possessed, in turn, their marital and social links and provided the prospect of new connections. Heath's antecedents further broadened their circle through the family vocation. Although they retained and in fact progressively expanded their land-holdings during the sixteenth century, the Heaths of Limpsfield were primarily lawyers. Heath's father, grandfather, and, apparently, his great-grandfather took up careers in the law.[6] Sir Robert's own career followed theirs.

Not surprisingly, the clearest direction came from Heath's father. Born at Edenbridge in 1535, Robert Heath the elder was admitted to Trinity Hall, Cambridge, in 1553, but he left without taking a degree. After spending several years at Clifford's Inn, he in 1564 entered the Inner Temple.[7] He was later to map out an almost identical scheme of education for his son.

Robert Heath the elder did not quickly gain either wealth or status from his vocation. As late as January 1587 he was, in an indenture, classed as a yeoman. However, in April 1592 he was designated a gentleman in a marriage settlement. His advance may have been tied to the death in 1590 of his older brother. The early 1590s found him enjoying not only a new rank, but prosperity. When a subsidy was collected in 1593 – 4, he was assessed at a relatively high figure.[8]

Of his first wife, Joan Foster, virtually nothing is known. Presumably their union was brief and if they had issue none survived to maturity. In February 1575 he married Anne Posyer of Guildford. His new wife, aged thirty, was an heiress, but her inheritance appears to have been small. The marriage may, however, have been inspired by motives that were far removed from both economics and romance. On 20 May 1575, only three

---

[5] W. S. Ellis (ed.), 'Genealogical Memoranda relating to the Family of Seyliard', *Miscellanea Genealogica et Heraldica*, second series, 1 (1886), 9 – 20, 117 – 20.

[6] Hasted, I, 379n.

[7] Venn, part I, vol. II, 348; SBT, DR 98/1282 establishes the Clifford's Inn tie.

[8] 'The Lay Subsidy Assessments for the County of Surrey in 1593 or 1594'; *Surrey Archaeological Collections*, 19 (1906), 44; PRO, C. 54/1257; Surrey Record Office, 78/10/1. On progress from the yeomanry to the gentry, see Mildred Campbell, *The English Yeoman under Elizabeth and the Early Stuarts* (New Haven, 1942), p. 34; J. T. Cliffe, *The Yorkshire Gentry: From the Reformation to the Civil War* (London, 1969), pp. 18 – 19; J. S. Morrill, *Cheshire 1630 – 1660* (Oxford, 1974), pp. 14 – 16.

months after the wedding, Sir Robert Heath was born at Brasted.[9]

Childhood and education

Anne Heath gave birth to at least three more children, a daughter in 1578 and sons in 1583 and 1591, but it does not appear that Sir Robert was ever close to his siblings.[10] Indeed, before either brother was born he had embarked on an educational programme that generally kept him away from home. There was little time for childhood. In a brief memoir that he prepared late in life, Heath recalled his youth.

> From the time of my birth, during the first 7 yeers of myne infancy, I was bred up in my fathers house, & there entred into the knowledge of the latin tongue; for the next seven years I was entred & constantly continued a scholler in the free grammer scoole at Tunbridge in the same countye, at the age of 14 yeers I was from thence sent to St Johns Colledge in the universitie of Cambridge, and at the age of 17 yeers I was admitted of Clifford's Inn one of the Inns of Cauncery, with a purpose to study the common lawes: at the age of 18 yeers I was admitted of the inner Temple.[11]

[9] I. H. C. Fraser, 'Sir Robert Heath: Some Consideration of His Work and Life' (unpub. M.A. thesis; Bristol, 1954), 1–3; 'Liber E. H.', 156–7. Heath was born at Brasted ('Anniversarium', 18) but baptised at Edenbridge (Fraser, 3n). Bridal pregnancy was not unusual in Elizabethan England, since it was common for espoused couples (which the elder Heaths may have been) to cohabit before marriage: P. E. H. Hair, 'Bridal Pregnancy in Rural England in Earlier Centuries', Population Studies, 20 (1966), 233–43; Peter Laslett, The World We Have Lost: England before the Industrial Age, second ed. (New York, 1973), pp. 150–3.

[10] Sir Robert's siblings were Anne (born in Sept. 1576), Matthias (Feb. 1583), and John (Jan. 1591): 'Liber E. H.', 162. The best evidence — though not conclusive — that Sir Robert was not close to them was that they appear not to have shared any business ventures, at least after 1610, when the records of his transactions become full enough so as to permit worthwhile analysis. In Elizabethan England, heirs were often close to their sisters, but friction between them and their younger brothers was common: Lawrence Stone, The Family, Sex and Marriage in England 1500–1800 (London, 1977), pp. 115–16.

[11] 'Anniversarium', 18–19.

The hours that Heath spent in study while a child were essential to his progress. At least according to the regulations, boys could hope to win admission to Tonbridge School only if they were able 'to write competently and to Reade perfectely both Englyshe and latten'. Once at Tonbridge, they found Latin to be the common language of instruction, and they were also expected to absorb the basics of Greek and Hebrew. The ambitious programme monopolised each day from morning prayers at seven until five or six in the afternoon. Just as the school days were geared to sober dedication, so was free time. Every effort was made to prevent the children from engaging in 'unthrifty pastimes and gaming'.[12] Despite strict discipline and hard work, Heath does not appear to have been discontented at Tonbridge. At least it may be said that he came to admire John Stockwood, the noted educator who was master 1574 – 86, for while still a student he wrote Latin verses in praise of him.[13]

In progressing from Tonbridge to St John's, Heath shed none of his trammels. The days when Cambridge would be associated with the soft life of the leisured classes lay in the future. During the Elizabethan period wayward students might still suffer in public the degradation of whipping. They were discouraged from associating with the townspeople and recreations of all sorts were strictly limited. Their days began at five, with morning chapel. Then followed a succession of tutorials, lectures, and disputations, before evening chapel and supper in hall concluded the formal routine some fourteen hours later. The schedule seldom varied. Residence was year-round and students were generally confined to their colleges. Supervision extended even to the area of private conversation, which was,

---

[12] Septimus Rivington, *The History of Tonbridge School from Its Foundation in 1553 to the Present Date* (London, 1925), pp. 63 – 70, 87 – 94. Perspective on the founding and purpose of the school is also provided by W. K. Jordan, *Social Institutions in Kent 1480 – 1660: A Study of the Changing Pattern of Social Aspirations; Archaeologia Cantiana*, 75 (1961), pp. 73 – 6; Joan Simon, *Education and Society in Tudor England* (Cambridge, 1966), pp. 308 – 9.

[13] W. G. Hart (comp.), *The Register of Tonbridge School from 1553 to 1820* (London, 1935), p. 121. On Stockwood, see Rivington, pp. 27 – 32. Stockwood included a dedicatory verse to Heath in his *Disputatiuncularum* (London, 1619). While Heath apparently admired him, he seems not to have felt much allegiance to Tonbridge: see p. 41.

except during leisure periods, conducted in Latin, Greek, or Hebrew.[14]

Cambridge served Heath in a practical fashion, playing its role in preparing him for the law. Like most boys who shared his vocational plans, he left university without taking a degree, and in 1592 he entered Clifford's Inn, eldest of the three inns of Chancery that were controlled by the Inner Temple. Clifford's Inn, like Cambridge, was a staging post. According to John Stow, the Elizabethan inns of chancery were largely populated by 'young students that come thither sometimes from one of the Universities, and sometimes immediately from Grammar schooles, and these having spent sometime in studying upon the first elements and grounds of the law, and having performed the exercises of their own houses . . . they proceed to be admitted [to the] Innes of Court'. So it was that in May 1593, on payment of the customary twenty shillings, Heath was admitted to the Inner Temple.[15]

Heath entered the Temple at a time when the method of training lawyers was in flux. The emphasis on moots, readings, and other traditional aural exercises was waning, as young members turned toward the study of printed legal literature or began to attend court sessions in the hope that they would profit more by seeing the law applied practically than by studying its theoretical applications.[16] Years after the close of his own

---

[14] Students broke the rules, however — enough, and in such ways, as to scandalise staunch Puritans like Sir Simonds D'Ewes. J. B. Mullinger provides a fine overview of Cambridge life in *Cambridge Characteristics in the Seventeenth Century* (Cambridge, 1867), pp. 26 – 31; see also W. J. Harrison, *Life in Clare Hall, Cambridge, 1658 – 1713* (Cambridge, 1958).

[15] Stow, I, 78; BL, Add. 6118, p. 712. The proportion of students entering the inns of court from the inns of chancery declined markedly, 1590 – 1640, though the Inner Temple consistently had the highest proportions of entrants from the lesser inns: W. R. Prest, *The Inns of Court under Elizabeth I and the Early Stuarts 1590 – 1640* (Totowa, N.J., 1972), p. 129. The decline reflected an overall diminution of the lesser inns' prestige, and they also suffered from falling membership. In May 1619 Heath was appointed to a committee of Inner Temple benchers that was charged with investigating the decrease in enrolment: *ITR*, II, 113. In Heath's day, about half of all entrants to the inns of court had some university experience: Lawrence Stone, 'The Educational Revolution in England 1560 – 1640'. *Past and Present*, 28 (1964), 54 – 5.

[16] Prest, *Inns of Court*, chs. 6 – 7; W. C. Richardson, *A History of the Inns of Court: With Special Reference to the Period of the Renaissance* (Baton Rouge, 1975), chs. 4 – 6. In Feb. 1627 the Inner Temple benchers, among them Heath, ordered students to stop ignoring their exercises: *ITR*, II, 160.

student days, Heath, having been informed that the son of his friend, Sir Edward Nicholas, might study the law, gave advice on how the boy should proceed. Quite possibly the programme that he suggested was similar to the one he had known as a student.

That he beginn with Littletons tenures; . . . with him studients doe usually beginn . . .; next it is fitt to reed Perkins, who writes of some particular tithes, in such a way as Littleton did; And I would wish he should reed the book of the Doctor & Studient, he shall find some pleasure in the reeding of it, being as a Dialogue: Then lett him reed Justice Stamfords pleas of the crowne, which will give a very good light for all criminal causes; and when he hath gone this farr, before he enters uppon any other of the yeer books (as we call them,) I shall advise him to beginn with mr Plowdens Commentarye, which debates the cases which he reports, with more clerenes & largnes, then other Reporters usually have done. This will be enough for a good while.

Sir Robert then offered young Nicholas the use of notes that he had compiled years before — specifically, the answers to 137 'queres' raised by Littleton, Perkins, and Fitzherbert, whom he added in an afterthought. Like all conscientious law students, Heath, while in training at the Inner Temple, must have compiled a vast store of notes. These notes he built on throughout his adult life.[17] In dedication and rigour, he paid the price necessary to master the law.

On 19 May 1603 — less than two months after the death of Elizabeth had brought the Stuarts to the English throne — the Temple's parliament of benchers promoted Heath and twenty-seven fellow-students into the ranks of the utter barristers.[18] By

---

[17] The letter quoted is from Heath to Sir Edward Nicholas, 1 May 1648, BL, Egerton 2533, f. 450. Late in the century, William Brown, a clerk in Common Pleas, collected, edited, and published a large proportion of Heath's notes in two works, *Maxims and Rules of Pleading* and *Praxis almae curiae cancellariae* (a collection of Chancery precedents), both of which appeared in 1694.

[18] *ITR*, II, 2. By a Privy Council order of 1574, utter barristers were barred from pleading in the central courts until they had been five years in their rank: A. W. B. Simpson, 'The Early Constitution of the Inns of Court', *Cambridge Law Journal*, 28 (1970), 252 – 3. Utter ('Outer') barristers were so called because they pleaded outside the bar; counsel were in some circumstances allowed the dignity of pleading within the bar — hence 'inner barristers'.

his call to the bar, Heath received official standing in the legal profession. He was now free to join the race for clients, a race that he was to run extremely well.

A protégé's progress

It is fair to assume that Robert Heath the elder not only decided that his son would be a lawyer, but also that he would use the law to find a patron. Father and son both maintained private practices during their respective careers, but the law also served them as a stepping-stone toward preferment. All great courtiers numbered lawyers among their servants. The litigiousness of the time in part explains this phenomenon, but lawyers also served to advise and to safeguard the interests of their patrons. The lawyer of a key favourite was himself a prime candidate for favour, including high office.

Heath's first known involvement with the patronage system clearly reflects the role of his father in shaping his career. During the latter 1590s Robert Heath the elder had as his prime patron Henry Brooke, Lord Cobham. Possibly they had come into contact through the offices of Edward Boys, the elder Heath's brother-in-law, for the Brookes were closely tied to the Boys family. All that may be said with certainty, however, is that by 21 September 1596 Heath had entered the service of Cobham, for on that date the latter sent a request to his brother-in-law, Sir Robert Cecil, through Cecil's aide, Sir Michael Hickes: 'This bearer my Servant Robert Heath ys an humble sutor unto my Lord for the next Eschetorship of kent wherin I am to praie your best furtheraunce, and he wylbe thankfull unto you for yt as he hath promised me.' Heath won the sought-for position, and presumably he chose the appropriate way in which to show Hickes — and possibly Cobham and Cecil as well — that he was indeed 'thankfull'. The year before, Hickes had received a gratuity of twenty-five pounds from the successful candidate for the escheatorship of Kent and Middlesex.[19]

On 29 May 1599 it was the future Sir Robert's turn to be appointed escheator, but the next day he deputed it to his father and assigned him all emoluments and responsibilities associated

---

[19] Cobham's letter is BL, Lansdowne 91, f. 36. On the escheatorship transaction of 1595, see A. G. R. Smith, *Servant of the Cecils: The Life of Sir Michael Hickes, 1543 – 1612* (London, 1977), pp. 78 – 80.

with the office.[20] This sequence suggests that the original grant was merely a device to permit the elder Heath to take the office for another year. That Sir Robert's first known office was his only in name does not depreciate the value of his relationship with Cobham. It may be that Cobham won other favours or offices for him, through dealings that are undocumented. Possibly he helped him to establish contacts at Court. Less conjecturally, it seems fair to say that Heath benefited from the relationship by seeing at first-hand, in his father's association more than his own, the manner in which master and servant interacted.

Robert Heath the elder continued to serve in Cobham's retinue at least until July 1601, when the latter asked Cecil to appoint Heath his deputy for the keeping of the royal manor court at Barking. Possibly the last years of Elizabeth's reign also found the future Sir Robert serving Cobham. The accession of James I, however, was soon followed by the disgrace of Cobham, an event that appears to have encouraged the younger Heath to come to Court in search of patrons.[21] The new monarch brought with him a train of Scottish favourites and hangers-on, many of whom were anxious to acquire the services of English lawyers. Heath was quick to take advantage. Sir James Whitelocke, a judge who included him in his long list of enemies, later accused him of being 'a man to well acquaynted withe the Scotts in the bedchamber'.[22] Although Whitelocke's remark is splenetic in origin, it probably reflects the truth of Heath's situation during the first fifteen years of James's reign. At one time or another, he probably served a number of Scottish courtiers, often several concurrently. Like any wise hunter of preferment, Heath knew better than to tie himself solely to one

---

[20] SBT, DR 98/1282. Possibly the reason for the circuitous handling is that it was unusual for one person to hold the office twice, in name, though father-son possession, in tandem, was common; note A. C. Wood (comp.), 'List of Escheators for England, With the Dates of Appointment' (PRO typescript), 71.

[21] Cobham's career and fall are surveyed by Peter Clark, *English Provincial Society from the Reformation to the Revolution: Religion, Politics, and Society in Kent 1500 – 1640* (Hassocks, Sussex, 1977), pp. 261 – 5. Cobham's enquiry about Barking is in *HMC*, Salisbury XI, 291. Robert Heath the elder held at least one post besides the escheatorship, that of clerk of the cheque of the Royal Guard — noted in a petition of March 1598: Lansdowne 86, f. 89 — but it is uncertain whether Cobham won it for him.

[22] 'Liber Fam.', 66.

lord and thereby face the danger that his patron would be unable or unwilling to do much for him. Besides, even the greatest courtier might suddenly fall from grace. Aware of the risks, Heath never gave himself over to exclusive clientage. For most of his career at Court he had a principal patron, but he consistently strove to ingratiate himself with other favourites. Of course, his efforts would have availed him little had he not satisfied the demands of his various masters. The probable nature of their demands is noted in passing by Whitelocke: 'This Robert Heathe was . . . a great agent in new suites and projects for greedy courteours.'[23] Naturally, any lawyer who aspired to favour had to be willing to further the 'suites and projects' of his present or prospective patrons. Judging from his ability to attract patronage, however, Heath appears to have been unusually successful in boosting the wealth and influence of the divers courtiers whom he served.

At some point between 1604 and 1607, Heath won the good graces of James Elphinstone, Lord Balmerino. Balmerino was a royal favourite and a member of the English Privy Council, but official duties and probably personal preference as well generally kept him in his native Scotland. He was therefore a man who needed agents in London, to manage his English affairs and to keep him informed of goings-on at Court. By 1607 one of these agents, perhaps the principal one, was Heath. On 16 June Balmerino and Heath were granted letters patent for the reversion of Sir John Roper's office, chief clerk for enrolling pleas in the King's Bench. Heath gave Balmerino £500 for his moiety and promised him an additional £1,000 within six months of their inheriting the office. Considering that possession of the clerkship was likely to bring Heath at least £2,000 per annum, the price he paid was small. In late October 1608 Balmerino assigned his moiety to a brother.[24] The assignment may have been linked to a deterioration in Balmerino's position at Court. In 1599 he had penned an amicable letter to the pope and James had signed it — by mistake, as both king and courtier

---

[23] *Ibid.*
[24] Egerton 2978, f. 5. On the value of the clerkship, see G. E. Aylmer, *The King's Servants: The Civil Service of Charles I 1625 – 1642* (London, 1961), p. 214.

explained when in 1608 it was suddenly published. After a treason trial in March 1609 he was forced to retire to his private estates, lucky to have escaped the block. In a desperate effort to retain the king's good will, on 10 May 1609 he wrote to Sir Robert Carr, begging him to intercede on his behalf. A gift — the messenger — accompanied the plea: 'I recommend to your discretion Mr Heath, whos sufficiencie will not frustrat your expection, and in trust will not prove inferior to any of his profession.'[25] The move did not save Balmerino, but it gave Heath a new patron.

Carr — later to be created viscount Rochester, then earl of Somerset — was not simply another favourite, but the greatest of James's early reign. Here was a man who could do much for his protégés. Unfortunately for them, however, he cared little for his servants and was less than avid in seeking out offices for them. Heath himself gained only one known office during his time in Carr's retinue, the recordership of Guildford — perhaps not a gift from Carr, and no prize in any case.[26] Carr not only failed to provide offices for his servants, but neglected another prime duty of a patron, that of protecting protégés. In the spring of 1610 Roper, one of his countless enemies, sought to hit back at him through his retinue, by challenging the validity of Heath's King's Bench reversion, but the situation, which from Heath's point of view amounted to a crisis, does not appear to have aroused Carr to aid his servant. Rather, it was Cecil, a man to whom Heath, by his own account, was 'a meer straunger', who came to the aid of the distraught reversioner. On 10 May Heath sent him a letter filled with effusive thanks, pleas that he work to prevent the Carr-Roper feud from again endangering the reversion, and strong hints that the writer wished to join his

---

[25] William Fraser, *Elphinstone Family Book* (Edinburgh, 1897), II, 183. D. H. Willson deals with Balmerino's career and his disgrace: *King James VI and I* (New York, 1956), pp. 146 – 7, 175, 234 – 5. Unlike most of Heath's patrons, Balmerino was generally popular with his contemporaries; note Anthony Weldon, 'The Court and Character of King James', *Secret History of the Court of James the First*, ed. (Sir) Walter Scott (Edinburgh, 1811), I, 328.

[26] He was recorder from Jan. 1615 to Oct. 1619. Although he was 'elected' by the town court leet, he actually arrived at the election armed with letters patent for the office. For this information, I wish to thank Miss G. M. A. Beck, of the Guildford Muniment Room. On the office itself, note Manning and Bray, I, 40.

retinue.[27] Cecil seems not to have accepted the offer, but since both his health and his influence were declining, his usefulness as a patron would in any case have been limited. So Heath remained with Carr, and the favourite continued to demonstrate his meanness and his ineptitude as a patron. In May 1612 he forced Heath to surrender his patent. Six weeks later a new one was drawn, but it left Heath a mere trustee to his patron, who received one moiety in the reversion, the other going to his partner, Lord Harrington. Heath and Whitelocke, Harrington's trustee, were to receive only one-twelfth of the profits apiece when the office came into the possession of their respective masters.[28] In 1616 Harrington died. Carr, after a series of manoeuvres, acquired his moiety and for £800 bought Whitelocke's agreement to dissociate himself from the management of the office.[29] Heath was now sole trustee, but little better off, with the same small share of prospective profits and the office still Carr's only in reversion.

Within weeks of acquiring Harrington's moiety, Carr, deeply implicated in the murder of Sir Thomas Overbury, fell from power, to the regret of few. One of the mourners, however, may have been Heath, for the disgrace of his patron, mean though he had been, removed him still further from the repository of gifts and offices that were the Court's to bestow. But by the close of 1616 his career had taken a decisive turn for the better for he had worked his way into the retinue of George Villiers, then viscount, presently earl, soon after marquess, and finally duke of Buckingham.

It was apparently the King's Bench office that first brought Heath to Buckingham's attention. The new favourite, reaching for whatever might augment his power or wealth, coveted the post, but unlike Carr and Balmerino he was not interested in a mere reversion. With the aid of the king and of Sir Francis Bacon, he forced Roper to surrender his office and at the same

---

27 PRO, SP 14/54/10. On Carr as a patron, see also P. R. Seddon, 'Robert Carr, Earl of Somerset', *Renaissance and Modern Studies*, 15 (1970), 48 – 68, *passim*. It may be argued that Carr was generous to some of his servants, and that Heath's lack of success suggests that he did not rank high in his patron's retinue. Nevertheless, considerable evidence, including contemporary opinion, suggests that Carr was ungenerous, at least as opposed to Buckingham.

28 The renunciation of Heath's patent is noted in C. 54/2150. Whitelocke describes the new patent: 'Liber Fam.', 27, 46.

29 'Liber Fam.', 46.

time directed both Heath and Whitelocke to deliver up their patents. He then divided possession, taking one moiety, leaving the other for Roper. A minion of long standing, Robert Shute, became Buckingham's trustee, while Heath was designated trustee to Roper. The new arrangement was, for a cut of the profits, agreed to by Sir Henry Montagu, who had recently replaced Sir Edward Coke as chief justice of the King's Bench, and on 11 February 1617 it was formalised in an indenture. When Roper died, in October 1618, Heath kept his place as joint trustee.[30] By then he was secure in Buckingham's service, and the months following were to see him established as one of the favourite's most important advisors and protégés.

The contest and the prize

On 1 November 1618 Richard Martin, recorder of London, died of smallpox.[31] Martin, the third recorder the City had known within two years, had held his post for only one month, and a trying month it had been. According to Whitelocke: 'He was made recorder by the solicitation of sir Lyonell Cranfield, master of the requestes, being tolde it sholde be done for him, but he must be thankful. He consented, but knew not in what manner, and being elected, bestowed sum two or three hundred pound in gratuities, but was afterward made acquaynted that 1,500£ was to be payd.'[32] Death cancelled Martin's debt, but not his patron's claim. Cranfield promptly put forward Whitelocke as his new choice for recorder. But then another courtier, the most influential of all, decided to press his own candidate for the vacant post; Buckingham, ever anxious to expand his power base, put forward Shute.

---

[30] Whitelocke claims that he would have been included with Heath in the new patent had not Buckingham and Bacon given Montagu £500 in order to win his agreement to the insertion of Shute's name instead: *ibid.*, 58 – 9. A text of the patent is SP 14/90/59. The battle for control of the chief clerkship has been used by several historians in an attempt to demonstrate that the level of morality in government was low during James's reign: Aylmer, pp. 214, 305 – 6; S. R. Gardiner, *History of England from the Accession of James I to the Outbreak of the Civil War, 1603 – 42* (London, 1883 – 4), III, 31 – 4.

[31] John Chamberlain to Sir Dudley Carleton, 24 Oct. and 7 Nov. 1618: McClure, II, 174, 180.

[32] 'Liber Fam.', 63. Chamberlain notes the £1500 debt in a letter to Carleton, 14 Nov. 1618: McClure, II, 182 – 3.

It appeared that there would be no contest. Buckingham was quickly able to win James's support for Shute, as Cranfield had won it for Martin a month before. The king's approbation was of central importance, for during the early Stuart period all but a few recorders were royal nominees.[33] Still, the votes of the aldermen were not gladly given. In November 1616, while James had vainly sought to persuade the solicitor-general, Sir Henry Yelverton, to pursue the recordership, then vacant, the corporation had sneaked in its own candidate, Sir Thomas Coventry, who was then disliked at Court.[34] Two years later, however, the situation was different, for Shute was a willing nominee. Nevertheless, when the aldermen assembled to hold the election, they quickly, perhaps eagerly, allowed the proceedings to be disrupted by some friends of Whitelocke's, who demanded a free election and levelled a series of charges against Shute.[35] Reinforced by the information that they received, the aldermen despatched a delegation to Court, to inform the king that Shute was less than an ideal candidate: 'The Aldermen tooke great exceptions to him as want of yeares, gravitie, learning in the law and that he had ben divers times out-lawed upon record, and ben bound to the goode behavior, so that he was altogether uncapable and insufficient for such an office.'[36]

James appears to have been genuinely surprised and disturbed by the aldermen's charges. For a moment there was confusion, but then Buckingham 'whispered the king in the ear. Then the king began againe with them, and told them he wold . . . commend an other to them, who as he was informed was a verye honest man, and a verye good lawyer, on mr. Heathe'.[37]

The delegation had hoped that James would permit a free election. Instead, he had put forward another nominee. Without committing themselves in regard to the new candidate the aldermen hurried off. According to Whitelocke, who can never

---

[33] Valerie Pearl, *London and the Outbreak of the Puritan Revolution: City Government and National Politics, 1625 – 1643* (Oxford, 1961), p. 66.

[34] Chamberlain to Carleton, 23 Nov. 1616: McClure, II, 39. Coventry's election may have been accompanied by anti-Court demonstrations; an anonymous biographer claims that Coventry 'became Recorder of London by a publique suffrage and suyte of the Cittizens': BL, Add. 3075, f. 2.

[35] 'Liber Fam.', 64 – 5.

[36] Chamberlain to Carleton, 7 Nov. 1618: McClure, II, 180. Further details on the outlawry are in 'Liber Fam.', 65; John Pory to Carleton, 7 Nov. 1618: SP 14/103/74.

[37] 'Liber Fam.', 66.

be accused of having been disinterested, the aldermen 'distasted' Heath, but in fact he seems to have been little known to them.[38] They did, however, know that he was Buckingham's man and the candidate of the Court, and if they did not 'distaste' him they may well have 'distasted' his connections.

Determined to stand up for their liberties, the aldermen met again at Guildhall, intending, if one accepts him at his word, to elect Whitelocke, who was then anathema at Court. But no sooner had they assembled than Cranfield entered with a message from the king, demanding that they 'chuse mr. Heathe, and no other', or else explain before proceeding why they would not elect him. 'Heerupon the counsell brake up, and they dispatched a committee of seven aldermen to the king, to desire him to withdraw his pressure, and to leave them to a free election. He gave them a milde answear, but told them, if they neglected him he wold neglect them.' James responded, 'aye', when the delegates yet again asked whether he would allow a free election, 'but still pressed his commendation, which he expected they sholde regard'. Hoping for compromise, the aldermen changed tack, asking James if there were any candidate, actual or potential, whom he particularly resented, and he responded that there was one — Thomas Crew, according to Whitelocke; Whitelocke himself, according to John Chamberlain — 'but still withe an item of his expecting their satisfying his request'.[39]

The delegation then left, a failure, but a number of aldermen remained ready to fight. Sensing their attitude, or perhaps being told of it, the Court maintained its pressure. Whitelocke claims that Sir France Bacon 'sent for diverse aldermen, and dealt with them'. John Parker, Buckingham's secretary, informed or reminded the corporation that James was opposed to Whitelocke's candidacy. Meanwhile, the king himself called in the lord mayor and again demanded Heath's election. Not every alderman was swayed or cowed, however. When the election was finally held, on 10 November, John Walter, Whitelocke's successor as candidate of the anti-Court faction,

---

[38] *Ibid.* According to Chamberlain, however, Heath was 'a man generallie approved and well spoken of': McClure, II, 182.

[39] The quotations are drawn from 'Liber Fam.', 66 – 7. While Chamberlain and Whitelocke do not concur on the identity of the man whose election was directly opposed by James, they agree that the Londoners pleaded with the king for a free election: McClure, II, 180 – 2.

received eleven votes. One alderman, after protesting 'that he had been at the chusing of ten recorders and never knew sutche proceeding', abstained. The opposition, though, fell short. There were still thirteen votes for Heath. That very day, he was sworn in as recorder.[40]

Heath now faced two problems. Within hours of the election Cranfield came forward to demand of him the £1,500 that had originally been Martin's debt. Secure in the knowledge that Buckingham could and would protect him, Heath denied that the obligation to pay was his, and there the matter rested.[41] His second problem could not be so easily resolved. The election that had brought him to office had been marked by an unusually open display of anti-Court sentiment. In all probability, the aldermen's fierce opposition did not result from hostility to Heath personally, but it is likely that some of those who had resented his candidacy transferred their resentment to him in the wake of the election. The corporation that he faced on becoming recorder was in large part antagonistic.

The nature of the recordership

When Heath assumed his new post he entered a world of great complexity, one that he was to know for almost thirteen years, first as recorder, then as solicitor- and as attorney-general. The similarity of the three offices is striking, even though the former, unlike the latter two, did not fall within the central administration. Each demanded omnicompetence. Each carried with it a range of tasks that was in fact great and in theory almost boundless. Each helped define the manner of life that Sir Robert knew during the period of his greatest influence.[42]

---

[40] Whitelocke provides the informational basis of this account, as well as all quotations: 'Liber Fam.', 66 – 9.

[41] Whitelocke gloats that 'Heathe must pay the £1500': *ibid.*, 69. However, Chamberlain, apparently working on the basis of inside information, writes that Heath had disclaimed 'all such contracts, wherfore [Cranfield] must find some other way to be restored': McClure, II, 183.

[42] The nature of the law offices is discussed in ch. 3. Neither that analysis nor this study of the recordership is intended to be comprehensive — if it is possible to be such — although they are the most intensive to date. Rather, they are intended to provide insight into the scope of Heath's authority and duties, so that one may judge something of his role in government and the nature of his day-to-day existence.

Heath's new office brought him high status, a fact that cannot have escaped or displeased him, for within the corporation the recorder yielded precedence only to the lord mayor and to aldermen who had previously served as mayor.[43] But his sudden boost in prestige was purchased at the price of heavy responsibility.

By tradition, the recorder's most basic duty was to advise the corporation. It was his charge to attend the Common Council, of which he was an officer.[44] More important, however, was his relationship with the Court of Aldermen, the main governing body in London. The recorder was expected to attend every session of the court, which met as often as twice per week, and to carry out its dictates.[45]

As an advisor to the corporation Heath generally played a passive role, responding to queries and complying with orders, but the situation could demand that he take the initiative. The recorder was the main repository of London's privileges. If he believed that the City's prerogatives were being infringed, by whatever body or individual, it was his duty to warn the corporation. When he did so, the force of tradition dictated that his word be respected: 'The Recorder shall or may ore-tenus, that is to say, by open speech, record and certifie the customs, being traversed. And his certificate shall be as strong in the Law as the verdict of 22 men.'[46]

It was as a lawyer that Heath served the City. Expertise in the law, not mere acquaintance with it, was expected of the recorder; in Stow's words: 'He shall be, and is wont to be, one of the most skilful and vertuous Apprentices of the Law of the whole Kingdom.'[47] Although generally the city solicitor pleaded

---

[43] Stow, I, 159.

[44] A List of the By-Laws of the City of London, Unrepealed (London, 1769), p. 79.

[45] Pearl, p. 58. Heath attended about two-thirds of all sittings during his recordership. When he was absent, the deputy recorder presumably substituted for him.

[46] Henry Calthrop, The Liberties, Usages, and Customs of the City of London (London, 1642), p. 23. Calthrop draws his authority from Sir William Fleetwood's 'Liber Fleetwood' (CLRO MS.); Fleetwood, in turn, cites (f. 30) Liber Albus. That both he and Calthrop concentrate on this power reflects its importance. The recorder's oath also dwells on his responsibility to protect the City's rights: H. T. Riley (trans.), Liber Albus: The White Book of the City of London (London, 1862), p. 268; 'The Elizabethan Book of Oaths' (CLRO MS.), ff. 4 – 5.

[47] Stow, I, 159. This is a paraphrase of Liber Albus; cf. Riley, 38.

London's cases in court, the aldermen often directed him to seek out the recorder's advice on pending litigation. Heath as recorded would also have been expected to advise on the drawing of bills to be presented to Common Council, another function that derived from his legal training, for it was his responsibility to warn the corporation if a proposed bill ran contrary to statute or precedent or if it contained any loopholes.[48] Only a lawyer could understand the subtleties of the law.

That the recorder was London's chief lawyer also qualified him to be its chief judge. The Lord Mayor's Court was his preserve, despite its name, for he acted as sole judge there.[49] He was expected to attend the Hustings, in order to advise on legal points, produce precedents, explain former verdicts, and pronounce judgements of outlawry.[50] Eight times each year he joined the lord mayor and select aldermen in constituting the Court for the Conservancy of the Thames.[51] As a concomitant of his office, Heath while recorder also served as a justice of the peace for London, Middlesex, Westminster, and Southwark. Being a justice, he probably performed some police duty, but again his main duties seem to have been judicial. Throughout his jurisdiction he served as a judge at sessions of oyer and terminer and of gaol delivery.[52] It was he, in his role as justice, who was responsible for taking recognizances for appearance.[53] It was he who, when the Privy Council asked whether a condemned prisoner was fit to be transported to the colonies rather than hanged, supplied the information.[54] When no

---

[48] F.F. Foster, *The Politics of Stability: A Portrait of the Rulers in Elizabethan London*, Royal Historical Society, *Studies in History*, 1 (London, 1977), p. 16.

[49] *Ibid.*, p. 77.

[50] CLRO, Rep. 21, f. 66; (Sir) Edward Coke, *The Fourth Part of the Institutes of the Lawes of England* (London, 1644), p. 247; Stow, 159.

[51] e.g., Rep. 34, f. 202.

[52] He held his commission by charter: Alexander Pulling, *The Laws and Customs of the City of London* (London, 1854), p. 118. The duties of a recorder, in his role of j.p., are well described in Fleetwood's letters to Lord Burghley, many of which are in print: Thomas Wright, ed., *Queen Elizabeth and Her Times: A Series of Original Letters* (London, 1838), esp. II, 37 – 41, 66 – 9, 184 – 8, 291 – 3. For a survey of Fleetwood's career as recorder, with concentration on his duties in law enforcement, see P. R. Harris, 'William Fleetwood, Recorder of the City, and Catholicism in Elizabethan London', *Recusant History*, 18 (1963), 106 – 22.

[53] Many of the recognizances that Heath prepared are extant: CLRO, Sessions Records; Odd Membranes from Missing Files, 1616 – 1622.

[54] Heath consistently favoured transportation; e.g., *APC*, 1618 – 1619, 418 – 19.

clemency was forthcoming, it was he who issued death warrants.[55]

Probably the most time-consuming of Heath's duties as recorder was refereeing. He was a referee, often sole referee, in dozens of cases during his recordership. Typically, the referral process began when an individual or group petitioned the Court of Aldermen in hope of gaining relief or redress for some wrong. The aldermen then referred the matter. An important or complex case might be passed on to a group of a dozen referees, including aldermen and perhaps even the lord mayor. Whatever the number, however, at least one member of the corporation counsel was certain to be included. Indeed, he would be of the quorum, and the referees' report was likely to be his handiwork. Heath, as the highest-ranking counsellor, naturally received a heavy share of references.

Often the issues that Heath dealt with were of no great moment. They might involve mediating between London officials who were battling over fees, status, or jurisdiction. December 1618 found him seeking to resolve a dispute between the 'Secundarye of the Poultrie Compter' and his former deputy.[56] Many of the cases that were referred to Heath were, nevertheless, quite significant in the eyes of the aldermen, particularly those that involved the companies. The government of London strove to protect the companies from competitors outside the City and at the same time tried to prevent them from weakening themselves through internal bickering or internecine disputes. When contention arose, the aldermen were quick to offer themselves as mediators, and they were no less quick to offer the corporation counsel, including the recorder. During his tenure Heath was frequently called on to mediate in company disputes. April 1620 saw the court order him to gather testimony from feuding whitebakers and brownbakers 'and to sett downe some order therein betweene for reconciliation of the differences if he can. And to certifie to this Court in writing under his hand of his doeing and opynion therein'.[57] Assignments like this meant many hours of work for Heath, and the

---

[55] In Nov. 1622 Heath interceded at Court to save sixty-seven condemned prisoners at Newgate, claiming that neither the present recorder nor he, during his term, had wished to issue death warrants for them. Largely through his efforts, all were pardoned: CSPD, James I, X, 462.

[56] CLRO, Letter Books, GG, f. 251; Rep. 34, f. 20.

[57] Letter Books, GG, f. 249.

final reports that he submitted to the aldermen tended to be lengthy and precise.

Sometimes his reports were themselves translated into petitions by the aldermen and were forwarded to the king or his Council. This was particularly likely when the issue at hand involved persons or associations that did not fall under the corporation's jurisdiction. When the City petitioned, its spokesman, more often than not, was the recorder. This role was already long established by Heath's time. Indeed, it antedated *Liber Albus* (1419), the great compilation of precedent and practice relating to the governance of London: 'The Maior and Alderman have therefore used commonly to set forth all other businesses, touching the City, before the King and his Council, as also in certain of the King's Courts, by Mr. Recorder, and eminent for eloquence.'[58] In most cases Heath may well have enjoyed his role as spokesman, suggestive as it was of higher status. However, occasionally he found himself required to protest against crown policy, an embarrassing position for a king's man. When in May 1620 the aldermen took note of frequent complaints over the issuance of bills of conformity — letters of protection from arrest for debt — they strongly implied that James himself was to blame, since he made it easy for debtors to obtain the bills. Heath probably did not approve of this criticism, and it is even less likely that he felt comfortable with the aldermen's order 'that Mr Recorder be entreated to drawe a petition to his Majestye on the behalfe of the Citye, Whereby they maye become humble suitors that his Majesty would be graciously pleased to be spareing in giving Countenance to such suitors'.[59]

In other situations, too, Heath as recorder represented the City. By tradition, the recorder was expected to take part in various ceremonies. It was, for example, his duty to introduce the new sheriffs at Exchequer each year.[60] When a great personage was honoured by the City, the recorder often addressed him on behalf of the corporation. Heath himself learned on one occasion that such speeches did not always win applause. In early June 1619 James entered the City for the first time since recovering from a dangerous illness and, according to

---

58 Stow, I, 159, derived from *Liber Albus* (Riley, 38).
59 Letter Books, GG, f. 251.
60 Fleetwood describes the ritual in a 'diarium' that he sent to Burghley in Nov. 1584: Wright, II, 241.

Chamberlain: 'The Recorder made a short speech in gratulation of his recoverie and excuse of the Lord Mayors absence whereto the King gave no great heed, making little shew of beeing pleased.'[61]

There was still another aspect of the recorder's representative function. He, probably more than any other City official, was responsible for conferring with the king or select courtiers and bringing to their attention problems that were particularly troubling to the corporation. The more distinguished the personage, the more likely it was that he would be accompanied by a delegation of aldermen, but in many instances he was sent alone. Seldom if ever was he merely a messenger, expected only to present the corporation's complaint and await a reply. In reality, he more closely resembled a negotiator, for he was supposed to explain what was at issue and to discuss possible remedies.

As though the duties peculiar to the recordership were not enough, Heath held collateral appointments that increased his workload. Besides the justiceships, there were various commissions that fell to each recorder in turn. So, for example, Heath was a commissioner of sewers.[62] He also served as an assistant to the Irish Society, a body that was helping to supervise the plantation of Ulster. Although the society was of recent vintage, the recorder's role in it seems to have become regularised by the time Heath assumed office. What that role was cannot be defined with precision, but it was sufficiently important that of the assistants, the recorder alone was reappointed from year to year.[63]

During more than two years as recorder, Heath certainly faced heavy responsibility and an awesome workload, but attendant upon his position was power. The recorder was a lawyer. The aldermen were not. Most of the issues that confronted the City involved legal problems. This was why they were so often referred to corporation counsel. Since the aldermen lacked legal

---

[61] McClure, II, 242. Chamberlain also claims that James thought that the speech made light of his illness.

[62] Rep. 34, f. 4.

[63] Heath was probably sworn an assistant on taking office as recorder, as was Shute (Rep. 35, f. 72), but the earliest recorded note of him as an assistant shows him as one 'formerly elected', 27 Aug. 1619: Letter Books, GG, f. 186. There is no evidence that Heath invested in the Irish Plantation, but Coventry did, during his term as recorder: Drapers Hall, Wardens' Accounts, 469/6, p. 45.

training, there was little likelihood that they would reject the advice of their lawyer-referees. When Heath, for one, recommended the solution to a dispute, his comments were often spiced with precedent and the language of the law. His lay audience, distinguished though it was, was likely to be overwhelmed. Even leaving the factor of legal training aside, there was good reason for the aldermen to rely on him. He was, first and foremost, a corporation official, while they remained company men who served the City only on a part-time basis. They depended on him to perform a host of functions for which they lacked the time, sometimes the will, and often the expertise.

The aldermen recognised their dependence on the recorder, not only as an advisor but in his other major capacities as well, and from time to time they acknowledged as much. Such was the case in July 1583, when they bemoaned the fact that outside obligations often kept the noted recorder Sir William Fleetwood from his post:

> At thys present thys Cyttye hathe dyvers & sundry sutes in lawe, aswell for theyre lybertes, theyre offyce and lande as other matters of great importance, the defence whearof cheefely dependeth uppon Mr Recorder, whos busynes & affayres aswell in her majestyes servyce, as thys Cyttyes ys suche . . . that he cannot be so often present at the Guildhall for his assistaunce to the Lord Mayor and Aldermen aswell as this Courte, as in the utter Courte withowt [the Lord Mayor's Court], and the Courte of Hustings as is requisyte . . . how needefull & Necessarye yt ys to have the conynuall presence & assistaunce of a man learned in the lawes of this realm wyse dyscrete & faythfull aswell for the furtheraunce of Justice to her majestyes subjects.[64]

Coupled with the sense of dependence was a sense of fear, that an incompetent, indifferent, or unscrupulous recorder might fail to warn the corporation of dangers to London's liberties or might provide bad advice. It was the recorder's job to speak up when the aldermen were unaware of a problem or were about to take a false step, and if he failed to warn them, he

---

[64] Rep. 21, f. 66.

could expect criticism. Not even his absence from court at the crucial moment served to excuse him. When in October 1619 Heath informed the lord mayor, Sir Sebastian Harvey, that the king was upset by a recent decision made by the aldermen, Harvey responded angrily 'yt was not myne error alone as you knowe for yt was done in open Courte, and yt was our misfortune, that you were then out of Courte whoe might have better advised us'.[65]

That the corporation relied so heavily on the recorder helps to explain why Heath's election was fiercely opposed. The aldermen wanted for the chief counsellor a man whose first loyalty was to the City. They realised that the recorder, like any local official, might be called upon by the central government to perform some duty that fell within the purview of his place, and they would not have objected when, for example, in May 1619 the archbishop of Canterbury ordered Heath to join with Yelverton in mediating in a dispute between the City and local ministers relating to tithes.[66] What did bother them about Heath was the fact that he was clearly more bound to the Court than he was to the City and that he was in a position to do London harm by either withholding advice or giving bad advice. Proceedings of the Court of Aldermen were secret, but Heath was well placed to report to the king or his councillors information on decisions that had been or were likely to be made. He might, in turn, be told what counsel to give, should the aldermen encounter a particular problem. The corporation resented having a potential informer placed in a key office. Then, too, the aldermen may have feared that Heath's deep involvement with the Court would make him an apathetic recorder, one who looked on his post as being a mere stepping-stone to better things. However, they would not have considered it entirely detrimental to have a courtier as recorder. In all probability they hoped that Heath would use his inside knowledge of the goings-on at Whitehall to aid them in their endeavours, as for example by reporting whether a certain move was likely to cause consternation at Court. And it was certainly an advantage to have a courtier serving as petitioner or intermediary in dealings

---

[65] BOD, Add. d.110, f. 180.
[66] Letter Books, GG, f. 185. On the central government's assignments to the recorder, see also Pearl, 30.

with the central government. Still, on balance the aldermen appear to have felt in November 1618 that they had more to fear than to hope for if they elected Heath. A king's man as recorder could do the City much harm.

Forbidden fruit

The furore that accompanied Heath's election reflected a broader, but generally subtler, quest for independence on the part of the City. Commonly, those who valued London's freedoms and wished to see them extended sought to buy the goodwill of eminent courtiers. In Jacobean society, the giving of gifts to gratify those who had done, or might be expected to do, a political or judicial favour was an accepted practice. Sometimes, certainly, the universality of gift-giving was overlooked by individuals who sought an excuse to condemn some lofty personage; the charges that brought down Bacon are a case in point. Many Englishmen believed that judges, who were so often presented with gifts, should be barred from accepting them. But it was nevertheless generally expected that anyone who sought a favour through an official would provide suitable recompense. The Londoners of Heath's day were quick to oblige.

Their gifts were dispensed through two main channels, the companies and the corporation. Companies that were not prospering could sometimes provide no more than an evening's fare for courtiers whom they hoped to win or keep as allies, but even in this case the cost could be considerable if the guests brought their friends.[67] The wealthy companies gave presents on a grand scale. In December 1620, on hearing that Sir Henry Montagu, a former recorder of London, had recently been promoted from the bench to the office of lord treasurer, the Goldsmiths resolved that a gift was in order for one 'whose favour and friendship this companie maye have often occasion to use. It was therefore moved . . . to be convenient for this

---

[67] E.g., in Nov. 1620 the Haberdashers invited Buckingham and his friends for a feast at their hall: Guildhall Library, Haberdashers CMB, L37 Ms. 15,842, III. f. 217.

companie to gratifie his Lordship with a peice of guilt plate'. The plate weighed 147 ounces.[68]

The corporation had a wider range of inducements. It, too, dispensed gifts from time to time. In early 1634 Charles I was given £1,000 in gold, £500 going to his queen, and shortly thereafter the corporation purchased a twenty-six carat diamond ring for him, at a cost of £4,000.[69] Lesser personages received lesser gifts. But the inducements were not always things material. Usually, in fact, they were favours, and while these sometimes went directly to some grand courtier more often they were granted to his servant. Typically, the process began when a high official petitioned the aldermen, requesting that one of his protégés be granted a specified office, in possession or, more generally, in reversion, or that he be granted the freedom of the City by redemption in one of the companies. If he were influential and had shown himself to be an actual or potential friend of the City — or, on the other hand, a potential enemy — he was likely to have his wish granted. His chances were particularly good if he were a judge, for the aldermen, their city being constantly involved in litigation, were quite ready to seek procedural advantages, and they knew that these, though not rulings, were for sale.[70]

The business of inducement was very much above-board and was discussed at length in the City records. When in October

---

[68] Goldsmiths Hall, Goldsmiths Company P, part 2, Wardens' Accounts and Court Minutes, f. 238. Montagu was quite close to both the companies and the corporation, probably as the result of his long term (1603 – 16) as recorder. In Sept. 1614 he lent the City £500: Rep. 31, f. 416. When he became treasurer the aldermen appointed a delegation, including Heath, to congratulate him 'and present unto him the some of Three hundred pounds in gould as a remembraunce of the Citties love': Rep. 35, f. 42.

[69] Rep. 48, ff. 103 – 4, 108 – 9.

[70] The judges and law officers who obtained redemptions and offices (usually in reversion only) for their protégés, 1618 – 30, included Montagu (three times, both as judge and as treasurer), Coventry (twice), Sir Henry Hobart, Sir James Ley, Sir Nicholas Hyde, Sir William Jones, and Whitelocke: Letter Books, GG, ff. 191, 295, 296 – 7; Rep. 34, f. 131; Rep. 43, ff. 278, 293. This list includes co-petitioners. In addition, judges sometimes received gifts from the corporation. For example, the aldermen gave wine to Chief Baron Tanfield in Nov. 1617 and to Chief Baron Davenport in May 1632: Rep. 33, f. 206; Rep. 46, f. 185. Included among New Year's gifts for 1635 were £22 for Coventry, £11 for Sir John Bankes, the attorney-general, and one sugar loaf apiece, total value £25 10s, to the two chief justices, the chief baron, and the master of requests: CLRO, City Cash 1/2, f. 57.

1597 the aldermen issued an order regulating the grant of reversions and redemptions they noted that:

> there appeareth a certen kinde of necessity to admitt some by way of redemption into the freedome of this Citty & . . . during these seaven yeres laste paste with the consent & good likeing of the Common Councell of this Citty and by themselves there hath bene aswell at the Contemplation of letters of divers great personages being privie Counsellors and other principall men whom this Citty for the great and Continuall need they have of their favours might not well denye, and for other juste and reasonable causes admitted into the freedome of this Citty by way of redemption.[71]

Heath himself was quickly brought into the circle of favours. Soon after his election as recorder he was, in keeping with tradition, given the freedom of the City, by redemption in the Ironmongers. In April 1619 the aldermen granted a similar boon to his servant, after Heath had petitioned on his behalf.[72] The following year, he won a reversion for an elderly relative.[73]

The tendency toward inducement was reinforced by the fact that the concept of conflict of interest was not well developed in early Stuart England. It is not therefore surprising that frequent conflicts of interest marked Heath's career as recorder. Even though he often acted as mediator between companies, he was not barred from accepting their fee, and was retained by several of them during his tenure, his closest association apparently being with the Plaisterers. Nor did he shy away from accepting

---

[71] Rep. 24, ff. 138 – 9. This order was often cited as a precedent when in later years the aldermen dispensed reversions or redemptions: e.g., Rep. 34, f. 226.

[72] Rep. 34, f. 119; Guildhall Library, Ironmongers CMB, L37 Ms. 16, 967. III, f. 142; John Nicholl, *Some Account of the Worshipful Company of Ironmongers* (London, 1851), p. 200. The tradition of giving each new recorder freedom may reflect the fact that in earlier years recorders were usually aldermen. Heath probably gained little by his freedom, since it was most useful to those who engaged in trade or manufacture within the City, which he did not. Nor does he appear to have enjoyed a close relationship with the Ironmongers, the company serving only to aid his entry into freedom.

[73] Rep. 34, f. 572. In March 1630 Heath obtained freedom for a protégé (Rep. 44, f. 167), and in Oct. 1631 he petitioned for freedom for another (Rep. 45, f. 536), with unknown results.

cases that involved disputes between companies. When the Plaisterers brought suit against the Bricklayers in June 1619, he advised them how to proceed.[74] Heath used not only his legal training to help his clients, but also the power of his office. In early 1621 a number of hot-pressers who were in Newgate petitioned the Commons, complaining that Sir George Douglas, patentee for the hot-press, had, in league with other pressers, sought to prevent them from plying their trade. When they had resisted, they had 'been imprisoned 15 dayes by Sir Robert Heath, then Recorder of London, notwithstanding he being a Counsell for Sir George Douglas against us'.[75]

The hot-pressers' revelations may have caused Heath some embarrassment, but at Court they appear to have been little noted, for behaviour such as the petitioners described was there accepted as the norm. Nevertheless, not even the Court held all conflicts of interest to be permissible. Not surprisingly, government officials were expected to refuse gifts from, or generally support for, parties that were working against the best interests of their patrons or superiors. Heath sometimes failed to observe this caveat, and on several occasions he suffered for his temerity. One such occasion, in 1620, saw him face the threat of disgrace and imprisonment for his part in an affair that brought down Sir Henry Yelverton, the attorney-general.

This affair had its origins in the statute of 1547 that abolished the chantries and delivered their wealth and property to the crown. Anxious to maintain their hold over chantry lands that entailed religious obligations, the City and the companies in 1550 purchased clear title to some properties, at a cost of almost £19,000. Soon, however, the Court began to claim — rightly, as it turned out — that the corporation and the companies had failed to report considerable property that served 'superstitious' purposes. Thereafter, the Court from time to time revived the issue, in order to extort money from London.[76] In June 1618 James granted John Murray, groom of the Bedchamber, all arrearages from concealed chantry lands, and a new crisis

---

[74] Guildhall Library, Plaisterers CMB, L37 Ms. 6122/1. Other City counsel were likewise retained by companies.

[75] *CD 1621*, VII, 553. In March 1620 Heath, acting on a government reference, reported in favour of the concept of a hot-press monopoly. Soon afterwards he and Yelverton recommended that hot-press apprentices be required to serve the full seven years: ibid., 378.

[76] R. R. Sharpe, *London and the Kingdom* (London, 1894), I, 424–5; II, 87–8.

seemed imminent. By the following January Murray and his agents had obtained certificates, relative to concealed lands, from at least one dozen companies and probably twice that number. Most if not all the certificates were prepared by Heath, and he geared them to the companies' favour, claiming that some companies owned no concealed lands and that while others, especially the larger ones, did, the property in question, regardless of the purpose for which it had originally been intended, was now being used solely to benefit the poor.[77] Murray was not moved, however, nor was James. The total of arrearages was set at more than £24,000.[78]

Even before the certificates came in, the wheels of negotiation started to turn. The aldermen quickly saw that neither the corporation nor the companies could entirely avoid being mulcted and began to seek a compromise with the Court. Twice during December 1618 they ordered Heath to confer with Yelverton 'touching the arrerages'.[79] For the next few months Heath was kept busy by the companies, explaining the law to them, reviewing wills to find the terms under which certain lands had been bequeathed, and relaying messages to and from the aldermen. Along the way, he seems also to have devised a new scheme: not only to compound, but to seek free and clear title to the concealed lands, so that there would be no similar crisis in the future.

The question of composition was dealt with first. Yelverton set the price at £6,000, part of which was to be paid to Murray, the remainder to the Exchequer. The corporation he held liable for £1,000, the companies for the balance.[80] From the beginning it was Heath who was responsible for determining what each

---

[77] SP 14/105/25 – 37. The Cordwainers' certificate is printed in C. H. W. Mander, *A Descriptive and Historical Account of the Guild of Cordwainers of the City of London* (London, 1931), pp. 71 – 2.

[78] S. W. Prideaux, *Memorials of the Goldsmiths' Company: Being Gleanings from Their Records between the Year 1335 and 1815* (London, 1896), I, 129.

[79] Rep. 34, ff. 18, 26. The Goldsmiths also sent a delegation to Yelverton: Prideaux, I, 129. The companies conferred among themselves during the winter, as is clear in Skinners' order of 14 Dec. 1618, that their counsel 'conferr with the Counsell of other Companies what is necessarie to bee done about the Composition required of the Companies for the Concealed lands': Skinners Hall, CMB, III, f. 30. On 4 Jan. 1619 Heath explained the issues to the Ironmongers and urged them to join the other companies in composing: Guildhall Library, Ironmongers CMB, L37, Ms. 16,967, III, f. 144.

[80] SP 14/105/38.

company was to contribute and from the beginning his decisions were uniformly unpopular. February 1619 found the Ironmongers complaining at being called on to pay £100 for their share in the composition, even though by Heath's own estimate the annual value of their concealed lands was only £3 4s 4d.[81] The companies were also concerned that James had not yet promised to give them clear title for their composition. That key issue, the Skinners noted on 11 March, was 'still in suspence'.[82] Finally, in mid-April, the City, with Heath probably serving as spokesman, petitioned James 'to secure them from feares for the quiet enjoying of their lands'. The king responded favourably and on 22 April ordered Yelverton to draw up the patents that would grant the City and the companies clear title.[83] Presumably he acted on the assumption that the £6,000 would be paid, although collection was still proceeding, and slowly, at that.

Then came the crunch, as the aldermen put pressure on the companies to contribute. Probably without exception, the companies welcomed the promise of clear title, but not the cost involved in obtaining it. Perhaps they feared that James would void the patents, in which case their contributions would not even serve the intended purpose of purchasing security. To the pleas of the aldermen they responded with complaints that they were being overcharged or that they were unable to pay. So, for example, the Brewers in early July resolved to retain the city solicitor and direct him to 'attend mr Recorder to shewe him the weake estate of this Companie and howe they are farr in debt alreaddie and not able to paye so great a sume'.[84] Other companies paid, but not what the aldermen had demanded. The Armourers, rated at £100 and frequently pressured to pay by the corporation, finally, on 5 July, persuaded Heath to send 'a note from him to mr Chamberlayne to receave . . . the some of fifty pownds with a submission to pay the rest if we should be thereunto pressed'.[85]

As the weeks wore on and the companies remained reluctant, the corporation became ever more desperate. In September the lord mayor went so far as to offer the Ironmongers an interest-

[81] Guildhall Library, Ironmongers CMB, L37, Ms. 16,967, III, f. 147.
[82] Skinners Hall, CMB, III, f.30.
[83] CLRO, Remembrancia, V, ff. 81 – 2.
[84] Guildhall Library, L37, MS. 5445/13.
[85] Guildhall Library, L37, MS. 12,071/2, p. 805.

free loan of £100, so that they could pay.[86] The corporation appointed the clerks of four companies, the Goldsmiths, Drapers, Grocers, and Haberdashers, to help collect the money, but most of the burden fell on Heath. It was his job to direct the collection, to make sure that all previously concealed lands were included in the proposed patents, and to see to it that the patents contained no loopholes that might serve to weaken the title of the companies and the corporation. At last, in late October, he was able to report to the aldermen 'that besides the Letters Patents to this City, 18 severall Letters Patents were obteyned from his Majestie for the securinge of Companyes and Parishes Landes'.[87]

His pains did not go unrewarded. During the latter half of 1619 the City and the companies treated him with exceptional generosity. On 1 July the aldermen, after being informed that he had been chosen Summer reader of the Inner Temple, resolved to give him £100, two hogsheads of claret, and a pipe of canary. At the same time they ordered the companies to follow suit.[88] Many, perhaps all, did, either in cash, the amounts ranging from five to twenty-five pounds, or in kind, normally wine, but in at least one case in sugar loaves. In voting the gifts, some companies referred to Heath's readership, others to his services in relation to the patents.[89] The latter reference was, however, probably more important in all cases. Almost certainly it was his work on the patents that inspired the aldermen, in January 1620, to present him with an additional £300, in recognition of his 'extraordinary good services to this Cittye'.[90]

---

[86] Guildhall Library, Ironmongers CMB, L37, MS. 16,967, III, f. 174.

[87] Rep. 34, f. 241. The Ironmongers' patent is printed in Nicholl, pp. 203 – 6. Some of the smaller and newer companies refused to take part in the scheme, since they had little if any concealed property. One company that held back was the Mercers: Mercers Hall, CMB, 1595 – 1629, f. 188.

[88] Rep. 34, f. 169. This order established a precedent that was followed, by both the corporation and the companies, when future recorders were made reader: Rep. 46, f. 39; Rep. 49, f. 283; Goldsmiths Hall, Goldsmiths Company P, part 2, Wardens' Accounts and Court Minutes, f. 300.

[89] Guildhall Library, Armourers CMB, L37, Ms. 12,071/2, pp. 809 – 10, Grocers CMB, L37, Ms. 11,588/3, p. 111, and Haberdashers CMB, L37, Ms. 15,842, III, f. 212. Skinners Hall, CMB, III, f. 41; Drapers Hall, Wardens' Accounts, 469/4, p. 40. Other City counsel also received gifts, though usually of small value.

[90] Rep. 34, f. 321.

33

But gifts given in gratitude for services rendered were only one aspect of inducement. Some, in giving to Heath, looked for future favours.

James had miscalculated. The patents had been drawn on the assumption that the £6,000 would be forthcoming. But with the documents in hand and their lands secured the companies that had not already paid their share in full had no desire to contribute further. Most found it simpler to provide inducement for Heath to plead their case to the aldermen or simply forget their remaining obligations. In early January 1620 the Drapers, on being 'much importuned by Mr. Recorder . . . to allow One hundred pounds towards the supplie of moneys wanting for defrayinge the Chardge of the Patents', offered Heath fifty pounds 'for the purpose aforesaid And over and above that . . . for his owne use tenne peeces as of the free & lovinge guifte of this Companie'.[91] On 19 January the Goldsmiths, who had been rated at £1,100, the highest of any company, were informed that they still owed £250 'for the discharge or instigation whereof it was heretofore promised by Mr Recorder that he wold doe his best indeavors'. The company wardens then resolved that in view of 'the good regard that of right' belonged to Heath 'for his greate and extraordinarye favors and paines in passeing of the Companies new Patent, to continue his favors heareafter have thoughte fitt and soe ordered that a peice of plate of 20£ value shalbe geiven unto him by way of gratification from this Companie'.[92]

In view of the companies' reluctance to contribute, and Heath's willingness to overlook their obligations, for a price, it is doubtful whether more than half the £6,000 composition was actually paid. For his part, James may well have felt cheated. Soon, however, he was presented with an excuse to void the patents, leaving Murray and the Exchequer significantly better off, at no cost to the crown.

In May 1620, or possibly earlier, the Privy Council launched an investigation into Yelverton's activities concerning the drawing of the London patent. The patent, it appeared, contained numerous clauses not covered by the attorney's

[91] Drapers Hall, CMB, IV, f. 153.
[92] Goldsmiths Hall, Goldsmiths Company P, part 2, Wardens' Accounts and Company Minutes, f. 215.

warrant. So dramatic were the departures that Coventry, who as solicitor-general examined the document, concluded that he could not: 'Conceive that there is halfe of one of these 27 skins that is within the Compasse of his warrante . . . It conteines things meerely newe, such as the city never had before. Thinges wherof if they had any usage, yet they had no Charter for them.' After listing a number of offending clauses, Coventry concluded that the patent, if allowed to stand, would enhance the City's profits at the expense of the crown and that 'the Kinge should be deprived of the partes of his Regall government, and the city so free, so independent upon him, that their successors in future time, would not expect any grace from his Majesty for any thing that concerns his Majesty'.[93]

With no hope of escape, Yelverton confessed that he had overstepped his authority and begged for mercy, but on 16 June the Council advised James to suspend him from office and to approve the filing of an information in Star Chamber 'against your Attorney as delinquent, against the Mayor, etc., as interested, and against the Recorder also mixtly with some touch of charge'.[94] On 27 June the king sequestered Yelverton's office and appointed Coventry acting attorney-general.[95]

One of Coventry's first assignments was to prepare the case for Star Chamber. By 29 June the aldermen had already heard the information and had ordered the city solicitor, Clement Moss, to prepare a defence of London and its recorder.[96] Perhaps the corporation at first intended to fight, but 4 July found it in a more placatory mood, for on that date the Common Council ordered a committee, including Heath, to draft and deliver a petition to the king.[97] Appearing before James, the

---

[93] BL, Stowe 159, f. 28. Several historians, notably Gardiner (IV, 23), have argued that Yelverton was just mistaken, or was at worst guilty of a peccadillo, and that the real reason for his fall was Buckingham's animosity. The favourite may well have helped to bring him down, but in fact Yelverton clearly hurt the king's cause by drawing the patent as he did, and he was almost certainly guilty of taking a bribe from the aldermen or some of the companies, that he might draft the document according to their wishes. On the first weeks of the investigation, see James Spedding, *The Letters and the Life of Francis Bacon* (London, 1874), VII, 99; McClure, II, 304 – 5 (Chamberlain to Carleton, 27 May 1621).

[94] *APC, 1619 – 1621*, 201 – 2.

[95] Chamberlain to Carleton, 28 June 1620: McClure, II, 309.

[96] Rep. 34, f. 473.

[97] Letter Books, GG, f. 258.

petitioners acknowledged that certain clauses had apparently been included in the new patent without the royal warrant, a misfortune:

> beyond our purpose and intention either to obteyne or retayne anythinge from his majesty which his highnes had not a cleare purpose to graunte and confirme unto us wee then not knoweing or imagininge that anythinge was conteyned in the said letters patents which was not agreeable with his majestys meaninge and for which his highnes had not given a full and effectuall warrante.[98]

James accepted this claim, perhaps with a straight face, and also acceded to the City's wish that all unobjectionable sections in the new patent be confirmed. In a second petition, the corporation asked James to have the case against the City withdrawn from Star Chamber, but on this occasion he gave an evasive reply, as he did when faced with another petition to the same effect. The investigation of the corporation's involvement in the affair continued and Heath, more than any other officer, remained in danger.

In early September the Common Council again petitioned the king. Claiming that the pending case was hurting London's trade and reputation, it begged him to order a halt to the proceedings against the City. This time James agreed, but only on condition that the offending patent be voided.[99] On 15 October, at the behest of the Common Council, Heath undid months of labour, largely his, by defacing and thus cancelling the patent.[100] About the same time, some if not all the companies' patents were likewise annulled.[101] The case against the City was dropped, but not the case against its recorder.

On the day of trial, 20 October, Yelverton heard out the charges and evidence against him. Then, in a move that shocked the judges, he admitted his guilt, claiming that he had acted in error on the patent business, rather than from base motive, and

---

[98] *Ibid.*, f. 272.
[99] *Ibid.*, f. 273.
[100] *Ibid.*, f. 282.
[101] The Drapers, e.g., had their patent annulled: Tom Girton, *The Triple Crowns: A Narrative History of the Drapers' Company 1364 – 1964* (London, 1964), p. 216.

threw himself on the mercy of the king. But the following day Bacon, with obvious satisfaction, reported that James had rejected the plea and had returned the case to its original judges. In swift succession Yelverton was removed from office, fined heavily, and imprisoned at pleasure.[102]

For his part, Heath stood charged with 'privitie and connivance' in the drawing of the patent. Through his attorney, Heneage Finch, he claimed that Moss had drafted the patent for Yelverton and that he as recorder had done nothing more than advise the solicitor on the nature of the City's liberties. Furthermore, he added, on learning that the proposed patent included clauses for which there was no warrant, he had at first refused to approve the sealing and had relented only after Yelverton had told him that he had obtained a new warrant that sanctioned the changes and addition. That Heath had failed to check out Yelverton's story showed him to be somewhat lax, but there was nothing implausible in his account, and he was acquitted.[103]

At least one observer felt he got off too lightly. According to Sir Simonds D'Ewes, he and Coventry were as guilty as Yelverton 'and yet did they not only remain unquestioned, but were also admitted to accuse him, and to plead against him'.[104] D'Ewes is patently incorrect, at least as regards Heath, who was after all tried, but it is more than possible that Sir Robert did not confront the proceedings of 20 October with the same sense of foreboding as Yelverton. The case against him appears to have been rather weak, and he probably realised that it could be overthrown by his own testimony. Then, too, he probably had Buckingham's support in this crisis, as in so many others. But the fact that he was forced to face Star Chamber, after the charges against all his codefendants except Yelverton had been dropped, suggests that he had some cause to fear. Quite possibly the Court was convinced that Heath had connived with the corporation and the companies, working against the interests of the crown in order that he might himself profit. If so,

---

[102] Bacon to Buckingham, 11 Nov. 1620: Spedding, VII, 140; BL, Stowe 159, ff. 28 – 37; BL, Stowe 423, ff. 51 – 69; ST, II, cols. 1135 – 46.

[103] BL, Stowe 423, f. 68. When interviewed by Coventry, probably in July, Heath had made a similar statement: PRO, St. Ch. 8, bundle 30, no. 5; SP 14/115/122.

[104] *The Autobiography and Correspondence of Sir Simonds D'Ewes during the Reigns of James I and Charles I*, ed. J. O. Halliwell (London, 1845), I, 155 – 6.

the trial may have been intended as a stern reminder of where his first loyalties lay.

His brush with Star Chamber behind him, however, Heath moved on to better things. Coventry advanced to the attorney-generalship, leaving the junior law office open, and on 19 January 1621 James sent a letter to the aldermen, telling them of his decision to appoint Heath solicitor-general. Three days later Heath obtained a patent for his new office.[105] On 28 January he was knighted at Whitehall.[106]

Succeeding him as recorder was Shute, Buckingham's choice, the king's nominee. That the aldermen were willing to accept Shute now may suggest that they wished to avoid a second confrontation, especially since they had failed in November 1618.[107] Also, the composition and leadership of the Court of Aldermen had altered since 1618, and perhaps the anti-Court faction was not as strong. Possibly, too, the aldermen's experience with Heath had made them less fearful of having a courtier as recorder, even one who was Buckingham's man. When taking leave of the aldermen, Heath did so 'with his verie lovinge thanks to this Court for their favours and love to him shewed, and with his faithful promise to contynue his freindship & heartie love to this Court and Cittie', and they responded by granting him a final gift 'as a kinde remembrance . . . of this

---

105   PRO, C. 66/2231; Rep. 35, f. 72.
106   W. A. Shaw (comp.), *The Knights of England* (London, 1906), I, 176. The knighting of law officers did not become automatic until 1720: J. L. J. Edwards, *The Law Officers of the Crown* (London, 1964), p. 283. However, it was the rule in Heath's day, even though there were exceptions, notably William Noy.
107   Ironically, Shute died within a few weeks of gaining offfice: McClure, II, 343 (Chamberlain to Carleton, 10 Feb. 1621). Chamberlain had heard that the reason why Heath and Shute were promoted was so that Buckingham might save their share, £700 – 800, of the King's Bench office: *ibid.*, 337 – 8 (letter to Carleton, 3 Feb. 1621). In fact, however, Heath retained his share in the office until 1629 (C. 54/2813), and the promotion from recorder to solicitor-general was common, having been given earlier to Coke and Coventry, among others. More plausible is Chamberlain's claim (*ibid.*, 337) that Shute has been 'so urged that [the aldermen] could not put him of'. Undoubtedly the court put pressure on the corporation, though it is still noteworthy that they did not take a stand comparable to the one they had in Nov. 1618. On 8 Sept. 1631 John Pory reported to Sir Thomas Puckering that the king had resolved to allow the City 'free choice of their recorder': Thomas Birch (ed.), *The Court and Times of Charles the First* (London, 1849), II, 130. If Charles reached such a resolution, he certainly was not true to it, then or in the future; note Pearl, p. 71n.

Courte'.[108] These last moments may have been formulaic, but in fact Sir Robert did retain a strong interest in City affairs, and for their part the aldermen and the companies too do seem to have been impressed by his efforts while recorder. From shaky beginnings, he had gained at least their approval, perhaps their esteem.

Clearly the most important effect that the recordership had on Heath's career was that it began it. Had he not, by a twist of fate, gained the office, he might well have passed his life toiling in obscurity. As it was, his first major office led neatly to his second and so paved the way to his central years of influence. It also served to enrich him — in cash, obviously, but also in contacts, for during his time as recorder he became close to a number of liverymen and other City notables.

Heath's term as recorder likewise serves the historian well. The records that relate to the position are full enough to provide insight into his work in an official capacity, as well to give some sense of his character. They reveal that he ably fulfilled the requirements of his place. The reports that he submitted to the aldermen were full and well-researched. His investigation of wills, relative to concealments, was meticulous, as the companies themselves recognised. In every respect, the records suggest a dutiful and diligent official, the only kind that could have mastered the rigorous duties that confronted Heath in London and later at Whitehall.

The same records, however, also reveal a man whose services could usually be bought. The notion that officials should be willing to do favours in return for payment grew side by side with the patronage system, which matched service and recompense in the same fashion. Both systems served Sir Robert well and seem to have had his wholehearted approval. During his time as recorder he profited as never before, because the favours that he could do in return for gifts were far greater than they had earlier been. As a law officer he was to profit even more, for his stock of favours continued to grow.

Heath was grasping, but there was also much of the idealist in him. In all probability, long before 1621 he had been anxious to serve his king and his nation. That he realised that crown office would also enable him to serve himself is undoubtedly true. Nevertheless, selfish aims were not his sole motivation in

---

[108] Rep. 35, f. 96.

39

seeking office. As solicitor-general, he had found his way into crown service. He could think of the profits that his new office would probably bring, and of the possibility of further promotion. But he could also think of the powers that attended his new place, and of the opportunities to serve that they provided. Indeed, he was to serve well. His road to Court had been long and not without its crosses, but now that he had found high office he was to establish a record of personal and public achievement that could be matched by few crown officials of his half-century.

2

Three Circles

The man who in January 1621 surrendered his place as recorder of London in order to take crown office was well into middle age, nearly forty-six. His basic philosophy and personality had long since been established, and the years in which they had developed are not well documented. But in spite of the paucity of evidence, it is possible to judge which elements were most probably responsible for moulding Sir Robert Heath. Like everyone, he was shaped by his environment. Dominating his world were, in turn, the Inner Temple, the Court, and his own household. Within these he found most of his close associates, the circles of friends and relatives that formed his attitudes. In order to understand him it is of paramount importance to determine how he viewed each institution and how he interacted with the members of each circle.

The Temple

It is likely that Robert Heath the elder was, almost from the moment of his son's birth, intent on directing the boy towards a legal career. The future Sir Robert therefore probably realised at an early age that his education would be centered not on grammar school nor on university, but on an inn of court. Perhaps this awareness explains why in later years he looked back on Tonbridge School and on St John's with some detachment. He sent none of his children to Tonbridge, and although he did, in 1630, provide St John's with a minor benefaction — a set of *Collections of the Councils of the Church*, valued at twenty pounds — all five of his sons were enrolled in other Cambridge colleges.[1] It is also noteworthy that he grew up, and probably always was, an orthodox Anglican, despite the fact that Tonbridge during Stockwood's term as master, and St John's, during the mastership of William Whitaker, years that included Heath's time as a student, were both staunchly Puritan.[2] Neither place can in fact be said to have retained a hold over Heath's mind, any more than it did over his affections. Likewise Clifford's Inn. Tonbridge, St John's, and Clifford's were all staging posts to Heath, and he seems to have framed his attitudes towards them accordingly. How different, from the beginning, were his feelings for the Inner Temple.

For nearly fifty years, from the time of his entrance until the civil war took him from London, the Inner Temple served Heath as a primary residence. Indeed, he probably spent more days and nights there than he did at any other address. His chambers, which became progressively more commodious as his stature increased, served him as study, office, and parlour. In most respects the Temple was his home, and he loved it.

Within that home, the residents were basically of two types. Many inmates had no intention of practising the law. Typically, they were the sons of large land-owners, and their responsibility while at the Temple, as determined by their fathers, was to learn such aspects of the legal system as might serve them in good stead when they came to manage the family property. Some parents, too, sent their sons to the inns of court in the hope that they would acquire the social graces, for London was the centre of fashion and culture, and the inns, with their pageants and masques, contributed mightily to its reputation.[3] Heath may well have been unimpressed by young men who sought only a smattering of law, or polish, at the Temple. He in any case is not known to have become friendly with any of them. It was to the serious students of law that he bound himself.

---

[1] Venn, Part II, vol. I, 347 – 8; Thomas Baker, *History of the College of St John the Evangelist, Cambridge* (Cambridge, 1869), pp. 340, 498.

[2] On Whitaker's career at St John's, see H. C. Porter, *Reformation and Reaction in Tudor Cambridge* (Cambridge, 1958), pp. 183 – 201.

[3] The pattern of life, particularly of entertainment, is best described in Richardson, chs. 3, 6. On the quality of membership, see Prest, chs. 2 – 3. T. G. Barnes claims that Prest is excessively critical in asserting that those who did not plan to practise the law learned little of it; instead, he believes, they learned by 'court-watching and routine contact with the profession': 'Star Chamber Litigants and Their Counsel, 1596 – 1641', *Legal Records and the Historian*, ed. J. H. Baker, Royal Historical Society, *Studies in History*, 7 (London, 1978), 23.

Heath's time as a member coincided with perhaps the greatest period in the history of the Inner Temple. Numbered among his fellow-members were Coke and Selden, the greatest juris-prudents of their age, and lawyers of only slightly less stature, men like Sir George Croke, whose family was in 1631 joined to Heath's by marriage. Although some of the finest legal thinkers at the Temple held anti-Court philosophies, a fact that occasion-ally brought them into open conflict with Heath, Sir Robert may well have been dazzled by the array of talent that he saw around him. He probably did not have a love of learning in the broad sense, caring little for the classics, for philosophy, or in general for subjects that did not have a practical use. However, he was rigorous in his study of the law, and he expected the men who shared his vocation to share his dedication. For the members of the Temple who were learned in the law, he had respect, if not always affection.[4]

Not only the erudition of his colleagues would have impressed Heath. Motivated as he was to serve the crown — in large part, so that he might serve himself — he was almost certainly impressed by the wordly success of his fellow-Templars. Under the first two Stuarts, the Inner Temple, the smallest inn by membership, won easily the largest share of appointments to the bench and to law offices.[5]

As a Templar, then, Heath shared the company of the great legal thinkers and high crown officials. Such association was probably a source of satisfaction to him, for it suggested that his inn held the central place in the legal world of England, and he held that world in reverence. Throughout his long life, he extolled the law and the practice of the law. When in 1627 he as treasurer of the Inner Temple responded to a reader's address, he: 'Commended the R. his speech for learning & discreet, & approved much, what he sayd of the study & profession of the

---

[4] Unfortunately, Heath's attitudes toward Coke and Selden as individuals are unknown. He was generally antagonistic towards critics of the crown: see pp. 219 – 20. But it quite possible that he respected those critics who could buttress their arguments with erudition, particularly in the law.

[5] Note the enrolment figures in Prest, pp. 244 – 5. The numbers of justiceships of the King's Bench and Common Pleas, baronages of the Exchequer, and law offices held, 1603 – 40, are as follows: Inner Temple, 28 (18 individuals), 39.7%; Gray's Inn, 20 (14), 27.4%; Lincoln's Inn, 15 (10), 19.2%; Middle Temple, 10 (10), 13.7%.

law (which he greatly praised) desiring the gent, & students to make use of it.[6]

Sir Robert's love of the legal profession was not generally shared by his countrymen. Many instead felt the anger that prompted Shakespeare's butcher, Dick, to demand of Jack Cade: 'The first thing we do, let's kill all the lawyers', and they would have applauded the resolve of More's Utopians to 'utterly exclude and banish all proctors, and sergeants of the law'. The poor especially, but members of all classes, commonly considered lawyers to be the oppressors, rather than the defenders, of justice. They held the law in little regard at best, and when it was in the hands of devious and subtle lawyers they thought it the scourge of honest men. In an age when both litigiousness and the number of lawyers were on the rise, many Englishmen saw legal chicanery at the root of the contention that was all around them. According to Sir Thomas Wilson, Heath's contemporary, only a few lawyers enjoyed a legitimate practice, while the others lived 'by pettifogging, seeking meanes to sett their neighbours att variance whereby they may gayne on both sides. This is one of the greatest inconveniences in the land, that the number of the lawyers are so great they undoe the country people and buy up all the the lands that are to be sold'.[7] In fact, it appears that increasing litigation created a demand for more lawyers, rather than vice versa.[8] But this reality is less important than what Wilson and his contemporaries believed to be the truth.

That his vocation suffered incessant attacks seems only to have reinforced Heath's devotion to it. And since the Inner

---

[6] Cambridge University Library, Dd. 5. 8., f. 167.

[7] 'The State of England Anno Dom. 1600', ed. F. J. Fisher, Camden Society, *Miscellany*, 16 (1936), 25.

[8] That the number of lawyers, and the amount of litigation, increased sharply in the late Tudor-early Stuart period is beyond question; note C. W. Brooks, 'Litigants and Attorneys in the King's Bench and Common Pleas, 1560 – 1640', in Baker, 40 – 59. However, the increase in the number of lawsuits, and consequently of lawyers, seems to have grown mainly from an increasing willingness of Englishmen, landowners especially, to use litigation to satisfy their greed or malice: *ibid.*, esp. 45 – 52; T. G. Barnes, 'Due Process and Slow Process in the Late Elizabethan-Early Stuart Star Chamber', *The American Journal of Legal History*, 6 (1962), 337 – 41. That the greed of clients, more than of lawyers, was responsible for many lawsuits was recognised by some non-lawyers of Heath's day; note *The Autobiography of Thomas Whythorne*, ed. J. M. Osborn (Oxford, 1961), p. 82. The increasing complexity of English life, as well as the rise in litigation, helps to explain the increase in the number of lawyers: Clark, pp. 279 – 84.

Temple represented, for him, the embodiment of that vocation, he was deeply loyal to the inn and its members. He regularly interceded with influential friends in an effort to win preferment for Templars.[9] And he was willing to fight for the prerogatives of his inn. When in 1628 Dr Paul Micklethwaite, master of the Temple, directed that members of the Temple inns were to take communion together at table — Inner Templars had been allowed to take the wine first, a procedure that had offended the members of the Middle Temple — Heath, acting as spokesman for his inn, demanded that he observe tradition. On meeting refusal, Sir Robert initiated a campaign, in the end unsuccessful, to have Micklethwaite removed by the Privy Council.[10]

Heath would probably have been devoted to the Inner Temple regardless of his status at the inn, but a series of Temple offices that he won during middle age provided him with both greater opportunity and greater motivation to fight for his society. During the early 1610s he held various minor posts at the inn, but his first significant honour did not come until May 1617, when the Temple benchers called him to their ranks. This promotion probably did not reflect a sudden recognition of his merits, but rather a desire on the part of the benchers to please his new patron, Buckingham, for that year saw another of Buckingham's protégés, Shute — scarcely a giant in the legal profession — elevated to the bench of Gray's Inn.[11] Of the twenty-eight members of the Inner Temple who were promoted

---

[9] Heath to Conway, 27 Nov. 1624, SP 14/175/63; petition of Heath (and others) to East India Company, 18 Feb. 1625: *Calendar of State Papers, Colonial Series*, East Indies, 1625 – 29, p. 31.

[10] The fullest discussion of the Micklethwaite affair in print is in *ITR*, II, lxxxi – ii. However, the best extant is John Wilde, 'A Treatise on the Duties of the Officers and Members of the Inner Temple', ff. 1 – 4: ITL, Inner Temple Miscellanea, XXXI. Ironically, it was Heath, then treasurer, who acted as spokesman for both inns in petitioning the king, on 30 June and 4 July 1627, to appoint Micklethwaite master: SP 16/118/39; SP 16/120/23. On Micklethwaite, see also Prest, *Inns of Court*, pp. 199 – 201.

[11] H. H. A. Cooper, 'Promotion and Politics amongst the Common Law Judges of the Reigns of James I and Charles I', unpub. M.A. thesis (Liverpool, 1964), 24. Historians have tended to assume that elevation to the bench reflected a recognition of merit, but such was true in only a minority of cases. Heath's early offices are noted in *ITR*, II, 69, 82, 103, 104; 'Anniversarium', 19. His appointment as reader of Clifford's Inn (1607 – 09) was probably made at the behest of the Inner Temple benchers; readers at inns of Chancery served as liaisons for parent inns: D. S. Bland, 'Learning Exercises and Readers at the Inns of Chancery in the Fifteenth and Sixteenth Centuries', *Law Quarterly Review*, 95 (1979), 250 – 1.

to the rank of utter barrister on the same day as Heath, in 1603, only six ever joined him on the bench, and at least five of them had significant Court links prior to their elevation.[12] When in November 1625 Heath was appointed treasurer of the Temple, a position that he was to hold for three years, political consider-ations may again have dictated the choice. Between 1617 and 1640, every Inner Temple treasurer was an occupant of one of the two law offices of the crown, and Sir Robert, newly appointed attorney-general, fit neatly into that pattern.[13] The years that saw Heath's rise at the Temple saw also a general attempt by the inns of court, and perhaps his most of all, to placate a crown that was increasingly demanding and inter-ventionist.[14]

Regardless of whether Heath's advancement at the Temple was due largely or even entirely to his Court connections, he seems to have valued the honours that came his way. The evidence indicates that he was conscientious in carrying out the duties of his places, and quite possibly his dedication was enhanced by the satisfaction that fellow-Templars recognised his achievements on their behalf. During his fourteen years as a bencher, 1617 – 31, he attended more than ninety per cent of the Temple parliaments, a record apparently unmatched during the period — this, despite the growing burdens associated with his crown offices. Nor were his duties restricted to attending parliaments, for he served on several committees of benchers and carried out various parliamentary directives.[15] One assign-ment that he may well have wished to avoid was given him in April 1619, when parliament appointed him Summer reader. Since the reader was required to provide a feast for his society, the office involved considerable expense, and during the seventeenth century a number of Templars, including Sir Robert's son John, in 1662, sought to evade this 'honour'.[16]

---

12 P. E. Kopperman, 'Sir Robert Heath (1575 – 1649): A Biography', unpub. Ph.D. dissertation (Univ. of Illinois, 1972), 70 – 2.
13 William Dugdale, *Origines Juridiciales* (London, 1666), pp. 170 – 1.
14 Prest, ch. 10; Richardson, ch. 9.
15 Relying on Inderwick's listings, which are not complete but include the most notable benchers, Heath attended 127, perhaps 128, of the 140 parliaments for which he was eligible: *ITR*, II, 105 – 90, *passim*. Examples of his assignments are *ibid.*, 108, 113, 148.
16 His petition to Hyde is included in SBT, DR 98/1652. He was in fact excused, on 11 May 1662, on the strength of a letter from Charles II to the benchers: *ITR*, IV, 9.

Heath seems not to have opposed the appointment, but he undoubtedly welcomed the wine and cash that the corporation and companies of London provided in 1619, for the gifts helped defray expenses.[17] Six years later, he faced a still heavier burden, because on his appointment as treasurer he assumed the single most demanding office at the Inner Temple. In keeping accounts, Heath as treasurer was assisted by a deputy, but he remained ultimately responsible for Temple finances. Furthermore, it was his duty to conduct parliament. Petitions were normally directed to the treasurer; society contracts were drawn by him. Finally, he was expected to carry out government directives regarding his inn, directives that most often dealt with problems of discipline or governance. For fulfilling these responsibilities, as well as a host of lesser tasks, the treasurer received no salary.[18] Nevertheless, Heath appears to have carried out his duties well. Some of the accounts that he kept while treasurer have survived, as have several petitions that he presented at Court on behalf of his society.[19]

Heath's willingness to work for the Inner Temple — even to fight for it, as he did in the Micklethwaite case — reflected a fierce dedication to his inn. Within the Temple he enjoyed the company of men who shared his vocation and his interests. While he was a young man a circle of Templars helped to form his philosophy, in his mature years they served to reinforce it, and throughout his life they provided support. Small wonder, then, that he was strongly attached to the Temple. With all sincerity he could write, as he did in February 1642, almost fifty

---

[17] See pp. 33 – 4.
[18] On the treasurership, see Dugdale, p. 200; Richardson, pp. 22 – 3. Prest claims (*Inns of Court*, pp. 75 – 6) that by 1640 the treasurers of all four inns had lost most real power, their duties instead being handled mainly by the sub-treasurer and other minor officials. However, the evidence suggests that, at least at the Middle Temple, both the power and the prestige of the treasurer increased during the seventeenth century: 'Rules & Government of the Middle Temple' (ITL, Inner Temple Miscellanea, XXXIII), ff. 7 – 8, 28. The nature of the office of sub-treasurer of the Inner Temple, as it existed in 1682, is discussed in 'Order &c. as to Officers & Servants of the Inn' (ITL, Inner Temple Records, XXV), f. 12.
[19] Some of Heath's accounts are noted in Egerton 2981, ff. 1 – 3; SP 16/39/21 is his complete audited account for 1625 – 6.

years after he had entered the inn: 'I esteem it my best title to be a member.'[20]

'The Duke's Creatures'

Heath's second circle was centred on the Court. It did not exclude his first, for a number of fellow-Templars were present there as well, seeking, as he did, the benefits of favour. Although the crown had many offices at its disposal, most were neither lucrative enough nor responsible enough to satisfy the demands of educated and capable men. For the scholars and the professionals of Heath's day, the search for office usually ended in frustration.[21] Nor did the gaining of place ensure a tranquil future. At the king's whim, even the greatest of courtiers might fall, and for the men who were cast out oblivion was a common end. As one of Heath's contemporaries noted: 'A cashiered Courtier is an *Almanack* of the last Year, remembered by nothing but the great Eclipse.'[22] If not even the greatest courtiers could rest easy in their places, how much sharper was the worry shared by lowly office-seekers. For them, the fear was not that they might be cast into oblivion, but that they might never rise out of it. In his early years, Heath presumably shared their concern. His eventual success in finding office merely brought him to the second stage of apprehension.

At the centre of this insecure world of the Court was, in fact as well as in theory, the king. Sir Robert served both of the first

---

[20] Heath to Nicholas Cholmeley, the Inner Temple treasurer, 4 Feb.: ITL, Miscellaneous Mss., f. 77. The letter was written to obtain a favour — the special admission of Francis Heath — but the request was fairly standard, and there is no reason to doubt Heath's assertion.

[21] M. H. Curtis suggests that the universities inadvertently helped to create a job glut for office-seekers by producing more qualified candidates than there were places to fill. In the end, he claims, the unemployed intellectuals became frustrated and alienated, a trigger for the Civil War: 'The Alienated Intellectuals of Early Stuart England', *Past and Present*, 23 (1962), 25 – 41. His argument is plausible.

[22] John Hacket, *Scrinia Reserata: A Memorial Offered to the Great Deservings of John Williams, D.D.* (London, 1693), II, 26. On the other hand, it was not unusual for a disgraced courtier to rise again, and Heath's own career represented a case in point: below, ch. 9.

two Stuarts, but he seems to have been close only to the second. James I appears not even to have been aware of Heath's existence prior to the day when, on Buckingham's advice, he nominated him to be recorder, for at that time he was able to tell the assembled aldermen only what he had just been 'informed' of concerning Heath. Nor did Sir Robert's elevation to the solicitor-generalship bring him much closer to the king, for James communicated with him primarily through the secretaries of state, while Heath generally spoke to the king through important courtiers, notably Buckingham. Although there is no reason to believe that Heath disliked James, surviving documents contain not a word written or spoken by Sir Robert to suggest that he had much affection for him. Charles I, on the other hand, he once described as being 'the best of men', and there is little question that he genuinely revered him.[23] As attorney-general and later as judge, he often attended Charles, finding him to be generally amenable to his requests and occasionally willing to praise him for jobs well done. Charles certainly did not return Heath's affection in full measure, and on several occasions disciplined him harshly. But the consideration and favour that he did show was enough to win him Sir Robert's devotion.

While Sir Robert revered Charles, it was not the king who forged his circle of courtiers. Within the world of the Court were many circles, each of which was established and dominated by some great favourite. The largest of the early Stuart period, and among the most cohesive, was Buckingham's. It was Heath's good fortune to hold a prominent place inside it.

Buckingham has generally served historians as a whipping-boy, and certainly his influence on government and policy was in some respects negative.[24] But he was an almost ideal patron, and it was primarily as a patron that Heath knew him. To be esteemed a great patron, a courtier had to be able to provide favours and offices for his protégés, and Buckingham, during the period 1616 – 28, easily excelled his rivals in providing for followers, a fact that in November 1625 caused Sir John North, a man not of his circle, to observe with apparent bitterness: 'My Lord Dukes Creatures are the men that rise, the Kings servants

---

[23] Quotation from Heath to Nicholas, 1 May 1648: Egerton 2533, f. 450.

[24] A more balanced account of Buckingham, and the most scholarly life to date, is Roger Lockyer's *Buckingham: The Life and Political Career of George Villiers, First Duke of Buckingham 1592 – 1628* (London, 1981).

having little hope of preferment.'[25] In writing as he did, North revealed a double truth: not only that Buckingham was powerful, but that he used his power to benefit his protégés. Some patrons, like Carr, were far from generous, doing little to find their followers places. But Buckingham was noteworthy for his generosity, so much so that even Roger Coke, who inherited a hatred of the duke from his grandfather, Sir Edward, conceded that, at least in his early years as favourite 'he was Affable and Courteous, and seemed to Court all Men as they Courted him, he promoted Mens Suits to the King *gratis*, which *Somerset* would not do, but for great sums of money'.[26]

It was through the patronage of Buckingham that Heath rose — recorder of London in 1618, solicitor-general in 1621, attorney-general in 1625 — 'to all which several places', he later claimed, 'I was preferred without my owne suite'.[27] Perhaps Buckingham did secure these three offices for him without prodding, but in general Sir Robert was quick to petition his patron for favours of all kinds. He was, for example, almost certainly behind a campaign to win the mastership of the Rolls for himself. In October 1621 Buckingham sought to persuade the master, Sir Julius Caesar, to vacate his place in favour of Sir Robert, but when Caesar refused he allowed the matter to drop. By early 1625, however, the duke was prepared to try again, this time aiming at the reversion, which was held by Sir Henry Wotton. Through promises of preferment and possibly through intimidation as well, he was able to persuade Wotton to surrender his reversion. Immediately courtiers began to bid for the prize, one offering £5,000, but as Wotton himself later claimed, Buckingham apparently had from the first intended to grant the reversion to Heath. For his part, Heath promptly petitioned James to direct that Coventry draw a grant of the reversion to him, and the king agreed, but for some reason the enabling warrant was not sent. In a move born of frustration, Sir Robert,

---

[25] Letter to the earl of Leicester: *HMC, De L'Isle and Dudley*, V, 441. On the extent of Buckingham's power at different stages of his career, see Lockyer, pp. 69 – 70, 275 – 6.

[26] *Detection of the Court and State of England during the Last Four Reigns* (London, 1696), vol. I, book I, 47. Coke claims the Buckingham became more venal with time; *ibid.*, vol. I, book II, 83.

[27] 'Anniversarium', 20. Even Whitelocke's testimony (above, p. 17) suggests that Buckingham acted on the spur of the moment in nominating Heath as recorder. His later promotions to solicitor- and attorney-general followed a common progression.

with Buckingham's blessing, himself prepared the warrant for Coventry, but the strategem failed, and Heath was soon reduced to complaining to his master: 'I suffer, in the opinion of the world, though not in myne owne.' James's death put a temporary halt to Heath's efforts. June, however, found Sir Robert jotting a memorandum to himself 'to put my Lord in mind to move his Majesty to be gratiously pleased to signe the warrant for the Revertions of the Rolls to my selfe'. His motion to Buckingham had the desired effect, for Coventry was soon ordered to prepare the desired grant.[28]

Protégés looked to their patrons not only for gifts and offices but for help in times of trouble. In 1610, Carr had demonstrated his indifference to the responsibilities of patronage by allowing Roper to threaten Heath's King's Bench reversion. Buckingham, on the other hand, was there when Sir Robert needed him, which apparently was often. In December 1621, for example, Heath lamented to his lord that: 'It hath been my folly to be too deeply ingaged for Sir Thomas Watson's dettes.' Watson having recently died, in debt to many, including the king, Heath feared losing his surety, and with a air of desperation he wrote: 'I humbly beseech your Lordship to be mine honourable good Lord and a Mediator for me to his Majesty.' True to form, Buckingham did intervene, and the problem was resolved. Indeed, Sir Robert was soon to be found soliciting Buckingham's aid in reclaiming his own debts from Watson's estate. In the end he was able to gain the entire estate for himself, probably with the aid of his patron.[29]

Had he been generous only with gifts, offices, and protection, Buckingham would have won the gratitude of his retinue. As it was, he had yet another virtue as a patron. Protégés were used to flattering their masters, but their blandishments were seldom returned. Buckingham, however, freely praised his servants. When in 1625 he offered to make the youthful Sir Edward Nicholas secretary of the Admiralty, a gesture pleasing enough in itself, he did so, according to Nicholas 'with many gracious Expressions of his esteem of my diligence & abilitie'.[30] Even

---

[28] Chamberlain to Carleton, 13 Oct. 1621: McClure, II, 399; L. P. Smith, *The Life and Letters of Sir Henry Wotton* (Oxford, 1907), I, 200, and II, 316 – 17, 400; SP 14/183/50, 66; SP 14/184/59; Egerton 2541, f. 55; Egerton 2551, ff. 1 – 2; Egerton 2552, f.14.

[29] 'The Fortescue Papers', ed. S. R. Gardiner, Camden Society, *Publications*, new series, 1 (1871), 171; SP 14/127/89; *CSPD, Charles I*, I, 365.

[30] BL, Add. 31,954, f. 3.

when his servants disappointed him, the duke often praised them for their efforts, and a case in point involved Heath. In late 1623 Buckingham ordered several of his followers at Court, including Heath and Coventry, to investigate Lady Purbeck, a sister-in-law with whom he enjoyed a mutual loathing, in the hope that they could prove her to be not only an adulteress, unfit to be his brother's wife, but also a witch, unfit to live. After a year of exhaustive investigation, however, the two law officers could only report that while she had in fact committed adultery the charge of witchcraft was groundless, and they further advised that whereas she had for some time been confined she should be set at liberty. Buckingham had obviously wished for a very different report, but he restrained his anger and wrote to them: 'I am beholding to you and do also understand . . . the Paynes [you] have taken in the Business concerning the Ladie Purbecke for which I thank you.' He wrote a second letter to Heath alone, to assure him that he and Coventry were two 'on whose Love to mee I principally rely'.[31] The consideration reflected in these lines, so little in keeping with the standard Buckingham portrait, reflects a quality that contemporaries recognised but many historians have forgotten: that the duke was as quick to love as to hate.[32] Buckingham felt genuine affection for some of his servants, perhaps most of all for Sir Edward Conway, to whom he once wrote: 'My dear friend: I have had a fever and let blood, yet I cannot forbear to tell you I shall shortly have you in my arms'.[33] His feelings for Heath appear to have been more muted, but they were warm nonetheless.

The keys to Buckingham's bounty and affection were three. The first was blandishment; included in the duke's retinue were

---

[31] Quotations are drawn from SP 14/183/65,66, as quoted in Laura Norsworthy, *The Lady of Bleeding Heart Yard: Lady Elizabeth Hatton, 1578 – 1646* (London, 1935), pp. 158 – 9. Norsworthy is incorrect in writing that SP 14/183/65 was written to Coventry alone. The fullest review of the case is *ibid.*, pp. 146 – 88.

[32] Clarendon claims that Buckingham's 'kindness and affection to his friends was so vehement, that it was as so many marriages for better or worse, and so many leagues offensive and defensive': *The History of the Rebellion and Civil Wars in England*, ed. W. D. Macray (Oxford, 1888), I, 39.

[33] BL, Harleian 6987, f. 166; quoted from R. E. Bonner, 'Administration and Public Service under the Early Stuarts: Edward Viscount Conway as Secretary of State, 1623 – 1628', unpub. Ph.D. dissertation (Univ. of Minnesota, 1968), 151. Regarding Buckingham's relationship with his protégés, see also Lockyer, 38 – 41, 112 – 13.

some of the ablest flatterers at Court, notably Sir George Goring.[34] The second key was loyalty. Buckingham particularly esteemed those who had served him in the years before his rise to power, men like Conway and Shute. His partiality for long-time servants sometimes caused him to prefer them to offices for which they were patently unsuited. So, for example, in 1623, shortly after having exclaimed that 'he knewe noe honnor that Conway was not woorthie of, nor noe place in the commonwealth to good for him', he had Sir Edward installed as secretary of state, and for his pains he was later, according to Clarendon, thanked by James for having preferred 'a secretary, who could neither write nor read'.[35] Finally, for his favours Buckingham expected recompense, in the form of cash, service, or both. In the demands that he placed on his servants, for flattery, loyalty, and recompense, he differed not at all from the other patrons who peopled the Stuart Court, but in his ability and willingness to reward good service, he far excelled them.

Heath willingly paid the price for preferment. Flattery he probably considered a patron's due, and he could proffer blandishments with the best of them. On 9 April 1623, in the course of a letter to Buckingham, he exclaimed: 'I owe soe much duity & service to your Lordship, & have found soe much Love, that the whole remayne of my life shall be divided into active parts to express my thankfulness.'[36] But there was also a limit to his flattery. Unlike Goring and his fellow-spaniels, Heath seldom if ever wrote to Buckingham for the sole purpose of expressing his reverence and willingness to serve. Rather, his letters concentrated on specific requests or counsel, with flattery adding occasional spice. Not surprisingly, he was more likely to flatter his lord in letters that contained pleas for help or thanks for favours than he was in those that were mainly advisory. If

---

[34] Something of the flavour of Goring's approach may be gleaned from his fawning letters to Buckingham and to other patrons, esp. in Harleian 1580, ff. 403 – 16.

[35] Clarendon, I, 80. A fuller version of the same story is provided by Sir John Oglander: *The Oglander Memoirs*, ed. W. H. Long (London, 1888), pp. 160 – 1. Oglander also provides the Buckingham quotation (p. 160). Conway's performance as secretary has won him the contempt of historians like Gardiner (IV, 410), but Aylmer (p. 92) and F. M. G. Evans (*The Principal Secretary of State: A Survey of the Office from 1558 to 1680* [Manchester, 1923], p. 79) give him slightly higher ratings, both writing that he was conscientious but that his inexperience left him unsuited for his office. Bonner provides a much more favourable appraisal.

[36] BL, Stowe 743, f. 44.

offering counsel, he could in fact be rather brusque. When in August 1621 Buckingham sought his advice on how James might best restrain the export of corn, Heath's response was pointed: the king should proceed by proclamation and he should 'act it speedily, whilst the uncerteynty of the success of harvest, may give just occasion of a restraint, lest our owne kingdom may want necessarye provision. for others his Majestys services, I shall be readye to give your Lordship an account when I shall have opportunity to wait uppon you'.[37] The tone is crisp and businesslike. There is nothing here of the servile flatterer.

To recompense his master for offices and favours, Sir Robert may in some cases have resorted or been compelled to resort to the medium of cash payment. Sir Anthony Weldon asserted that *'Heath* Atturney paid a pension' to Buckingham for his place, and while Weldon, a frustrated office-seeker, seldom had kind words for men who succeeded where he failed, his claim is plausible.[38] It appears, however, that in the main Heath repaid Buckingham through service. During most of their time together as master and man, Sir Robert was one of the duke's chief advisors. Not surprisingly, many of the problems that he dealt with were legal in nature. There were Buckingham's lawsuits to pursue, notably the Purbeck case, but the uses of a lawyer extended far beyond litigation. Heath was often called upon to explain to the duke which powers attended some office or commission held by the latter. Sometimes he took the initiative, as in June 1627, when, as Buckingham prepared to sail on his ill-fated La Rochelle expedition, Sir Robert sent him not only a commission of martial law but also a set of instructions on its uses and limitations.[39]

Much of Heath's value to the duke, indeed, lay in his vigilance. He was constantly on the lookout for opportunities to augment his master's powers and profits — the two were usually linked — and when he found them he was quick to follow them through. June 1625 found him making a note for himself regarding 'the mine in Cardiganshire, to obteyn his Majestys warrante for a lease to Sir Hugh Middleton for 31

---

[37] Berkshire Record Office, DEHy01, f. 255.
[38] 'The Court and Character of King James', 129. On 10 April 1624 Chamberlain informed Carleton that Heath would pay Buckingham for the Rolls reversion: McClure, II, 352. His assertion is highly credible, for Heath was behind the campaign.
[39] SP 16/66/4.

yeers, & for his Majestys consent to contract with my Lord the Duke'.[40] He served the duke well not only by providing him with opportunities to increase his wealth, but by warning him of threats to his income. In 1619 or 1620 he and Shute, as trustees for the King's Bench office, wrote to Buckingham that attorneys in Common Pleas and Exchequer were stealing cases from King's Bench 'to the injurye of . . . that office especially, which by your honourable favour wee serve in to your use'.[41]

When Buckingham was absent from Court, his numerous enemies tended to attack. It was then the duty of his servants to do what they could to forestall any action that might prove detrimental to his power or profits. Sometimes the battle was fierce. In April 1623 Sir Robert wrote to his master, then with Charles on their famous embassy in Spain, that: 'Some of your Lordships affaires committed to my trust, and communicated for your service, doe chill in your absence, my hope is only to preserve them, not to perfect them till your retourn.'[42] Usually, however, Heath was successful in holding back Buckingham's enemies. In November 1625 the duke was at Plymouth when word reached him that Sir Thomas Harris, a man whom he had supported, on the advice of fellow-courtiers, for the post of chief justice of Chester, was not to be trusted politically. Immediately he wrote to Heath, calling on him to oppose the Harris nomination. Sir Robert dutifully informed Conway that the candidate was a man of 'mean deserts & . . . ill Report', and he called on the secretary to 'make it nowe sure with his Majesty that [Harris] may have noe more hope of it; but that it may thus rest until my Lords retourn'. In taking his stand against Harris, Heath had carried out the specific assignment that Buckingham had given him, but he went further, voicing his concern that, even if Harris were denied the chief justiceship, Buckingham's position might be endangered, for the earl of Northampton, who was trying to build up his own power base at Court, might 'press for one, whom my Lord duke would not wish the place unto'. The next day, Conway wrote to Heath that no nominations for chief justice would be entertained at Court prior to Buckingham's return.[43]

---

[40] Egerton 2541, f. 55.
[41] BOD, Add. d.111, ff. 96 – 7.
[42] BL, Stowe 743, f. 44. The main object of Heath's concern was probably the aliens' commission; below pp. 119 – 20.
[43] SP 16/9/41; *CSPD, Charles I*, I, 148.

The 1620s saw Buckingham's men dominant at Court. Some, like Coventry and Sir Richard Weston, came to feel so confident of their position that they began to move independently, without regard to their patron's orders. For such temerity, the threat or the fact of dismissal was often the price.[44] Most of the duke's followers, however, served him loyally, whether motivated by love or by fear. Their private counsel and their public offices were alike at his disposal. Heath could depend on their aid when the need arose to help their common master. He could also depend upon them when it was he who needed a favour.

Given the size of Buckingham's retinue, it is only natural that the members resolved themselves into a number of cliques. Heath had powerful friends, including Coventry and Goring, but none was closer nor more important to him than Conway. Heath's superior in the governmental hierarchy, Conway also controlled the actual distribution of much of the vast store of patronage that was in theory Buckingham's.[45] It would seem that Heath had little to offer him. In fact, however, their relationship was dominated by Sir Robert. Conway was a kind man, but weak. As Sir John Oglander wrote of him 'he woold tender his service to all, and denie noe man a courtesie or favor in woordes; but in deedes he never woould nor could p'forme itt'.[46] Heath found in Conway a man whom he could manipulate. In their correspondence as secretary and law officer, Heath was usually the aggressor, coolly informing his superior of his resolve in some matter or telling him that he had decided to delay taking a mandated action. Usually, Conway accepted Heath's decision. In March 1624 he put into words the spirit contained in much of his correspondence with Sir Robert: 'I am soe confident, in your goodness aswell as in your good judgement as I pursue readily whatsoever you recommend.'[47]

---

[44] Weston was far more independent than were most of Buckingham's protégés: M. V. C. Alexander, *Charles I's Lord Treasurer: Sir Richard Weston, Earl of Portland (1577 – 1635)* (Chapel Hill, 1975), p. 41. But there is no evidence that Buckingham challenged his independence. Coventry, on the other hand, fell foul of the duke, according to Weldon, when he opposed Buckingham's pretensions to the place of prince of Tipperary, and, despite Coventry's claim that he owed his place to the king, Buckingham threatened to remove him from office; Weldon believes that only Buckingham's death saved Coventry: 'The Court of King Charles', *Secret History*, ed. Scott, II, 31 – 3.

[45] Bonner, 146 – 51.

[46] *The Oglander Memoirs*, p. 161.

[47] SP 14/161/58.

Conway prized Heath's friendship, and he showed as much with presents, including, in 1628, a New Year's gift of plate, worth forty pounds.[48] He and Sir Robert freely exchanged favours, defining as they did so the nature of a relationship that was beneficial to both. When Heath was absent from Court, he relied on Conway to keep him abreast of developments.[49] When he fell foul of the king, he looked to Sir Edward to plead his case.[50] Conway, in turn, regularly asked favours of Heath, more often for his friends than for himself. Occasionally he asked Sir Robert to prefer someone using his own store of patronage. Thus in August 1624, he sent the noted coloniser, John Pory, to Heath, with a message that in part read: 'I would not loose the opportunitie to tell you, that all the favours you doe to him are obligations upon mee.'[51] Perhaps more often, Conway called on Sir Robert to use his office to aid an acquaintance, as he did in April 1630, when he requested Heath, as attorney-general, to include one Gillian Goad in a general pardon that he was preparing. Sir Robert promptly added the name — another of the countless favours that one servant of Buckingham did for another.[52]

While Buckingham's retinue included its factions and internal alliances, it was clearly the duke himself who was the linchpin. Hundreds of courtiers and crown officials, high and low, looked to him for patronage. Most of his protégés openly acknowledged their indebtedness, Heath not least: 'I knowe well on who I relye', he once wrote to his master.[53] Their power, they knew, largely derived from his, and his disappearance was likely to leave them vulnerable. Buckingham's death in August 1628, at the hands of John Felton — that 'wretched villaine

---

[48] SP 16/90/4.
[49] Heath requested intelligence from Conway, 23 Sept. 1626: SP 16/36/68. Sir Robert himself provided information to members of Buckingham's retinue, e.g., Endymion Porter: Heath to Buckingham, Oct. 1622, BOD, Add. d.111, f. 215.
[50] See pp. 172 – 3.
[51] SP 14/171/47. The gift that Conway was looking for in this case was probably not an office.
[52] SP 16/164/66; SP 16/165/8. On 11 Feb. 1629 Conway asked Heath to show leniency toward one of Sir Edward's kinsmen, whom he had charged with usury: SP 16/135/35. The outcome of this plea is unknown, but it is noteworthy that Conway submitted it only a few days after he had helped Heath through a personal crisis (see pp. 172 – 3 below). Possibly Conway then felt that Heath owed him a favour.
[53] Letter of 13 Feb. 1625: SP 14/183/50.

Felton', as Sir Robert described him — sent his protégés scurrying to find new patrons.[54] A number of them, including Heath, Conway, and Goring, concentrated their attention on James Hay, the amiable but indolent and hedonistic earl of Carlisle, for they apparently considered him to be Buckingham's heir-apparent to the mantle of chief favourite. Carlisle welcomed many of them, including Heath, to his retinue and he was not ungenerous, but his laziness and his lack of interest in Court intrigue prevented him from becoming the patron that Buckingham had been.[55] After August 1628 Sir Robert probably never again knew the security that he had enjoyed while the duke lived.

The patronage system encouraged selfishness. Protégés looked for favours, and they were as likely to turn on patrons who could not satisfy them as on those who would not. When in 1612 Heath surrendered his patent for the King's Bench office, prior to becoming Carr's trustee, he claimed that Balmerino had granted him his share on 21 October 1608, when in fact the moiety had gone to Balmerino's brother.[56] In his prevarication, he probably acted no worse than most other men in his position, for it was then the case that Balmerino was no longer able to help him, and Carr was. But while the patronage system bred selfishness, it did not exclude sentiment. Successful courtiers in particular tended to think well of the patrons who had done most to help them, and they remained loyal even if their benefactors were removed from the Court scene. On being sworn chief justice of the Common Pleas in October 1634 Sir

[54] Heath quotation drawn from his letter to Carlisle, 28 Aug. 1629: SP 16/114/42.
[55] There are among the State Papers perhaps 100 letters that courtiers of every rank wrote to Carlisle in 1628 – 9 in hopes of winning his patronage. Heath, who always liked to have several patrons at any given moment, offered the earl his services even before Buckingham's assassination. On 20 July he wrote to Carlisle, 'I receaved soe much honor, by your noble letters you lately voutsafed to write unto me, that I could not but take this opportunitie to express my thankfulnes, & to engage my uttermost service unto your Lordship': SP 16/110/45. On Carlisle's character, note Clarendon, I, 76, 78.
[56] Balmerino's assignment is Egerton 2978, f. 5. Heath's misrepresentation surfaced when Balmerino's son petitioned the Lords against him in 1642; a summary of the younger Balmerino's petition is printed in HMC, Fifth Report, 26, and a copy of the full petition is in the Kent Archives Office, U55 E101. Balmerino himself misrepresents the truth by claiming that as of 1612 his father had owned a moiety, when in fact his uncle had owned it.

John Finch recalled that it had been Sir Frances Bacon, a courtier dead and disgraced, who had first raised him up.[57]

If Bacon could arouse such loyalty, it was only natural that Buckingham, the greatest patron of his age, could inspire more. Here was a man whom his protégés could admire for power, generosity, and kindness alike. Within his retinue, Buckingham's death brought general sorrow. Nicholas spoke for two mourners when he wrote to Conway on 24 August 1628: 'I . . . do beseech you to be pleased to excuse the scribbling of a trembling hand guided by the sad heart of your Lordship.'[58] Two days later William Laud, a man not given to grief, informed Conway that he had shortly before learned of 'that abominable murder . . . to my great sorrow and grife of heart. My Lord, it is the saddest accident that ever befell me, and should be so to all good Christians'. But Laud recognised that his sorrow was shared by few who were outside the duke's circle. On 12 September he wrote to another correspondent: 'I propose not to write these either to declaim in [Buckingham's] commendations, which so few would believe, or to express my grief, which as few would pity.'[59]

Like Laud, Sir Robert grieved for his patron. Like him, too, he realised that most Englishmen felt no sorrow, but rather joy, on learning of the duke's murder. To this broad audience he spoke at Felton's trial, reminding them that for the most part they had not known Buckingham, while he had.

> I know well what a weight not only of affaires, but of envy, which accompanyes great places & great persons, lay uppon him, and with what disadvantage I speake to many to give him but his due . . . Many thinges I can speake of him knowingly; & for my self, who doe fully & truly profess that I was much bound unto him for his noble favours, . . . I should boldly say this of him: I had many times access unto him . . .;

[57] BL, Sloane 1455, f. 12.
[58] Donald Nicholas, *Mr. Secretary Nicholas (1593 – 1669): His Life and Letters* (London, 1955), p. 67.
[59] H. R. Trevor-Roper, *Archbishop Laud 1573 – 1645*, second ed. (London, 1963), p. 456; *The Works of . . . William Laud . . . Archbishop of Canterbury*, ed. James Bliss and William Scott, *Library of Anglo-Catholic Theology*, VII, 16.

I observed in him many excellent partes & indowmentes & can truly report many good thinges of him, of knowledge but I can say noe ill of him, of knowledg . . . I am sure I flatter him not, nor well cann nowe he is dead, And I speak it with confidence I never did flatter him whilst he lived.[60]

Some twenty years later, at Brasted, an inventory of Heath's household possessions was prepared. Included in the list were a number of portraits. Most were of Heath's family. In one hall hung a painting of Charles I and his queen, as though to challenge the Roundheads. Apart from the royal couple, only one person outside the family appeared in portrait: that was Buckingham.[61]

Heath at home

It was Heath's education, particularly his legal education, that made him attractive to patrons and prepared him for public service; it was the patronage system, personified in Buckingham, that propelled him to high position; but it was his family, first and foremost, that gave him a sense of direction. Robert Heath the elder had the greatest influence on his son's education and ambitions, and introduced him to the world of patronage. But Sir Robert's family in general had a great impact, for it provided him with friends and partners, with love and security, with a sense of identity. Throughout his life it was this family, nuclear and extended, that claimed his first loyalty.

Sir Robert was always close to his cousins. Two of them, Robert Titchbourne and Robert Seliard, relatives by marriage, but treated as blood-kin, were among his chief partners, while other cousins became his associates in individual business ventures.[62] As he rose at Court his store of patronage increased, and he freely used it to help promote the careers of his relations.[63] The use of influence on behalf of one's family was so much expected that it would have been almost inconceivable

---

[60] SP 16/121/78.
[61] Egerton 2983, f. 86.
[62] Below, pp. 252 – 4, 265.
[63] Below, pp. 114 – 15, 117, 286 – 7.

that a noteworthy courtier would not have tried to see to the preferment of his kin. Female relatives as well as male looked to Heath for favours. It was the duty of a wealthy man to provide dowries for poor girls in his family, and during the 1620s and 1630s Sir Robert, by then the richest Heath family member as well as the most influential, willingly shouldered the burden. July 1639 found him writing to John Hurst, an acquaintance, on behalf of a cousin, Ann 'that if you marry with her besides the tenement I have assured her in Croydon in Surry, & the money she has already I will give you a hundred & twenty pounds'.[64]

Heath was deeply devoted to his extended family, but his strongest affections, at least after the death of his parents — his father in 1615, his mother in 1626 — naturally centred on his wife and children. In his memoir, he wrote that the greatest 'comfort' he had enjoyed in life had come from 'soe discreet, soe virtuous, soe religious & soe loving a wife, and the hopes, and more than hopes of the children I have had by her'.[65]

He was married on 10 December 1600. His bride, Margaret, was then approaching twenty-one. She was the daughter of John Miller, who had died in 1589, leaving her, his sole surviving child, considerable property in and around Tonbridge. Her estate probably attracted the Heath family; likewise her connections, for the Millers were linked by marriage to the wealthy Crow family of Brasted, who were in turn linked to the Seliards and, more remotely, to the Heaths.[66] Whatever her attractions, it is probable that she was chosen not by Heath himself, but by his father. It would have been unusual for the heir to a gentleman's estate to be allowed to make his own match. The most he could hope for from his father, generally

---

[64] U. of I., Heath Papers. The possibility exists that Heath was Ann's godfather; if true, this situation would further explain his generosity.

[65] 'Anniversarium', 17. Unfortunately, little may be said with certainty about Heath's attitude toward his parents. He did allow his father to shape his career: see pp. 6, 11. As his mother lay dying, in Sept. 1626, he left the Court to visit her: Heath to Conway, 23 Sept., SP 16/36/68. Of course, this is scarcely remarkable.

[66] 'Anniversarium', 20; 'Liber E.H.', 162, 164; will of John Miller, PCC 75 Leicester; John Cave-Brown, *The History of Brasted, Its Manor, Parish, and Church* (Westerham, Kent, 1874), p. 16; Ellis, 'Genealogical Memoranda on Seyliard', 11.

speaking, was permission to veto a choice that he considered unpalatable.[67]

Margaret Heath appears to have been a strong woman, willing to speak her mind and often able to achieve her end. Her influence over her husband is reflected in two letters that Thomas Locke wrote to his master, Sir Dudley Carleton, on 30 April and 12 May 1619. In the first, Locke expressed the hope that Heath, then recorder of London, would rent Carleton's house at Emworth in Hampshire 'if his wife be not more addicted to a howse at Micham', but in the second he could only report: 'Mr Recorder's wife had more mind to a howse at Micham bycaus it is neerer London & hath gone through for one there.' Margaret also advised her husband in matters relating to his public offices. In May 1629 Sir Robert wrote to his eldest son, Edward: 'Assure your Mother, that I am very mindful of the kings business & have made a very good stepp in it, & will not forgett her counsell, & I think I see my way fully thorough it.'[68]

Heath stated in his memoir that Margaret had borne him 'many' children.[69] This claim may suggest that an extant list of their offspring, prepared by Edward, includes only reference to children born alive, not to miscarriages or stillbirths. Edward's list does suggest, however, that Sir Robert and his wife were fortunate by the standards of the time, for six of the nine children noted in it lived to adulthood, indeed, to at least fifty-five: Mary, 1608 – 69; Edward 1612 – 69; John, 1614 – 91; George, 1617 – 72; Robert, 1620 – 97; and Francis, 1622 – 83.[70]

Owing to the demands of office, particularly during the period 1618 – 31, Heath was able to spend little time with his children during their formative years. Margaret was presumably respon- sible for the day-to-day management of the children. It was probably she who handled their early education, and indeed when in September 1615 Heath prepared a will — a document never to be proved — he assigned to her the task of educating the children, especially Mary, in the event of his death.[71] However, Sir Robert himself sought to dictate the general

---

[67] On marriage arrangements during the period, see Stone, *Family, Sex and Marriage*, pp. 180 – 91; Miriam Slater, 'The Weightiest Business: Marriage in an Upper-Gentry Family in Seventeenth-Century England', *Past and Present*, 72 (1976), 25 – 54.

[68] U. of I., Heath Papers; SP 14/108/85; SP 14/109/23.

[69] 'Anniversarium', 11.

[70] 'Liber E.H.', 164.

[71] SBT, DR 98/1511.

direction that his children's lives would take, and he seems to have decided early that his sons, or at least most of them, would follow in his footsteps, as he had followed in his father's. Those footsteps led to Cambridge for all five sons. Heath decided to send the boys in pairs, probably so that they would have natural helpmates. Edward and John went off to Clare College in Easter term 1626 and George and Francis entered Corpus Christi in 1633, where they were joined by Robert the following year.[72]

Heath did his best to influence the boys during their student years at Cambridge. In letter after letter he poured forth the platitudinous advice that fathers in his circumstances were so fond of, the sort that Shakespeare presented, perhaps parodied, through the medium of Polonius. To Sir Robert, of course, playing the sage was serious and vital work. While at university, the boys were freer of parental influence than they had previously been, and rowdiness and licentious behaviour were not unknown at Cambridge.[73] Heath was anxious that his sons should hold to the straight and narrow, and lost no opportunity to provide guidance. In June 1627 he wrote to Edward and John:

I take comfort in nothing more than in the hope of your well dooing, wherein your selves will find the greatest comfort, nowe is your seed time, your harvest will be hereafter, & yet be assured that the reputation of religious, industrious & sober carriage which you shall sett in these your younger days . . . will more availe to your preferment in this world, and the true and not fleeing substance thereof in the world to come then any thing which you or I or any of our friends can imagine for your good. Please god religiously & use the means in publike & private prayers & other publike exercises of religion & private reading of the scriptures & other good

---

[72] Venn, part I, vol. II, 347 – 8. George, who entered the Church, was the only son who remained to receive a degree. A record of John's and Edward's expenses at Cambridge is in Egerton 2983, ff. 11 – 13; of Edward's, at the Inner Temple, 1629 – 31, ff. 13 – 23.

[73] D'Ewes recalls that 'swearing, drinking, rioting, and hatred of all piety and virtue . . . did abound . . . in all the University. Nay, the very sin of lust began to be known and practised by very boys'; quoted by Mullinger, p. 30. D'Ewes, a strict Puritan, probably exaggerated considerably.

books; Apply your studys both in your private reading of the scriptures & in frequenting the publike lectures; harken with all due respect to the counsell and instructions of your worthy tutor.[74]

The 'worthy tutor' was Henry Dean. A year before, Heath had told Edward and John that he was sending Dean to them to 'attend you as your sister, & look to your apparrell & all other things which are necessary for you . . . & to help you in your lerning also'.[75] In addition to these stated reasons, Sir Robert probably hoped that Dean would police his sons and generally act in loco parentis. To compensate him for his pains, he paid Dean's way at Cambridge. For awhile, the relationship between the boys and their tutor appears to have been smooth, but April 1628 found Dean writing a desperate plea to Richard Stacy, who was his friend and Heath's cousin:

> I perceived by my Father & Mother that some complaints had beene made to my Lady [Margaret Heath] of mee, & that my Lady mentioned some dislike, as though I had carried my self undutifully, carelesly & negligently towards my younge Masters. . . I replyed . . . that they might happily thinke that I writt to my Lady somethinge concerninge them, in regards, that sometimes when they squabled, I should mention writinge to my Lady of it.

Wondering 'who would have thought that of so small a Mole-hill should be made so greate a mountain?', Dean concluded by begging Stacy to intercede with the Heaths on his behalf.[76] How the problem was resolved is unknown, but Dean did eventually receive a degree at Cambridge, suggesting that Heath continued to patronise him.[77]

While Dean's future still hung in the balance, Edward and John left Cambridge, like their father without taking a degree,

---

[74] U. of I., Compton-Verney Book, no. 20.
[75] U. of I., Heath Papers. On the rise of the tutor, see Lawrence Stone, 'The Size and Composition of the Oxford Student Body 1580 – 1909', *The University in Society*, ed. Stone (Princeton, 1974), I, 25 – 6.
[76] U. of I., Heath Papers.
[77] Venn, part I, vol. II, 26.

and took up residence at the Inner Temple, where they had as early as July 1626 been granted special admission at Sir Robert's request.[78] The promotion apparently did little to improve their behaviour. In the autumn of 1631 they were suspended for taking part in a brawl at the inn, and it may well have been only their father's intervention that saved them from expulsion. As it was, they and the other brawlers were forced to submit to certain penalties, including paying a fine and personally petitioning each bencher for pardon.[79]

By obtaining membership of the Inner Temple for Edward and John, Sir Robert had set his sons well on the road to careers in law. His next aim was to find a good match for his heir. Heath's first experience with marriage negotiations, at least as a father, came in 1627, when he contracted a match on behalf of his daughter. By his decision, Mary was joined to Sir William Morley, of Halnaker, Sussex, the son of one of Heath's business associates.[80] At the time, and for years afterwards, the Heaths believed this match to be a fine one. Only in the late 1640s were they to learn otherwise, to their sorrow.[81] In the meantime, they had been allied to yet another family, through a marriage that was a failure almost from the moment it was solemnised.

The autumn of 1630 saw Sir Robert avidly seeking a bride for Edward. In November of that year Sir Robert Harrison wrote to his relative by marriage, Sir Dudley Carleton: 'There is a motion of a good marriage for my sonn sett a foote in London by some friends of mine.' He had earlier asked Carleton to solicit the aid of Heath, a friend and fellow-courtier, in promoting the match, and he now requested that Sir Dudley again encourage him to intervene, since Heath might 'strike a stroake in the business'. But Harrison was also wary of Sir Robert: 'I am tould that hee is like to speake one word for mee and two for his own

---

[78] *ITR*, II, 115. Robert was granted special admission in Jan. 1638, Francis in Feb. 1642, both at Sir Robert's behest: *ibid.*, 240, 264. Presumably at the instance of Heath, Edward and John were from the start given preferential lodging: Wilde, ff. 44 – 5.

[79] Wilde, f. 45. Students at the inns of court (like those at university) had a reputation for riotous behaviour and debauchery, but their critics probably exaggerated: W. R. Prest, 'Legal Education of the Gentry at the Inns of Court, 1560 – 1640', *Past and Present*, 38 (1967), 25 – 6. On violence at the inns, see also Prest, *Inns of Court*, ch. 5.

[80] Sir John Morley is noted as an associate of Heath's in a deposition, SP 14/ 115/43.

[81] See p. 293.

sonn.'[82] Harrison need not have worried, for Heath had already decided on a match for Edward. The girl he had chosen was Lucy, the daughter and heiress of Paulus Ambrosius Croke.

Heath knew Croke from the Inner Temple, where both were benchers, and the fact that they shared a vocation may have prompted amity. The marriage of two children was often encouraged by their fathers' friendship. It appears, however, that Heath was more impressed by Croke's property than he was by Croke himself.[83] The proposed marriage promised to be profitable for the Heath family. By the marriage articles, which were finalised on 17 February 1631, Croke agreed to convey the great manor of Cottesmore, in Rutland, to Edward and Lucy, as well as the manors of East Hanny and Barrow, in Berkshire, and various lesser properties. In turn, Sir Robert pledged to give them Soham, a large but inundated manor in Cambridgeshire, and to build them a house at Colliweston, in Northamptonshire. Colliweston and several minor properties were to pass to Edward and Lucy on Heath's death. The marriage articles likewise bound both fathers to bestow plate and jewelry on the young couple, all of a prescribed minimum value, and to provide them with other expensive gifts as well. All in all, the articles reflected the importance of the match to both Heath and Croke. Here was the joining of two wealthy gentry families, embodied in an heir and heiress. The fathers' generosity was intended to further the happiness of Edward and Lucy, certainly, but Heath and Croke probably looked beyond their own children. Through the agreement, and through the consequent linking of their families, they sought to ensure the prosperity and the worldly success of their descendants.[84]

Had the parents looked more deeply into the prospective marriage, they might have acted with greater circumspection.

[82] SP 16/175/13.

[83] Some biographical notes on Croke, as well as excerpts from an account book that he kept during the 1610s (the original is now boxed with the Heath Papers, U. of I.), are in print: J. H. Bloom (ed.), 'Paulus Ambrosius Croke: A Seventeenth-Century Account Book', *Notes and Queries*, twelfth series, 4 (1918), 5 – 7, 36 – 8.

[84] SBT, DR 98/1287. Further data on Heath's obligations is included in a document dated 1 Feb 1630 and endorsed, 'Sir Robert Heaths agreement upon the mariage': SG Top. Mss., under 'Rutland, Cottesmore'.

On the day of the wedding, 26 February 1631, Edward was only eighteen, and his bride was barely thirteen.[85] By contrast, Sir Robert had been twenty-five when he married Margaret, and she had been nearly twenty-one, ages that almost exactly represented the norm for first marriages during the period.[86] The new pair was not only young, but temperamentally ill-suited: Edward was dour and self-centred, Lucy highly-strung and possessive. In their haste to make a match, Heath and Croke had concentrated too much on material aspects of the union. They were soon to suffer for their short-sightedness.

Still, it was not the children, but their fathers, who first brought the marriage to grief. Within a few weeks of the wedding they began to feud, for two basic reasons as Heath later wrote: 'Some differences have been betwene us, since the intermariage of our children; partly about assurances of our Lands, accordinge to the communication betwene us before this marriage, but especially about the abidinge with us, wherein the greatest contention hath been; out of our Loves, with which of us they should abide longest.'[87] Perhaps the ordering was as Heath claimed. Particularly in view of the ages of Edward and Lucy, both fathers undoubtedly wanted them to remain with them for long stretches during the early years of their marriage. But most documents relating to the feud suggest that the main cause of contention lay in disputes over property. Although the marriage articles had been drawn before the wedding, apparently no attempt was made to effect the undertakings made within them for several months after it, and by then Heath and Croke each began to fear that the other was attempting to renege on the promises that he had made earlier, especially those involving the conveyance of lands.

The feud apparently originated with Croke. After the wedding, he and his wife, Susanna, took Lucy home with them, on the understanding, Sir Robert later claimed, that she would soon return to her husband and parents-in-law. But not long after Heath was notified that Croke had no intention of returning her, and on 17 April he wrote angrily to Sir George Croke, Paulus's older brother: 'If my sonn will be advised by me, he shall not

[85] 'Liber E. H.', 158. Lucy's trousseau was highly elaborate, costing £179 3s 8d: J. H. Bloom, (ed.), 'Wedding trousseau of a Lady c.1630', *Notes and Queries*, twelfth series, 4 (1918), 291 – 2.
[86] On ages at first marriage, see Stone, *Family, Sex and Marriage*, pp. 46 – 54.
[87] Quoted from an agreement between Heath and Croke, dated 18 Aug. 1632: SG, Unbd. Mss., under 'Heath'.

hazzard his portion with his wife, & his wife also: he is sure of a wife, & I hartily pray she may prove a good & a loving wife, but if he desire the ende he must use the means.'[88] Heath's suggestion, or at least threat, that it might be best for all concerned if the union were dissolved was not opposed by his brother-in-law, and in fact Croke himself began to reconsider the match. Uncertain whether Lucy and Edward should remain joined, he temporised, informing Heath, through Sir George, that 'for avoyding inconveyencyes, it is agreed that they shall for this summer at least forbear to be bedfellows together'.[89] All parties apparently realised that if the union were not consumated, it was not technically a marriage, but only an espousal, which might easily be terminated.[90]

For some reason, the talk of annulment soon ended, and Lucy was allowed to rejoin Edward at his parents' house. But 12 June 1631 found Sir Robert again angered by the attitude of his brother-in-law: 'You write a strange language to my understandinge, that you would be contented to receave your daughter, but if my sonn her husband should bring her downe to you, you should take it as a scorne put uppon you by me; who is soe fit to come with her as her husband I knowe not.' Then, in a statement that reflected well his sense of values, he added: 'I knowe [not] how it will stand with our reputations that she should be sent downe or carried downe without her husband.' But there were matters of property at stake, as well as matters of honour. For that reason, he concluded by informing his brother-in-law that he was bringing suit against him in Exchequer.[91] Once again, the eruption was followed by comparative calm, and on 15 May 1632 Edward heard from his father that: 'My Brother Croke & I have talked togeather & talked ourselves frends & I hope we shall reconcile all our differences.'[92] But only eight days later Sir Robert wrote again: 'Your father Croke . . . did write, that he would be content to receave his daughter; But if you should bring her downe to them, he should take it as a scorne put uppon him, & he hath in his passion sayd, if you come in at one doore, he would you out at another.'[93] The feud might have continued for many years, but

[88] U. of I., Heath Papers.
[89] U. of I., Heath Papers.
[90] On espousals, see Laslett, pp. 88 – 9.
[91] U. of I., Heath Papers.
[92] SG, Unbd. Mss., under 'Heath'.
[93] U. of I., Heath Papers.

it was soon brought to a close by Croke's death, on 25 August 1632.

Despite the bitterness of the feud, it does not appear that Heath turned against Lucy personally, as Croke turned against Edward. On 23 May 1632 he wrote to Edward:

> I doe assure you both I have & shall love you both very really until I shall find you will not deserve it . . .; yee shall be both wellcome at my house, and shall not want any thing . . . Even if you never shall have a penny with your wife, as yet you have not had I will nevertheless doe that to & for you both, as shall be fitt & worthy.[94]

But despite his protestations, he did not behave in a way that won Lucy's trust. One week before Croke died, he and Heath agreed to have the dispute over property mediated by Sir Humphrey Davenport, chief baron of the Exchequer, and Sir Richard Hutton, a justice of Common Pleas.[95] Later that year, however, Heath, with the permission of the Court of Wards, personally assumed jurisdiction. He then apparently held back from concluding the matter. By 1635 Lucy had lost her patience with him, and in a letter to Sir George Croke she complained 'concerning my land in barkshire you know my father in law was to have had it for present portion but then he was to setle 300 pounds a yeare which I am never likely to have'. She then begged her uncle to intervene, and he complied. By the close of 1636 he and Davenport had settled most of the contested property.[96] Lucy seems thereafter to have been at peace with her father-in-law, though on her part the relationship was probably always more respectful than loving.

In any case, it was apparently not her father-in-law's behaviour that was of greatest concern to Lucy, but her husband's. Edward seems never to have shown much interest in the marriage. He had played little if any part in making the

---

[94] U. of I., Heath Papers.

[95] Heath's agreement with Croke, together with a note dating Croke's death, is in SG, Unbd. Mss., under 'Heath'. The Wards' order is in Unbd. Mss., under 'Croke'.

[96] Lucy's letter is in U. of I., Heath Papers; like all of her letters, it can be dated only approximately, through internal evidence. Information on the settling of the property is included in an answer to a Chancery deposition — the case pitted Edward against his son-in-law — prepared by Edward sometime during the early 1660s: U. of I., Heath Papers.

match and indeed prior to the wedding had not been allowed significant contact with Lucy or her family. When on 19 January 1631 Sir Robert, having heard that Lucy was ill, wrote to Susanna Croke to express his concern, he added 'were my sonns hands & penn, and tonge at libertie, which are yet bound up by consent, it were his proper part, which he would willingly have performed, but that I have at this time taken it uppon me, & directed him to forbeare'.[97] The eighteen-month feud between his father and his father-in-law also found Edward a bystander and, by all appearances, a rather detached one. After the death of Paulus Croke prospects for the marriage brightened, but Edward's behaviour soon destroyed the opportunity. By 1634 he was involved in an affair with a woman in London, and it appears that he was often unfaithful thereafter. Adultery was not uncommon at the time, but not surprisingly this fact was of little consolation to Lucy. When first she suspected that Edward was being unfaithful, she pleaded with him to return from London: 'If any intreaty of mine be of sufficience power to prevaile, let me beg your company this week. I pray you will make haste for you have tarried allready longer than you promised me.' By 1635, however, her attitude was hardening: 'I know you are now in the place and with the companie you like . . . I intreate you not to come till you canne bringe your hart with you; for excepte both harte and body may be joyned together I care not whether I see you, either ever or never.'[98] That year found Lucy feeling totally isolated. In 1633 her mother had died, and she considered both her husband and her father-in-law to be indifferent to her, perhaps hostile. The same letter that contained the plea that her uncle mediate the land dispute also contained the complaint: 'I am now an orphan sente into the world destitute of freindes except you will be pleased . . . to helpe as my stedfather.'

Lucy's marriage was also a failure in that it did not result in the birth of an heir. During the period 1632 – 44 she endured twelve pregnancies, but most ended in miscarriages or stillbirths. Only two infants, both daughters, survived the first year, and only one, Margaret, lived to adulthood.[99] This failure must

---

[97] U. of I., Heath Papers.
[98] U. of I., Heath Papers. These letters are also quoted in Reginald Hine, *The Cream of Curiosity* (London, 1920), pp. 81 – 2. Adultery, particularly between gentlemen and their servants, was not unusual: Slater, 38 – 49.
[99] 'Liber E. H.', 158 – 60.

have worried Lucy and Edward. It undoubtedly concerned Sir Robert, for he cannot have been indifferent to the prospect that the wealth and property he had worked so hard to accumulate might pass from his line. Interestingly, however, he seems not to have put pressure on his younger sons to marry, in the hope that one of their marriages might prove fruitful. In fact, only one of them, John, ever married, and he did not do so until 1664, fifteen years after his father's death. His marriage, too, produced only daughters.[100]

The 1630s saw contention not only between Heath and his in-laws, but also between Edward and his mother. The latter conflict may have been developing for some time. As a mother, Margaret was quite vigilant. At her behest, for example, Heath wrote to Edward, at Cambridge, in May 1627: 'Your mother hath heard you have had an ague & although she heareth also that you have lost it again, she is not well satisfied until she heare & knows certeynly how you . . . doe.'[101] Her solicitousness, however, encouraged interference, and Edward may well have resented her meddling. By the late 1630s a feud had developed between mother and son, a feud that Sir Robert sought desperately to resolve. Although he tried to play the honest broker, his correspondence from the period reveals that his highest loyalty and love rested not with his heir but with his wife. March 1642 found the dispute particularly bitter, and Heath could do no more than plead with Edward for a truce: 'You shall not lose by being just & kind to your mother. We are both old: neather of us by all possibility can live longe, much less is it likely that both of us shall live many years together.'[102] The dispute soon died down, but it does not appear that Edward and Margaret were ever again as close as Sir Robert would have wished them to be.

That Edward would brazenly abuse his mother reflects the fact that by the late 1630s Sir Robert had little control over him. Heath's other sons, too, early on gave indications that they did not feel bound by their father's plans for them. George became a divinity student at Cambridge and, upon receiving his master's degree, entered the ministry. Sir Robert, who was deeply

---

[100] *Ibid.*, 164.
[101] U. of I., Compton-Verney Books, letter no. 19.
[102] U. of I., Compton-Verney Books, no. 54. The dispute seems also to have arisen from differences relative to the settling of Heath family properties, notably Colliweston.

religious himself, may not have opposed the move, but it should be noted that in his correspondence he tended to slight George, a characteristic that perhaps suggests displeasure. Francis and Robert dutifully followed their father to the Inner Temple, and had the civil war not quickly taken them from their studies they might have become practising common lawyers, as he had intended. In fact, Francis did practice after the Restoration, but as a civilian. His father apparently supported him in his endeavours, for he left his books on civil law to him. Robert strayed entirely from his father's plan, becoming a poet, published and moderately celebrated in his own day, almost entirely forgotten by later ages. Edward, who diverged sharply from the way his father had chosen even while the old man lived, became a gentleman farmer. Only John embraced the common law as a vocation, and only he entered crown service.[103]

The independent spirit that characterised Heath's sons did not make them unique. Children of the time, sons especially, did sometimes resist the authority of their parents.[104] Still, the norm was for a child to accept his father's dictates, and the lives and careers of most sons ran roughly parallel to those of their fathers. As Sir Robert followed in his father's footsteps, so John followed in his.

Heath's apparent failure to control his sons' lives may be explained in several ways. Firstly, he seems to have been a rather indulgent father, instead of a disciplinarian, and it may be that he did not exert much pressure on his sons to follow the careers he had mapped out for them. Secondly, the fact that

---

[103] Generally on the younger Heaths, review Hine's essay, pp. 52 – 180. The essay contains numerous mistakes, however, and should be supplemented with Margaret Toynbee and Peter Young, *Strangers in Oxford: A Side Light on the First Civil War 1642 – 1646* (London, 1973), pp. 2 – 6 (on Edward), 260 – 1; on John, see (Sir) Robert Somerville, *History of the Duchy of Lancaster*, II (privately printed, London, 1970), pp. 62, 66, 77 – 8; on Robert, the introduction to *Clarastella, Together with Poems Occasional, Elegies, Epigrams, Satyrs (1650) by Robert Heath*, ed. F. H. Candelaria (Gainesville, Florida, 1970). Candelaria's appraisal of Robert Heath's poetry (p. viii) is quite just: 'Heath's poems are often better than those Herrick did not blot, though on the whole Herrick is so far superior to Heath as to make a detailed comparison unnecessary.'

[104] The relationship between Ralph Josselin and his second son, John, was strained for many years: Alan MacFarlane, *The Family Life of Ralph Josselin, A Seventeenth-Century Clergyman* (Cambridge, 1970), pp. 120 – 3. Edward Heath's daughter Margaret married without his permission: 'Liber E. H.', 161.

crown service often kept him away from home, particularly during the 1620s, may have prevented him from establishing a close relationship with his children during their formative years. Finally, the tumult created by the civil war may have negated Sir Robert's attempts to set his sons on a clear course. Whatever the explanation, it seems apparent that Sir Robert was not able to influence his sons' lives to the extent that his father had influenced his.

But however much he may have failed as a model, Heath generally enjoyed a happy family life. He sincerely loved his wife and children, and appears to have felt secure in their love. Like most of his contemporaries, he drew his greatest strength from his family. In return, he was prepared to make every sacrifice to better the lot of his wife and children. Judging from his known activities, he seems to have believed that the greatest boon he could provide for them was prosperity and material comfort. Consequently he strove to accumulate wealth, and by his efforts ruined himself.[105] To understand Heath's behaviour as a businessman, indeed, to understand his behaviour generally, it is necessary to remember that he was first and foremost a family man.

As others saw him

The product of Heath's three circles was a sombre man, who tried to face the world stoically and usually succeeded. A profound faith helped him to hold up well in tragic circumstances. When his first-born son, Robert, died in 1615, at the age of thirteen, he wrote 'god, as I assuredly hope, hath given a better inheritaunce' than he could hope to provide.[106] However, he also drew strength from his intimates, many of whom, in all likelihood, shared his faith and encouraged him to look to God in times of trouble. Reverses, then, did not cast Heath down, but neither was he elated by success. Seriousness was his general mood, and the written evidence that he left behind, including his correspondence, provides few traces of humour.

---

[105] See ch. 8.
[106] Noted in a codicil to the will that he prepared in 1615: SBT, DR 98/1511.

Indeed, when once he attempted to define the virtues of a perfect judge he noted in part:

> *Sobrietie* is a pretious link in this chayne; noe time, noe place, noe occasion, noe company, may put this virtue off. Bring the person of a magistrate, or suffer him to be brought into an occasion of levitye, and soe into contempt; let him speak like an angel, or otherwise live like a saint, yet he cann not redeem this one error.[107]

Nor, apparently, was Heath a sportsman.[108] Clearly, he did not fit the mould that great courtiers set for their boon companions. He was neither witty nor charming, neither a physical marvel nor a buffoon.

Despite his reserved personality, however, Heath was far from friendless. He had his enemies, men like John Vicars, the Roundhead historian, who wrote angrily of him as 'that dry and barren Heath the Judge', and Bulstrode Whitelocke, who, with Heath's career as attorney-general chiefly in mind, saw him as having been a 'fit instrument' to pursue the policies of Charles I.[109] But both Vicars and Whitelocke were enemies largely on ideological grounds, and the latter was also influenced by his father's grudge. Those who shared Heath's world generally liked him. In February 1632 Sir Edward Moundeford, a minor courtier, informed a cousin that Heath was winning 'much love' at Court.[110] Sir Richard Hutton, who for three years was Heath's colleague on the bench of Common Pleas, spoke for his fellow-judges when in September 1634 he commented that Sir Robert

---

[107] 'Collar of SS', ed. E. P. Shirley, *Notes and Queries*, 10 (1854), 357. 'Sobrietie' is one of the 24 words beginning with 's' — one for each 'SS' link in the judicial collar — that Heath included in this jeu d'esprit (written during his exile), as being characteristic of the perfect judge. Many of Heath's contemporaries shared his feeling that a judge should be sober. Sir Thomas Richardson was commonly disparaged for his flippancy: Edward Foss, *The Judges of England* (London, 1857), VI, 360 – 2.

[108] Hine claims (p. 60) that Heath was 'not a little fond of playing on the ''Peccadillo bowling-green'' ', but, as usual, he cites no source — his work is an essay, rather than strict history — and he often misinterprets his data. The possibility exists that he had some documentary basis for his statement, but in all of the letters and papers that I have seen there is not a single suggestion that Heath enjoyed or participated in sports.

[109] *Memorials of the English Affairs* (Oxford, 1853), I, 37; Vicars is quoted by G. N. Godwin, *The Civil War in Hampshire (1642 – 45)* (Southampton, 1904), p. 40.

[110] *HMC, Gawdy*, 138.

was 'bien beloved d'nous'.[111] And in June 1655 Nicholas, who alone of Heath's friends from the Buckingham retinue survived him, wrote to the earl of Norwich, an exile like himself, that the young man who was carrying his message was to be trusted 'being of the good Lord chiefe Justice Heaths family'.[112]

Heath was able to inspire affection because he himself welcomed intimacy. Individuals who took no part in his world may have seen him as being aloof and unfriendly, and in fact he probably would not have felt close to them. Within his three circles, though, he was kind, generous, and loving. To these circles he owed his happiness, and he repaid them with intense devotion.

---

[111] Microfilm of Hutton's diary (the original is in Cambridge University Library, Add. 6863), YCPH, f. 71. Hutton made his comment in the wake of Heath's dismissal as chief justice of the Common Pleas.

[112] 'Correspondence of Sir Edward Nicholas, Secretary of State', ed. G. F. Warner, Camden Society, *Publications*, new series, 50 (1892), 326.

3

Law Officer of the Crown

On 9 July 1626, as so often before and after, Sir Robert boomed forth advice to his sons at Cambridge: 'Although yee be young in yeers yet yee must not be so in behavior, remember that yee are the sonns of such a father as is soe well known in the world that your faults will be more observed then of others.'[1] The words were those of a man who believed that the office of attorney-general, an office that he had occupied for some eight months, carried with it great honour. Many an Englishman disagreed.

Actually, the reputation of law officers of the crown during Heath's time was quite low. That these officials stood at the pinnacle of a profession, the law, that was unpopular at all levels probably contributed to popular hostility, but to a great extent they brought condemnation on themselves by their behaviour. Most harmful to their reputation, perhaps, was a tendency common to many of them, to vilify and intimidate those whom they prosecuted. One of the worst offenders was Coke, who during the trial of Sir Walter Raleigh continually assailed the defendant: 'Thou art a monster; thou hast an English face, but a Spanish heart . . . I protest before God, I never knew a clearer Treason. Thou art the most vile and execrable Traitor that ever lived.'[2] Many law officers were milder than Coke, but they were tarred with the same brush. Small wonder, then, that an early writer on Bacon should have claimed: 'The offices of Attorney and Solicitor-general have

---

[1] U. of I., Heath Papers.
[2] *ST*, II, cols. 7, 26. Many contemporaries were shocked by Coke's behaviour. Aubrey writes, 'He shewed himselfe too clownish and bitter in his carriage to Sir Walter Ralegh at his Triall, where he sayes *Thou Traytor* at every word, and *Thou lyest like a Traytor*': *Brief Lives*, ed. O. L. Dick (Ann Arbor, 1957), p. 68.

been rocks upon which many aspiring Lawyers have made shipwreck of their virtue and human nature. Some of those Gentlemen have acted at the bar as if they thought themselves, by the duty of their places, absolved from all the obligations of truth, honour and decency.'[3]

While early Stuart England was willing to judge its law officers primarily on the basis of their behaviour in court, probably the most visible aspect of their work, pleading constituted only a small, though important, part of their range of duties. Apart from the secretaries of state, they were the two officials who were most responsible for the day-to-day function of government.[4] There were few aspects of the central administration with which they did not deal. Such ubiquity was characteristic of several major crown offices. The duties attendant on the occupants were myriad, and areas of purview overlapped in all directions. High officials were expected to be omnicompetent, even if the actual performance of some might suggest that they should be described with a different prefix.

As offices were poorly defined, so were modes of supervision. Some officials were bothered by the chaos, but it appears that most accepted it as a fact of life. When on 4 January 1641 Charles was notified that a proclamation that had been drawn up on 27 March 1629 had not gone into effect, he showed no surprise: 'Wee doe perfictly call to mynde that wee gave our then Atturney Generall Sir Robert Heath . . . warrant to drawe that proclamation in such sort as it is penned & if that warrant be either mislaid or not entered into our Councell booke, yet we

---

[3] David Mallett, *The Life of Francis Bacon* (London, 1760), xix; as quoted by Edwards, p. 56.

[4] Edwards is easily the best study of the law offices, and it contains much material that is relevant to the Tudor-Stuart period. J. W. Norton-Kyshe, *The Law and Privileges relating to the Attorney-General and Solicitor-General of England* (London, 1897), is geared to the nineteenth century. No published work deals at length with the law offices as they existed in Heath's day, but an extensive study of the attorney-generalship is provided by R. A. Swanson, in his unpublished Ph.D. dissertation, 'The Office of Attorney-General in England, 1558 – 1641' (Univ. of Virginia, 1976). While the term 'law officers of the crown' is variously defined, it is most commonly taken to apply to the attorney- and solicitor-general only, and it is so used throughout this book.

doe and in Justice and honor must avowe the same.'[5] Depending on the efficiency, motivation, and diligence of the leading crown officials, Stuart government ran well or poorly.

In the capable hands of Sir Robert, the law offices were among the best run branches of government. And they, in turn, ran him. During the ten years that he served as a law officer, ten years that were in many respects central to both his life and his career, the offices defined the way he lived, just as the recordership of London had previously. As far as possible, then, it is desirable to know the law offices as he knew them.

The stopcock

The conditions in which the law officers served were far from glamourous. They worked from their private quarters, in Heath's case the Inner Temple, and there kept considerable quantities of official correspondence and records. That they had no regular headquarters was in keeping with their status. Only when they were actually engaged in government work were they crown officials. Otherwise, they were private persons.[6]

Just as Heath, while solicitor- and attorney-general, would have had no official headquarters, so would he have had no official staff. Each law officer hired his own clerks and was responsible for paying them.[7] There was, in addition, a deputy attorney-general who headed the Outlawry Office and may have provided assistance.[8] Beyond such subordinates, the law

---

[5] Egerton 2978, f. 49.
[6] Edwards, p. 141.
[7] *Ibid.* Most of the clerks' income came from the fees that they received for drafting documents. A table of their fees, and the attorney's, as of 1693, is included in Lincoln's Inn Library Ms. 582, pp. 5 – 6 (part of a small collection of manuscripts relative to the attorney-generalship, kept by Sir Edward Ward). Heath's staff carried out functions other than drafting. They also served him as messengers and, when he wished to interview a party to a case or to see certain property confiscated, carried out his orders: *APC*, 1627 – 1628, 32; SP 16/96/50,51 (Robert Charnock to Conway, Conway to Heath; both 19 March 1628).
[8] William Johnson, who had been appointed deputy in 1592, held the post until at least Nov. 1623, when he prepared a schedule of fees — and, in passing, discussed the nature of his office — for the benefit of the commissioners on fees: PRO, E. 215/1.

officers, the attorney-general particularly, depended on a number of officials, high and low, to advise him or to carry out his bidding. From the attorney-general's point of view, his most important aide was the solicitor. The remembrancers of the Exchequer prepared for him several kinds of commissions, processes, writs, and injunctions.[9] The attorney could also, in various circumstances, look to the judges for advice. Local officials did his bidding in the field of law enforcement. Indeed, any official but the very highest was liable to receive an order from Heath for aid — sometimes accompanied by a royal warrant, but more often not — and the tone was apt to be peremptory. On 15 March 1627, for example, Sir Robert Cotton heard from Heath: 'For a present & an extraordinarye service for his Majesty I pray lett me intreat that you will serch out your antiquitys & Records: what hath been done & in what manner, when any have refused to serve the king in his warres.'[10]

Ironically, despite the fact that he could have counted on the service of many, Heath as a law officer was not in a position to delegate much responsibility. His staff was capable of little but preparing documents.[11] Not even drafting jobs could automatically be turned over to clerks, for there was always the chance that a poorly drafted document would be returned by some angry superior. The Stuart government, so chaotic in nature, demanded precision in its official instruments. Heath himself was well aware that documents had to follow strict patterns. In December 1630 he wrote to Carleton:

I receaved a warrant for the drawing up of a patent for mr wigmore for a place in the Marches; without a fee it will not be good in lawe, but the warrant mentioneth none, therfore I must drawe it with a blank, & humbly submitt it to his Majestys good pleasure to bee filled up with his owne hand.[12]

---

[9] (Sir) Thomas Fanshawe, *The Practice of the Exchequer Court* (London, 1658), p. 92.

[10] BL, Cotton Julius 103, f. 192. Heath had made a similar demand of Cotton in a letter that he wrote to him on 2 Aug. 1626: *ibid.*, f. 193. These letters related to crown schemes for raising cash; note Kevin Sharpe, *Sir Robert Cotton 1586 – 1631: History and Politics in Early Modern England* (Oxford, 1979), p. 141.

[11] Ward's schedule of fees (see n. 7) provides insight into the clerks' duties, as of 1693.

[12] SP 16/177/28.

Similarly on 31 March 1624 he complained to Conway that although the day before he had received from him the draft of a commission 'made by mr Read [i.e., Thomas Read, the Latin Secretary] . . . Of this draught I would make noe use, the body of it, was not legall enough, & the preamble was of too fine a makinge to peec with any courser stile'.[13]

While a law officer, Heath received his orders from two main sources. First there were those that came from the king, usually communicated by a secretary of state. Second were directives from the Privy Council or from individual councillors.[14] It was fairly common for an order to be sent to 'Mr. Attorney or Mr. Solicitor', perhaps meaning that the law officer who was more available at the time was expected to handle the assignment, perhaps only that the messenger was to present the directive to the first one he encountered. More common were orders directed to both law officers. They were most likely to come in relation to matters that were complex, suggesting that the recipients were somehow expected to divide responsibility. The orders themselves were often hazy. After hearing a report on corn from the commissioners of trade, the Privy Council on 10 July 1623 ordered 'his Majesties Attorney Generall and Solicitor shall drawe up bookes for the forme of commissions and corporacions to be in each countie, cittie and place where it shalbe found nedefull, and the draught of a proclamation for publishinge the magasins of corne'. The haphazard fashion in which orders were communicated naturally created confusion. In July 1624 Coventry informed Conway that although he had received from him 'a proclamation with directions for amendment thereof . . . because that proclamation was not drawen by me but by mr Solicitor I sent it together with the letter unto him to whom it properly apperteyned who will amend & returne it to yow'.[15]

Among the more common orders for drafting that Heath received from the king, almost invariably forwarded by a secretary of state, were warrants to draw pardons. These, he saw almost daily. They could be directed to either law officer, but most pardons, being formulaic in nature, were in any case at least partially drafted by clerks. During his decade as a law

13 SP 14/161/57.
14 Heath occasionally attended meetings of the Council and received his orders directly; note *APC*, 1623 – 1625, 297.
15 SP 14/170/44; *APC*, 1623 – 1625, 53.

officer, Heath received warrants to draw up pardons for recusancy, adultery, usury, theft, and many other offences. Charles refused to warrant pardons for murder, but he freely pardoned manslaughter.[16] Quite often pardons were tied to prior investigation. Sir Robert was frequently given carte blanche to prepare a pardon if, upon examination, he found the convicted party to be deserving. Since almost all pardons were initiated by petition, his investigation usually consisted of nothing more than verifying that what the petitioner had claimed was true. In rare cases, petitions were rejected, but there was a good reason for accepting them: the money paid for pardons helped to swell the royal coffers. When investigating the possibility of granting a pardon, Heath may sometimes have been swayed by humanitarian sentiments. If not, however, material arguments may have moved him, for he, like most courtiers, was anxious to see the crown prosper.

Perhaps the most important type of document drafted by the law officers was the proclamation. Most proclamations were drawn up by the attorney-general or his staff, but some were assigned to the solicitor.[17] The proclamation was the main method by which the king communicated with his subjects, and in consequence great care was taken in its preparation. Normally, it was the Council that decided whether a given problem should be dealt with by proclamation and if so what form the document should take. It then sent one of the law officers an order to draft, accompanied by fairly precise instructions on wording and content. A high proportion of the proclamations that Heath prepared were based on earlier ones, and the Council often noted which predecessor might serve as a model, meaning that clerks could handle much of the drafting and that, since the Council was specifying what it wanted, there was only a slight chance that it would reject the finished product. Frequently orders to draft proclamations were accompanied by advice as to the tone to use — normally, a strong one, the aim being intimidation. So, for example, when in January 1628 the Council learned that certain individuals had been

---

16 In a letter to Conway, 2 Feb. 1627, Heath alluded to Charles's policy against pardoning murder: SP 16/53/14.

17 Even when proclamations were drawn by the solicitor, the attorney may have remained responsible for the style and content, for he had to sign the draft in any case: Robert Steele (ed.), *Tudor and Stuart Proclamations 1485 – 1714* (Oxford, 1910), I, xv.

smuggling in goods from the East Indies, to the detriment of both the crown and the East India Company, it ordered Heath to prepare a proclamation 'to prohibite and terrifie all others from like practices'.[18]

That Heath as a law officer usually acted under orders when preparing documents does not mean that he lacked room for manoeuvre. He often anticipated need and drafted documents of his own volition. In July 1628 Conway informed him that vicious rumours about Buckingham were spreading in the north, and Heath responded that he would immediately 'drawe a proclamation, such as uppon the like occasion was in king James time & wait uppon your Lordship with it, before the kings retourn this afternoon'. His willingness to work without warrant, however, occasionally led him to unwise moves. June 1624 found him apologising profusely for having drawn up, without warrant, a pardon for a man who had been charged with 'the fowle crime of buggerye'. Significantly, he defended himself by claiming that Sir Ralph Freeman, the master of Requests, had told him that James favoured a pardon.[19] He may have misjudged in this case, but to have drafted a document in anticipation of the appropriate warrant reflected a common practice.

Just as Heath was quick to prepare documents that he believed were needed, warrant or no, so was he quick to question an order for drafting that he considered ill-advised. In June 1625 he wrote to Buckingham,

> I have receaved a warrant to drawe a proclamation about the office of Survey of Seacoles, in favour of the Duke of Lenox & am much pressed for a present dispatch. I find the busines it self one of thos things which was preferred amongst the greivaunces the last Sessions. And now another Sessions is neer at hand. . ... I nowe humbly offer it to his Majestys wisedome & judgment wheather it be a reasonable time to publish such a proclamation.[20]

---

[18] APC, 1627 – 1628, 236 – 37.
[19] Documents relative to this affair are Heath to Conway, 15 May 1624, SP 14/164/82; same to same, 31 May 1624, SP 14/165/68; same to same, 12 June 1624, SP 14/167/49; same to same, 19 June 1624, SP 14/168/12; and Heath to the earl of Holderness, 17 Sept. 1624, SP 14/172/35. Heath's letter to Conway is SP 16/110/28; on this document see also p. 222.
[20] Egerton 2541, f. 55.

In making known his reservations, Sir Robert was behaving as duty required, for law officers were expected to speak up when they felt that their superiors were about to blunder. Even when they did not openly question, or when their arguments were rejected, they were usually in a position to delay, sometimes to prevent, the preparation of a document that did not have their approval. Neither king nor Council had a good memory regarding orders for drafting, particularly when the document in question involved a trivial case. Of course, petitioners and others who were depending on a given instrument to aid them sometimes pressed the law officers and their superiors for despatch when the desired document was not forthcoming, but their pleas, to a Court that was inundated by petitions, did not necessarily bring prompt action.[21] Furthermore, the need for the document might pass, making a second petition superfluous.

Far from being a mere functionary, Heath, even in his clerical role, served as a 'stopcock', often free to decide which documents would be drawn and how promptly. But in another role he exerted a far greater influence over the workings of government: as a law officer, he was a prime advisor to king and Council. When a petition arrived at Court, it was seldom acted upon immediately by the addressee. Instead, it was referred, frequently to a law officer. While recorder of London, Heath had gained considerable influence through his role as referee and as a law officer, he played that part more often and in affairs of greater moment.

Generally referees were told which course of action to follow. Sometimes they were merely supposed to advise whether a petitioner's request might legally be granted. More often, however, they were ordered to report not only on the legality of a grant, but on its advisability, particularly on whether the king's prerogatives, profits, or popularity might suffer, should the request be approved.

If a second party opposed the granting of a petitioner's request, the referee's task was likely to be complicated by the need to interview and to mediate. Petitioners who were not

---

[21] In about April 1631 Donough O'Connor Sligo claimed in a petition that eighteen months before he had petitioned that he receive a renewal of a grant of lands, but that although Heath and another referee had promptly approved his request no further action had been taken: *Calendar of the State Papers relating to Ireland, of the Reign of Charles I*, ser. IV, vol. I, 607 – 8. Sligo's experience was not unusual.

challenged, however, usually saw their wishes satisfied, largely because they almost always had to pay to get what they wanted, and the fees benefited crown and crown officials alike. The more innocuous requests were granted as a matter of course. It was probably custom, not credulity, that in November 1630 caused Heath to report favourably on a petition for a patent on inventions that could, according to their creator 'make any sort of mills to goe on standing waters, by continuall motion without wind weight or horse . . . make all sorts of Tapestrie without any weaving loome . . . make boats shipps and barges to goe against strong winds and tide . . . make the Earth fertill more than usual'.[22]

The powers of the referee were considerable. Generally speaking, his advice on whether to grant a petition was accepted as the final word. A petitioner might question an unfavourable decision and possibly succeed in having it reconsidered, particularly if he were a great personage or if he could demonstrate that the referee had decided the matter on the basis of prejudice or incorrect or insufficient information. But second chances appear to have been rare.

Two principal factors determined the power that Heath enjoyed as a referee. Firstly, the king and Council were altogether incapable of handling the number of petitions that poured into Court during the 1620s, and the fact that most of the requests were of a trivial nature made them disinclined to try. Secondly, while neither the king nor, typically, his councillors, apart from the chancellor or lord keeper, were trained in law, many of the petitions revolved around legal questions. The volume of business and a lack of legal expertise made high officials anxious to refer most petitions.

A deep weariness is evident in an order that Heath received in February 1624. On examining a certificate that various officials of Guernsey had prepared, relative to the cause between a petitioner to the Council and a second party, the councillors:

fynding the same to be verie long and to consist of many particulars referred it to be further perused by his Majestie's Atturney and Sollicitor Generall requireing them to take into

---

[22] SP 16/175/58. The attorney reviewed all applications for patents for inventions.

theire due consideracion aswell the said certificate as all other proceedings had in this case and lykewise to call the said parties before them and to heare what could be further alleadged on either side and thereupon to make certificate to the Board of theire opinions touching the same.[23]

This order is characteristic in that it provides the referees with considerable leeway. Lacking interest in the case, lacking comprehension of its legal intricacies, the councillors were only too happy to give the law officers virtual carte blanche in deciding it.

On questions that the king or his councillors considered trivial, the advice of referees was heeded as a matter of course, and it was in fact quite common for their reports to serve as the text of a decision. Even if the substance of a petition or the identity of its author gave it special importance, the referee's counsel was generally accepted.

Heath's advisory function was not limited to his work as a referee on petitions. King and Council regularly ordered him to investigate and report on issues that troubled them. In addition, he sometimes submitted memorials that had not been requested by his superiors. Because the government seldom showed interest in unsolicited advice, it tended to ignore his gratuitous counsel. When superiors asked him to advise, however, Sir Robert knew that his suggestions would probably be accepted.

In large measure, the law officers' power derived from their advisory duties. Most work that the early Stuart government, like any government, faced was routine and mundane, and the king and his councillors were quite willing to accept the advice of referees on matters that they regarded as trivial. Furthermore, while great issues piqued their interest and their sense of duty, even these often involved complexities that they felt ill-equipped to handle. It was officials like Heath who dealt with difficult cases, and their reports decisively influenced government policy.

The king's lawyer

In advisory and clerical duties the law officers were more or less on an equal footing, but legal functions placed the solicitor-general in a strictly subordinate position. His job was to unearth

---

[23] APC, 1623 – 1625, 189. Cf. ibid., 179, 188; ibid., 1630 – 1, 273 – 4.

precedents for the attorney and to help him prepare cases. Sometimes he pleaded the crown's case in court, as did other members of the king's counsel. He also acted as liaison between the attorney and the judges, carrying messages, helping them to coordinate their activities.[24] These were the chief legal activities that Heath would have known during his time as solicitor, and they helped to prepare him for the senior law office. It was not coincidental that when, in Stuart England, the office of attorney-general fell vacant, it was usually the solicitor who advanced to fill it, for he was well qualified.[25] And the tasks that faced the attorney were complex and arduous, not the sort that a stranger to the law offices could quickly master.

To a great extent the attorney-general stood to the crown in the same relationship that the recorder of London did to the City. He was the Court's first line of defence, the champion of royal prerogatives. If possible, he was expected to help the king to magnify his power, but more important was his duty to note and report any event or action that seemed to endanger prerogative to even the slightest degree. If through oversight or choice he failed to expose a challenge, the king's power in some particular might forever be diminished. Coventry, during the course of his information against Yelverton, made clear the danger that was posed by an attorney who violated his trust: 'This office is one of the greatest, and largest, concerning the possessions of the Crowne, an extraordinary place for the preservation of the kings royall prerogatives, and inheritances, so that by this diligent care, he may increase them, and by the neglect of his duty, he may more diminish them, then any other of his Majesties ministeriall officers.'[26]

Just as the attorney was expected to defend the king's prerogatives, so was he expected to defend the king against all enemies within the realm, for he was the crown's chief prosecutor. By patent he could appear for the crown in any court of record; by Heath's day, however, the senior law officer usually practised in only four courts, they being, in descending order of usage, Exchequer, Star Chamber, King's Bench, and

---

[24] Fanshawe, pp. 94 – 5.
[25] Edwards, p. 125. According to Roger North, by the 1680s the solicitor-general had become 'almost a peer to the Attorney': *The Lives of . . . Francis North, Baron Guilford . . . Sir Dudley North . . . and . . . Rev. Dr. John North*, ed. Augustus Jessopp (London, 1890), II, 140.
[26] BL, Stowe 159, f. 28.

Common Pleas. Elsewhere, the king's business was handled by other counsellors.

In building his cases, the attorney often made use of the statements of informers. Heath probably had no higher a regard for informers than had Coke, who called them 'viperous vermin'; in fact, in 1630 Sir Robert prepared a list of instructions for them, with the object of providing tighter regulation.[27] Still, he undoubtedly realised that no law officer could efficiently defend the king's interest without them. When a case involved the crown, the attorney, not the informer, regularly exhibited the information, and he always did so if the case at hand were such that all resultant fines or forfeitures might go to the crown, rather than in part to the informer. If an informer died while pursuing a cause or refused to proceed, the attorney had the option to take over.[28] But never could he carry through his responsibilities entirely without informers, much though he might wish to do so.

Despite the assistance of professional informers and of individuals who informed for reasons that, while not necessarily admirable, were not pecuniary, it was often necessary for the law officers to run an investigation in order to build a case. Normally, at least in Star Chamber, a defendant who proclaimed his innocence would not be convicted on the testimony of a single accuser.[29] One informer's word, therefore, was not enough. Nor was it reasonable to assume that corroborative testimony from one or two additional witnesses proved the informer's case. Subornation was common, and malice caused many a person to bear false witness against his neighbour.

Probably the most thoroughgoing investigation that Heath conducted came in the wake of Buckingham's assassination. From August to October 1628 Sir Robert, prodded by Charles, worked feverishly to determine whether Felton had acted alone or had, as the king and his attorney believed, been part of a

---

[27] BOD, Ashmoleon Ms. 1148, IX, 17. This document may represent just part of a broader programme. On 15 May 1631 Charles ordered the two chief justices, the chief baron, and all other common law judges to 'set down orders for preventing abuses of clerks & informers in their prosecutions upon penal laws'; he further prodded them on 19 February 1633, noting that they had failed to act: SP 16/232/71.

[28] Edwards, pp. 262 – 4; Fanshawe, p. 91; Heath, *Maxims and Rules*, pp. 329 – 30. The informers were less active in Star Chamber than they were in quarter sessions, assizes, and Exchequer: Barnes, 'Due Process', 331 – 2.

[29] Heath reminded Conway of the rule, 27 Feb. 1627: SP 16/55/29.

conspiracy. Along the way, Heath interrogated individuals who ranged in status from the poet laureate, Ben Jonson, down to a baker's roundsman. Early in the investigation he encountered Robert Savage, who claimed that he and several others had joined Felton in a conspiracy. On 24 October, however, Heath felt compelled to report to Charles that the day before he had visited the Tower '& spent two or three houres in the examination of Savadge . . . he is and of longe hath bene an incorrigible rogue, & as such a one he ought to be punished . . . he hath noe knowlege at all of Felton, but all that he said . . . was fictious & untruthes'.[30] Heath, even though outraged, refused to charge an innocent man with conspiring to murder. Instead, he admitted failure in his search for conspirators.

Sir Robert was willing to discount the bogus confessions of eccentrics like Savage, but like crown prosecutors generally he sought to persuade accused parties to confess before the trial. If he succeeded, he knew that he had virtually won his case and that only the sentence remained to be determined.[31] It appears that when Heath had adequate time to prepare his case he was usually able to procure a confession prior to the trial. This was despite the fact that he did not have at his disposal the instruments of torture that were available to many a prosecutor on the continent. The common law did not sanction torture, as the judges reminded Charles when he suggested that Felton be racked. In rare cases, the king and his Council did authorise torture as a method of extracting information and ironically it was Heath who, in May 1640, was called upon to act as a witness to the last officially sanctioned racking in English

---

[30] SP 16/119/24. On 30 Sept. Carleton, in a letter to Carlisle, had also dismissed Savage as a liar: SP 16/117/83. On 31 Oct. Savage was tried in Star Chamber (SP 16/119/63) and, although the outcome is unknown, he presumably received a severe penalty. Other documents that reveal Heath's role in the investigation of Buckingham's murder, all being records of interrogations that he conducted, are SP 16/114/32, SP 16/117/33, SP 16/118/16, SP 16/119/30, SP 16/119/33.

[31] In Star Chamber, the attorney-general also gained an advantage in pleading if he appeared armed with a confession, for he could then proceed ore tenus, since the confession was accepted as the defendant's answer; nevertheless, the attorney still had to construe the confession so as to prove the charge: Barnes, 'Due Process', 230 – 1. Defendants sometimes disavowed their confessions on being tried, and occasionally they were then acquitted. Swanson, 202.

history.[32] But by then he was a king's sergeant, and furthermore the decision to use the rack was not his. There is no evidence that while attorney-general he ever sought to secure a confession through torture.

Heath needed no rack to win confessions. He was an able interrogator, who seems to have been sensitive to the psychological complexion of those whom he interviewed. His techniques are perhaps best delineated in the recollections of Alexander Leighton.[33]

Leighton, a deranged zealot, wrote a tract in 1628 which called on parliament to abolish the episcopacy and hinted that the bishops should be executed.[34] Shortly after he was apprehended, in February 1630, he was interrogated by eight members of the High Commission, but refused to cooperate, being unwilling to recognise their authority. Seeing that the commissioners were not winning Leighton's cooperation, Sir Robert took over the questioning. He confronted him at Newgate and told him 'the King was informed that I would not be examined'. This challenge to his loyalty shocked Leighton, and he protested that although he did not recognise the authority of the High Commission he would gladly cooperate with any representative of the king, including, of course, the attorney-general. Heath, giving no appearance of being mollified, made clear to Leighton that his crime merited severe punishment. The prisoner responded that he was willing to

---

[32] SP 16/454/39; *ST*, III, col. 371; J. H. Langbein, *Torture and the Law of Proof: Europe and England in the Ancien Régime* (Chicago, 1976), pp. 134–9. Although the racking was authorised, it is not certain that it took place.

[33] The following record of Leighton's interrogations is, except where otherwise noted, based on his memoir, *An Epitome or Briefe Discoverie . . . of the Many and Great Troubles that Dr. Leighton Suffered in His Body, Estate, and Family* (London, 1646), pp. 10–12. Three strictures should be noted in dealing with the *Epitome* as a source: Leighton's level of emotional stability was clearly less than would be desirable in an eyewitness; he was recalling events that had taken place some years before; not surprisingly, he detested Heath, an attitude reflected in his recollection (*ibid.*, p. 30) that at his trial it had been 'an easie thing for a man of his place and gifts, with nipping Scoffes, to tryumph over an absent and prostrate man'. Nevertheless, there is nothing implausible in Leighton's account itself.

[34] There is a considerable body of secondary literature on the Leighton case. The most recent work on the subject, and in many ways the best, is Stephen Foster, *Notes from the Caroline Underground: Alexander Leighton, the Puritan Triumvirate, and the Laudian Reaction to Nonconformity; Studies in British History and Culture*, 6 (Hamden, Conn., 1978), chs. 2–3.

suffer any penalty that he deserved, but begged to be permitted bail, for his circumstances were miserable. Sir Robert's demeanour now changed. His manner highly solicitous, he told Leighton that:

> if I would discover what I knew, it would be acceptable to the King . . . yea if it intrenched upon my selfe, I shoulde finde as much favour as I could wish. To which I answered, if it were a thing so pleasing unto his Majestie, and if he would be pleased to lay a particular command upon me, I would discover what I knew by my selfe in that.

Sir Robert, according to Leighton, was 'well content with this, and in words regretting my distresses, he went away withall making offer'. He soon returned with a specific question, ostensibly the king's: Who had written the tract? Leighton claimed sole authorship. Changing his tack, the attorney again challenged his loyalty, as 'he told me that it was given out that I should deny the Kings *supremacy*; I answered, that it was an unjust aspersion'. Leighton signed a statement approving of the royal supremacy and Heath left, returning yet again that day to announce that Charles was pleased with the affirmation.

At their next interview Heath again asked who had helped Leighton to disseminate his tract. The divine responded that 'some well-affected people' had helped him, but he refused to name them. In the face of this obduracy, Sir Robert's bearing softened: 'The Atturney urged me to give up the names of those Approvers, with faire promises of liberty, and what not.' What was this 'what not'? Years later, Leighton told the Long Parliament that during the interrogation: 'By Sir Robert Heath great gifts were offered to accuse others that approved of the booke.'[35] The 'gifts' were probably promises of mercy and perhaps of the king's favour. Whatever they were, they did not bring Leighton to name his confederates. As he steadfastly refused to inform, Heath again appealed to his loyalty: 'After a pause, hee told me that the king would take it [as] an argument that I loved him not, I replyed, that I would not for a Kingdome

---

[35] *The Journal of Sir Simonds D'Ewes: From the Beginning of the Long Parliament to the Trial of the Earl of Strafford*, ed. Wallace Notestein (New Haven, 1923), p. 17.

give him just cause of offence, but obedience must be ruled.' Unimpressed, Sir Robert sought to intimidate the prisoner: 'In conclusion, he began to bee rough, and to threaten me with the Rod: To which I answered, the *rod was in Gods hand, and he should doe well to looke to it;* . . . and for his threatenings I hoped they should never bring me to be an accuser of the Brethren.' On such a note did the interview end. The two next met in Star Chamber.

His sessions with Leighton saw Heath play on the loyalty of the accused. In an age when Englishmen uniformly revered the crown, if not always the king, such appeals to loyalty were probably common at interrogations, and it is likely that they were frequently successful. As attorney-general, Sir Robert partook of the crown's mystique, and he could with advantage tell prisoners that if they failed to cooperate with him they would thereby demonstrate disloyalty to the king. He could also hope to awe prisoners with his title. Undoubtedly, many subjects of interrogation, especially those of humble circumstances, were overwhelmed when confronted by the king's chief counsel and meekly did his bidding.

Besides playing on his loyalty, Sir Robert sought to obtain Leighton's cooperation by alternating threats with promises of mercy. This was probably a standard device in the interrogation process, likewise a potent one. Nor was its use limited to pretrial investigations. Appearing in Star Chamber, Heath advised that Leighton receive corporal punishment: 'Because he hath refused to confess his coadjutors', but he added the hope that the divine might yet be 'redeemed . . . by confession of the names of his complices'.[36] Through intimidation crown prosecutors extracted not only confessions but abject pleas for mercy. When in the wake of his conviction Leighton escaped, to enjoy a few precious days of liberty before being apprehended, Heath launched an investigation to determine who had freed him. On 26 November three prisoners appeared in Star Chamber, accused of aiding in the escape. The question of their guilt had already been settled, for Sir Robert appeared with full confessions. Still he kept up the pressure, railing against the accused, demanding severe punishment. His seeming rabidity may actually have been a ploy, intended to drive the defendants to new depths of remorse. If so, it was successful, for when they

---

[36] 'Leighton', 10.

were asked to respond, they all humbly admitted their guilt, recognised the right of Star Chamber to punish them severely, and begged for mercy. The members of the tribunal responded by recommending sentences that did not include the dreaded corporal punishment. Laud stated that he would have called for heavier penalties if the three had been 'stubborn', and probably most of his colleagues were impressed by the contrition of the accused. They saw before them three penitents, who would not soon challenge the authority of the crown.[37]

Heath's conduct in both Star Chamber cases recalls Coke's vilification of Raleigh, and in fact attorneys-general were usually free to depart from the norms of court behaviour that applied to most lawyers. Furthermore, they possessed advantages in pleading. For example, while defence counsel normally had the right to the last word, attorneys-general claimed it as a prerogative, and Heath himself considered the last word to be so important that he objected strongly when a lawyer who was defending one of the 'Five Knights' attempted to speak after him. When involved in a jury trial, the attorney enjoyed a signal advantage, for if the panel seemed unimpressed by his case, he had a right to quash it.[38]

Nevertheless, there were limits to the attorney's prerogatives. He was not free to ride roughshod, even in Star Chamber, where he probably enjoyed his greatest advantage over opponents. William Hudson, in his noted treatise on that court, states that the attorney-general was 'not tied to any strict rule of prosecution, but only to the order which the court shall make, or the lord keeper', but adds that the exemption extended 'only to strictness of time, for saving men's dismission, for he must

[37] 'Star Chamber Cases, 1618 – 1631', Gray's Inn, Add. Ms. 31, ff. 69 – 85. On 19 June 1631 Charles, noting the three men's contrition, ordered Heath to draw a pardon for them: SP 16/194/33.

[38] Fanshawe, p. 90; ST, III, col. 50. Edwards claims (p. 272) that Heath's complaint at the Five Knights' hearing marked the first time an attorney-general had ever asserted his right to the last word. However, the practice was long established. On 17 April 1628 Heath told the Lords that in the upcoming debate at a conference of both houses, his opponents would 'have this advantage which never any had against the Kinge, vizt. to be herde laste': 'Notes of the Debates in the House of Lords Officially Taken by Robert Bowyer and Henry Elsing, Clerks of the Parliaments, A.D. 1621, 1625, 1628', ed. F. H. Relf, Camden Society, Publications, third series, 42 (1929), 115. Litigants in Star Chamber sometimes retained the attorney-general to proceed by relation in their cases, so that they could share his procedural advantages: Barnes, 'Star Chamber Litigants', 16.

make a good bill, in matter and form, as a common person; he must join issue, give convenient time for examination of witnesses, as a common person; . . . and make as pregnant, manifest, and direct proof, as any common person whatsoever'.[39] Heath's own experiences in Star Chamber reveal that the attorney-general was indeed bound by rules. For example, during the spring of 1626 the court heard a case involving forgery, but decided that the information that had been exhibited was insufficient to convict. Heath, then in attendance, immediately sought to take over the case from the informer, only to be told by Coventry that he would not be allowed to go on unless he could produce a new and more incriminating information. He did so, and only then did the court permit him to proceed.[40]

Nor was the attorney-general assured of a favourable verdict when he pleaded for the crown. Star Chamber itself, often thought of as having been the attorney's preserve, occasionally saw Heath defeated. One case, during the autumn of 1627, followed the attempt by John Wallis, a justice of the peace, to persuade the tribunal to convict two men of rioting. The defendants were acquitted, and Heath, who had observed the proceedings, then conferred with them. On the strength of their statements, he soon presented his own information, alleging that Wallis had pressed false charges in the hope of extorting money from the defendants. Despite Heath's rank and the allegations of his informants, the court dismissed his case.[41]

That Sir Robert should even have troubled himself with so trivial a matter may seem surprising. He was, after all, the king's chief prosecutor, and one might imagine that he would have dealt mainly with litigation that involved important issues. In fact, however, while he undoubtedly devoted more time to preparing cases that the crown seemingly could not afford to lose, cases that involved the king's leading critics or greatest

---

[39] 'A Treatise of the Court of Star Chamber', *Collectanea Juridica*, ed. Francis Hargrave (London, 1792), II, 135, 137. Hudson has been accused of having been an apologist for Star Chamber, but the evidence tends to support him on these points.

[40] ITL, Inner Temple Miscellaneous Ms. XIX, 'Reports of Star Chamber Cases H.T. 1629 – T.T. 1639', ff. 75 – 9. Heath's assignment may have been made more difficult by Coventry, who instituted various reforms in Star Chamber and generally kept the court under a tight rein during his term as lord keeper: Barnes, 'Due Process', 344 – 6.

[41] 'Reports of Star Chamber Cases', ff. 91 – 3.

prerogatives, most of his appearances in court came in connection with apparently small matters. It was a duty of his place to project himself into any case that seemed to involve the interests of the crown, and he was expected to interpret his mandate broadly. So, for example, the charge of extortion that he levelled against Wallis was, more subtly, a claim that the defendant had perverted the king's justice. He was also expected to detect, across the breadth of the kingdom, activities that seemed to endanger stability. Seditious words or writings, riots — these were danger signs, and Heath was duty-bound to make certain that the people responsible did not go unpunished. As attorney-general, he possessed an arsenal of powers that aided him in his quest. To cite one example, if he discovered that litigation involving the crown was held up, for instance, by supersedeas, he could demand that the case proceed or even personally assume its pleading.[42] To a great extent the legal machinery of England was at his disposal and he was expected to use it to the king's advantage.

A second reason likewise brought Heath into court on cases that might be considered trivial. The attorney-general, more than any other member of the king's counsel, was called upon to uphold the ideal that all the king's subjects might look to the government for justice. On 24 October 1631, Sir Thomas Richardson, in the course of welcoming Heath, newly appointed chief justice of the Common Pleas, to the bench, reminded him: 'When you were Attorny generall yow had a Porter to keepe suitours from comeinge in to you, least by the multitude of Suitours you might be Oppressed.'[43]

Sir Robert's part in law enforcement was not limited to his duties as prosecutor. It was his responsibility to coordinate police and judicial activities throughout the kingdom. His role as coordinator saw him attempt to enforce government policies that often contradicted one another while themselves meandering maddeningly. The inconsistency of policy, as well as his performance in that maze, is amply evident when one examines his activities relative to the recusancy laws.

---

[42] Fanshawe, p. 93.

[43] The speech is drawn from Hutton's diary, which is printed in J. H. Baker (ed.), *The Order of Serjeants at Law*, Selden Society, *Publications*, supplementary Series, 5 (1984), 365. I wish to thank Dr Baker for having brought this source to my attention. Technically, Richardson was addressing Heath as a serjeant-at-law, but his speech concentrates on the chief justiceship.

Even as solicitor-general Heath played a significant role in the enforcement of anti-Catholic legislation. When in August 1623 James commanded that Catholics be treated less harshly, Conway ordered Sir Robert to confer with Coventry on how best to carry out the royal directive. James went still further in December 1624, himself ordering his law officers to cease entirely from enforcing the recusancy laws. Shortly after becoming king, Charles issued a similar directive, this time to the lord keeper.[44]

The virulently anti-Catholic posture of the parliament of 1625 forced Charles to back down from his policy of toleration. On 3 November 1625 the highest legal officials of the realm — the lord keeper, the judges, both law officers — were commissioned to superintend enforcement of the recusancy laws. While he did not serve alone, Sir Robert, now attorney-general, appears to have been primarily responsible for mapping out strategy, and the nature of his office placed upon him the burden of seeing through the commission's schemes. He moved quickly. On 19 November he was to be found interrogating an alleged priest.[45]

The six months that followed were hard for the Catholics of England, the hardest that they were to know until the 1640s, and Heath was in charge. On 1 March 1626 he sent a circular letter to the justices of the peace, enjoining them to enforce the laws that were aimed at recusant wives of communicant husbands and insisting that while such women might be shielded 'by the love of theire husbands . . . yet it is not fit that these Women [who] were contented to be more dangerous to the perverting of theire Children & Family then the husbandes should escape the penalties of the law'. His order was accompanied by an observation: 'In examinacion of Records for the Recusants Convict I finde there are many marryed women in that number [whose] goods are not to be seized nor theire landes.' Had he not reviewed the records carefully he would probably not have discovered what seemed to him to be a problem. His vigilance reflected a strong sense of responsibility. In a second circular letter, dated 7 March and directed to the judges riding circuit, he made clear what he considered to be his

[44] SP 14/150/45; SP 14/157/10; SP 16/2/1.
[45] *CSPD, Charles I*, I, 142, 151; SP 16/10/8. A more detailed discussion of the convulsions in policy, 1623 – 25, is in M. J. Havran, *The Catholics in Caroline England* (Stanford, 1962), ch. 2.

95

role in the campaign. At the same time, he reminded the judges of their own duties:

> Haveing received a spetiall Commandement besides the duties of my place to see the lawes against Recusants (as much as me lieth) to put in due execution being very loath that any parte of that service which soe concernes the church & state all hath beene recomended to his Majestie & soe gratiously entertained by his highnes should suffer by the error or negligence of my ministery. I am therefore bolde to put your Lordships in minde of these few following things which may advance the service & humbly entreat your Lordships that in the severall Counties of your Circuit you will be pleased to make such use of them as in your wisdom you shall thinke fittest & at your retourne out of the Circuit you will give me leave to waite upon you & understand from you how well these or any other your Lordshipps have bin observed by those who are to bee your Lordshipps eyes and eares.

He then called on the judges to spread word of the king's initiative, praising it as they went, and to see to it that local authorities enforced the recusancy laws.[46]

Despite Heath's efforts, the campaign was only moderately successful. English Catholics were experienced in handling persecution, and they met the government's offensive with a range of devices. Particularly successful was their tactic of conveying lands to communicant friends, in order to avoid forfeiture. Sir Robert was aware of the device, but apparently neither he nor other officials were able to blunt its efficiency. On 28 April 1626 a frustrated justice of the peace, John Newdigate of Cambridgeshire, apologised to Heath for his lack of success: 'I have done my best, to raise those monies which I had direction to distraine the convicted recusants goods for, & though there be not so much levied as was found by the jury that their goods were worth, because they were for the most part conveighed away before the seizure was made.'[47]

Sir Robert's main role in the campaign was that of coordinator, but as late as 21 April he could be found personally

---

[46] Cambridge University Library, MM. 4. 38, ff. 12, 13 – 14.
[47] SBT, DR 98/1652.

interrogating an alleged recusant.[48] Certainly he was zealous in pursuit of his duty. But suddenly the nature of that duty took a drastic turn. Late in the spring of 1626 Charles decided to reverse his recusant policy, from persecution to toleration. The royal will manifest, Sir Robert, too, changed course. A letter that he wrote to Conway on 29 July reflected the switch:

> I have received Advertisement from your Lordship that I should informe you particularly what Course his Majesty hath taken for the moderate execution of the Lawes against Recusants: in answer whereof your Lordship may be pleas'd to remember that his Majesty at the Councill Table was pleas'd to aske an account of me before all his Lords whereunto I then answered as I shall now doe.

After listing nine specific areas in which, at the order of the king, moderation was to be shown, Sir Robert concluded: 'This I know to be true because in the duty of my Place, It is most proper for me to take knowledge of his Majestys Pleasure and to observe it.'[49]

In directing the new campaign Heath was sometimes called upon to counter the very zeal that he had fostered during the old one. In March 1627, on the king's orders, he directed that the trial of the earl of Arundel and his son, alleged recusants, be delayed. The next eleven months saw four more letters in similar vein. March and July 1629 found him intervening yet again on behalf of a Catholic peer, this time Lord Petre, whose trial he ordered to be postponed.[50]

While Sir Robert accepted and even superintended the new policy, he did not approve of it. Like most of his countrymen he distrusted the English Catholics, seeing them as a corrupting force and potential fifth column. He feared that official

---

[48] SP 16/25/40.
[49] SP 16/36/80.
[50] *HMC*, Various Collections I, 96–7; Essex Record Office, Q/SR 266–117 (another copy D/DPZ 30/18), A/SR 264/108. Some persecution continued, with Yelverton being particularly harsh: Havran, pp. 111–14. In addition, the machinery for fining recusants and for sequestering their estates was streamlined, pulling more of them into the system: T. S. Smith, 'The Persecution of Staffordshire Roman Catholic Recusants: 1625–1660', *Journal of Ecclesiastical History*, 30 (1979), 330–3.

toleration would permit them to increase their numbers, strength, and wealth. His concern manifested itself in several pleas to Charles to permit somewhat stricter enforcement of the recusancy laws. Generally he tried to appeal to the king in monetary terms, arguing that the crown could profit from the spoliation of the Catholics. His arguments probably interested Charles, pressed as he was for money, but they did not sway him.

Heath's campaign may be traced through three documents. On 5 September 1627 Charles informed him that:

> Although we understand by you, that such Recusants as either to themselves or to others to theire use have obteyned graunts or leases of their lands estates, in the time of the raigne of our late deare father Kinge James, might by lawe be againe questioned and made a subject to their forfeitures, wherby we might encrease our profitt. yet consideringe it weere against the honour of our father to frustrate his graunts, and men might justlye suspect that we or our successors would in like manner avoide our graunts, we have resolved with our selves that all such graunts and leases shall stande firme.

Late in 1628 Sir Robert tried again. In a petition to Charles, he argued that annual crown revenue deriving from recusant forfeitures had fallen below £6,000 and that 'the great fault hereof, hath been in some of your Majestys officers, & other ministers of Justice'. He went on to advise the king to 'committ the trust to oversee this part of your Majestys just Revenewe, to some trustworthy person'. By coincidence, Sir Robert had just such a 'trustworthy person' in mind: himself. For the proposed office Heath was willing to pay £20,000 per annum, plus one-third 'of the surplusage which shall be raised by his industrye'. In the course of his petition, Heath noted that the recent parliament had bemoaned the fall in value of forfeitures and had propounded measures 'to prevent the practises, and to discover wher the error hath been for the times past & to advance your Majestys profite'. His tone suggests that Heath approved the members' stance, but Charles was not to be swayed, least of all by reference to a parliament that he detested. Nevertheless, Sir Robert continued his drive to turn the king away from toleration. In 1630 he called on Charles to command that 'the legal proceedings against Recusants, be directed, to goe on in a

due course (I say not severely and vigorously,) but constantly &
equally against them all, which will stopp the growth of
poperie, & yet take away the unjust sclaunder of persecution'.[51]
But not even an appeal for what Heath considered a middle road
swayed the king.

Despite his reservations, Heath enforced Charles's policy of
moderation as carefully as he had the earlier campaign of
harshness. Sometimes he moved on the king's express order,
but frequently he followed his own initiative. February 1627 saw
him advising Conway that two imprisoned priests be freed.[52] A
year earlier, he might well have attempted to send them to the
gallows.

The formulation of policy was the work of king and Council,
but its enforcement, like all routine matters, for the most part lay
in the hands of lesser men, who as a group had it in their power
to make a success of some crown initiative — or at least, to give it
a fair chance of success — or to defeat it through disobedience,
favouritism, or apathy. As a law officer, particularly as attorney-
general, Heath bore a heavier share of responsibility for the
implementation of policy than did all but a few officials. He
responded to the challenge with ability and dedication. That the
policies he helped to enforce were not always to his liking does
not mean that he was protean, for he was quite willing to let his
superiors know that he disagreed with them. Once the
government's course was set, however, and while it remained
set, he worked hard for its furtherance. Loyal service he saw as
his duty.

The profits of power

While devoted to his duty, Sir Robert was likewise devoted to
the interests of his family and himself. There were many
avenues that promised enrichment to a crown servant, and
during his years as a law officer he explored most of them.

The years 1621 – 31 saw Heath occupy not only the law offices,
but also a considerable array of other governmental posts, and
in addition he was many times a commissioner and a justice of

---

51 SBT, DR 98/1665; SP 16/43/27; SP 16/178/4.
52 SP 16/54/59.

the peace.[53] Most of these positions were either collateral to his central offices or were merely honorary, but all illustrate the complexity of his position. Furthermore, while a law officer he was also a private lawyer. Despite the importance and the burdens of their respective places, the attorneys- and solicitors-general were both crown officials only when they were actually involved in the king's service. Otherwise, they were private parties and, as lawyers, normally enjoyed a large clientele. The duality of their position was sufficiently well known to be reflected in the world of legal protocol. As Roger North noted in the 1680s: 'The Attorney General in the Kings Bench is an officer by the Constitution, and hath a place under the Chief Justice when he sits, and puts on a round cap like the prothonotary and chief clerk of the Crown, but profit calls him away, and to take place of a pleader within the bar.'[54] Some limits were set on the law officers' rights in the private sphere. By their oaths, they were barred from accepting retainers from any party to a case in which the king was involved on the opposite side.[55] In specific cases, too, their rights might be circumscribed, as Heath's were when in December 1626 the Council ordered him not to accept as client any party to a dispute that he was helping to mediate.[56] But on the whole both law officers were left free to pursue their own advantage. In an age that failed to define and seldom condemned conflicts of interest, Heath the law officer, like Heath the recorder of London, enjoyed the right to use his

53 As attorney-general, Heath was automatically steward of the court at Kingston upon Thames: Lincoln's Inn Library, Ms. 582, p. 7; Manning and Bray, I, 339 – 40. He also served, with Coventry, several judges, and other lawyers, as a governor of the hospital at Charterhouse: SBT, DR 98/1286.

54 *Lives of the Norths*, II, 141. By a precedent established in 1615, attorneys-general had precedence over serjeants when they pleaded for the king in Common Pleas, but not when they pleaded for other clients: Edwards, pp. 278 – 9. note also Baker, *Serjeants*, 112. According to George Gresley (to Sir Thomas Puckering, 27 Oct. 1631), Noy, on being informed by Charles that he was the king's choice to succeed Heath as attorney, demanded to know the wages associated with the office, 'for he was now well cliented; & when he was his Majesty's sworn servant in that place, he held it very unfitting to dishonour his Majesty or the place so much, as to be called & run from bar to bar to gain fees from other clients': Birch, II, 137. On the overall value of Heath's private practice during his time as a law officer, see pp. 249 – 50.

55 Lincoln's Inn Library, Ms. 582, p. 4.

56 *APC*, 1626, 436. When Heath was not acting as mediator, however, he did sometimes appear before the Council in service to a client; note *ibid.*, 1623 – 5, 168.

public office to benefit private parties. Moreover, as his power increased so did the store of favours at his disposal and the amount of recompense that he might expect from satisfied clients.

The wheels of government were oiled by inducements. An individual who sought some action, particularly one who wished for speed, was well advised not to come empty-handed. Gifts could be small and usually were so if the favour that was involved was minor or if it could be delivered without great effort. In 1627 the corporation of Exeter sent Robert Tooker to London, to seek a new charter. Since it was the attorney-general who was responsible for preparing charters, Tooker deemed it desirable, perhaps essential, to wine and dine Heath. In an evening at the King's Head Tavern, Sir Robert, the petitioner, and two king's sergeants consumed 'a sholder of mutton and a loyne . . . a fatt capon . . . a copell of robetts . . . 2 woodcocks . . . a dosyne of larks . . . bredd . . . ale . . . wyne . . . fruyte and bysketts'. The entire meal, including charges for preparation and service, cost Tooker 11s 6d, a small enough price to pay for Heath's good offices.[57]

While Exeter's expense was small, Sir Robert was often well rewarded for his favours. In June 1629 the earl of Cork noted in his diary that:

> I sent Sir Robert Heath, the Kings Attorney generall, one hundreth pownds in golde for his Fees in passing my two pattents from his Majesty, the first being a Release towching all suche proportions of yron as I sent from yoghall to Amsterdame: the later a graunt confirmation & Release to me & my Feoffees of truste of the best & greatest part of my lands in Ireland. This money, with a further promise of thanck-fulnes, I sent Sir Robert Heath . . . I having formerly gratefied him with a former C£ in golde.

Two months later Cork sent Heath another £100 'which make CCC£ given unto him for his favor & fees in passinge my pattents for my lands and yron'.[58]

---

[57] HMC, Exeter, 91 – 2. Exeter also gave Heath 10s for drawing the charter, his servant 12d for reminding him: *ibid.*, 92. Giving small gifts for favours was common practice; note B. Cozens-Hardy (ed.), 'Presents to the Sheriff of Norfolk, 1600 – 1603', *Norfolk Archaeology*, 26 (1936), 52 – 8.

[58] *The Lismore Papers of Sir Richard Boyle, First and 'Great' Earl of Cork*, ed. A. B. Grosart (London, 1886), II, 326, 339.

Tooker and Cork came to Sir Robert for particular favours and were not regular clients. Other groups and individuals, however, routinely retained him in fee. Sometimes they sought only his legal services. The prestige of a law officer, even if he served merely in a private capacity, could not but help his clients in court. But more often the parties that retained Heath hoped he would also serve them by interceding on their behalf with king and Council. Thus the East India Company engaged Heath as both lawyer and intercessor. The company regularly retained attorneys-general, but apparently no other crown counsellors. To some extent, it used the senior law officer as it might have any lawyer. Sir Robert regularly advised it on how to proceed in litigation, and on at least two occasions he represented it in court. However, perhaps his greatest service involved aid of a different kind. April 1627 found the company court resolving 'to be humble suitors to his Majestie for his proclamation to restraine all private trade into the Indies'. The court then directed its counsel to draft the necessary bill and 'to attend mr Atturney gennerall therewith for his advice and furtherance in procuring thereof'. Heath seems to have cooperated, for in February 1628 the company awarded him twenty pounds 'for his paines in drawing of the Proclamation for prohibiting of private Trade & for procuring his Majestys hand thereunto'. The company next sought to have a certain statement appended to the proclamation, and again it looked to Heath for aid: 'The Court being informed that the Declaration . . . cannot be done without his Majestys hand thereunto, Ordered that their Secretary shall attend mr Attorney Generall therewith, & desire his favor to procure the same.'[59]

How did Heath go about his task of 'procurement'? Sir John Heydon, lieutenant of the Ordnance, provides insight in his recollections of 27 March 1627, a day when, according to him, he met Sir Robert at Whitehall, where both men hoped to obtain the king's signature on a contract for the disafforestation of Neroche and Selwood forests. The request itself was to be put by Heydon, and he was to hold the document. Nervously, he asked 'what if the king should aske me who made me his

---

[59] Foreign and Commonwealth Office, India Office Records, CMB of the East India Company, B/11, IX, 502, and X, 270, 309; *CSP, Col.*, East Indies, 1625 – 9, 263, 280, 458, and *ibid.*, 1630 – 4, 79.

Attorney?' and he heard Sir Robert, uncharacteristically flippant, respond: 'Say that I did', and add that 'if he [Heath] then lost his place he might thanke himself.' The king soon appeared and Heath stepped into the royal withdrawing chamber, returning promptly with a standish. It was then the matter of a few moments for Heydon to make his case that Charles sign 'which his majestie was pleased then to doe . . . where Sir Robert Heath had formerlie placed the sayd Staundish & did then put the pen into the kings hand'.[60]

Heydon's account shows how easily the royal signature could be obtained. The king was not likely to withhold his hand when a high-ranking courtier requested it, particularly if the matter seemed trivial or routine. He was quite used to having his law officers approach him, document in one hand, pen in the other. Only the deviation from normal practice prompted Heydon's question 'what if the king should aske me who made me his Attorney?' Given the power of the king's signature and the ease with which it was procured, it is not surprising that those who needed favours were willing to pay crown officials to seek it. As a law officer, Heath could provide his clients with special advantages. He was skilled at drawing up instruments for granting any of a vast range of favours, and public as well as private business caused him to seek the king's signature routinely. Many a client might be satisfied by the stroke of a royal pen, and Sir Robert might even provide the standish.

Heath's offices promised him profit not only as a lawyer but as a referee. Interested parties were often willing to pay for reports that favoured them, and it appears that Sir Robert was not deaf to offers. There is certainly cause for suspicion in the record of his relationship with John Blanch, lawyer from Guernsey. During the 1620s Blanch, sometimes in association with his son, was party to eight disputes that were dealt with by the Council, while the total of petitions and counter-petitions that were prepared in consequence reached the dozens. Small wonder that on one occasion a party of petitioners from Guernsey characterised the Blanches as being two 'who for these 20 years have been the Common enemies of the Quietnesse of that

---

[60] SP 16/299/78. This document, drawn about 1635, is apparently an affidavit, prepared for a case in which Heath and Heydon were parties. On the disafforestation of the two forests, see also T. G. Barnes, *Somerset 1625 – 1640: A County Government during the 'Personal Rule'* (Cambridge, Mass., 1961), pp. 156 – 7.

Countrey'.[61] Heath's decade as law officer saw most of the Blanch cases referred to him. He received the petitions, interviewed the parties, and recommended a course to the Council. At first he generally sided with Blanch's antagonists, but after August 1627 he approved of every Blanch petition that came his way. In September 1628, furthermore, he asked the Council to appoint Blanch to a potentially lucrative post in the Channel Islands.[62] Finally, on 20 December 1630, two islanders complained to the Council that within the past fourteen months Heath had issued reports supporting the Blanches in their petitions against them, without first having heard their side. Without directing accusations at Heath, but probably believing that his actions were suspicious, the Council re-referred the cases, and in at least one of them the new referee decided against the Blanches.[63]

Although Heath may well have given in to temptation in the Blanch case, on the whole he seems to have been a capable, thorough, and honest referee. A case in 1626, involving a petitioner's claim that certain local officials owed him money, reflects his conscientiousness. He attempted to hear both sides, and when the officials failed to appear he advised the Council to order that the petitioner be paid, unless the officials demonstrated within four months that they were not liable. It was not unusual for Heath to make every effort to interview both parties to a case, as he did here, or to delay his report in order to give them time to appear. Nor was it unusual for the Council to take his advice without question, as it did in this instance. All that made this case exceptional was that the councillors, in framing their order, took note of the fact that during his enquiry Heath had taken 'much paines'.[64] In reality, he generally did.

As a referee, Heath normally followed fixed procedures. The same may be said of his general activities while a law officer. Even within a government that was in many ways chaotic, there were rules that determined the precise wording of documents, the precise nature of protocol. Where these rules existed, Heath was sensitive to them, and he could be adamant in their defence. In January 1626 he complained to Conway that

---

[61] All Souls Library, Oxford, Ms. 204, pp. 5 – 6.
[62] SP 16/117/15.
[63] APC, 1630 – 1631, 163 – 4; PRO, Privy Council Registers, PC 2/41, pp. 16 – 17.
[64] APC, 1626, 17 – 18.

although the archbishop of Canterbury had informed him that Charles wanted the Ecclesiastical Commission renewed, it was improper for the prelate to bear such a message, since he himself was a member of the commission.[65]

There were rules, but there were also gaps. In many areas, there were no fixed patterns of behaviour, and even where there were, lax supervision permitted abuse. Furthermore, a Court philosophy that favoured the acceptance of gifts by crown officials almost guaranteed abuse. Heath, for that matter, was probably less grasping than many courtiers.[66] Certainly, he gained much wealth through the law offices, but had he been entirely without scruples, he could have gained much more.

---

[65] SP 16/19/47.
[66] Of course, it is impossible to quantify rapacity. Generally on gratuities, and on the related question of corruption, see Aylmer, pp. 178 – 81, 246, 468.

4

An Economist as Counsel

Among their many duties, the law officers were charged with safeguarding crown income. As attorney-general, Heath was required to certify annually to the clerk of the estreats, an Exchequer official 'all the kings moyties recoveries, and fynes, for compositions made in the Kings Bench upon all penall Sumes or penall Statutes, and pay the Sumes yearley into the Receipt by taile'. He was also responsible for overseeing the payment of rents due to the king. When a will was challenged in court, the attorney-general was duty-bound to examine the deposition and to prevent its publication if it seemed in any way to endanger the king's interests.[1]

The law officers were responsible not only for maintaining the king's right to established sources of income, but for attempting to uncover new means of filling the often empty crown coffers. 'Fiscal feudalism', although most often identified with the 1630s, was practised throughout the early Stuart period, and the law officers, particularly the attorney-general, were notable among the researchers who ferreted out the precedents that gave the policy its direction and its legal basis. Furthermore, they served as the instruments of its enforcement. For the diligence with which they searched ancient records in an effort to justify new levies, they won the contempt of their countrymen and of historians. None suffered more in reputation than did William Noy, who died, it was said, with 'a bundle of olde moathe eaten records in his mawe'.[2] The contents of Heath's maw are unknown, but he, like Noy, did much to forward fiscal

---

[1] Fanshawe, p. 90; W. J. Jones, *The Elizabethan Court of Chancery* (Oxford, 1967), p. 262.

[2] Robert Ryece to John Winthrop, 1 March 1636: 'The Winthrop Papers', ed. R. C. Winthrop et al., Massachusetts Historical Society, *Collections*, fourth series, 6 (1863), 418.

feudalism. When, during his last months as attorney-general, he launched several lawsuits that were aimed at winning the reafforestation of Waltham Forest, he initiated thereby the crown campaign to expand the purview of the forest laws, a campaign that promised to increase both the king's wealth and his power.[3] While he may not have actively supported reafforestation — the lawsuits may have been entirely the result of orders handed down by his superiors — he probably played some role in shaping the policy. Certainly he did so in regard to the implementation of distraint of knighthood, since in July 1631 he prepared a memorial in which he argued that the best means of persuading men to compound was to try a few recalcitrants 'for to make an example'.[4] Heath may also have advocated expanding the geographical scope of ship-money levies. In early 1628 the Privy Council ordered the levying of ship-money in all maritime counties. The order was soon rescinded, and the identity of the man who inspired it is not known.[5] However, considering the role that Noy and Sir John Bankes, his successor as attorney-general, were later to play in the implementation of ship-money policy, Sir Robert may well have encouraged the scheme, and he would certainly have been largely responsible for coordinating and enforcing collection.

Besides overseeing crown income and seeking means to augment it, the law officers had a third, more complex, role to play in the field of government finance: the formulation and implementation of economic policy. The early Stuart government did not blithely intervene in economic affairs, save in areas that obviously pertained to it, like the customs. Nevertheless,

---

[3] SP 16/206/10-13, 17. Nevertheless, Noy, rather than Heath, has generally been viewed as the instigator of the campaign: George Hammersley, 'The Revival of the Forest Laws under Charles I', *History*, new series, 45 (1960), 89.

[4] SP 16/196/9.

[5] R.J.W. Swales, 'The Ship Money Levy of 1628', Institute of Historical Research, *Bulletin*, 50 (1977), 164 – 76. Ship-money was on several occasions levied during the Elizabethan period, over a progressively greater area; in 1603 the government decided to extend the levy to inland towns, but the plan was abandoned on Elizabeth's death: A. H. Lewis, *A Study of Elizabethan Ship Money* (London, 1928), *passim*. While Noy was a proponent of ship-money, he does not appear to have envisaged a levy that would include inland communities, so his plan was not as innovative as were those of 1603 and 1628.

the paternalistic philosophy that was common to the period encouraged intervention when national prosperity seemed endangered, and the government also knew that economic distress meant smaller crown revenues and increasing unrest. The Court was seldom indifferent in a time of depression. But before acting, it looked for guidance.

During his time as law officer Heath wrote a number of proposals and reports on economic matters. Most of them date from his years as solicitor-general, a disparity that may be explained in either of two ways. Firstly, the distribution of assignments and responsibilities gave the attorney-general a workload that was in most respects heavier than the solicitor's, so it may have been considered more the duty of the junior law officer to deal with complex problems, such as the formulation of economic policy. Secondly, Heath's term as solicitor coincided with the greatest depression of the early Stuart period. During the years 1620 – 4 trade slumped disastrously. The result was a massive outpouring of proposals on how to cure the nation's ailing economy. In this time of crisis Heath was often called on by his superiors to report or advise on economic matters. His years as attorney saw a healthier economy so the government was less in need of his counsel.

Not only did Sir Robert write a great deal on economic matters, but he wrote well. Moreover, the key period 1620 – 4 saw his economic philosophy rapidly mature. At the same time, however, the government paid steadily less attention to his ideas. Heath's economic schemes may therefore be studied to gain insight into the man, while their fate says much about the Court.

The cloth trade

Hardest hit by the depression of 1620 – 4 was the textile industry. During 1620 the market for textiles collapsed, and the Court was deluged by petitions from desperate clothiers and merchants. In mid-May, having heard the outcry, the Council concluded: 'The cloathing of the kingdome, wherein so many sortes of people are interested as namely the woollgrower, clothier, merchant, weavour, spinner, fuller and divers others, is of farr more generall consequence than any other mistery or trade whatsoever.' Eleven councillors were then appointed as a standing committee to deal with problems in the textile industry. High-ranking courtiers all, they were ill-prepared for their assignment. In the end, the only remedy that the Council proposed was discipline and self-denial: 'The wooll-growers may not . . . expect such hiegh rates at all tymes for wooll as are given some times [and] every man must beare a part as may best conduce to the good of the publicke and the maintennance of generall trade.'[6]

Having taken its stand, the government retired into inaction. It was moved by neither the worsening situation in the textile industry nor the demands for relief that shook the parliament of 1621.[7] As the depression deepened, however, progressively more workers were laid off, increasing popular discontent and anxiety, frustration, and, finally, potential for mass violence. Tumult the government feared, and on 9 February 1622 the Council ordered the justices of the clothing counties to end the depression by punishing those who allowed it to continue:

> Wee do hereby require you to call before you such Clothiers as you shall think fitting and to deale effectuallie with them for the imployment of such weavers, Spinners, and other persons as are now out of work . . . So may wee not indure that the Clothiers . . . should at their pleasure . . . dismisse their work folks who being many in number and most of them of the poore sort, are in such cases likely by their clamours to disturb the quiet and Government of those parts wherein they live.[8]

Such a ham-handed policy could not succeed. As tactfully as possible the justices informed the Council that England's economic ills were not curable by fiat, some citing the example

---

6 *APC, 1619 – 1621*, 197 – 8, 205 – 6.
7 *CD 1621*, II, 75 – 8, 214 – 17, and IV, 95 – 8. James did, however, as part of a lengthy proclamation issued 10 July 1621, reaffirm an earlier ban on the export of wool, woolfells, and fuller's earth, and in the same document he, at the urging of Parliament, opened up the trade in Welsh cloths: J. F. Larkin and P. L. Hughes, (eds.), *Stuart Royal Proclamations* (Oxford, 1973), I, 516 – 18. In Nov. 1621 the Council appointed a 20-man committee on the decay of trade, but the body, which was dominated by MPs, seems to have accomplished little: J. P. Cooper, 'Economic Regulation and the Cloth Industry in Seventeenth-Century England', *Royal Historical Society, Transactions*, fifth series, 20 (1970), 78.
8 *APC, 1621 – 1623*, 132.

of William Benett 'a very ancient & good Clothier', who had offered 'to live by browne bread & water rather then his great number of poor people should want work, yf he had meanes to keep them in worke'.[9]

The government's course of action was not only naive but confused. On 2 March 1622 the Council informed the judges of assize that James was about to issue a proclamation 'for the generall wearing of cloath and stuffs made of wooll growing in his Majestie's dominions for the better ventinge of that commoditie within this realme'.[10] No such proclamation was published, apparently because a new decision had been reached: that the status of the cloth trade was to be reviewed before any further steps were taken. On 10 April the Council reported to the sheriffs and the justices of the peace of each clothing county that a committee would soon be appointed to investigate all problems relating to textiles, and it ordered them to designate two clothiers apiece to appear before the projected panel.[11] Thirteen days later the committee was named and the members directed:

> to treate and conferr aswell with the Marchant Adventurers of London as with the said clothiers (who shalbe ordered to attend you) and such others of experience as you shall thinke meete to call unto you touching the efficient cause of this great decaye and abatement of trade in the vent of cloth, together with all particular greevances and objecttions which the said clothiers can make. Whereof, when you shall have found out the true groundes and motives, you are then to consider of the aptest and fittest remydie how such exceeding losses and inconveniences to the realme may hereafter be eschewed and avoyded and how the cloth may be readely taken off from the clothier.[12]

Beneath the peremptory tone was vagueness. Although required to interview the Merchant Adventurers and the

---

[9] SP 14/128/49; as quoted by R. H. Clutterbuck, 'State Papers relating to the Cloth Trade, 1622', Bristol and Gloucestershire Archaeological Society, *Transactions*, 5 (1880 – 81), 157.

[10] *APC, 1621 – 1623*, 153.

[11] *Ibid.*, 190.

[12] *Ibid.*, 201 – 2.

designated clothiers, the committee was generally left free to gather and to weigh information as it chose. Such imprecision was typical of Council assignments.

Heath was a committee member. So was Coventry. The law officers were regularly included on panels that were intended to advise on policy, probably for any of three reasons: as lawyers, they were aware of precedent and were competent to translate committee reports into legal instruments, notably proclamations; as crown servants, they were bound to recognise and protect royal prerogatives; as courtiers, they were aware of general government policy and could take it into account when they advised on remedial action. With Heath and Coventry on the committee were ten others, some of them courtiers, all sharing some link with the mercantile world, as money-lenders, as merchants, or as active members of trading companies. When the Council sought advice on complex issues, it looked to experts.

Over the course of several weeks the committee heard a number of spokesmen. Only one set of notes taken at an interview is known to have survived, Heath's, dated 6 May. Speaking that day were delegates from the clothing counties. This was not their first appearance, since Heath mentions at the head of his notes that: 'The Clothiers again presented themselves.' They were prepared with statistics and analyses, and Sir Robert dutifully recorded their statements.[13] Undoubtedly the session of 6 May was only one of many. There is no reason to doubt the committee's assertion, made in its report to the Council, that during its investigation there had been 'manie Conferences had with the Merchants Adventurers and the Merchants of other Societyes and Companies with the Gentlemen of quallitye of severall clothinge shires with the officers of his majesties Custom-howse in the port of London and the drapers and dyers of London And . . . manie daies spent in this weightie service'.[14]

Like its investigation, the committee's final report, issued on 22 June, was wideranging. After reviewing possible causes of the malaise, the committee proposed several dozen specific remedies, under eight heads. The government, it suggested,

---

[13] SP 14/130/28. On clothiers' complaints, see also Cooper, 'Economic Regulations', 78 – 9.
[14] SP 14/131/55; quoted from Clutterbuck (whose citation is incorrect), 161 – 2.

should ban all exportation of raw wool and order: 'That the meaner sort of people, as Apprentices, Servants, or Mechaniks be enjoyned by proclamation to the weare of clothe and stuffe of wooll made in this kingdome.' Next, the committee urged that illegal dyeing be actively combatted, while at the same time the 'intricate' mass of laws dealing with the manufacture and dressing of cloth be reduced to 'one Clere Lawe'. With well-advised timidity, the panel then noted that some clothiers blamed the trade slump in part on pretermitted customs on cloth, but it did not go so far as to suggest that the king forego this source of revenue. More forthrightly, it argued that the Merchant Adventurers should be forced to open their membership and that no new joint-stock companies should be established. The committee next dealt with the drainage of coin from the kingdom, calling on the government to demand that the East India Company, which many Englishmen saw as the primary exporter of coin, should bring into the kingdom as much bullion as it removed. Finally, it urged that a commission be established, to oversee the management of the textiles industry.[15]

The report provided clear direction, and the government in large part accepted it. On 28 July James paraphrased many of the committee's proposals when in a proclamation he forbade the export of wool and ordered his subjects to wear more woollens. On 21 October he implemented another recommendation by appointing a commission to superintend the manufacture of textiles. It is noteworthy, however, that he did not crack down on either the Merchant Adventurers or the East India Company in the ways suggested by the committee. Perhaps company pressure discouraged the government from acting. Not surprisingly, the king also in no way reduced his customs.[16]

---

[15] SP 14/131/56. The report is printed entire in G. D. Ramsay, *The Wiltshire Woollen Industry in the Sixteenth and Seventeenth Centuries* (Oxford, 1943), pp. 147 – 53.

[16] Larkin and Hughes, I, 547; Thomas Rymer (ed.), *Foedera, conventiones, literae et cuiuscunque generis acta publica* (London, 1720), XVII, 410 – 15. The relationship between the crown and the great companies, notably the Merchant Adventurers, 1621 – 4, is dealt with by Robert Ashton, *The City and the Court 1603 – 1643* (Cambridge, 1979), pp. 106 – 20. Ashton claims that 1621 found the Court friendly to the companies, while parliament was hostile; by 1624, he believes, James, swayed by the anti-company sentiments of Buckingham and Charles, had turned on them, even as parliament had grown more moderate.

For Heath, the committee report marked both an end and a beginning. He had apparently helped to supervise interviews for the panel, although the fact that the only record of a hearing is written by him does not indicate that other committee-men did nothing. Heath was also assigned the task of drafting the report, possibly an indication that his fellow-members thought him an able and accurate spokesman. But undoubtedly most committee-men contributed suggestions to it and Heath's own role in shaping the finished product cannot be determined. Be that as it may, it is certain that his experience on the committee helped him, since the breadth of the investigation brought him into contact with an array of problems that beset the English economy. Furthermore, one outcome of the committee report put him in a prime position to investigate the problems further — he was included on the commission that was appointed on 21 October.[17] Until that time, his involvement with economic issues had depended on personal interest and on specific assignments. Thenceforth, he would, for as long as he remained in government, have reason to observe the economy and to analyse it.

Strangers

The problem of how to deal with England's alien community was ever-present in Heath's day. Admired for the religious convictions that had caused them to flee their homelands, strangers were at the same time seen as a threat to native industry. A petition submitted by the City to the Council in 1616 succinctly stated the complaints of the mercantile community:

> Theire chiefest cause of entertainment here of late was in charity to shroud them from persecution for religion; and, being here, theire necessity became the mother of theire

---

[17] Several historians have claimed that this commission evolved into the Board of Trade; e.g., B. E. Supple, *Commercial Crisis and Change in England 1600 – 1642* (Cambridge, 1964), p. 67. As a group, however, the commission seems to have been rather inactive, and James criticised it for this; note the transcription of his letter in William Cunningham, *The Growth of English Industry and Commerce*, fifth ed. (Cambridge, 1912), pp. 900 – 1. Under Charles, also, the commission appears to have done little, especially after 1626: Cooper, 'Economic Regulation', 84.

ingenuitie in deviseing manye trades before to us unknowne. [They have been] bould of late to devise engines for workinge of tape, lace, ribbin, and such, wherein one man doth more amonge them then 7 Englishe men can doe; soe as theire cheape sale of those comodities beggereth all our Englishe artificers of that trade and enricheth them.[18]

In times of economic depression, the anti-alien campaign intensified. During the parliament of 1621, some of the most heated language was reserved for denunciations of the strangers. That same year of depression saw London petition the king for help in combatting the economic danger allegedly posed by alien craftsmen. Reacting at last, on 4 August James appointed a commission to deal with the problem. The mandate that he provided was vaguely defined, in keeping with common practice:

[You are] by such waise and meanes as you in your judgements and discretions shall hold most convenient, to enquire of all and every the Premisses, and to consider of all the Lawes and Statutes any way touching the same, and to treate with the Strangers . . . either to draw them to a Conformitie unto our said Laws and Statutes . . . or at least so to moderate them as may best stand with their Conveniences . . . and the good and welfare of our owne People.[19]

Among the thirteen commissioners were Heath and Coventry. Their membership was to be expected. More surprising was the designation of Robert Titchbourne and Robert Seliard. They do not appear to have been experts on the alien problem and their

---

[18] SP 14/88/112; as quoted by W. D. Cooper (ed.), 'Lists of Foreign Protestants, and Aliens, Resident in England 1618 – 1688', Camden Society, *Publications*, 82 (1862), v. On native English attitudes toward the strangers, see C. W. Chitty, 'Aliens in England in the Sixteenth Century', *Race*, 8 (1966), 129 – 45; Patrick Collinson, 'The Elizabethan Puritans and the Foreign Reformed Churches in London', Huguenot Society of London, *Proceedings*, 20 (1964), 528 – 55. Throughout the seventeenth century, as in this section, 'stranger' was used interchangeably with 'alien', although it was actually a looser term, covering denizens as well.

[19] Rymer, XVIII, 318 – 19; *CD 1621*, III, 427 – 9, and VII, 267 – 9, 282 – 6. In June 1621 London petitioned the Council, demanding that the strangers be more strictly supervised: SP 14/121/148.

links with the government were weak, but both were Heath's relatives by marriage, as well as business associates of his. That they were included in the commission suggests that Sir Robert played a role in the choice of members.

During its investigation, the panel heard from a number of interested parties. Among them was the Goldsmiths Company, which had long been vocal in criticising alien competition. On 2 January 1622 the company assistants, noting that Heath had recently told a delegation of wardens that the Goldsmiths should 'sett downe in wryteing theire perticuler greivances suffred by the saide Aliens and Strangers with theire number', designated a committee to enumerate grievances. Only four days later the report was read out in company court. Heading it were the names of almost two hundred aliens who were, the authors alleged, involved in 'buyeing selling & makeing of gold & silver wares jewells pretious stones & other imployments within this citie & suburbs'. Disciplining these men would be difficult, they conceded, for the strangers worked 'in chambers garretts & and other secret places, where the wardens of this companie may not have convenient access & recourse to searche'. Nevertheless, they called upon the government to order that the alien craftsmen 'not take anie servants or apprentices, but by the approbation & allowance of the wardens of the companie . . . and be subject unto them and theire ordenances in all matters of government concerning theire misterie', to forbid aliens to sell any jewelry or plate except to members of the company, to 'duely & strictlie put in execution' statutes and City ordinances that regulated strangers' business practises, and finally, most broadly, to take some action 'that the great multitude of such Aliens & strangers maye be reduced to a farre lesse nomber'.[20]

Besides the Goldsmiths, several other London companies reported to the commission, as did officials of the City and of other communities that had significant numbers of aliens. The reports that have survived are uniformly hostile to the strangers, but it is entirely possible that some parties, whose statements are not extant, took a more sympathetic line. Furthermore, the strangers themselves were heard, or at least,

[20] Goldsmiths Hall, Goldsmiths Company P, part 2, Wardens' Accounts and Court Minutes, ff. 266 – 7.

as Heath reported, 'the Elders of the French & Duch congregations'.[21]

From beginning to end, Heath dominated the aliens' commission. Apparently all reports were addressed to him and Coventry or, as in the case of the Goldsmiths, to him alone. Moreover, the central task of making recommendations seems to have been left entirely to him. During the first half of 1622 he sent the Council several sets of proposals regarding the alien issue. All of them were in his hand and were probably his work alone. They seem, however, to have been accepted as being not merely his reports, but the commission's.

Heath's sympathies lay with his countrymen, and this bias is reflected in his reports. With obvious indignation he told the Council that strangers were actually profiting from their foreign birth, whereas in justice they 'should be servantes to the english'. To his mind, they gained an unfair advantage because they, unlike their English competitors, were not limited to a fixed number of apprentices and were largely free from the charges and the supervision that the City and the companies imposed on London craftsmen. They profited further, he claimed, by ignoring statutes that barred them from certain handicrafts and that forbade them to sell by retail. The remedies that Heath suggested were for the most part direct responses to these perceived wrongs. No alien craftsman, he advised, should in future be allowed to sell any item of manufacture whose quality had not been approved by the company that shared his trade. Laws against retailing were to be strictly enforced. Strangers were to be allowed only as many apprentices as their English counterparts.

As he wrote, Heath bore in mind the king's interest. His proposed settlement, he believed, should serve to augment the royal income. He therefore advised 'because the Straungers are not subject to the publike charges of the Citty or Companys as the Englishe are: That every straunger using any Trade or profession, whereby he acquireth his living shall pay quarterage to his Majestys use'. The same motive, at least in part, inspired Heath to further suggest that laws barring strangers from certain

---

21 SP 14/121/61. In the following analysis of Heath's proposals, all references are derived from this account, SP 14/121/50, SP 14/121/160, or SP 14/121/163. SP 14/121/146 – 69 includes several reports attacking the strangers, as well as proposals for dealing with them. Although undated, these documents likely date from Heath's enquiry.

trades should not be enforced, provided the alien craftsmen paid 'a smale proportion out of ther labors, . . . whereby the Straunger may be secured from damage or trouble, the english receave some incouragement, [and] the King receave some benefit, in thankfullnes for his grace extended to the Straunger'.

The problem of enforcing the proposed regulations remained. Realising that the government knew little of the alien community, a fact that made both supervision and taxation difficult, Heath recommended that a register of strangers be established, and revised annually. The cost of maintaining this register was to be borne by the aliens themselves, but the fee that Sir Robert recommended, 12d annually for householders and 6d for other strangers, was much higher than cost, suggesting that his proposal was partly intended to provide yet another source of income for the crown. To direct the preparation of the register, as well as generally to oversee the enforcement of whatever policy the government established, Heath advised that a new commission be created, with a jurisdiction that would include not only London, but other cities that had significant alien communities, namely, Norwich, Colchester, Canterbury, Sandwich and Dover.

On 1 June 1622 the commission was reconstituted, the new membership differing from the old only in one addition. In the course of instructions to the commissioners the king detailed his policy. The commission was to prepare a register of strangers. Aliens were to pay quarterage to the crown and those involved in trades that they were barred from by statute were to be allowed to purchase the 'Royal Protection'. Foreign-born craftsmen could employ no more apprentices than their native-born counterparts. Strangers would no longer be allowed to sell by retail, nor would they be allowed to sell items that had not been approved by company representatives.[22] Everywhere, Heath's influence was evident. It was also evident in a grant of 14 May 1622, by which Seliard and Titchbourne were empowered to receive the aliens' quarterage and 'protection' money and to pay the same to Buckingham and to his associate, the earl of Montgomery. Presumably, Heath's two relatives profited by the arrangement, if not as much as did his patron, or the king.[23]

[22] Rymer, XVII, 372 – 4.
[23] SP 14/130/71.

Heath incorporated into his scheme a large measure of moderation. In both his temperament and his philosophy, Sir Robert was given to a via media, and it was entirely in keeping with his predilections that he wrote in one of his reports: 'To restreyne the straungers wholy, were too hard & and not fitt for the present times, & therfore ther is noe middle way but this.' The same sense of moderation also drew him to past practice. Suspension of anti-alien statutes in return for protection money was by no means unprecedented, he argued, but rather parallelled medieval crown policy toward the Jews. However, few of the precedents that he looked to were so ancient. Almost all his major proposals were, in fact, similar to others that had been made in recent years. For example, in 1618 the Council had ordered a register of strangers to be prepared; while nothing had come of the scheme, it is entirely possible that Heath bore it in mind when he framed his own proposal.[24] That his suggestions were grounded in precedent made them all the more acceptable to Heath's superiors, for the government was reluctant to make moves that were unprecedented. Of course, it was not at all reluctant to take up advice that promised to augment the royal income, a fact that strongly favoured an acceptance of Heath's proposals.

King and Council alike, however, avoided decisions that might antagonise any influential element of the nation. It appears that Heath's proposals did not at first arouse significant opposition. However, in choosing a moderate path he had angered both the strangers, who resented the required payments and the limitations on their trade, and the companies, which wanted still stronger measures. The corporation of London, which closely reflected company sentiment, soon joined in attacking the aliens' commission. On 23 December James informed the commissioners: 'London have cast a doubt, beyond our Expectation, whether the proceeding uppon this our Commission may not be extended to the Prejudice of our said Cittie contrarie to our intention; and that some Straungers have alsoe claymed the Priviledge of former favors.'[25] Another apparent complaint of the commission's critics, an unspoken one, was that it gave Buckingham additional revenue and

---

[24] Cooper, 'Lists of Foreign Protestants', viii – ix; *APC*, 1618 – 1619, 249.
[25] Rymer, XVII, 440.

power. The duke was not a commissioner, but he played an important, though perhaps undefined, role in the panel's activities, and he undoubtedly retained a large share of the strangers' fees. So long as he remained on the scene his enemies were muted in their criticism of the commission. However, when in February 1623 he accompanied Charles on his ill-conceived journey to Madrid, he left behind him a commission that was unpopular and weakly defended.

On 7 March the French and Dutch congregations petitioned the Council. Heath was present by order, so that he might play devil's advocate. The strangers explained the nature of the commission to councillors who first feigned surprise, then, according to Sir Robert 'condemned the busines, before they herd me speak a word to maynteyn it'. Concluding its business, the Council gave Heath until the following Tuesday to prepare a defence of the commission, and it hinted, perhaps stated, that if he were unpersuasive the panel might be abolished. Sir Robert, understandably concerned, soon despatched a letter to Montgomery. After acquainting his patron's partner with the situation, he begged him to seek to persuade James to order the Council to postpone action on the strangers' complaints. In passing, he revealed a personal fear, that if the commission were quashed, he, whose duty it was to defend it at this juncture, would stand smaller in the eyes of his patron: 'If my Lord himself were here . . . it would less trouble me; but my care is now doubled.' Apparently Montgomery did intercede, for Conway soon informed Heath that the king had reached a decision on the matter.[26] It seems, however, that James's decision was that the Council might proceed with its investigation.

The danger increased on 13 March, as the Common Council of London appointed a committee to review the activities of the commission and determine 'howe farre forth the same may be benificiall or prejudiciall to the Citty'.[27] It was at Haberdashers Hall that Heath received word of the Common Council's decision — a circumstance that suggests his continuing ties with the City — and he immediately wrote to Sir Humphrey Handford, sheriff of London, an old acquaintance who was a member of the committee. His letter was an impassioned plea

[26] APC, 1621 – 1623, 443; SP 14/139/60; SP 14/139/72.
[27] CLRO, Letter Books, HH, f. 212.

for the commission and more generally for the government's policy on aliens. No stranger, he assured Handford, would 'be capable of any liberty of the Citty'. The commission would in no way endanger the corporation's control of aliens in London. Finally, for purchasing the royal protection, strangers would 'be only free from informations uppon penall lawes'.[28] Heath's plea availed him nothing. On 29 March Handford's committee reported that the commission was 'very prejudiciall not only to the Citty but to the wholly kingdome', and the Common Council ordered that a petition was to be presented to the Privy Council, to 'pray their lordshipps favor for the suppression of that Comission'.[29] Before such determined antagonists, Heath had little chance. The commission was soon abolished, and Stuart policy on aliens reverted to the confused state that had characterised it prior to 1622.[30]

Although not without their virtues, Heath's proposals represented a narrow solution to a narrow problem. Certainly, he could have argued that more stringent measures be taken against the aliens, and the companies would have applauded. On the other hand, despite his efforts to find a middle course, the policies that he inspired hit hardest at the strangers. Wealthy aliens could well afford to pay the fees and the subsidies that he proposed, but, contrary to their critics' imaginings, most strangers were poor.[31] Furthermore, the tax burden was not the only new danger that they faced as a result of Heath's proposals. Sir Robert's system, by giving the

---

[28] SP 14/139/94. While recorder, Heath had served with Handford on several committees.

[29] Letter Books, HH, f. 214. Judging from the statements of the committee and of Common Council, it is apparent that the City believed the commission threatened its prerogatives. The issue of jurisdiction may have been central in this respect.

[30] On 1 April 1623 the corporation of London petitioned the Council 'touching the late commission' (*APC*, 1621 – 1623, 458), indicating that the panel had already been dissolved. Thereafter, the government did not have a coherent policy on strangers: Irene Scouloudi, 'Alien Immigration into and Alien Communities in London, 1558 – 1640', unpub. M.Sc. Thesis (London, 1936), 273 – 6.

[31] Of course, some members of the alien community were wealthy; note Robert Ashton, *The Crown and the Money Market 1603 – 1640* (Oxford, 1960), pp. 20 – 2. However, as the lists that were submitted to the aliens commission during 1622 indicate, most strangers were involved in lowly occupations; note Cooper, 'Lists of Foreign Protestants', iv – vii, 1 – 27. Scouloudi also provides an occupational profile, ch. 5 and app. 3.

companies power to regulate the quality of alien manufacture, gave to the strangers' harshest critics the ability to cripple their trade. It is probably fair to say, therefore, that if the policies that Heath advocated had remained in force long the alien community would have suffered economic hardship. Native craftsmen, particularly those within the London companies, might for their part have profited, but the impact on the nation at large would probably have been negligible. In a time of depression, broader vision was needed.

Coinage

Sir Robert's views on strangers and on the cloth trade were traditionalist and unimaginative. The same depression that inspired them, however, eventually encouraged him to take a broader view of the economy, and the result was a scheme of thought that was, by the standards of the day, sophisticated and boldly innovative. Heath's development as an economic thinker is well reflected in his writings on the coinage.

For years prior to the 1620s the English government, the mercantile community and the articulate populace had almost universally espoused bullionism, convinced that the national economy could remain healthy only so long as more specie entered the country than left it. James regularly ordered his subjects not to export specie or plate without licence, and Parliament passed bills of like intent. Those who took coin abroad without proper authorisation faced prosecution and, often, harsh penalties.[32] The crisis of 1620 – 4 raised popular condemnation of exporters of specie to a new height, for it was widely felt that they were in large part responsible for the depression. Gerard de Malynes played a major role in the campaign, upholding the traditional bullionist stance in a series of writings, published and unpublished. These years also saw a challenge to the accepted position, however, as some writers argued that England's wealth was determined not by the level of specie, but rather by the trade balance. Among those who

---

[32] Supple, pp. 178 – 92, provides an excellent survey of policy regarding coinage.

upheld this position, later to become standard, probably the most important was Thomas Mun.[33]

An important element in the Malynes-Mun debate was the question of how, or whether, the value of English coins should be adjusted. It was generally believed, with justice, that English coins were exceptionally fine and were therefore particularly welcome in international exchange. The end result, many argued, was the drainage of specie from the kingdom, and consequently the bullionists insisted that the value of English coinage should be somehow lowered. There were two basic ways to depreciate the currency. The first, the crudest, was through debasement. The second, enhancement, was slightly more complex. Enhancement was a device for raising the exchange rate of coins relative to their bullion content. The desired alteration might be achieved by reducing the weight of coins, leaving their fineness constant, or by a governmental order that coins were to circulate at a higher rate.[34] Not surprisingly, Mun held out against any depreciation, insisting that *'The Exportation of our Moneys in Trade of Merchandize is a means to encrease our Treasure'*.[35] Malynes, on the other hand, argued for enhancement, preferably through proclamation, so as to enforce par, that is, ensure that English and foreign coins be exchanged at rates that reflected their intrinsic values.

The problem of what to do about the value of coinage vexed king and Council. During 1622 the Council appointed several committees to study the issue, but since the panels were usually dominated either by Malynes and his supporters or by Mun and his, their recommendations clashed sharply. Not being given a

---

[33] On the Malynes-Mun controversy, which also involved other noteworthy theorists, such as Edward Misselden, see Supple, esp. ch. 9; J. O. Appleby, *Economic Thought and Ideology in Seventeenth-Century England* (Princeton, 1978), pp. 35 – 51.

[34] Technically, enhancement by proclamation constituted a change in the domestic valuation of coins, as expressed in 'monies of account'; foreign coins were then rated in accordance with the new valuations. Regardless of how the coinage was depreciated, the usual result was that there was more money in circulation, causing inflation.

[35] 'England's Treasure by Forraign Trade, or the Ballance of Our Forraign Trade is the Rule of Our Treasure', *A Select Collection of Early English Tracts on Commerce*, ed. J. R. McCulloch (London, 1859), p. 134. Mun's theories, it should be noted, accorded well with his vested interests. He was a director of the East India Company, which during the early Stuart period was often attacked for exporting specie. His critique of bullionism also served as a defence of company policy.

clear line of action, the government threw the management of the coinage to the commission that was established, primarily to oversee the cloth trade, on 21 October 1622.

Sir Robert was a member of the commission, but even before his appointment he had become involved with the coinage issue. On 29 August 1622 an unidentified individual petitioned the Council 'touching Spanish ryalls', and an order quickly followed for Heath to enquire of the officers of the Mint, the Spanish merchants, and the Goldsmiths 'of the true waight, finenes, and value of all sortes of Spanish ryalls' and to report their answers. For once, the instructions were specific, but Heath broadened them to suit his purpose. On 31 August he submitted to Sir George Calvert certificates from the three groups he had been ordered to interview, but in his covering letter he went on to advise:

> The way to restore us out of this consumption is, as I conceave; by bringing some supply of mony from other parts, which must be by some assurance of a competent gaign to the merchants; & by reteyning it here, which cann not be, but by making our coyne in some proportion equall to other States, to which ende I humbly offer to your honors Judgment the last lines of the Goldsmiths certificate.[36]

Looking for further support, Heath that same day wrote a lengthy letter to Buckingham, in which he detailed the Goldsmiths' proposals. What they, and he, wanted was enhancement through lightening. Specifically, they advised that, just as Elizabeth had ordered that the shilling be cut sixty-two to the pound, rather than sixty, so now should the Mint be directed to cut sixty-five. By this step, par would be established with Spanish coinage, the most important medium of European trade, and the outflow of English specie would be reduced.[37]

As he wrote, Heath apparently bore in mind that recent precedent boded ill for his scheme. In 1618 the Goldsmiths, in combination with the Spanish merchants and the officers of the

---

[36] SP 14/132/110. The three sets of answers are SP 14/132/107–09.
[37] BOD. Tanner 73, vol. I, f. 175. The entire letter is printed, with spelling modernised, in Godfrey Goodman and J. S. Brewer (eds.), *The Court of King James the First* (London, 1839), II, 244–7.

Mint, had advised the government to order the cutting of shillings sixty-six to the pound, but the Council had refused to act, claiming that the scheme had three main drawbacks: the king and other great landlords would suffer a reduction in the value of their rents, which would remain fixed in a situation that was likely to be inflationary; the value of silver would be increased, thereby enriching Spain; other nations would retaliate by raising the prices of their silver, placing England once again at a disadvantage.[38] Hoping to counter at least one of these arguments, perhaps the one that he considered the most important, Heath, in his letter of 31 August, assured Buckingham that the proposed enhancement would not reduce the value of rents, because domestic exchange rates would remain unchanged. In the very next sentence, he contradicted himself, conceding that enhancement would lessen real revenue from rents, but, he argued, the reduction would be only one thirty-second, and that loss had to be balanced against the probable outcome if current trends continued:

> Let every man examine truly his revenewe as the case nowe standeth with us, & will be every day worse if the drayne of our mony be not stoppt, whosoever shall nowe lett his land for an improved rent, must abate a 5th part, & yet shall hardly have his Rents well payd in mony for the other 4 parts.

Buckingham may or may not have been impressed by these arguments and may or may not have related them to his fellow-councillors. All that is certain is that the Council failed to approve the Goldsmiths' proposals.[39]

Although in most respects the depression abated after 1624, the government continued to express concern over a presumed drain of specie. In a sweeping proclamation of May 1627 Charles renewed the old bans on exporting coin or bullion.[40] But neither it nor two other proclamations of similar intent had much effect,

---

[38] Rogers Ruding, *Annals of the Coinage of Great Britain and Its Dependencies* (London, 1840), I, 372 – 3; BL, Hargrave 321, f. 11 (part of a document, ff. 10 – 18, that was likely prepared by Heath, although the Hargrave draft is not in his hand).

[39] It was not only the landowners who feared depreciation. Mun also predicted that if the coinage were debased or enhanced 'all mens estates (be it leases, lands, debts, wares or mony) must suffer in their proportions': 'England's Treasure', McCulloch, 150.

[40] Rymer, XVIII, 896 – 900.

and in February 1628 he ordered a commission to be established, including Heath, to uncover 'all or any such Frauds, Abuses, Contempts, Corruptions, Deceipts and other Things which at any Tyme hereafter shalbe . . . practised upon or befall Our Moneys'.[41] The wording was typically vague, and Heath was not pleased with it, nor was he satisfied with the proclamation that announced the forthcoming establishment of the new commission. And since, as attorney-general, he was charged with drafting the proposed instrument, he had an opportunity to make his complaints known. As he did so often when faced with orders that he disapproved of, he delayed final action and instead informed superiors of his reservations. On 1 March he wrote to Conway that the two documents could not be completed 'until the King be pleased to declare his Resolution'. What he wanted Charles to approve was a more strongly worded commission, one that would make clear that the panel's 'charge [would] be to observe all accidentes both at holm & abroad touching coynes'. The proclamation, he argued, should be published simultaneously with the commission, rather than before it 'that both at holm & abroad it may appeare, it is not wordes but actes'. In writing as he did, he informed Conway, he expressed not only his own suggestions, but those 'of the officers of the Mint'.[42]

At about the same time as he wrote to Conway, Sir Robert prepared a lengthy memorandum on the coinage.[43] In it, he informed his unidentified audience, presumably the king, that the drainage of specie remained a grave problem. Such an expression of concern was not, of course, unusual, but having made his formulaic complaint he went on to make proposals for reform that were among the most far sighted that the 1620s produced. First, he argued that the two most often suggested remedies could not succeed. Laws against the export of specie had to fail, he argued, because 'hope of gaigne, & an opinion that [coin might be] secretly carried' would encourage merchants to disobey. Nor, he added, would the balancing of trade be a satisfactory solution, partly because it would reduce the king's customs revenue, partly because it would be 'as difficult

[41] *Ibid.*, 971.
[42] SP 16/95/7.
[43] SP 16/460/16. This document is considerably miscalendared.

to bring to pass, as to persuade all men to be thriftye'. Heath's criticism of the theory that a better trade balance would slow the specie drain may have been a vague challenge to arguments that were coming from Mun and his circle. In any case, Sir Robert's own proposals placed him solidly in the ranks of Mun's critics. He insisted that the only viable answer to the specie outflow was to enforce 'a paritye' between English and foreign coinage. Par was not to be achieved: 'By lesseninge the weight of the pees to make it lighter nor by abasinge the Allay to make it worsen', but by altering the value of English coin, through the medium of proclamation. In arguing as he did, he renounced the position that he had taken six years earlier, that enhancement should be brought about by lightening. The switch had some justification. During the 1620s most European nations had depreciated their currency, often through debasement.[44] England could not renew the coinage every time that it was overvalued on the international market. However, the king could alter its exchange rate through proclamation, as need arose. Sir Robert's change of heart may also have been inspired by the fact that in August 1626 Charles, desperate for cash and perhaps more willing to tamper with the coinage than his father had been, had ordered that silver was to be cut 70s 6d to the pound, only to rescind the decree in the face of public outcry.[45] Heath may have reasoned that enhancement by proclamation was less likely to encounter strong opposition than lightening. Indeed some shift in exchange could be effected through proclamation. The position that he now assumed was certainly wiser than the one he had taken in 1622, and his line of argument was more cogent.

Had Sir Robert's memorandum of 1628 concluded with his plea for enhancement, it would have been a moderately impressive document. He went further, however, and the result was excellence. Through his links with the mercantile community he was painfully aware of the problems that arose owing to the fact that no small coins were being minted. Because all English coins were cut from bullion, the inflationary spiral of the sixteenth century has resulted in coins that were so tiny and fragile as to be worthless. Eventually, the minting of coin below the sixpence had ceased. As a remedy for the lack of small coins,

[44] Supple, pp. 73 – 81.
[45] Ruding, I, 382 – 3; John Craig, The Mint (Cambridge, 1953), p. 138.

Elizabeth had been advised to allow the minting of copper, but she had refused. Small merchants in particular had then found it necessary to establish their own medium of exchange for lesser transactions, sometimes using farthing tokens cut from base metal, or exchanging mere sticks of wood in lieu of money. In May 1613 James had tried to solve the problem by allowing the stamping of farthing tokens from copper and by limiting the production of tokens to a few projectors, including Malynes, but in 1621 the enterprise had collapsed, owing to popular hostility to monopolies generally and to the fact that tokens tended to be greatly overvalued.[46]

Bearing in mind both recent history and present need, Heath continued his memorandum, advising the king:

> to coyne a Basis of a meaner sort, & of smale monyes of 2d 1d, & ½d only, by which the greater moneys shall be served & accounted. The proportion which in this case should be held, must be concluded uppon, when the true intrincecall difference betwene our monyes & the monyes of our neighbore nations & States, are justly calculated . . . That the coyninge of thes smaller coynes [be] of a baser alley.

What Sir Robert was advocating was the regularisation of small coins. Hereafter they would be struck at the Mint, rather than by private individuals. Furthermore, while they might be of 'baser alley', their weight would be calculated in terms of intrinsic value, so as to avoid overvaluation.

In conclusion, Sir Robert tried to sell his reform package as a panacea. Perhaps he actually believed it to be such, but more probably he was actuated by the realisation that a balanced analysis would probably not impress his superiors. He knew that his proposals would face fierce criticism from the great landowners, notably the king himself, owing to their persistent fear that devaluation would reduce their income from rents. To calm them, Heath insisted that enhancement would not lower the value of rents 'but will hold them up, whereas nowe we

---

[46] C. E. Challis, *The Tudor Coinage* (Manchester, 1978), pp. 199 – 208; Craig, pp. 123, 128, 139 – 42; Larkin and Hughes, pp. 287 – 90; E. A. J. Johnson, *Predecessors of Adam Smith: The Growth of British Economic Thought* (New York, 1937), pp. 43 – 4.

find, that the scarcitye of mony doth decay every mans rents visibly. But to be secured herein The same proclamation, which shall direct the values of thes coynes, may also appoint, that all contracts past shall be payd in such monyes & at such values as they were before'. But persuading landlords was only part of Heath's problem. What he was proposing meant change, and there was a pervasive conservatism to be overcome. He was therefore quick to state that enhancement should take place only after representatives of the mercantile community had fully considered his proposals. Change, therefore, would not be precipitate. He knew, however, that many Englishmen feared any policy for which there was no precedent, even if it were slow to be effected. Defending his proposal for enhancement before them, through the king, he argued: 'If it be further objected, this will be an Innovation, & all Innovations are daungerous, The answere is, uppon the like occasion ther have been alterations in the like kind in this kingdome, with good success.' Heath devoted less attention to trying to win over Charles on the minting of small coins, noting mainly that his proposed reform could mean 'a very great yearly profite of the kings mint, beside a round sume at ther first coynage without hurt to the private estate eather of the kinge or his people'. To argue that a suggested change would profit the crown was generally good politics, especially when the audience was the king himself. Unfortunately for Heath, however, he could not also call precedent to the aid of his proposal on small coinage, for if Charles had ordered the stamping of coins, as opposed to tokens, from base metals, it would have been an entirely new procedure.

In fact, the king gave no such order, nor did he issue a proclamation giving a mandate to enhancement. Assuming that he considered Heath's proposals seriously at all, apparently he decided in the end to stand on the arguments that his attorney had sought so hard to counter — the danger to landlords, the hazard of change. Sir Robert had failed to win his case, but considering the nature of the opposition it is doubtful that any proponent would have fared better.

The banking scheme

Heath's 1628 memorandum on the coinage is a fine piece of work, but still more impressive is a proposal that he put forward during the spring of 1624.[47] In a petition, of which four drafts are extant, he called upon James to establish a national bank. An air of mystery surrounds Heath's proposals. Why they were written is unclear. Almost certainly they did not result from a direct assignment by king or Council. Sir Robert may have written under the broad mandate of some committee or commission of which he was a member. It is, however, entirely possible that he wrote as a private individual, for he often gave unsolicited advice to his superiors.

His reasons for desiring the establishment of a bank are referred to in each draft, but are most clearly delineated in the second, entitled, 'A means layd downe for the inlarging of Trade':

> Experience shewes that Trade cann not be liberally mayntayned both at holme & abroad: but by credite, as well as by mony: & by a fitt way to make use of both when ther is need of it. For want whereof it comes often to pass, that a marchant of good worth; uppon some suddeyne losse at sea, or by ill dettors; or uppon a suddeyn pressing of his creditors is driven into great stresses, his owne monyes being dispersed abroad . . . This may be holpen; if by command, or by a voluntary consent, a *Bank* may be raised.

The bank was therefore intended to improve credit, in hopes of boosting commerce. To ease tight credit, he argued, it would first be necessary to legalise the assignment of debts, that is, to allow creditors to use the various instruments of indebtedness as credits, which might be given over to other parties in the process of completing business transactions. The bank was then to act as a clearing house for assignments. Beyond that, assignments might be deposited. As Heath explained in his third draft:

---

[47] None of the drafts is dated, but marginal notations in SP 14/130/29, the roughest draft, suggest tentative dating; the calendaring, under May 1622, is in any case too early. Judging from style, content, and neatness, the four drafts should be ordered SP 14/130/29, SP 14/130/32, SP 14/130/30, and SP 14/130/31 (apparently the final draft; in a polished hand, not Heath's), and this is the ordering that will be followed in the present discussion. All four drafts are in print: F. G. H. Price, *A Handbook of London Bankers: With Some Account of Their Predecessors, the Early Goldsmiths* (London, 1876), pp. 145 – 51.

They which receave ther mony at the *Bank* shalbe at ther owne libertye, eather to carry it away; or to leave it ther for ther owne use at ther need; If they leave it ther, they shall by way of assignation pay it over, only be entring it in the *Bank*; which shall goe as an actuall payment, & soe a 100 may be assigned from man to man to serve for payment of tenn several hundreds or more: . . . what his occasions requires, he shall take it out, or assigne it; to supply this turn, eather in mony or credite.

An individual's bank balance, therefore, would include not only the cash that he had deposited, but also the credits that had been assigned to him.

Heath's proposals regarding the creation of the bank were marked by inconsistency. In his first draft he recommended 'The king to doe itt by a declaration of his pleasure by an instrument under the privy seale', but in his third he wrote 'it may be established by parliament'. In both drafts he called on the king to establish a commission to lay the groundwork for the bank and to govern it once it had been founded, but his final advice on governance was that: 'A Cowncell of trade aswell as a Cowncell of warre is fitt to be established to governe this aswell as other partes of Trade.' As soon as the bank was established several facilities would be opened, the main one in London, lesser branches in other cities and in port towns.

To stock the bank, wrote Sir Robert 'the kings owne example would prevaile much . . . If the monyes nowe to be receaved from the Cittye & others, uppon the sales & the monyes uppon the Coustomes & Imposts & for Prize goods &c be all appointed to be receaved & payd out in this Bank'. Heath also expressed the hope that 'some principall merchants, who understand the use of the Bank', would be willing to 'paye & receive ther', for if that happened, he suggested, many lesser merchants would likely follow suit. To further encourage deposits, he proposed, in his second draft, that 'The owners [i.e., depositors] shall have a certeyn allowance of 4£ p cent', but he then crossed the comment out and did not raise the issue of interest in either later version. Perhaps he felt that persuasion was not necessary, for capital might be raised by other means. As he informed James 'the kinge, if he soe please, may compell all thos who lend mony at interest, to receave it & pay it in the Banke, or else to forbidd the taking of interest, which is but tollerated, not allowed by Lawe'.

Heath's reference to coercion was not casual. He sensed that his proposal would arouse opposition, particularly from the very group that it was directed toward helping, the London mercantile community. The merchants' fears were several, as he explained during the course of his petition. Firstly, they shared with their countrymen the fear of innovation. He responded to this concern much as he did in the document on the coinage that he wrote in 1628, claiming that what might seem innovative really was not. The bank would not be new, he wrote in the final draft, but rather an English 'imitation of Venice as Amsterdam, Hamburgh, Danske & Nurenburgh'. Many merchants feared not only innovation, however, but also the exposure of their true worth. Heath also spoke to this fear in his final draft: 'Yf it bee objected that this wilbee a meanes to discover mens estates which els might subsist being weake; the answere is, it will not discover any estate but mony & trade only, which is now more discovered by the entryes of all goods made in the Custom-howse; & monyes registred in every Scrivenors booke.' But his next statement was of the sort that could only redouble the merchants' concern, for he suggested that the bank would in fact serve as 'a meanes to discover mens estates'. The bank, he argued, would be 'a good meanes to prevent banckerupts, which is a benefitt for the Common wealth that men whoe deserve Creditt may be supported, and such as deserve noe Creditt maie not secretly Cosen others of greate somes of mony'.

Above all, however, the merchants feared that James would take advantage of the bank, to their detriment. Sir Robert's final draft contained a response to both their concern and their suspicion: 'Yf it bee objected that a Ritche man maye bee thus discovered & his mony in the bancke taken awaye, the answer is, to what purpose should the kinge take awaye the monye for hee Can make les use of yt by takinge yt awaye; then by leavinge yt there.' His stand was ironic, for in 1640 Charles, faced with economic disaster, was to seize the money that merchants had deposited in the Mint.[48] In 1624, however, Heath believed that such an act would never take place, and he was

---

[48] Ruding, I, 392.

upset that anyone could so distrust the king as to imagine it would.

While in his memorandum Heath suggested responses to the complaints that might be raised by critics of the bank, he bore in mind that his immediate audience was not the merchants, but the king. It was James whom he had to impress if the bank were to become a reality. He therefore made much of the advantages that his scheme offered the crown. The bank, he claimed, would improve credit within the mercantile sector; easier credit meant greater trade, which meant higher customs revenue. Furthermore, since the bank would serve to simplify the flow of cash, there would be 'noe disturbance of trade thowghe a greate some of monie were upon a sodayne to be advanced to the kinge', as by a forced loan. Finally, the bank would provide James and his agents with an opportunity to keep the English financial system under surveillance. One advantage was that the outflow of coin could be halted: 'Exportation is already punishable by lawe, but the meanes wanting to discover. Yf a Banke were erected . . . yt would prevent the exportation of Coyne: Yf all payments exceeding v£ or 10£ were enjoyned to bee made at the bancke & entred there; exportation would be discovered.' Of course, it was just such interference that the merchants feared, but Heath was more concerned with winning over the king than he was them.

James, however, was not converted. Possibly he was cool to Heath's proposal from the moment it was presented. Possibly his advisors turned him against it. Possibly he gave way in the face of complaints by the London mercantile community. Whatever the reason, Heath's banking scheme sank without trace.

Sir Robert's failure does not diminish the impressiveness of his plan. During the Elizabethan period a number of writers called for the establishment of banks, and early Stuart England saw more such proposals, before and after Heath's. But although Sir Robert was not alone in advocating the creation of a bank, the nature of the institution that he envisaged was unusual, perhaps unique. The banks that his contemporaries projected were usually of two kinds. Some writers favoured the *mont de piété*, that embodiment of medieval idealism and concern for the poor. Others advocated banks that were in essence reservoirs of ready cash for the crown, coffers filled with money that had been deposited by wealthy men — forced to be generous by heavy government pressure — and could be emptied by the king, if he saw fit.[49] Heath's proposals said nothing about the poor, and although he listed the advantages that the king might derive from establishing a bank, he made it clear that the institution that he advocated was primarily intended to serve business and trade. With freer credit, the economy would improve, and eventually both the king and the nation at large would benefit. That the depression of 1620 – 4 was largely due to a credit crisis has been supported by modern scholarship.[50] Heath was one of the few government officials of that time to recognise the problem, and the solution that he advocated was generally wise, especially as compared to other schemes that were then being advocated at Court. It was the work of a perceptive man, and a creative one.

Inferences

For the most part, the economic proposals that Heath laid before the government did little to influence the course of events in England. His report on the wool trade had an impact, but only a slight one, and in any case Heath penned it as a mere member of a committee. His advice regarding strangers was influential only as long as the aliens commission remained in existence. Neither his proposals on the coinage nor his advocacy of a national bank bore fruit. Nevertheless, the plans that he put forward during the 1620s for dealing with the economy, and their fate, are significant, in that they reveal much about central government in early Stuart England, about Heath's milieu and about the man himself.

The attitude of the government towards Heath's proposals, both those it accepted and those it rejected, says a great deal about its general stance. Although contemporary political theory favoured paternalism, king and Council were not blindly interventionist. They were quick to intervene when major acts

---

[49] Besides Heath's drafts, Price includes the text of two other memorials on banks, pp. 142 – 4, 152 – 4. Other schemes are dealt with by R. D. Richards, *The Early History of Banking in England* (London, 1929), pp. 11 – 13, 93 – 5; Ashton, *Money Market*, p. 189.

[50] Supple, pp. 40 – 1, 55, 198; R. W. K. Hinton, 'The Mercantile System in the Time of Thomas Mun', *The Economic History Review*, second series, 7 (1955), 285.

of domestic violence occurred, for in them they saw a threat to national stability, and they usually handled crises in foreign policy with despatch. Furthermore, the king's personal biases and attitudes regularly resulted in the making and unmaking of specific policies, sometimes with dizzying speed, a case in point being recusant policy during the 1620s. But quite often the government held back when confronted by crisis, in the hope that the problem would disappear. The more complex the issue, the less willing Whitehall was to deal with it. Given the complexity of the problems that faced the cloth trade during the period 1620 – 4, it is not surprising that the Council procrastinated for more than two years of crisis before appointing a committee of experts to deal with the depression, and it did so only after events had made it clear that the industry could not right itself nor be righted by the intervention of local officials.

When the government did act, it tried to hold to well-trodden paths. The suggested remedies that Heath included in his reports on the cloth industry and on the strangers, reports that won favourable notice from the Council, were for the most part strongly grounded in precedent. In both these reports, as in his proposals on the coinage and on banking, Sir Robert himself claimed that the reforms he was advocating were in no way innovative, for he understood the traditionalist bent of his audience. But despite his protestations, it was obvious that some of his schemes, especially those that involved the minting of coins from base metals and the establishment of a national bank, represented radical departures from tradition, and that realisation may have done much to bring them down.[51]

That Heath's proposals were filled with arguments intended to counter potential criticism also reflects the nature of his audience. King and Council were, in the early Stuart period, not the immovable megaliths that many of their critics claimed them to be — a characterisation that some modern historians continue to foster — but were, on the contrary, rather flexible. If a

---

[51] The fear of innovation, it should be noted, was not likely to prevent the government from taking a step that it regarded as being clearly necessary, or one that promised to be profitable. Some historians have argued that the broad policy of Thorough was in many ways innovative. For a specific example of the government's willingness to innovate when there was the possibility of profit, see J. L. Malcolm (ed.), 'Charles I on Innovation: a Confidential Directive on an Explosive Issue', Institute of Historical Research, *Bulletin*, 53 (1980), 252 – 5.

powerful group challenged a given crown policy and the Court did not feel that for some reason it had to stand fast, the policy was likely to be scrapped. So it was that the aliens commission was brought low by the attacks of the strangers' congregations, the companies, and, perhaps most important, of the City.[52] So it was that Heath sought to defend his banking scheme against the criticisms that he expected to be levelled by the mercantile community. He realised that if the Court were only moderately attracted to his various proposals, it was likely to succumb when outside interests challenged them.

The proposals that Heath put forward on economic issues were seldom his alone. Obviously, his report on the cloth trade represented the statement of a full committee, and beyond that it reflected the statements of a number of clothiers and merchants. His proposal on strangers was more independently drawn, but it, too, was based upon the testimony of interested parties. From Heath's own statement, it is clear that the report on the coinage that he penned in 1622 was, as the Council had directed, derived from the statements of the Goldsmiths, the officers of the Mint, and, perhaps less importantly, the Spanish merchants. The sources for his most impressive statements on economic issues, his 1628 petition on the coinage and his several proposals to establish a bank, are more difficult to pinpoint. It is, however, probable that behind them lay the Goldsmiths, the Mint-men, and Malynes. Heath's relationship with the Goldsmiths seems to have been close throughout the 1620s, probably a result of his days as recorder. He was likewise close to several officers of the Mint, so much so that when in September 1626 they begged him to delay drawing the grant of the mastership to Sir Robert Harley, so that they could close their accounts — and, in all likelihood, find time to cover some chicanery — he readily complied.[53] Both the Mint-men and the Goldsmiths were interested in revaluing the coinage, and Heath's 1628 proposal, as well as the one he wrote in 1622, would for the most part have

---

[52] Buckingham's involvement with the commission also played a role in bringing it down, by encouraging his enemies at Court to move against it.

[53] Sir William Pankhurst, Richard Rogers, and Andrew Palmer to Heath, 27 Sept. 1626, SP 16/36/71; Heath to Conway, 2 Oct. 1626, SP 16/37/11. Some higher-ranking courtiers, notably Cranfield, were economically astute by the standards of the period, and it is possible that one of them may have influenced Heath. However, Heath does not appear to have been close to any of them.

pleased them. The Goldsmiths may very well have questioned the desirability of minting coin from base metal, but the Mint-men were probably prime advocates of the reform that Heath proposed, for it promised them greater profits.[54] For his part, Malynes, who was an assay master of the Mint, had long hoped to see England somehow freed from the necessity of importing bullion, and he had in consequence begun to advocate the minting of base coinage.[55] Just as Heath's proposals on the coinage seem by and large to have accorded well with the desires of the Mint-men, the Goldsmiths, and Malynes, so do his bank schemes. Individual officers of the Mint and Gold-smiths were by the 1620s becoming interested in banking, and it appears that some of them were themselves serving as petty bankers.[56] Although Malynes was highly critical of continental bankers, blaming them in large part for England's problems in foreign exchange, he also saw advantages in a regularised banking system. In particular, he advocated the assignment of debts through the medium of a bank, as a means by which to expand credit. Assignment was unknown in common law, but law merchant allowed it, and Malynes championed the latter system.[57] The evidence therefore suggests that Heath may well have been acting as a spokesman for Malynes, and very likely for the Goldsmiths and the Mint-men, also, when he submitted his proposals on banking to the Court.

---

[54] The profits of the Mint were low, 1619 – 23, and the income of the officers there undoubtedly suffered in consequence; note J. D. Gould, 'The Royal Mint in the Early Seventeenth Century', *The Economic History Review*, second series, 5 (1952), 244 – 6.

[55] Johnson, p. 43; Ruding, I, 370n.

[56] On early Goldsmith banking, see Richards, pp. 35 – 7; A. V. Judges, 'The Origins of England Banking', *History*, 16 (1931), 138 – 45. There is some disagreement over the question of whether the early Stuart Mint actually stored bullion for merchants and other wealthy men or merely held it until it was coined; note Ruding, I, 392n; J. R. Bisschop, *The Rise of the London Money Market 1640 – 1826* (London, 1910), p. 42.

[57] *Consuetudo vel lex mercatoria* (London, 1604), 132. Malynes tended to equate law merchant with mercantile practice: J. H. Baker, 'The Law Merchant and the Common Law before 1700', *Cambridge Law Journal* 38 (1979), 296. Many of the principles of law merchant were incorporated into the common law during the Tudor-Stuart period: L. S. Sutherland, 'The Law Merchant in England in the Seventeenth and Eighteenth Centuries', Royal Historical Society, *Transactions*, fourth series, 17 (1934), 163 – 8; Baker, 'Law Merchant', 320 – 2.

A spokesman Heath was, but probably not a mere parrot. Just as he left behind the extreme counsel of the Goldsmiths in framing his proposals on strangers, so it is likely that his petitions on banking and the coinage contained, besides the views of others, large measures of originality, and it is highly probable that they represented his own synthesis. The end-products, therefore, clearly bear Sir Robert's stamp, and they reveal much about his personality and his philosophy.

Heath believed in a strong, paternalistic government. Still more basically, he believed in order, order within the State, within the Church, within the nation, and within the economy.[58] He had no compunction about calling on the government to intervene in economic matters, whether the issue at hand was the state of the cloth trade, the seeming threat posed by strangers, the drain of specie, or the credit crisis. But it was not the government alone that he looked to as a buttress against confusion in the economy. Heath tended to support the central institutions of trade and business. His career as recorder of London made him aware, or enhanced his awareness, of the problems they faced. For example, in January 1619 he petitioned the Privy Council on behalf of the City to restrict the activities of the Shrewsbury Drapers, who, he alleged, were challenging some of London's monopolies.[59] Even after he had entered crown service he generally remained opposed to 'free trade', which at the time meant the extension of trading rights to the outports, at the expense of London and the great trading companies.[60] He did, during the parliament of 1621, support a bill for the free buying and selling of Welsh cloth, and during a debate in 1624 he advocated extending the trade in coloured cloths to the outports.[61] However, he may have been moved to take these stands by the trade crisis of the moment, and in any case neither position was typical of him. More in keeping with his general philosophy was the attack on wool brokers that he

---

[58] Chapter 6.

[59] APC, 1619 – 1621, 115. The petition was rejected: ibid., 129 – 30.

[60] There is some dispute as to the motivation of the early Stuart free traders: Robert Ashton, 'The Parliamentary Agitation for Free Trade in the Opening Years of the Reign of James I', Past and Present, 38 (1967), 40 – 55; T. K. Rabb, 'Free Trade and the Gentry in the Parliament of 1604', Past and Present, 40 (1968), 165 – 73.

[61] CD 1621, III, 65; CJ, I, 699. In arguing as he did on Welsh cloth, Heath may have been inspired by his pro-London bias. The Shrewsbury Drapers had a monopoly over Welsh cloth, and the City was anxious to break it.

launched in the Commons in 1621. He demanded that the activities of the brokers be curbed by law, and in so doing he took a position that accorded well with the stance taken by the leading cloth interests and by the greater London merchants, one-third of whom were involved in the cloth trade.[62] He was also reasonably consistent in supporting the great companies, and 1624 found him, as a member of the Commons, defending the prerogatives of the East India and the Eastland Companies, even as other speakers demanded the opening up of trade.[63] In yet a third speech, in support of the Merchant Adventurers, he went beyond the case in hand, to discuss the proper role of government *re* commerce: 'Trade cannot enlarge without government. The merchant must not venture where he will; the adventure is not his own but the stock of the kingdom.'[64]

Heath himself profited through government paternalism. He was a monopolist, though not a major one, owning, at least from 1620 to 1630, a small share in a seacoal farm.[65] In 1624 he became a surveyor of the soapworks, and during that year he also began to play a role, presumably to his profit, in the management of the 'new draperies' industry.[66] Sir Robert was never backward in making moves to enrich himself and his family, so the income that he gained through his role in the management of the economy was an inducement to support paternalism. But it is likely that even if the prevailing economic system had done nothing to boost his fortune, he would still have supported it, for in it he would have seen both a reflection and a cause, of the orderliness that he loved.

Nevertheless, Heath's proposals do not show him to have been a hidebound traditionalist. On the contrary, his call for minting of coins from base metal and his banking schemes took him far from precedent. He did, of course, claim that the reforms he advocated did not demand innovation, and while the nature of his audience encouraged such a stance it is quite

---

[62] The links between the greater merchants and the cloth trade are discussed in R. G. Lang, 'The Greater Merchants of London in the Early Seventeenth Century' unpub. D.Phil. dissertation (Oxford, 1963), 396 – 415.

[63] YCPH, Nicholas's diary, transcript (the original is in the PRO, SP 14/166), p. 253.

[64] YCPH, Pym's diary, transcript (the original is in the Northamptonshire Record Office, Finch-Hatton 50; and, BL, Add. 26,639), p. 322.

[65] Egerton 2978, f. 43.

[66] SP 14/149/15; SP 16/1/23 – 24.

possible that he wrote with conviction. Still, he must have realised that the precedents were weak. They served him mainly as a means to an end, as an excuse for the reforms that he was convinced were needed. He might not have been willing to propound totally unprecedented solutions to national problems, but he was willing to find security in even the most tenuous precedents, when the situation demanded it. By such means he found a rationale for change.

5

A Decade of Parliaments

By a custom dating back to the mid-fifteenth century, whenever a parliament was in the offing London returned the recorder as one of its four members, and in November 1620 the City, having received writs of election, named Heath to a place in the Commons.[1] But when the session finally opened, on 30 January 1621, he sat as solicitor-general. Londoners may have felt that this promotion deprived them of a representative, though there is no evidence that they complained openly. Sir Robert's career in the Commons, thus launched, was impressive, but brief. East Grinsted, Sussex, returned him to the parliaments of 1624 and 1625. The same borough returned him in 1626, but at that session he was not allowed to take his seat, owing to the fact that he was by then attorney-general.[2] In 1614, the Commons had resolved that no senior law officer could sit, and the ban was to hold until 1670.[3] While the rule kept him out of the Commons during the

---

[1] A. B. Beaven, *The Aldermen of the City of London* (London, 1908), I, 276; Foster, *Politics of Stability*, pp. 27, 62. Significantly, in 1640 the City did not return the recorder, a Court appointee, to either the Short or the Long Parliament: Pearl, pp. 175, 193.

[2] *CJ*, I, 871. Possibly, East Grinsted returned Heath only because of pressure brought to bear by the duchy of Lancaster: R. E. Ruigh, *The Parliament of 1624: Politics and Foreign Policy* (Cambridge, Mass., 1971), p. 52. However, Heath did own land in the area (Kopperman, 'Heath', 205n), and he may have been well known to the voters.

[3] Edwards, pp. 36 – 7. The reason for the ban is uncertain. During the 1660s Lord Guilford wrote, 'The reason [for it] was, becaus it was presumed that the king would call [the attorney-general] to the assistance of the hous of lords, & therefore to prevent a vain chair was the order made': BL, Add.

tumultuous parliaments of 1626 and 1628 – 9, Sir Robert remained a part of the parliamentary scene. He was, first of all, the main legal advisor to the Lords, and in that capacity he helped to frame many a bill and probably influenced many a vote. The Lords also made him their primary messenger to the Commons.[4] During the seventeenth century a number of attorneys-general served in similar ways, but what distinguished Heath's relationship with parliament during the years 1626 – 9 was his role as prosecutor of those peers and members whom the Court wished to see cast down. In parliament itself, in King's Bench and in Star Chamber, he upheld the crown cause against leaders of the opposition — Holles, Selden, and, most important of all, Eliot. And when he was done, that opposition was, for the moment, cowed and scattered.

For the abilities that he displayed while a member of the Commons, Heath has received the near-unanimous approbation of historians.[5] Not surprisingly, his part in the government campaign against the radicals has won him less praise.[6] Yet, in essence, his functions were analogous; as a prosecutor of radicals, and an active member of the Commons, he served the king's cause, and in both roles, he demonstrated an ability that set him far above the usual run of crown servants.

32,518, f. 220. His assertion may reflect the Commons' rationale, but probably not its reason. The 1614 debate is noted, but not well reported, in *CJ* (I, 456, 459 – 60). Clearly, the members were concerned that, prior to that parliament, no attorney-general who had been appointed to his post before the election, had sat in the Commons. But among arguments adduced for banning future attorneys — Bacon was allowed to retain his seat — perhaps the most telling was Sir Dudley Digges's expression of fear (*CJ*, I, 460) of the attorney's 'Power, his Means (being here) to observe all, or requite any, that shall oppose him.'

4   On the role of the attorney in the Lords, see Edwards, pp. 32 – 3, 39 – 40.

5   D. H. Willson compares Heath's talents to Bacon's: *The Privy Councillors in the House of Commons 1604 – 1629* (Minneapolis, 1940), p. 214; note also pp. 53 – 4. Gardiner, with his parliamentary career mainly in mind, observes, 'No man . . . showed himself a stouter champion of the prerogative than Heath': *History*, IV, 248.

6   Note John Forster, *Sir John Eliot: A Biography 1590 – 1632* (London, 1864), book 11; Foster, *Caroline Underground*, chs. 2 – 3. With some exceptions, criticism has died down during the twentieth century, in part because of the decline of the Whig mentality.

In the Commons

Even before he entered the Commons, Heath's career in Parliament had to some extent been determined. Precedent dictated that as solicitor-general he was bound to perform certain functions. So it was that on 27 February 1621 the Commons ordered 'that because the King's Solicitor the last convention brought in the bills of grace, that therefore Mr. Solicitor that now is should take care to see them new written (which they must be) and brought in'.[7] It was probably more than coincidental that on at least one occasion in each of his three parliaments Sir Robert was designated to report a royal speech to the house, for Yelverton had likewise been obliged to do so in 1614.[8] Normally, the king's speeches were reported only by privy councillors, the Speaker, or messengers from the Lords. The fact that the solicitor-general was added to this select circle reflected the prestige of his place.

Past practice inspired the crown, as well as the Commons, to look to Heath for service. Since the attorney-general was barred from the lower house, the solicitor stood as the unofficial leader of the king's counsel, that somewhat amorphous agglomeration of crown legal servants. If properly led, the counsellors could play an important role in debate, a central role in committee. The king expected his solicitor to provide that leadership. He also expected him to help direct the affairs of the Commons generally. Three Elizabethan solicitors had, at the queen's behest, been appointed Speaker.[9] James and Charles chose not to designate their solicitors as nominees, though they regularly supported the candidacy of other counsellors.[10] The switch in strategy may have resulted from a sense at Court that the solicitor could better serve the crown cause if he were allowed to join in debate, which the Speaker was not. However, there was no guarantee that he would cut a strong figure in debate. In 1614

---

[7] CD 1621, II, 144.
[8] CJ, I, 458 – 9.
[9] These were Richard Onslow (the first solicitor to sit in the house: 1566 – 7), Sir John Popham (1581 – 3), and Coke (1593).
[10] The early Stuart Speakers who were members of the king's counsel were Sir Edward Phelips (Speaker, 1604 – 10), Sir Ranulph Crew (1614), Sir Thomas Richardson (1621), and Sir John Finch (1628 – 9). Phelips and Crew were king's serjeants, Richardson chancellor to the queen and Finch the queen's attorney.

Yelverton spoke seldom and with seeming reluctance.[11] In 1626 and 1628 – 9 Sir Richard Shelton, the man Buckingham chose to succeed Heath as solicitor, displayed ineptitude in debate, as well as occasional timidity.[12] Heath, unlike both his predecessor and his successor, used his office to great advantage in the Commons.

Both the advantage that he drew from his place and his ability to magnify that advantage may be seen reflected in his career as a committee-man. During his three parliaments he served on well over one hundred committees, more than any other courtier.[13] His assignments came about in any of several ways. In choosing committees the Commons often made use of a procedure so chaotic as to defy the word 'system'. According to William Hakewill, Heath's contemporary: 'Every one of the House that list may call upon the name of any one of the House to be a Committee, and the Clark ought in his journal to write under the title of the Bill the name of every one so call'd upon, at leastwise of such whose names (in that Confusion) he can distinctly hear.'[14] Some of Heath's assignments undoubtedly came through this awkward route, as one of his supporters, probably a courtier, shouted his name loudly enough to be heard above the din. But it is possible that the shouting out of names was not the only method of choosing committees. By some means the house also named committees that were small and exclusive. These bodies were typically charged with handling some complex matter, and the men who were designated as members were 'experts'. When the problem in hand was a legal one, the members were almost certain to be lawyers, around ten in number, and Heath was likely to be included among them, not necessarily because his fellow-

---

[11] Williams Mitchell, *The Rise of the Revolutionary Party in the House of Commons 1603 – 1629* (New York, 1957), p. 53; T. L. Moir, *The Addled Parliament of 1614* (Oxford, 1958), pp. 59, 90, 111.

[12] For an assessment of Shelton, see Willson, *Privy Councillors*, p. 215n.

[13] A list of Heath's committee assignments, as well as abstracts of his speeches, is included in Kopperman, 'Heath', 372 – 7. Recent and projected publications of material on the parliaments of the 1620s, particularly a forthcoming YCPH volume on the parliament of 1624, have, however, pointed up significant gaps in the list. On the distribution of committee assignments in general, see Mitchell, pp. 91 – 2, 97; in judging the numbers of speeches cited by Mitchell, however, one should note that he relies primarily on *CJ*, rather than on the wide range of sources available.

[14] *Modus tenendi Parliamentum: or, The Old Manner of Holding Parliaments in England* (London, 1671), p. 145.

members believed him to be notably learned in the law, though perhaps they did, but because his high office made him a natural choice to represent the interests of the crown in committee.

But Heath's own activities, and not his place, helped to put him on a number of committees. Some of his colleagues seem to have recognised that he was interested in, or at least had experience of, economic issues, since prior to his maiden speech he was appointed to several committees that dealt with aspects of the depression.[15] His contributions in debate, too, brought him assignments. The usual practice in the Commons was to include on committee most members who had joined in debating a bill at its second reading, except those who had spoken against the body of it.[16] Sir Robert was active in debate, and the number of his assignments increased commensurately. On 17 February 1621 Coke asked to be added to a subcommittee on courts. Heath, quickly following, suggested that the subcommittee should expand the scope of its enquiry and gave his reasons in detail. Without making the same request as Coke, Sir Robert thus demonstrated to the house that he was interested in the subcommittee and had a definite conception of how it might best serve. Soon both he and Coke were added to it.[17]

That Heath spoke up, and spoke up forcefully, in this instance was typical of him, for during his three parliaments, the first two especially, he was the most active debater for the Court interest. On more than two hundred occasions he rose to speak. Sometimes his speeches were brief, but not infrequently they were quite lengthy. In keeping with contemporary practice, most were probably extempore, delivered without the aid of notes. Like lawyer-members generally, Heath often cited statutes and precedents in the course of turning his arguments, and, being as religious and as well versed in Scripture as most of his colleagues, he often alluded to the Bible. The Commons emphasised performance in debate, and an ineffectual speaker was liable to be shouted down, as was one who took an

---

[15] Heath's main work on economic issues (see ch. 4) began in 1622, but his career as recorder had seen him address many of the basic problems the committees dealt with.

[16] CD 1621, IV, 104. The rule was regularly enforced; note CJ, I, 526 – 7. A committee member could, however, oppose a bill after it had been reported: Hakewill, p. 146.

[17] CJ I, 525.

unpopular position. It was, therefore, an act of courage to speak, and most members, perhaps realising their limitations, spoke seldom or never. Heath not only spoke, but spoke well. In particular, two abilities distinguished him from most colleagues. Firstly, he had an excellent sense of timing. Generally members were allowed to speak only once to a question, and the evidence suggests that he tended to save his contribution until it seemed likely to have maximum impact. Secondly, he knew his colleagues well enough to know which line of argument was most likely to appeal to them. As he spoke, he consistently played on the psychological composition of the membership.

Heath's abilities as a debater are evident in a speech that he delivered on 5 August 1625. His task that day was difficult. Charles had demanded a huge subsidy from parliament but had refused to divulge how he intended to use the money. Had he revealed his plans the appeal might have been more popular, for in fact he was intent on attacking Spain, the very action that the Commons had long been calling for, but he declined to commit himself, apparently because he believed that to explain his scheme in order to win the subsidy would lead parliament to expect similar accounting in the future. So he demanded the subsidy and then sat back silent, ready to forgo it rather than commit himself as to its use. The burden of persuading a puzzled and angry parliament to vote the subsidy fell on the courtier-members, and they were restricted in their approach in that, given the king's own silence, they were not free to assure the Commons that war with Spain was imminent, even if they knew. When Heath rose to address the house on the subsidy issue, therefore, he did so with a marked handicap.[18]

It was not the king alone who was suspect, Sir Robert knew, but also his servants in the house. By 1625, many members already doubted that crown officials in the Commons could serve the nation. Such officials, the reasoning went, necessarily served the king's interest, which was somehow not the nation's interest. Heath recognised the concern, and therefore as he

---

[18] The following summary, including all quotations, is drawn from the two versions included in 'CD 1625', 87 – 8, 133 – 5. Assessing Heath's effort, Gardiner comments: 'The important speech of the day on the Government side was that of Heath, who in this session exhibited qualities which, if his cause had been better, and if his professional advancement had not early separated him from Parliamentary life, would probably have placed him in the front rank of Members of the House of Commons,' *ibid.*, xi – xii.

opened his speech he moved quickly to establish his own credibility. Although in the king's fee, he did not, he assured his audience, speak only as a courtier: 'By way of preamble, intimatinge that besides the common difficultyes their [were] some particuler to himselfe, being to act both a publicke and private parte; wherein yet he ment to shew himself so indifferent as not to hold either of Cephas or Appollo.'

Then he addressed the key question: How would the subsidy be used? Although privy to the king's designs, he could not announce to the house that Charles was planning war. But he could hint as much, and he could hope that the members, knowing him to be close to the centre of power, would believe that he spoke with certain knowledge. 'Hee doth move that the King would bee pleased [after the subsidy were voted] to declare the enimyes, and hee thinketh it would much moove us, and hee makes noe doubt but it wilbe the same enimy we all desier — Spayne.' While obliquely stating that the subsidy would be spent on a war with Spain, he also pricked the conscience of the house by reminding the members that only the year before many of them had demanded that the treaties with Spain be broken, and some had called for war: 'Hee holdeth wee are engaged by our word, which is to bee kept unles wee be unable: hee doth not thinke the treaties were broken before our desier signified unto his Majestie in the last Parliamente.' It was not bad enough, he went on, that by withholding funds the members were breaking an implied promise to support the king if he moved against Spain, but they were violating the trust of the very man who a year earlier had championed their cause: 'Hee that was then our advocate for the breache, is now our judge.' This judge, he asserted, stood for the nation. If the projected war turned out badly, then the king's shame would be England's: 'Either they will saye his hart fayled him, or his people fayled him; whereof the last is the worst.'

Moving on to parry a possible threat to the subsidy, Heath noted that, according to some members, it was too late in the year to launch an invasion and so there was no need to be hasty in granting supply. Delay, he argued, worked to the benefit of Spain: 'The deferringe of tyme disadvantageth the cause, by the King of Spayne's preparation against us either to bee in Ireland, or att home, and how dangerous it would bee, yf the seate of the warre should be att home . . . he will not put it upon a peradventure, for jealousey and feare of relapse of other Princes by our coldnes.' By these words he suggested that what many members were confidently expecting to be an offensive war might prove to be a struggle for home and hearth, if they did not do their part. And what was their part? Heath concluded with a flourish: 'The King's estate, like a shippe, hath a great leake. If a shipp be assaild, all must not goe to mend the leake, and none to defend her. For the particular propositions delivered to this purpose, he referd them to a future consideration, and concluded that it was fit to give.' By identifying the impending war as both the king's cause and the nation's, he had made possible, indeed logically necessary, his final call: to fund the war was the Commons' duty.

Even in a day of great speakers, few members, and probably none in the Court faction, could have delivered a speech of equal cogency or eloquence. Nevertheless, Heath's efforts went for nought, for the Commons refused to vote supply. No amount of brilliance in debate could serve to make an unpopular demand popular. By 1625, the cleavage between king and Commons was already apparent. Four years earlier, even one year, it had not been so, and a courtier-member who was an effective debater could expect to win some minds. Heath had done that but could no longer.

The question of how the anti-Court faction was able to win control of the Commons has been a favoured one among historians. Among the explanations often given is that James and Charles, unlike Elizabeth, ignored the fine art of parliamentary management. While the queen had ensured that there were enough able high officials in the Commons to guide proceedings, the first two Stuarts, so the theory goes, rewarded too many of their great servants with peerages, leaving only a few of them, often the least competent, eligible to sit in the lower house.[19] Heath's own career in parliament, however, suggests

---

[19] As usually stated, the theory is that the Stuarts' primary blunder lay in not keeping enough privy councillors in the Commons: Wallace Notestein, *The Winning of the Initiative by the House of Commons* (London, 1926), passim, esp. 33; *The House of Commons 1604 – 1610* (New York, 1971), pp. 497 – 9. Other historians, notably Willson, have followed Notestein in keying on the privy councillors. However, the councillors were not the only courtiers whose rank impressed — at least until the 1620s — the Commons. Others included the solicitors-general. With regard to the parliaments of the early 1620s, Conrad Russell writes: 'Though Solicitor General Heath was not a member of the Privy Council, the King had few more loyal servants, and few more dependable Parliamentary spokesmen': 'Parliamentary History in Perspective, 1604 – 1629', *History*, 61 (1976), 19 – 20.

that it was the general attitude of the house toward crown policy, rather than a decline in the ability of courtier-members, that determined how much influence crown officials might exercise. His experience during the parliament of 1621 is a case in point.

That parliament ran a dichotomous course. During the first session, which ended in adjournment on 4 June, the relationship between king and Commons was generally harmonious, despite a few disagreements. But a range of differences brought this amity to an end during the second session, 20 November – 18 December.[20] Heath's own fortunes during the parliament reflected the dichotomy. Prior to the adjournment, the opinions that he expressed seem to have weighed heavily in debate. On 24 May a member recommended that in future all bills should be prepared by lawyers, who were to meet daily for the purpose. Heath answered succinctly 'Then we must have no Lawyers in the house', and the proposal got no further.[21] Even in moments of crisis, he possessed the ability to sway his fellow-members. On 29 May a message arrived from the Lords, stating that James, despite a plea from the lower house, had decided that the session would not be extended. His resolve raised the spectre of dissolution, and many members wished to adjourn the debate and devote the remainder of the day to planning strategy, even though the house was faced by important and pressing business. According to one diarist: 'The discontent of the Howse could hardly bee restrayned till the Messengers might goe out, and presently after was expres't by a generall crye *Rise, Rise,* which Mr. Sollicitor began to temper by a fayre and mild speech.'[22] Heath subdued an angry house and in so doing impressed the diarist, a man who was even then not generally fond of courtiers — John Pym.

But the second session saw Heath's success turn to failure. On 4 December, when word arrived that James had rejected a petition that called on him to enforce the recusancy laws, there

---

[20] A considerable number of books and articles, many of them excellent, deal in depth with the parliament of 1621. The most thorough study of that parliament is Robert Zaller, *The Parliament of 1621: A Study in Constitutional Conflict* (Berkeley, 1971). See also ch. 2 of Conrad Russell, *Parliaments and English Politics 1621 – 1629* (Oxford, 1979), Russell also deals well with the other parliaments of the 1620s. And Ruigh's study of the parliament of 1624 is truly extraordinary.

[21] *CD 1621,* III, 294.

[22] *Ibid.,* IV, 390.

was, as there had been on 29 May, a loud call to adjourn the debate. Heath opposed the move, but the decision of the house went against him.[23] A second petition, dealing again with recusancy but also with the rights of parliament, which the Commons believed James had derogated, was drawn up and sent out, and the house then resolved to cease debate pending the king's reply. Heath opposed the decision to forgo further business, but he was unable to win over his colleagues.[24] He then tried a device to renew debate, when on 10 December he 'Moved to goe on with the bill of contynuance of Statutes at this time, if not in the howse yet as A Committee, because it was of very great Consequence.'[25] The Commons refused him. Two days later he again attempted to revive debate, this time by claiming bluntly: 'It is not in the power of the howse to impose silence upon our selves.'[26] Again he spoke in vain. Finally, on 14 December James, who had earlier refused to receive the second petition, sent a message of moderate tone, announcing that while he would not receive the petition he had seen it and he would respect parliamentary liberties, so long as they were not abused as he implied they had been during the session. Heath was quick to approve the message: 'as the Stile of the King's Answer doth carry in it Gravity and Majesty, so doth it espress, that the King is a Father to us'.[27] But the radicals demanded that the house should issue a protestation, reaffirming its rights. Heath supported this move, but not the further resolve of the house to ignore business that did not relate to grievances or to the protestation. James had announced that he would prorogue parliament on 22 December, and Sir Robert repeatedly begged his colleagues to divert their attention from grievances long enough to prepare for a session by passing key bills. With prorogation looming, he could not await the strategic moment for speaking out, but instead had to inject his pleas into debates that by their nature put them out of place. Many members seem to have been annoyed by his interruptions, for when on 18 December he put forward 'a short Bill for to continue all the Statutes that depend on Continuances', he felt compelled to

---

[23] (Sir) Edward Nicholas, *Proceedings and Debates in the House of Commons in 1620 and 1621* (London, 1766), II, 278 – 9.
[24] *CD 1621*, II, 500.
[25] *Ibid.*, VI, 230.
[26] *Ibid.*, 234.
[27] Nicholas, II, 329.

add: 'If 20 men should say tis not his duty, he would not believe them.'[28] The members refused to heed his plea, and the following day, as if to scorn him and his king, they voted to adjourn the house.

In marked contrast to these days of acrimony, the parliament of 1624 was for the most part characterised by close cooperation between king and Commons, owing largely to the fact that the members believed James to be making ready for war with Spain. Taking advantage of the harmony, Heath markedly influenced the proceedings in the Commons. No courtier, and few members of any persuasion, spoke as often as he did, sat on as many committees, or chaired as many.[29] Although he had some difficult crosses, probably no member enjoyed greater success. His influence was readily apparent during the debates on the subsidy. Even though the Commons generally felt well disposed toward James, the anti-Court faction sought to block funding, at least until the king had dealt with grievances. Against them, Sir Robert called for the prompt passage of a subsidy bill that would provide the crown with £300,000. On 19 March he argued that the house should not, on the one hand, demand that James make war on Spain, while on the other, refuse him funds: 'We desire the King should presently declare the breach of the treaties, then we must presently resolve to provide for the consequences of such a declaration. This business is as much ours as the King's.'[30] Sensing that his sentiments were shared by a majority of the members, the anti-Court faction proceeded against the subsidy by manoeuvre, rather than by frontal assault, persuading their colleagues to commit the bill. The commitment threatened prolonged delay, perhaps defeat. On 19 May, however, Heath moved that no new business should be dealt with until the subsidy had been voted on, and the house supported him. Two days later, the bill passed.[31]

During 1624 amity prevailed between king and Commons, but 1625 saw animosity the rule. The lower house was outraged by a

[28] *CD 1621*, VI, 337.
[29] Mitchell, pp. 97 – 8.
[30] YCPH, transcript of Nicholas diary, p. 149. It is noteworthy that this reasoning apparently impressed the members, for on 5 Aug. 1625 it failed to move them.
[31] *CJ*, I, 706. Heath also suffered some setbacks during the subsidy debate; note Ruigh, p. 248.

host of grievances, not least among them, that there was no war. Many members felt that they had been duped the year before, and from the beginning seemed bent on binding the new king to their collective will. Charles, for his part, was scarcely placatory, quickly proving himself to be at least his father's equal in the ability to antagonise parliament. Faced with an angry house, Heath could accomplish little. In debate, he often found himself on the losing side, even when his contributions were of the calibre of his 5 August speech.[32] The two short sessions of 1625 saw a fine career in the Commons end in anticlimax.

Heath's failures in 1625 were not his alone, any more than were his earlier successes. What happened during these few years was that the courtier-members, who had earlier enjoyed respect and even deference, came to be widely distrusted by the house. In 1621, except towards the close of the tumultuous second session, and in 1624, the house generally favoured courtiers. This was neatly reflected in committee assignments, particularly chairmanships. In 1621, for example, Sir Miles Fleetwood, sheriff of Buckinghamshire and son of the noted recorder, was appointed to five committees and chaired three, despite the fact that he seldom spoke in debate, while four leading radicals did not have a chairmanship between them, even though each spoke at least eighty times.[33] In honouring the courtiers, the members were probably motivated in part by simple respect, for most Englishmen, in parliament and outside, still revered the crown and saw its servants as an extension of the king himself. Members probably also believed that the king would be more kindly disposed towards an institution that honoured his servants than towards one that did not, and that as long as he knew that courtiers played an important role in conducting Commons business, there was some chance that he would be less suspicious of house decisions. To reassure him further, the Commons used its courtier-members to convey official communications to the king. The same members would then relate the royal response. Even when relations between king and Commons were at a low ebb, the house thought it expedient to have courtiers plead its case. So when on 4

---

[32] He was, however, occasionally able to sway the Commons; note Russell, *Parliaments and English Politics*, p. 221.

[33] The four were Sir Edward Giles, Edward Alford, Sir James Perrot, and Sir Thomas Wentworth.

December 1621 members prepared to send a petition to James on his recusant policy, they decided that the document should be presented to the king by 'suche persons as might *captare benevolentum*, all Courtiers'.[34] Finally, the house may have hoped that if it treated the courtiers well, they might reciprocate. They might, for example, report significant information that they discovered through official contacts. The house did not shrink from asking courtier-members to gather intelligence. On 29 April it urged Heath to use his Court connections to determine, for the information of the Commons, whether James would soon issue a proclamation directed against the Jesuits and whether he planned to dissolve Parliament.[35]

But there seemed to be a price to pay for any benefit that the Commons might hope to gain through courtier-members. Always fearful that its activities would be disclosed to the king, the house naturally assumed that it was courtiers who were most likely to violate secrecy. On 4 December 1621, even as the courtiers who were supposed to *'captare benevolentum'* were preparing to depart with the petition, a messenger from James arrived to inform the house that the king had learned of the petition and would refuse to receive it. Immediately members began to complain bitterly that some courtier had told the king of their intended petition and, worse still, had placed it in a bad light. For the remainder of the session, courtiers were generally regarded with suspicion by their colleagues.[36]

---

[34] *CD 1621*, V, 237.

[35] Ruigh, pp. 251 – 2. Heath occasionally served the court and the Commons as a go-between for a series of messages. On 20 May 1624 he informed the house that 'the Prince commanded him' to report that James was willing to allow the session to continue for an extra week, provided that the Commons would agree not to address any new business during that period. The house then ordered that only the perfecting of old business would be dealt with and that 'Mr. Solicitor is to acquaint the Prince presently with this order'. The next day Heath reported 'from the Prince . . . that his Highness seemeth very willing to embrace our desire': YCPH, Nicholas diary, pp. 341, 343. In matters involving Buckingham, members may also have looked to Heath, as the duke's spokesman.

[36] Zaller, pp. 160 – 1. In point of fact, many courtiers, both in and out of the Commons, were hostile to parliament, and the counsel that they gave James was to a great extent responsible for his poor relationship with parliament; note R. C. Munden, 'James I and "the Growth of Mutual Distrust": King, Commons, and Reform, 1603 – 1604', *Faction and Parliament: Essays on Early Stuart History*, ed. Kevin Sharpe (Oxford, 1978), 43 – 72, *passim*.

In 1621, it still took a crisis to cause most members of the Commons to turn against the courtiers in their midst. The radicals, however, were always suspicious of them, regarding them as being, by the very nature of their affiliation, enemies of reform. Even Coke, who held to a popular line from the opening of the parliament of 1621, was shunned by many radicals until it became clear that he was almost a pariah at Court, and as late as 4 May, one of them impugned his integrity. Heath, loyal crown servant that he was, never gained the radicals' favour — this, despite that fact that during his three parliaments he often joined, even led them in taking popular positions on such issues as parliamentary prerogatives, recusancy, foreign policy, monopolies, and court reform.[37] In 1621 and 1624 the radicals were generally too weak to move against the courtier faction at large, but they gained control of the parliament of 1625, and subsequently the position of all courtiers, including Heath, began to deteriorate, as progressively more members took up the radical line, that one could not simultaneously serve Court and people. Heath came up against the new bias on 23 June 1625, when, on being named to chair a committee of the whole house, he heard Edward Alford, a radical, complain 'because hee was sworne to the Kinge and of his fee'. A courtier-member angrily responded that he 'dislikt that exception, as tendinge to division by setting markes of distrust upon the King's servants', but it was a second radical, Sir John Popham, who secured the chair for Heath, and he did so by relying on a technicality: 'That it is against precedent that he that sits in that chayre at a Committee should be named by the House.' He then added, perhaps sarcastically 'whomsoever wee employ, wee are too many witnesses to suffer wronge'.[38]

The animosity towards courtiers that Heath saw that day continued to grow. By 1629 courtiers in the house were regularly meeting with hostility, even derision, with privy councillors suffering the most.[39] Given the course of history in the 1620s, it appears doubtful that even Elizabeth and her courtiers, capable though they were, could have held back the radical tide. Heath

---

[37] See ch. 6. The attack on Coke is noted in Zaller, p. 109.
[38] 'CD 1625', 8. In Feb. 1621 a member opposed allowing Coke to chair a committee of the whole, ostensibly because there was no precedent for giving a privy councillor the chair: CD 1621, IV, 16. On 12 Aug. 1625 Heath assumed the chair without apparent opposition: 'CD 1625', 148.
[39] Russell, Parliaments and English Politics, p. 413.

certainly could not. Although a fine parliamentarian, he, like any member in any period, was successful mainly when circumstances favoured his cause. Once the radicals had taken control of the Commons, his parliamentary abilities meant little. He had to fight back by different means.

Attorney-general v. the Commons

During the latter half of the 1620s radicals in both houses pushed on relentlessly, determined to bind the king to the will of parliament. For his part, Charles, with enemies real enough, tended to assume that anyone who did side with him was an enemy and to treat him as such. The weapon that he used most often and to most devastating effect was his attorney-general, Sir Robert Heath.

First to feel the weight of the king's wrath was Thomas Howard, earl of Arundel.[40] Arundel, long hostile to Buckingham, vented his spleen during the first weeks of the parliament of 1626 by roundly criticising the duke for his handling of the attack on Cadiz, that notable failure of the preceding autumn. Soon neither the king nor his favourite could stand more. On 4 March, acting on the pretext that Arundel had permitted his son to marry into the royal family without first obtaining the king's license, Charles had the earl confined to the Tower. The Arundel affair was essentially a contest, an important one, over the parliamentary claim to freedom from arrest, and it left Heath ambivalent. As attorney-general, he was duty-bound to defend Charles in his decision to detain Arundel, and he may furthermore have felt some animosity towards Arundel, because of the earl's attacks on Buckingham, a man Sir Robert both served and admired. On the other hand, Heath appears to have believed that the detention of Arundel was unwise, because it harmed the relationship between Charles and the Lords. He may also have doubted its legality. In early May, apparently on his own initiative, he

---

[40] The fullest treatment of the affair is V. F. Snow, 'The Arundel Case, 1626', *The Historian*, 26 (1964), 323 – 49. Heath's role is discussed by Fraser, 'Heath', 93 – 7.

drafted a model answer for Charles to send in response to one of the Lords' petitions. The answer was placatory in tone. At its core was a promise that the Arundel matter would be turned over to the judges and that Charles would abide by their decision, whether it was to proceed against the earl or to release him. The answer was not sent, however; Charles was in a combative mood. In early June Arundel was finally freed, but the king, while allowing him to reclaim his place in the Lords, in no way conceded that he had been wrong to take him from it.

By then, the Court was faced with a far greater danger than the Arundel case. John Digby, earl of Bristol, had for a decade prior to 1624 been ambassador to Spain. Charles and Buckingham blamed him for the failure of the negotiations for the Spanish match, and since his return to England in 1624 he had frequently been harassed by the Court. Sensing that he might retaliate, Charles was reluctant to issue him a writ of summons in 1626, but Bristol stood on privilege and the king gave in. The concern of the Court increased when on 19 April Bristol announced in a petition to the Lords that he intended to bring accusations against Buckingham. Apparently to thwart him, Charles decided to have Bristol tried by the Lords, for treason.[41] On 1 May Heath charged the earl before the upper house, only to see the accused respond by exhibiting articles of treason against Buckingham. To the consternation of the duke and his supporters, the Lords then ordered: 'That the King's Charge against the Earl of *Bristol* shall be first heard; and then the Charge of the Earl against the Duke; but yet so as the Earl's Testimony against the Duke be not prevented, prejudiced, nor impeached.'[42] In reality, neither Bristol nor Charles had an impressive case to make. Bristol claimed that Buckingham had been responsible for the breakdown in Anglo-Spanish relations and that during the embassy of 1623 he had sought to convert the then prince to Catholicism, while Charles, through Heath, accused him of precisely those two offences, but neither side

---

[41] On 21 April Charles sent a message to the Lords, requesting that Bristol be sent for as a delinquent, to answer for his behaviour in Spain and for slandering Buckingham. The message was prepared by Heath, for there is a draft (SP 16/25/41) in his hand. The best coverage of the background to the Bristol affair is Ruigh, ch. 7.

[42] *LJ*, III, 576 – 8.

could do much to substantiate its charges. The Court, however, feared that the Lords might convict Buckingham, given the number of peers who hated him. If Buckingham were toppled, Charles would lose not only his greatest favourite, in itself unbearable, but also credibility, for although Bristol spoke of him reverently it was probably clear to all parties that the king was deeply implicated in the wrongdoing that was being laid at the door of the duke. It was therefore the court as a whole, rather than Buckingham alone, that now faced a crisis.

To deal with Bristol, the king looked to Heath, Sir Robert was, as attorney, the individual responsible for drawing and exhibiting the articles against the earl. Now circumstance forced him to assume a defensive role too. On 2 May Charles ordered him to help Buckingham prepare answers to Bristol's articles 'and because you are our Servant and by oath bound to do us service in all our affaires to free you of any scruple in this case and to secure you against ourselves and all others, that you doe nothing contrary to the duty of your place or oath and fidelity to us'.[43] Heath may not have been entirely reassured by the wording, but he proceeded. On 6 May he presented the Lords with the articles against Bristol. The earl quickly blunted his initiative by forcing him, through pointed questioning, to divulge that Charles was the main informer in the case, and Bristol insisted that the king could not be both his judge, as with the Lords he technically was, and his accuser. The house then directed that the judges rule on this issue. Heath went off to counsel the king, and later, probably on his advice, Charles ordered the judges not to deliver an opinion 'as it was very hard and dangerous to give a general Rule'.[44] Sir Robert's stratagem was successful. Never again did Bristol publicly question the king's right to inform. Otherwise, however, advantage clearly lay with the earl, for the case against him was weak and the peers were sympathetic. As he proceeded against Bristol, Heath was on several occasions stymied by the upper house. On 6 May the peers denied his request to allow the clerk of the crown in

---

[43] SP 16/523/110.
[44] LJ, III, 594.

King's Bench to be present when the charges against Bristol were read. Eleven days later, despite the king's express opposition, they decided to permit Bristol counsel. On 14 June, after the earl had petitioned the house, requesting an order that Heath restrict his investigation — the implication being that he had not done so — to 'Proofs of his Charge, or the Earl's Answer', the Lords promptly complied.[45]

By 14 June, however, the Bristol case was probably of secondary importance in the eyes of both the upper house and the Court. On 2 May the Commons had impeached Buckingham, and the following week, in an intense meeting that lasted for two days, eight spokesmen from the lower house, led by Sir John Eliot and Sir Dudley Digges, levelled a dozen charges against him.[46] The Court quickly retaliated by arresting Eliot and Digges, and while the latter was soon freed the former was interrogated at least once by Heath before he was released.[47] Meanwhile, Sir Robert found himself in the ironic position of being forced, by virtue of his office, to proceed against Buckingham in the Lords, while at the same time, more in keeping with his sympathies and loyalties, helping him to frame his defence. On 19 May the duke answered Bristol's charges and on 8 June he spoke to the Commons' articles. In both cases, his lengthy refutations were undoubtedly prepared by Heath.[48]

On 13 June Sir Robert wrote to Buckingham. He had heard that the following day the Commons intended to deliver a

---

[45] Ibid., 582, 627, 680 – 1.

[46] CJ, I, 846 – 54. Excellent coverage of Buckingham's impeachment is provided by C. G. C. Tite, Impeachment and Parliamentary Judicature in Early Stuart England (London, 1974), ch. 7.

[47] Harold Hulme, The Life of Sir John Eliot 1592 to 1632: A Struggle for Parliamentary Freedom (London, 1957), pp. 139 – 46.

[48] LJ, III, 632 – 45, 655 – 67. It appears that Buckingham, who had never wanted the contest with Bristol, was attempting to effect a reconciliation with him. On 12 June 1626 Andrea Rosso, Venetian Secretary in England, reported to the Doge and Senate 'there has been an attempt to reconcile the earl with the duke, but the earl has steadfastly refused this': Calendar of State Papers and Manuscripts relating to English Affairs, Existing in the Archives and Collections of Venice, XIX, §618, p. 440.

remonstrance to Charles, calling on him to dismiss the duke from Court and promising him a large subsidy if he complied. Counselling Buckingham to display 'patience & wisedome & moderation', Heath proposed an answer for the king, which by implication, he hoped that the duke would forward:

Gentelmen, you have offered unto us, this Remonstraunce wherein you express your apprehension of many errors & misdemenors of high natures committed by the Duke of Buck, and with all you express much Love & duity to our person. The particulers consist of many hedds, to which I knowe yee cann not in reason expect a suddeyne awnswere . . . I will doe it with that speed which I cann . . . But I must put you in mind of your former promisses to supplye my present & pressing occasions not for my owne particuler use, but for the service & defence of us all, & for our honor & Religion, which is more then all.[49]

Heath hoped that this answer would serve to place the blame on the Commons, particularly the radical members, for the deteriorating relationship between king and parliament. As he told Buckingham, if the royal answer failed to resolve the problem, '(as I dare not be confident of the success) it will justly cast the blame of the breach upon them'. His letter was also an indirect plea to the king, for he feared that Charles would respond to the remonstrance by dissolving parliament, and he wished to see the session continue. Dissolution would not only deprive the king of his subsidy, but it might signal to the nation that the Court doubted Buckingham's ability to defend himself successfully against the charges that had been brought against him. Heath seems to have been convinced that the charges, though many and emotive, were weakly supported, and that the Lords would acquit Buckingham if the trial were completed. Charles, however, was in no mood to compromise. He refused

[49] SP 16/524/28.

to receive the remonstrance, and on 15 June dissolved parliament.[50]

Heath now developed a new strategy to clear his patron, and with the support of Charles and the duke he sought to implement it. On 17 June he wrote to each of the twelve members who had drawn up the Commons' charges against Buckingham, including the eight who had reported them to the Lords, and requested that they come as a group to his chamber at the Inner Temple, there to learn 'his Majestie's further pleasure'. That pleasure, as it turned out, was to acquaint Heath with the evidence that they had used in framing the charges and to identify the witnesses against Buckingham. Acting as spokesman for the group, Eliot soon afterwards wrote to Heath that 'some proofes were delivered to the Lords with the charges but what other proofs the house would have used . . . we neither know, nor can undertake to informe'. Heath was dissatisfied with this, and he interrogated each of the twelve individually. Eliot, in his statement, was uncharacteristically cautious, being neither inflammatory nor enlightening. Pym blustered 'he cometh not to his answere by his owne Free will but inforced by his Necessary Dutie and obedience to his

[50] Whether Charles over-reacted — in essence whether Heath's counsel was wise — is a subject of some controversy. It is noteworthy that apart from Buckingham all privy councillors, including some of his political allies, opposed the dissolution: Willson, *Privy Councillors*, pp. 53 – 4. Buckingham himself seems to have been little worried by the investigations by the Commons, but the attitude of the Lords concerned him: Kevin Sharpe, 'The Earl of Arundel, His Circle and the Opposition to the Duke of Buckingham, 1618 – 1628', *Faction and Parliament*, ed. Sharpe, 232 – 3. J. N. Ball claims that the grounds for the impeachment were weak, but does not discount the possibility that the impeachment or the impending contest between Buckingham and Bristol provoked the dissolution: 'Sir John Eliot and Parliament, 1624 – 1629', *Faction and Parliament*, ed. Sharpe, 191 – 3. Russell argues that the dissolution came because Charles was convinced that the Lords would not convict Bristol and that the Commons would not give him the subsidy he desired, at least not before wringing still more concessions from him: *Parliaments and English Politics*, pp. 320 – 2. J. S. Flemion asserts that the Lords would have convicted Buckingham in the impeachment trial, and that Charles was in fact forced to dissolve Parliament to save his favourite: 'The Dissolution of Parliament in 1626: A Revaluation', *The English Historical Review*, 87 (1972), 784 – 90. It is doubtful, however, that the prosecution of Buckingham would have succeeded in the face of royal opposition, and indeed after 1626 Parliament seems to have realised that it could not successfully move against crown ministers if the king were adamantly opposed: C. B. Anderson, 'Ministerial Responsibility in the 1620's', *Journal of Modern History*, 34 (1962), 389.

Majesties Commande', and then turned to an apparently purposeful vagueness, insisting: 'That he doth not remember any other Witnesses examined in his presence, because he did seldome attende the Comittees to whome these Examinations were refered. But . . . whatsoever was Conteyned in the same Charge . . . he then Conceyved [to be] uppon very good and sufficient proofe, although the particulars of the proofes then insisted uppon, he doth not further remember.' Digges produced a timid statement: 'I am not able sufficiently to Recollect those Thinges which gave me satisfaction . . . I that use to Take no notes in Parliament, and had no particular charge Comended to my care foreseinge how slight information, my weake memory, is like to give, doe pray you to valew it accordingly.'[51] The rash of 'weake memory' allowed Digges and his fellows to avoid divulging to Heath the secret business of the Commons, but it also furthered Sir Robert's argument that the case against Buckingham was, as the Commons' charges had earlier suggested, demonstrably weak.

The next step was to file informations in Star Chamber against both Buckingham and Bristol. By moving against the duke as well as the earl, Heath may have hoped that the public would perceive the Court as being even-handed, but the fact that Bristol was confined to the Tower as he awaited trial, while Buckingham went about his normal business, probably destroyed any hope that the ruse would work. Bristol soon fell ill, which gave the Court an opportunity to delay both trials. Finally, in early March 1628 the earl petitioned to be freed, and Buckingham, with whom he had now been reconciled, supported his appeal. With parliament due to meet soon, the release of Bristol seemed also a prudent step politically, as it removed a potential grievance. On 19 March Heath informed Bristol that he would soon be free and added, by way of admonition: 'I am very confident that your Lordshipps wisedome is such as that both to his Majestie and to your Noble freind and Intercessor your further carriage wilbe such as shall dailye more and more increase and enlarge those beginnings of favours your Lordshipp hath receaved.'[52] The Bristol affair was over at last. But a still greater crisis was just beginning.

---

51 Gloucestershire Record Office, D185/1X/9; Egerton 2978, f. 14; *De Jure Maiestates . . . and the Letter Book of Sir John Eliot*, ed. A. B. Grosart (London, 1882), II, 6 – 11; Egerton 3779.
52 BL, Stowe 365, f. 101; Ruigh, pp. 378 – 81; Hulme, pp. 150 – 1.

In the wake of dissolving the parliament of 1626, Charles used various expedients to raise funds. Particularly galling to many of his subjects was the forced loan, and some of them refused to pay. By the autumn of 1627 a number of men had been imprisoned for non-payment, and in early November five of them moved the King's Bench to grant them writs of habeas corpus. The Five Knights' Case, the most important constitutional contest of the 1620s, was under way.

Charles at first opposed granting the writs. He finally gave in, at the urging of the judges, but left moot the question of whether habeas corpus was allowed of right or of grace.[53] On 13 November, Sir Thomas Darnel, one of the five prisoners, appeared in King's Bench to hear his return.[54] Heath was there, representing the crown, and he quickly took the offensive by complaining 'these gentlemen gave out in speeches, and in particular this gentleman, That they did wonder why they should be hindered from Trial'. When Darnel protested that he was having difficulty obtaining counsel, because lawyers feared the king's wrath, Sir Nicholas Hyde, the chief justice, responded 'no offence will be taken against any man that shall advise you in your proceedings at law', but Heath, after affirming Hyde's statement, added, perhaps by way of warning to both Darnel and his prospective counsel: 'If it shall be conceived, as is rumoured, that there was a denial of justice on the king's part, you must know that his majesty is very tender of that.' Sir Robert's surliness may have been genuine, but it also served well as a device, for Darnel appears to have been intimidated. And he was completely taken aback by the return submitted by the warden of the Fleet, which noted only that he had been 'committed by the special command of his majesty, &c'.

---

[53] The defendants apparently could not demand the writ as a right: E. R. Adair, 'The Petition of Right', *History*, new series, 5 (1920), 99. However, it was common practice to grant the writ, for as Charles noted he acted on advice 'that it was agreeable to Justice, & to the Lawe of the Land that such writtes should be graunted in thes cases': Fraser, 'Heath', 113, quoting SP 16/85/2.

[54] The following summary of the proceedings involving Darnel and other knights, including all quotations, is drawn from *ST*, III, cols. 1 – 59. Analysis of the Five Knights' Case is constantly evolving. Important new direction, particularly as regards the nature of source material available, has recently been provided by J. A. Guy, 'The Origins of the Petition of Right Reconsidered', *The Historical Journal*, 25 (1982), 289 – 94.

Apparently uncertain of how to proceed, Darnel asked that his writ not be filed, and his case came to an end.

The real challenge to Heath and to the crown came a week later, when the other four prisoners came to King's Bench to hear their returns, all of which were identical to Darnel's, as they had probably guessed they would be. It appears that by now, they and their counsel had planned a joint strategy: to argue that, while the king might be free to order the arrest of an individual, his command alone could not justify lengthy detention. Were the knights to win their freedom by so arguing, the king's power to enforce his policies would be substantially reduced. They had more than cause to hope, because representing them were four of the finest lawyers in England: Selden, the greatest legal mind of his age; Sir John Bramston, a future chief justice; Sir Henry Calthrop, later to serve as recorder of London; and William Noy, the brilliant radical fire-brand who was to succeed Heath as attorney-general. Perhaps never before had a crown lawyer faced the talent that Heath now did.

Bramston led off, and he set forth the argument that the other three counsellors were to follow:

> I will not dispute whether or no, a man may be imprisoned before he be convicted according to the law; but if this return shall be good, then his imprisonment shall not continue for a time, but for ever; and the subjects of this kingdom may be restrained of their liberties perpetually, and by law there can be no remedy for the subject.

He then called on the justices to grant bail and cited statutes and precedents to support his request. Most potent was his citation of the twenty-ninth chapter of Magna Carta: 'No freeman shall be taken or imprisoned . . . but by lawful judgement of his peers, or by the law of the realm.' Heath for the moment declined to respond, instead asking the justices to settle one issue at least, by approving the returns in respect to form, but Hyde answered: 'I think it is not best for us to declare our opinions by piece-meals' and one of the puisnes, Sir John Doddridge, added: 'This is the greatest cause that ever I knew in this court; our judgements that we give between party and party, between the king and the meanest subject, ought to be maturely advised on.' Still more ominous, from Heath's point of view, was a question that a second puisne, Sir William Jones, asked towards the close of the day's proceedings: 'Mr.

Attorney, if it be so that the law of Magna Charta and other statutes be now in force, and the gentlemen be not delivered by this court, how shall they be delivered? Apply yourself to show us any other way to deliver them.' Doddridge echoed Jones's concern: 'Yea, or else they shall have a perpetual imprisonment.' It was now Heath who was on the defensive.

On 26 November the parties reassembled, and Heath responded to the knights' counsel. He began with a clever attempt to weaken the impact of the lawyers' assertion that Magna Carta was relevant to the case at hand:

> No freeman can be *imprisoned* . . . But will they have it understood that no man should be *committed*, but first he shall be indicted or presented? I think that no learned man will offer that; for certainly there is no justice of peace in a county, nor constable within a town, but he doth otherwise, and might indict before an indictment can be drawn, or a presentment be made.

He realised that the knights and their lawyers had not challenged the king's right to commit, but only to detain for an extended period, without promise of trial or deliverance. Still, he was able to make the point that the twenty-ninth chapter, if rigidly applied throughout England, would destroy the apparatus of law enforcement. In essence, he was calling on the judges to use their common sense in determining whether the chapter should apply in the present situation, while at the same time implying that it had to be taken literally or not at all. Having dealt with the knights' most serious challenge, he went on, attempting to demonstrate that each of the precedents and statutes that had been cited in favour of bail was somehow irrelevant.

As Heath spoke, his demeanour appears to have been sullen, at times surly. He knew that many Englishmen were deeply interested in the case, and he believed that the knights' counsel were using it as a device to stir up anti-Court sentiment. At one point he commented bitterly:

> I will answer their precedents with precedents; nay, I will shew your lordship that the precedents which they have cited are no precedents for them. — And, my lord, it is a dangerous thing for men in matters of weight to avouch precedents with confidence, when they make nothing for them: for, my lord,

163

precedents are now become almost proclamations, for they are already run up and down the town.

After long hours of speaking, Heath completed his attack on the precedents and statutes that had been adduced in favour of bail. He then cited several precedents that he believed would show that the knights were not bailable. One in particular was damaging to the opposition, and it seemed clearly pertinent: a resolution of all the judges, dating from 34 Eliz. and recorded in the notes of Sir Edmund Anderson, then chief justice of the Common Pleas. Heath conceded that he could not introduce the precedent 'with so great authority as I have the rest, because I have not the thing itself by me'. Still, citing Anderson's notes, he claimed: 'The Judges were desired to shew in what cases men that were committed were not bailable, whether upon the commitment of the queen or any other. — The Judges make answer, That if a man shall be committed by the queen, by her command, or by the privy council, he is not bailable.' By all appearances the judges were little concerned by Heath's inability to produce the resolution, for it was apparently widely known. As Sir Robert mentioned: 'I will put it to your lordship's memory, I presume you may well remember it.' Only Noy complained, demanding that Heath produce the original resolution. Seemingly testy even in his moment of triumph, Sir Robert responded: 'I will shew you any thing; but, my lord, I shall be bold to claim the privilege of my place, as the king's counsel; when the king's Attorney has spoken, there ought to be no arguments after that; but if you ask to see any thing, you shall have it.'

The next day Hyde delivered the opinion of the court. Like Heath, he disparaged the precedents produced by the knights' counsel and claimed that the resolution of 34 Eliz. was pertinent and significant. Far from granting the prisoners victory, he suggested what to them would have been the ultimate defeat — a petition to the king for deliverance. He then concluded with the most famous words he was ever to speak: 'If in justice we ought to deliver you, we would do it; but upon these grounds, and these Records, and the Precedents and Resolutions, we cannot deliver you, but you must be remanded.'

In January 1628 the knights were freed, as were all others who had been imprisoned for refusing to contribute to the forced loan. Shortly thereafter, Charles ordered the issuance of writs of election. Presumably he hoped that by approving the release of the prisoners he would reduce anti-Court sentiment in England, but the electorate returned radicals in large numbers. On 22 March, soon after the opening of parliament, the popular leaders chorused a determination to reverse the decision on the five knights. If they failed, the king would be left free, as one member of the Commons saw it, 'to take from his subjects what he will'. A second speaker was even more vehement: 'This is the crisis of parliaments. We shall know by this if parliaments live or die.' And Sir Thomas Wentworth announced that he would soon introduce a set of motions, including 'for our persons, the freedom of them from imprisonment . . .; for our goods, that no levies may be made, but by parliament'.[55] From these was born the Petition of Right.

In mounting their campaign to nullify the judges' decision, the radicals were helped unwittingly by Shelton. Heath's successor as solicitor-general had also inherited his role as unofficial leader of the king's counsel in the Commons, but he was as inept a parliamentarian as Sir Robert had been able. On 27 March he first joined the debate on the ramifications of the Five Knights' Case, providing his interpretation of the judges' ruling. He made no great blunders in this instance, but in passing he mentioned a form of entry for the decision that differed from the one Selden believed to be appropriate. The next day, Selden reported that he had checked the controlment roll and had confirmed the form was as he had imagined it. He also called on the Commons to appoint a subcommittee to check all the precedents cited in the Five Knights' Case, and the house complied.[56]

On 29 March Shelton really started to blunder badly, unnecessarily and foolishly claiming that he could produce forty

---

[55] CD 1628, II, 56, 58, 61.
[56] On the question of the entry — specifically, whether it was a *remittitur* or a *remittitur quousque*, etc. — see Guy, 295–6; F. H. Relf, *The Petition of Right* (Minneapolis, 1917), pp. 3–5. Relf may exaggerate the impact of Shelton's statement. It certainly did not cause consternation, and indeed Sir Dudley Digges, after hearing him, said that 'he was glad to hear of these quousque's': *CD 1628*, II, 156.

precedents that supported the king's right to detain at will. Two days later Selden reported to the house:

> He remembered the House of Mr. Solicitor's intimation that he had 40 cases to this effect making for the King. He says that Mr. Solicitor brought a book but not any case more to the subcommittee, with the notes of students quite mistaken. But he much commended the ingenuity of Mr. Solicitor that brought to the subcommittee the case of Sir John Heveningham in a copy of a record of judgement.

For all his trumpeting, Shelton had produced only one relevant case, and that of one of the knights. Up to this point in his remarks, Selden had been sarcastic, as contemporaries often were when they discussed the solicitor-general, but now he turned to a more serious issue, noting that Shelton's copy of the entry had been 'full of blanks. The beginning was confessed to be written by the clerk, the latter end by another hand, and so foiled in, and certainly intended to have been recorded and the blanks filled up'. Shelton may have been unnerved by the proceedings, which were making a perfect fool of him. In any case, soon after Selden had completed his report, the solicitor volunteered that John Keeling, secretary of the Crown Office, had prepared the draft, but that Heath had given 'direction to drawe a forme of a judgment'. Shelton was recklessly unwrapping a major scandal. The next day Selden reported that Keeling had informed him:

> after Michaelmas term last, the Attorney wished him to make a special entry of the habeas corpus . . . Mr. Keeling . . . went to the judges, and at that time they would not assent to any special entry, but the Attorney divers times sent to him, and told him there was no remedy, but he must draw it . . . and not long since . . . (though it went against his heart) yet he gave it to Mr. Attorney as he drew it, but never heard more of it since.

In the wake of Keeling's statement, it was obvious that the Court, or at least Heath, had attempted to enhance the value of the Five Knights' Case, making it an assured precedent for the king's right to detain, by altering the entry to cause it to appear a final judgement. Selden's reports of 31 March and 1 April magnified the power of the radicals, and on 3 April the Commons passed Wentworth's resolutions.[57]

On 12 April, Heath gave the Lords his version of the Keeling affair:

> That he dyd dyrecte the Clerke to make this draught out of the duitye of his place for the Kinge . . . I never shewed yt to any, nor coulde I have entred yt without acquaintinge the Judges. Yt came forth now by misfortune, and hathe gyven much distaste, which I am sorry for. But perusing the olde precedents with theis, I founde noe difference but a fewer words and therefore resolved never to enter yt.

Two days later, however, the judges provided the upper house with quite a different account. According to Whitelocke: 'As for endeavouring to have a judgment entered: it is true Mr. Attorney pressed the same for his master's service; but we, being sworn to do right betwixt the king and his subjects, commanded the clerk to make no entry, but according to the old form.'[58]

While they differed on the question of whether there had been an actual attempt to change the entry, Heath and Whitelocke both implied that the king's order lay behind the entire proceeding. Furthermore, after Sir Robert had completed his version, Buckingham added: 'The Att had a check from the Kynge bycause he had not entred that draught.' Had the members of the Commons been given any excuse to believe that Heath had acted of his own volition in the Keeling affair, they might well have moved against him. As it was, in all probability a number of them were suspicious of him for the part he had played, and, in truth, it is quite possible that Charles, when he issued the fateful order, was acting on the advice of his attorney,

---

[57] *CD 1628*, II, 229, 217–18; Relf, pp. 5–7; Guy, 296–8. Shelton defended himself by telling Selden (*CD 1628*, II, 218): 'You charge me that I should say I had 40 precedents to prove this case. I hope you do not expect that I should have them about me, but that there are such I make no question, and Sir Edward Coke himself says, in Reports, if reason should be expressed, it would swell the records.'

[58] 'Notes of the Debates in the House of Lords', 93.

who understood far better than he did the nature of the issues involved.

Heath's statement on the entry was overshadowed by a new crisis. On 7 April delegates from the Commons, led by Selden, addressed a committee of both houses, devoting several hours to citing statutes and precedents in an effort to demonstrate that the judges' decision of the preceding 27 November had been misguided. Five days later Heath responded, in the Lords, much as he had in King's Bench, by claiming that the specific references cited by the Commons delegates did not apply to the knights' case, nor generally to the king's power to detain.[59] His rebuttal lasted through the entire morning's sitting and well into the afternoon, but nothing was settled, and he was forced to cover much the same ground yet a third time, in perhaps the most dramatic circumstances of all. Appearing at a conference of the two houses, 16 - 17 April, he led the king's counsel against a delegation of lawyers from the Commons in the celebrated debate 'On the Liberty of the Subject'.[60] Once more the two sides batted back and forth precedents and statutes, philosophy and constitutional theory. Finally, the leaders of both delegations concluded in a diplomatic vein. Coke, briefly recalling the work of two days, requested that the 'Noble Lords' place, 'in the one Balance, Seven Acts of Parliament, Records, Precedents, Reasons, all that we speak . . . and, in God's Name, put into the other Balance what Mr. Attorney said, his Wit, Learning, and great Endowments of Nature. And if he be weighty, let him have it; if no, then conclude with us'. Heath was more modest in his request. He seems to have realised that the king's power to detain was going to be somehow defined by parliament, and

---

[59] *Ibid.*, 87 - 95.

[60] Perhaps the best treatment of the conferences of both 7 and 16 - 17 April is provided by S. D. White, *Sir Edward Coke and "The Grievances of the Commonwealth," 1621 - 1628* (Chapel Hill, 1979), pp. 237 - 51. The fullest text of the latter conference is in *LJ*, III, 746 - 63; both quotations in the following review are p. 763. Heath was entirely responsible for directing the king's counsel at the conference; however, Sir Francis Ashley, a king's serjeant, went beyond the text that he had cleared with him, and his added statements were so high-prerogative in nature that he was detained by parliament: 'Notes of the Debates in the House of Lords', 117 - 18. During the conference of 16 - 17 April, as in a Commons' debate of 1 April, Coke and other Commons speakers devoted considerable effort to reducing the significance of 34 Eliz. as a precedent for the king's right to detain. To their own satisfaction, they succeeded, although it appears that they in turn may have overestimated the extent of their success: Guy, 298; Relf, pp. 16 - 18.

he was mainly intent on seeing that the definition did minimum damage to the prerogative. To that end, he called on the Lords:

> to weigh (as Sir *Edward Cooke* desired) both in equal Balance, Reasons, Precedents, and Resolutions of Judges. This Manifesto of the House of Commons takes the Matter upon great Advantage, as resolved by that Body; but this is our Comfort that are of Counsel for the King, that you are all now Counsellors of the King and Kingdom. If all can be so ordered as you shall not destroy the Rights of the King, and shall favour the Liberties of the Subject, as the Cause requires, Mr. Attorney hath the very utmost of his Desires.

Heath's address was excellently turned, appealing as it did to the vanity of the peers, the 'Counsellors of the King and Kingdom', and to their royalism and sense of moderation in constitutional matters. Thus encouraged to seek a middle ground, the Lords proposed that a clause, affirming that parliament recognised the sovereign powers of the king, be affixed to the Commons' resolutions.

The lower house refused to compromise, and it was able to persuade the peers to accept the resolutions of 1 April virtually without alterations or additions. The Petition of Right went on to the king. Having viewed the petition, on 2 June Charles affirmed: 'The King willeth That Right be done, according to the Laws and Customs of the Realm. And that the Statutes be put in due Execution, that His Subjects may have no Cause to complain of any Wrongs or Oppressions contrary to their just Rights and Liberties.' The Commons refused to accept his answer, deeming it evasive, and by threatening to censure Buckingham it managed to induce Charles to assent to the petition in the standard form.

The same concern that caused the king to give in on the petition, however, soon aroused him to strike out at parliament. When the Commons pressed its advantage by calling on Charles to, among other things, remove Buckingham from all offices, in return for a large subsidy and tunnage and poundage for life, he decided that, despite his pressing financial needs, he would not sell his favourite. As early as 12 May he had ordered Heath to draw up a prorogation speech. Perhaps at the time he had thought that by proroguing parliament he might avoid dealing with the Petition of Right. For some reason he had held back, but now he put the speech to use, ending the session. The king's prorogation speech — and Heath's — was marked by a subtle repudiation of the portion of the Petition of Right that dealt with commitment. While the petition had specified that 'no man hereafter be compelled to make or yield any gift, loan, benevolence, tax, or such like charge, without common consent by Act of Parliament; and that none . . . be confined, or otherwise molested or disquieted concerning the same or refusal thereof', in his speech the king conceded only 'neather we nor our privye counsell shall or will, at any time hereafter commit or command to prison or otherwise restrein the person of any, for the not lending of mony unto us, or for any other cause, which in our consciences doth not concerne the State the publike good & safety of us & our people'.[61] It was therefore on a note of ambiguity that the session came to an end.

When parliament reassembled the following January, several members of the Commons warned their colleagues that during the prorogation Whitehall had worked to undo the Petition of Right, by having it printed with the king's original, evasive, answer, as well as his formal assent, and with portions of his prorogation speech appended. Bristling, the house on 21 January appointed a committee to discover who had been responsible for appending the king's statements, and the following day Selden reported that the royal printer had told him 'there were 1500 copies printed without any addition at all, which were published in the time of the last Parliament; but since the last Parliament other copies have been printed with the additions and those suppressed and made waste paper, which the printer did, as he said, by command from Mr. Attorney, which he received from his Majesty'.[62] Despite these revelations, the Commons did not attack Heath for his involvement, possibly because, as in the Keeling affair, it was generally felt that he had acted under the king's own orders. But the anti-Court faction, which was by now solidly in control of the Commons, was becoming ever more convinced that Sir Robert

---

[61] *LJ*, III, 789 – 90. Fraser appends Heath's draft, SP 16/138/45: 'Heath', 221 – 32.
[62] *CD 1629*, 8 – 9.

was an important figure in the clique of crown officers and advisors that, to their mind, worked against the people. Allegations concerning his role in the printing of the petition did nothing to reduce their suspicion. And still more revelations were soon to place him high on their list of enemies.

On 4 February the house received a petition against Dr John Cosin, prebendary and later bishop of Durham, for practices 'tending to the introducing of Popish doctrine and Popish ceremonies into the Cathedral Church at Durham'. Speaking to it, a member reported: 'There were two affidavits that Cosin should say, That the King had no more to do with Religion than his horsekeeper; and that by the appointment of Mr. Attorney these affidavits were taken, and he said, to the end a bill in Star Chamber might be filed against him. But since Cosin hath his pardon.' A second member added that in addition to Cosin, three other churchmen, Richard Mountague, Roger Manwaring, and Robert Sibthorpe, all of whom had been attacked by the Commons in 1628 — Mountague for his anti-Puritan writings, the others for their Arminianism and for having supported the forced loan — had been pardoned. Aroused by these revelations, speaker after speaker demanded that those who had procured the pardons be identified, and the house appointed a deputation, headed by Sir Robert Phelips, a leading radical, to interview Heath. Within hours, Phelips reported that Sir Robert had said: that Carleton and the earl of Dorset had pressed him 'to hasten the pardons'; that he had received two warrants to draw the documents; and that, when Heath had completed a rough draft of Mountague's pardon, 'being often urged to expedition' by Richard Neile, the Arminian bishop of Winchester, the prelate 'underlined and corrected the same, adding the names of Cosin, Manwaring, and Sibthorpe to the pardon'. Not satisfied that they had heard the whole story, the members sent Phelips and his colleagues back to question Heath further, particularly on the question of who among the 'procurers' of the pardons had known of the affidavits on Cosin. Two days later Phelips reported that Heath had, by his account, shown the documents to Charles, 'whereupon the King charged him to make a strict inquisition herein; but the King would not believe the same to be true'. After receiving contradictory testimony from several persons who had been present when Cosin had allegedly made his remarks against the king, Phelips added: 'Mr. Attorney finding the busines lessened and some malice: proceeded not in it.' Phelips concluded his report by stating that

Heath had told him that he 'had not given the King any account of this business because he thought it wod come to nothing'.[63]

That Sir Robert had, by his own admission, discontinued the investigation without informing Charles caused consternation in the Commons, for many members had long suspected that the king, although himself honourable, was being deceived by evil ministers, who misrepresented affairs to him and worked behind his back to undo his good policies. As Phelips concluded, Eliot quickly rose to demand that 'the persons that made the affidavits may be sent for and that Mr. Attorney shod be questioned upon what reasons he soe slightly passed this over: and if the Attorney or others are found guilty that we spare them not'. Other speakers followed Eliot in calling for further investigation, but in fact most of them had already convicted Heath in their minds. As one complained: 'Neyther Mr. Cosens nor Mr. Atturney fitt to sleepe.' At length, the house ordered Selden and Sir Edward Littleton, 'being of the same Inns of Court', to inform Heath that, 'there being an accusation against him, he may here answer and satisfy the House on Monday next'.[64]

But the house was to hear no more from Heath on the Cosin affair. On Saturday, 7 February, Charles, angered by the revelations that his attorney had already provided and perhaps fearing still more disclosures of what he regarded as private Court business, confined him to his chambers. Never before had Heath faced such a crisis, and there was the very real possibility that he might be dismissed from his place. In desperation, he wrote to his friends, that they might intercede with the king, and they responded. Particularly helpful was Conway, who on Sunday informed Heath of what he and Weston had done on his behalf:

I desired his Majesty that the Lord Treasurer might read your Letter and prayed his Majesty that he would observe

---

[63] *Ibid.*, 39 – 40, 44, 175. For background on this affair, especially as regards Mountague, Sibthorpe, and Manwaring, note Hillel Schwartz, 'Arminianism and the English Parliament, 1624 – 1629', *The Journal of British Studies*, 12 (1973), 41 – 68.

[64] *CD 1629*, 47, 175 – 6.

your Last humble suite to him, which I did the rather that it being opened by another of more eminent condition then myself, I might then humbly use the freedome to speake something of that request of yours, which for ought I could perceave his Majesty receaved with his accustomed Grace.[65]

The intercession had its desired effect, for the following day Charles freed him and restored him to active service, but not before admonishing him to 'feare God and the King and none els'.[66]

The house presumably did not forget Heath's involvement in the Cosin case, though it moved on to other matters. Soon yet more damaging revelations came to light. On 14 February the Commons was informed that the year before Heath had been ordered by the king to proceed against ten alleged Jesuits, but that he had turned the case over to a justice of the peace, George Long. Furthermore, the report went on, he had instructed Long:

to indite three of them for Priestes and to offer the oath of allegiance to the other seven, upon refusall whereof they might afterward be indited. By this meanes whereas they might have beene all convicted for Jesuites which is no lesse Capitall then being a priest, one of them onely who professed him selfe a Priest was condemned, and he reprieved too, the other two were acquitted for want of proofe of their being priests, and the seven were all bayled upon slight bondes.[67]

---

[65] U. of I., Heath Papers. In search of help, Heath wrote to Carlisle and Carleton, besides Conway: SP 16/135/17, 20, 22. After he was freed he wrote again to Carlisle, to thank him for having played the largest part in obtaining his release and to beg him to intercede again so that Heath might personally attend the king '& tender my most humble submission & thankfullnes to his sacred person uppon my knee, & receave his owne absolution': SP 16/135/ 27. That Heath gave Carlisle the main credit for winning him freedom may suggest that the earl did in fact play the leading role, but Heath may also have written as he did in order to flatter his patron.

[66] As reported by Sir Francis Nethersole to Elizabeth of Bohemia, 14 Feb. 1629: CD 1629, 250.

[67] Ibid., 249 – 50. The alleged Jesuits had been taken prisoner during a raid, in 1628, on a recently established Jesuit college in Clerkenwell. The raid, and the holdings of the college, are described in 'The Discovery of the Jesuits' College at Clerkenwell', ed. J. G. Nichols, Camden Society, Miscellany, 2 (1853). This narrative was at one time ascribed to Heath, but Sir John Coke is now generally recognised as the author.

With that last revelation, Eliot rose to demand that those who had been responsible for freeing the Jesuits would not themselves go free. One man especially he saw a danger:

> What could be their purpose that laboured so to find a way to free them, but still to work our ruin? I fear the drawing of the indictment was maliciously done. The persons that I look at are first the Attorney, whom we still find faulty in this matter of Religion, when he saw the importance of the cause, and had directions from the King and the Council-board, and yet in a cause that so much concerns the King and people and Religion and all, he must take his own hand away and put it to another; this negligence renders him inexcusable.

After several speakers had echoed his sentiments, the house ordered a delegation headed by the radical Sir Francis Seymour to interview Heath.[68]

Two days later Seymour reported to the Commons that he and his colleagues had called on Heath and had asked him to respond in writing to certain questions. Sir Robert had written the answers, but then had 'seemed timerous to deliver in that paper before he consulted with the King'. Given Heath's experience of the past week, it should have surprised no one that he was 'timerous'. Seymour continued, reporting that at a second meeting Heath had given over the written answers. He had probably seen the king in the interim, though Seymour did not speculate on the possibility. In his answer, Heath attempted to exculpate himself, blaming the failure of the prosecution on Long. 'I did receive order from the Council to proceed against the priests', he recalled, 'and I did accordingly proceed against them, and I gave directions, and took the examinations and informations, and I sent for Mr. Long, and desired him to take special care therein . . . I understood an indictment was preferred against three of them for treason, and the rest for praemunire.'[69] Unfortunately for Heath, his account was undone by his own hand, for Seymour had also called upon Long, who had shown him an order from Sir Robert 'to

---

[68] CD 1629, 77.
[69] Ibid., 79, 215.

proceede against the said three of the said recusantes as priests and not otherwise, and against the rest for the oath of allegiance'.[70] That Heath had misrepresented his role in the affair seems not to have bothered the Commons, but the nature of that role did. Moreover, since the king was still upset with him, he could not look for strong backing at Court. As one observer remarked, Heath 'now being fallen into the ill opinion of the House of Commons is in danger to be crushed between two rockes'.[71]

Yet, just having cornered Heath, the hunters moved on. After 16 February the radicals uncovered scandals that implicated courtiers still higher-ranking than he, and they set out in pursuit of this big game, striking out wildly as they went.

After six weeks of lurching from crisis to crisis, the session reached a dramatic climax. On 2 March, in a justly famous scene, Sir John Finch, the Speaker, attempted to adjourn the house, but was held in his chair by Denzil Holles and Benjamin Valentine. At that moment 'notwithstanding the Speakers extremity of weeping and suplicatory oration quaintly elo- quent', Eliot rose and began a lengthy attack on Court personnel and policy. He capped his performance by tendering three resolutions, that anyone who encouraged innovations in religion — papist or Arminian innovations were meant — or who counselled the payment of, or himself paid, any customs or taxes not approved by parliament, 'be reputed a capital enemy to his Kingdom and Commonwealth'. His resolutions were acclaimed by the house, and the shaken Finch then led an exodus from the chamber. Eleven years were to pass before that chamber would know another parliament.[72]

The reaction at Court was swift. On 3 March Eliot, Valentine and Holles were called before the Council, as were six other members whom the government suspected of having connived with them: Selden, William Coryton, Sir Miles Hobart, Sir Peter Hayman, William Strode, and Walter Long. Their initial

---

[70] *Ibid.*, 152. Heath's memory may have failed him as he gave his statement. However, in several other instances he was likewise caught up in deception: see pp. 58, 275 – 6.

[71] Nethersole: *CD 1629*, 250. In his letter Nethersole expresses sympathy for Heath and mentions to Elizabeth that Sir Robert is 'much your Majestys servant'. Unfortunately, no other material exists that bears on Heath's relationship with the electress.

[72] Hulme, *Eliot*, pp. 308 – 15.

statements did not satisfy the Court, and before the month was out all had been imprisoned.[73]

It was up to Heath to make a case against them, and he stood more than ready. Only a few weeks before it had been these men, along with others of their faction, who had nearly brought him to ruin. Almost certainly, he felt vindictive. But he did not blame them for his misfortune alone. To his mind, they were enemies of the Commons and the commonwealth. He was convinced that their faction was but a small one, though vocal, and that it had seduced the majority of members from their natural alliance with the king. As he pondered the coming legal contest, he stood determined to discredit the nine and their cause. On 7 March he wrote to Carlisle:

> The untoward disposition of a fewe ill members of the Commons house of parliament, hath given a just & such an unhappy occasion, for the dissolvinge of this parliament, that my selfe, amongst many thousands of other well affected to the King & State, am truly sorrowful for it. But the deserved punishment of the Authors thereof, may make such an example of better obedience, that the ages yet to come may be warned by ther follye, not to runn into the like error, and whatsoever shall be suggested to the contrarye, his Majestye shall never find me, faint or remiss in this or any other service which may concerne him.[74]

Even before the last of the nine had been arrested, Heath had prepared a list of thirty-five interrogatories for use at anticipated interviews. The questions fell into three categories. First, he wanted to know who, if anyone, had helped Eliot to frame his resolutions. Had some or all of the nine met privately prior to 2 March? If indeed they had, to what end? A second series of questions dealt with the proximity to the Speaker of Valentine and Holles on 2 March. Were they in fact seated next to the chair? Where did they normally sit? Finally, the proposed

---

[73] Notes on the Privy Council examinations of Hayman, Holles, Eliot, and Hobart are included in Edward Hughes (ed.), 'A Durham Manuscript of the Commons Debates of 1629', *The English Historical Review*, 74 (1959), 674 – 5.
[74] SP 16/138/45.

questioning turned to the scene of tumult. Had Eliot, on seeing the Speaker held, thrown down a piece of paper bearing his three resolutions? Had Holles repeated the resolutions after Eliot had first stated them? Had Coryton meanwhile assaulted one or more fellow-members? Had Hayman demanded that the Speaker be punished for attempting to rush the house towards adjournment? While some questions were to be asked of all nine prisoners, perhaps half were intended for just one or a few.[75] But regardless of its nature or intended employment, every interrogatory had a common purpose: to elicit evidence that the events of 2 March had been the culmination of a conspiracy that involved the nine and perhaps others. In framing his questions, Heath obviously used information given him by pro-Court members who had been in the house that day, for he had quite a clear idea of what had gone on and was concentrating on fine points, particularly the aspects of the nine radicals' behaviour that he considered suspicious and seemingly orchestrated.

By the time he actually interrogated the prisoners, on 17 – 18 March, he had learned that they had met at the Three Cranes, a local tavern, one evening in late February.[76] There was no need now for Heath to ask broad questions. He could sit back, read out his pointed interrogatories, and wait for the prisoners to incriminate themselves or their colleagues. He could not, however, expect all nine to cooperate, and certainly several did not. Eliot and Valentine, and probably Holles as well, refused to answer, arguing that what had taken place in parliament should remain there. Coryton pleaded faulty memory, but at least he did answer, in itself a minor victory for Heath. And Selden was quite forthcoming, recalling, for example, that 'he was at dinner at the three Cranes in London, when Sir John Eliott & divers other parliament men were present, & that was a fewe dayes

---

[75] Egerton 2978, ff. 39 – 41; Egerton 3779. Fraser appends the questions: 'Heath', 213 – 20. He also provides a fine analysis of them: 'The Agitation in the Commons, 2 March 1629', Institute of Historical Research, *Bulletin*, 30 (1957), 86 – 95, passim.

[76] Fraser asserts ('Agitation', 94 – 5) that it was Coryton and Selden who, in their answers to the interrogatories, let slip information that the meeting had been at the Three Cranes. While it is true that extant copies of the interrogatories (SP 16/138/87, SP 16/139/6) do not include questions specifically naming the tavern, it is probable that prior to 17 March Heath was aware that the meeting-place had probably been the Three Cranes, and that he altered the questions accordingly. Otherwise, Coryton's answer in particular is almost ludicrous.

before the 2d of March last', and although he added, 'ther was not a word spoken of any parliament busines, or matters concerning parliament, to his knowledg or in his hearinge', his admission helped to confirm reports that Heath had heard earlier.[77] Selden may have hoped that, since he had not actively participated in the disturbance of 2 March, he would be released if he cooperated. However, the government had many scores to settle with him, and his detention continued. Soon he returned to his hard line, unwilling again to play the part of Court informer.

The evidence in, Heath prepared his case. The surest means of gauging the likelihood of success was to question the judges about their opinions on key legal points that would probably be introduced in court. It was not unusual for the judges to be questioned by the attorney-general prior to an important case, and they seldom complained about the practice.[78] On the other hand, they often refused to respond to specific questions, and their answers were sometimes not what the attorney wanted to hear. Heath faced both these problems as he questioned them on the legal implications of the Eliot case. On 27 April he interviewed the two chief justices and the chief baron, hoping to gain firm guidance on two points: 'Whether a Parliament man offending the King criminally or contemptuously in the Parliament House, and not there punished, may be punished out of Parliament'; 'If two or three, or more, of the Parliament shall conspire to defame the King's government, and to deterr his subjects from obeying or assistinge the King, of what nature is this offence?' Somewhat hesitantly, the three judges responded to Heath's first question as he had hoped, by saying that a member who misbehaved in parliament could be punished outside it. However, they refused to commit themselves on the nature of the offence, saying that it would vary from case to case. What Heath had hoped to hear was that the offence was treasonable conspiracy. Two days later he tried again, this time questioning all the judges. While on 27 April he had asked general questions — although the judges had certainly known which particular case was at issue — he now referred specifically to Eliot and his fellows. Still the judges hedged, refusing to

---

[77] SP 16/138/88, 89; SP 16/139/7, 8.
[78] Bulstrode Whitelocke, however, claims that his father 'did often and highly complain against this way of sending to the Judges for their Opinions beforehand': *Memorials of the English Affairs*, I, 13.

commit themselves when they did not have all of the particulars. At last, apparently in frustration, Heath simply read out Eliot's speech of 2 March and his resolutions and he asked 'if the substance of this be proved whether he were to be censured or not?' No longer able to justify reticence by claiming that they were unaware of the details, the judges changed their tack, replying that: 'They desire to be spared to give any answer to a perticular case which might peradventure come before them judicially; but they all disliked manie parts of the speech, and did conceave it to be not accordinge to a parliamentarie proceedinge.'[79]

Despite the judges' fears that they might have to rule on the case that they were being called to advise on, the government, possibly concerned that they might prove reluctant to convict the alleged conspirators, had decided to proceed in Star Chamber. On 7 May Sir Robert presented his information, accusing the nine members of having met outside parliament at some point between 25 February and 2 March, for the purpose of composing a document that contained various assertions that tended to bring the government into disrepute.[80] On 22 May a plea and demurrer was submitted by each of the defendants. In his, Eliot signalled that he would refuse to cooperate in the proceedings, arguing that 'by the lawes of this kingdome' no one was to divulge outside parliament what had gone on inside it and that 'every member of the howse hath and ought to have freedome from all impeachment imprisonment and molestation other then by Pleasure of the House it selfe for or concerninge any speakinge reasoninge doeinge or declaringe of any matter or matters touchinge the parliament'. Holles and Valentine did not echo Eliot's claim that only parliament might judge the behaviour of its own, but did insist that they were bound not to discuss publicly events that had taken place in the Commons. In his information Heath had attempted to nullify questions of parliamentary prerogative by alleging that the members had hatched their conspiracy outside the house. But the defendants claimed that parliamentary freedom from arrest extended to all activities that members engaged in while parliament was sitting, and to counter a possible move by Heath to claim that the

[79] This summary, including all quotations, is drawn from 'The Autobiography of Sir John Bramston, K.B.', ed. Charles, Lord Braybrooke, Camden Society, *Publications*, 32 (1845), 49 – 54.

[80] Hulme, *Eliot*, p. 320.

session had ended, along with such protection, at the moment Finch attempted to rise, Selden insisted that the house had remained in session until the members had actually begun to exit from the chamber on 2 March.[81] Heath found the defendants' case dangerously strong, and on 29 May he petitioned Star Chamber to be allowed to alter his information, but his amended version was met by a new set of pleas and demurrers, which left him with no advantage. On 6 June Coventry advised the king that Heath's case was too weak to succeed in Star Chamber. Three days later Charles interviewed each of the common law judges individually, and seven of the twelve advised him to stop the Star Chamber proceedings. With some reluctance, he agreed. The prisoners had scored a notable victory.[82] Within a few weeks, they enjoyed still another success, as Hayman and Coryton were released.[83] Heath's case against them appears to have been particularly weak, and they were not accused of having played a major role in the conspiracy. The possibility also exists that they had been particularly cooperative.

Bolstered by their recent success, it was the imprisoned members who made the next move. On 6 May six of them applied to King's Bench for writs of habeas corpus. Eliot alone held back, perhaps out of a sense that his comrades would have a better chance of succeeding without him. The returns were soon sent down, citing the king's warrant 'this commitment was for notable contempts . . . against us and our government, and for stirring up sedition'. Heath, who had undoubtedly advised on the wording and had probably framed the warrant, had wisely encouraged ambiguity, for the return said nothing of parliament and therefore weakened the prisoners' claim to privilege. Nevertheless, Bramston, the chief counsel, made a strong argument that bail be allowed the six. In reply, Heath asked only that the court delay its decision on bail. His request was granted, and he went off to see Charles. Soon the judges received an order from the king, that they must not allow bail before conferring with their judicial brethren. Heath had again

---

[81] Eliot's plea and demurrer is SP 16/143/4; others are SP 16/143/6, 9, 11 – 14. Meanwhile, the prisoners were being interrogated. According to the notes of one of Heath's subordinates (SP 16/142/74), all nine appeared before Sir Robert between 1 and 22 May.

[82] Hulme, *Eliot*, pp. 321 – 2.

[83] *Ibid.*, p. 317.

advised his royal master well, for he knew that the other common law judges would be unwilling to discuss the issue of bail in a case that they had not themselves heard. The king's order therefore served the purpose of delaying bail, and soon the term was over, allowing the government time to plan its next move.[84]

On 9 September Heath, in conference with Coventry, Carleton, and Sir Henry Montagu, now earl of Manchester and lord privy seal, agreed that bail should be allowed to the seven prisoners — Eliot had recently joined the others in their request — but only on condition that they offered security for good behaviour. The courtiers knew their antagonists and therefore knew that they would probably not accept the condition, because it would demean them, and parliament as well; normally, only common criminals were required to give security. Charles supported the decision of his advisors, and on 30 September the King's Bench judges accepted the condition for bail. Thereafter, the scene was played out as Heath had imagined it would be. On 3 October the prisoners appeared in court and heard the terms. Selden contended that bail was a right and that he and his fellows could not offer security 'without great offence to the parliament', but Hyde rejected the first point and to the second replied: 'The Return doth not make mention of any thing done in parliament', thereby attesting to the cleverness that Heath had shown in framing that document. Stymied, the prisoners refused to accept bail on the conditions offered, and they were remanded.[85]

As they left the court, Hyde warned them that, having once refused bail, they might not have a second opportunity, and that they might spend the next seven years in prison. During the early months of the contest he had been reserved and seemingly disinterested, but with the proceedings of 3 October, his bearing changed. Possibly he feared that the crown case against the seven members was too weak to hold up in court, and he wished to save the government the embarrassment of an acquittal. Whatever inspired him, his position had become well defined by 13 October, when Heath informed Carleton: 'My Lord cheif justice thinketh the best way were to despose of them

[84] *Ibid.*, p. 323.
[85] *Ibid.*; *ST*, III, cols. 289 – 90. Long did accept the conditions and post bail, but when he realised that the others had refused to do so, he returned to prison: Joseph Mead to Stuteville, 17 Oct. 1629, Birch, II, 30 – 3.

eather wher they nowe are, or to other prisons, at the kings pleasure, & ther leave them as men neglected until ther owne stomacks come down, not to prefer any Information at all, they being nowe safe & soe shall continue.' But Sir Robert was confident that his case would succeed, so he added, 'I dare not subscribe totally to his opinion, to forbeare the information.'[86]

It was Heath's opinion that prevailed. But he did concede that his case was not strong enough to convict all seven imprisoned members, and therefore he resolved to proceed only against the three who were most clearly involved in the tumultuous passages of 2 March: Eliot, Valentine, and Holles. His course set, he decided to move them from the Tower to Marshalsea, the usual prison for those awaiting King's Bench appearances. Charles was reluctant to order the transfer, being unaware of the reasoning behind it, but after Sir Robert explained his decision, he quickly approved. Beyond approving, he assured his attorney, as Carleton related on 15 October: 'We very well approve your reasons for the remove of the three prisoners (against whome the imformation is ready) from the tower to the kings bench, as likewise the course you propose for the remove, which his Majestie would have you follow, and likes very well of your care in the whole businesse.'[87]

The informations that Heath exhibited in King's Bench on 4 November differed little from the ones that he had prepared for the earlier Star Chamber proceeding. But while he had failed in Star Chamber he could afford to feel confident now, for he was moving only against the three men who were most obviously and deeply implicated in the tumultuous passage of 2 March. As events transpired, however, his case became almost irrelevant. The three defendants refused to plead on 4 November, claiming that the court had no jurisdiction over events that had taken place in parliament. They again refused to plead when the parties reassembled on 25 January. Finally, on 2 February 1630, all three were adjudged guilty as charged, the basis being a *nihil dicit*, and they were consigned to the Tower.[88]

Although Heath had decided not to proceed against Selden, Long, Strode, and Hobart for their involvement in the alleged

---

[86] SP 16/150/53.

[87] SP 16/150/67. Also relevant to the transfer issue are SP 16/150/53; Carleton (Dorchester) to Heath, 13 Oct. 1629, SP 16/150/55; and Heath to Carleton, 15 Oct. 1629, SP 16/150/66.

[88] *ST* III, cols. 293 – 310; Hulme, *Eliot*, pp. 328 – 36.

conspiracy, he was not about to see them released. January 1630, the same month in which he faced Eliot, Valentine, and Holles in King's Bench, also saw him act against three of their comrades. He prosecuted Long in Star Chamber, the charge being that, by standing for election, he had violated his oath as high sheriff of Wiltshire, for an old rule barred sheriffs from sitting in the Commons. The ban had originally been designed to exclude a class of king's officers that the house deemed particularly obnoxious, but now Heath used it to the court's advantage, and Long was fined and imprisoned.[89] Next, Sir Robert brought Hobart and Strode into King's Bench and charged that during the previous year they had left their confinement and returned home, hoping thereby to escape the plague, which was then in London. Although they had obtained the gaoler's permission before departing and had soon returned to gaol voluntarily, they were punished by the court.[90]

By mid-February, therefore, Heath had managed to convict six of the seven prisoners, even though three of them had been brought to trial on seemingly petty charges. Now only Selden remained. In May he, along with Cotton, Oliver St John, and the earls of Clare, Bedford, and Somerset — all of whom had fallen foul of the Court, generally for their political proclivities — were brought into Star Chamber, where Heath accused them of having circulated 'A Proposition for His Majesty's Service to Bridle the Impertinence of Parliaments', a memorial that advised the king on methods for breaking the power of parliament so that he might, if he chose, establish an autocratic government. Heath feared that critics of the Court might claim that the 'Proposition' represented the sort of advice that Charles was receiving and heeding. But all that he was able to demonstrate was that Cotton had kept a copy of the memorial in his library and that several of the defendants, not including Selden, had read it. For their part, the defendants were able to show that the memorial had lain dormant for many years, having been written by Sir Robert Dudley, the disgraced and exiled son of the earl of Leicester, who had hoped through it to win James's patronage, but had instead earned his contempt. Heath had no proof that the defendants planned to publish the memorial or otherwise disseminate it. His case was, in fact,

---

[89] ST, III, cols. 233 – 6; Harold Hulme, 'The Sheriff in the House of Commons', Journal of Modern History, 1 (1929), 370 – 3.
[90] ST, III, cols. 291 – 2.

weak, and it may have been on his advice that the king, to celebrate the birth of the future Charles II, ordered a halt to the proceedings.[91]

Despite his failure to convict Selden, Heath could look back with satisfaction on his prosecution work in 1629 – 30, for he had helped to bring low several men whom the king numbered among his chief enemies. Around him, England was tranquil, and he could hope that, with leading radicals in prison, their followers in the provinces would be too cowed or too disorganised to foment unrest. Indeed, the anti-Court faction was little heard from during the first half of the 1630s. Possibly the successful prosecution of Eliot and his fellows helped to account for this uncharacteristic silence. Certainly it provided the impetus for Heath himself to rise. From the slough of February 1629, when Charles's anger was sufficient almost to bring his ruin, he soon regained a position of honour at Court. By October his stature was such that the king granted him a vast tract of land in America, by far the largest proprietary created during the Caroline period.[92] Charles was determined that the leading parliamentary radicals, particularly Eliot, be punished. That Heath was the chief instrument of their downfall brought him to a position of favour and influence that he had never known before, nor would know again.

Close-run things

Despite Heath's overall record of success in casting down the king's enemies, some historians might disparage, and in some cases have disparaged, his efforts, using any of three criteria. Firstly, they might claim that he acted in the service of an evil system and that he therefore deserves no credit, but rather

---

[91] *Ibid.*, cols. 387 – 400. The case aroused considerable attention at the time, a fact reflected in the abundance of copies of the petition for a subpoena that Heath sent Charles in late 1629, prior to moving against the alleged conspirators. In 1642 Heath's petition was printed as a Royalist pamphlet, his only piece of writing published while he lived: *A Machavillian Plot, or, A Caution for England, Presented in a Time when Princes were so Pious, and Judges Durst be Valiant against Unhonest Slaverie.*

[92] See p. 191.

condemnation, for his victories. Secondly, some might suggest that while during the various trials Heath served as Court spokesman, he was really a small cog in a great wheel, following the directions of others. Finally, it could be argued that Sir Robert's efforts in building his cases contributed less to his success than did the pro-crown bias of the courts. The first reservation is so grounded in value judgements as to preclude a simple response. It is probably best to say simply that Heath believed that in moving against the radicals he was helping to promote unity and tranquility in England and that the only men who were likely to be hurt by his actions were the ones who were attempting to forment unrest.[93] The other two reservations may be dealt with more positively. The major prosecutions were in most respects directly under his control, and his success in court derived not from the judges' bias, but from the strength of his presentation.

The prosecution of Bristol, of the five knights, of Eliot and his fellows were all directed by Heath. As attorney-general, he was of course the king's chief prosecutor, and in practice as well as in theory he handled Charles's litigation. When the king gave commands in a case of major proportions, he usually did so on his attorney's advice, and when Heath changed his mind on strategy, Charles tended to follow suit. On 24 June Sir Robert advised the king to allow Selden and Valentine to attend the King's Bench judges the next day, as they pursued the matter of bail, and Charles complied with the appropriate order. Within hours, however, Heath notified Carleton that:

> Since I waited uppon his majesty, I have been with my Lord cheif Justice; & uppon conference I find, it is not safe, to adventure the bringing of any of thes prisoners to the kings bench to morrowe, least they should be delivered: Therfore I beseech you acquaint his Majesty therwith presently, & intreat him to countermaund that part of his letter to mr Lieutenant of the Towre.

Soon after, Charles wrote to the judges that, whereas earlier he had intended to allow the two prisoners to appear in court:

---

[93] See pp. 220 – 2.

'Now upon more mature deliberation wee have thought good to treat them all alike.'[94]

The great cases of the late 1620s not only found Heath mapping out strategy, but also handling details. He could have looked to any one of various officials for help, notably the solicitor-general, but in practice he appears to have done almost all the case-work himself. On that crucial day in November 1627 when he appeared in King's Bench to discuss the precedents and statutes that had been cited earlier by the knights' counsel, he told the judges that there was one precedent that he would not deal with, because the document containing it 'came not to me before Saturday last, about candle-lighting; and yesterday was no time fitting to search out precedents, and how could I then search for this?'[95] It was he, not some assistant, who generally searched out precedents, be they to cite or to refute; and it was he who delivered the case for the king. What that presentation might entail, in terms of physical strain, may be seen in a letter that he wrote to Carleton on 4 June 1629, the day after he had appeared in Star Chamber to give his ill-fated information against Eliot and the eight other imprisoned members: 'All the fornoon, was spent by my self, for the kinge, which was uppon the point of three houres in continuall speech, til I was almost tired, which I hope I shall never be in the kings service.'[96]

As attorney-general, Heath enjoyed great advantages over defence counsel in cases that he prosecuted. He had the right to confer with judges prior to trial, and in these meetings he might test out his planned strategy. Furthermore, by eliciting the king's order he could force the judges to do or not to do certain things. It was, for example, Charles's command that prevented King's Bench from granting bail to Selden and his comrades in May 1629. Finally, he could depend on a sympathetic hearing from the bench, for the judges tended to be staunch king's men.[97] But despite all of these advantages, he could by no means take victory for granted. When the knights' counsel first made their case in King's Bench, the judges were impressed by their arguments for bail. Two years later, Hyde felt compelled to warn the Court, firstly, that Selden and his fellow-prisoners

---

[94] *ST*, III, cols. 286 – 7; SP 16/145/40.
[95] *ST*, III, col. 47.
[96] SP 16/144/37.
[97] See pp. 227 – 48.

might be bailed, and secondly, that if the radicals were tried, King's Bench might be forced to acquit them. There was no assurance that Heath would win his cases even in Star Chamber, that bastion of the Stuart Court, for he was unable to convict Eliot and his comrades there.[98] What the courts seem to have demanded of Heath, as of any attorney-general, was that his cases be as strong as those presented by defence counsel. He did not have to present a superior case in order to win, but neither could he be bested and expect the judges to support him. In the Five Knights' Case, for instance, he was victorious not because he presented a devastating argument in favour of the king's right to detain at will, but because he showed to the judges' satisfaction that the precedents produced by the knights' counsel were weak or inappropriate. Had the case made by the petitioners for bail been stronger, they might have carried the day. Hyde's famous comment may well have had this emphasis: 'upon *these* grounds, and *these* Records, and the Precedents and Resolutions, we cannot deliver you'. Later, Doddridge told the Lords that he had expected the prisoners to sue out fresh writs and reopen the case, and he added: 'I wish they had, because it may be they had seen more, and we had been eased of a great labor.'[99] Neither these words, nor Hyde's, suggest that their speakers were men who were determined not to grant bail. They felt, however, that Heath had made at least as strong a case as the knights' counsel, so he gained the decision.

During the early 1620s Heath's relationship with parliament was based on his place as a member of the Commons. The latter half of the decade saw him influence parliamentary history primarily as a prosecutor of the king's enemies. In both roles, he performed with exceptional ability. In both, he served his king well.

---

[98] In fact, attorneys-general sometimes lost in Star Chamber, even in cases of moment; see p. 93.
[99] Relf, p. 9.

6

Mind of a King's Man

In a period dominated by localism, Heath had a national perspective. True, his associations with Kent were deep, as he was born in that county and in middle age established his chief residence there. He seems to have felt a particular kinship with Kentishmen and it is probably more than coincidental that most of his major business associates had roots in the county.[1] Nevertheless, Heath was truly an Englishman. At an early age he left his home county to study at Cambridge, and then he went on to London, where he spent the bulk of his days as an adult. Nor did he necessarily head toward Kent when business or pleasure took him from London. For more than thirty years he had his principal residence outside the county, first at Worth, Sussex, then at Mitcham, Surrey, and he occasionally visited his other properties, which by the 1630s were spread throughout England. The nature of his career also prevented him from fixing his attention on Kent. At the Inner Temple and later at Court, he was brought into contact with people from every corner of the realm. During the 1620s his duties as a law officer forced him to take charge of problems that were national in scope. His horizons may, in his early adulthood, have been local or regional. By middle age, however, they had expanded to encompass all England.

That his vision was nation-wide does not mean that it was clear. Sir Robert was not a systematic thinker, and he never attempted to regularise his thought. He seldom commented on politics in his personal correspondence, so the historian must be content to study his ideas primarily through the medium of his

---

[1] On Heath's domiciles and his partners, see pp. 251 – 6. The Kentish gentry was quite cohesive and had a strong regional pride: Clarke, pp. 219 – 20; Alan Everitt, *The Community of Kent and the Great Rebellion 1640 – 60* (Leicester, 1966), pp. 33 – 45.

public stands, and these were usually inspired by a particular situation. Different circumstances sometimes prompted different arguments. Unlike the 'virtuosi' of his day, he did not read widely, but rather concentrated on works that dealt with religion or law. Neither did he commonly associate with scholars, who might have broadened his outlook.[2]

All reservations aside, however, it may be said that the body of Heath's political ideas, at least, merit the term 'philosophy'. Broadly speaking, he believed that his nation was in danger, from elements internal and external, and he was convinced that the best way to overcome the danger was through unity. For this he looked to the Church, to the law, and, most of all, to the king. It was in his emphasis on, and search for, unity that his scattered ideas acquired a system.

National strength and the national enemy

Early in 1624 England was shocked to learn that the preceding year the Dutch in Amboina had executed ten English East India Company merchants. The people cried for vengeance, and Heath quickly joined them, submitting a petition in which he urged James to demand restitution. But he also looked beneath the current issue, to the basic question of national security:

This being an Island howsoever inhabited by a warlick people, of able bodye, & full of courage, yet our strength &

---

[2] The standard study of the 'virtuoso' movement in England is W. E. Houghton, Jr., 'The English Virtuoso in the Seventeenth Century', *Journal of the History of Ideas*, 3 (1942), 51–73, 190–219. Some lawyers who were educated during the Elizabethan period may have qualified as virtuosi — Bacon, obviously, and also Ellesmere: L. A. Knafla, *Law and Politics in Jacobean England: The Tracts of Lord Chancellor Ellesmere* (Cambridge, 1977), pp. 40–3. But the lawyers of Heath's generation seem to have had little interest in the Classics, or generally in scholarship. Probably, he himself had not; a rather extensive inventory of his library at Brasted (1647) reveals mainly religious books, with a few works on medicine and other subjects: Egerton 2983, f. 79, transcribed in Fraser, 'Heath', 199–201. His law books were presumably elsewhere. In 1643 a library owned by 'Mr Heath of the Temple' was seized and sold by the Committee for Sequestrations, and a list of the books is extant (SP 20/B.7, pp. 60–63), but these books were probably Edward's. The only true scholar among Heath's known acquaintances at Court was Sir William Boswell, and their relationship was business-oriented; note P. E. Kopperman, 'Profile of Failure: The Carolana Project, 1629–1640', *The North Carolina Historical Review*, 59 (1982), 9–13.

safety under gods blessinge lye in our walls, which is our shipping, & thereby to maynteyn the kings undowted right of Lord of the narrowe seas . . . to lett our neighbor kingdomes knowe, not by words, but by acts: that we are resolved to mayteyn the auncient honor of our nation; & although we will not take an occasion, before it be offered, yet . . . we shall make our peace assured, when we are prepared for warre.[3]

When Sir Robert found England's strength to 'lye in our walls, which is our shipping', he echoed a national consensus, for most of his countrymen likewise believed that security was to be found in a strong navy. The navy was looked to, primarily, for protection against invaders. But Heath, again like many of his contemporaries, had a bellicose streak. On 19 March 1624 he complained to the Commons 'it is better to have a war than a deceitful and dangerous peace'.[4] The peace that he denounced that day tied England to Spain in a relationship that most Englishmen considered unnatural. In his great speech of 5 August 1625 he may well have made some statements entirely for effect, but not his claim that war would soon come against 'the same enimy we all desier — Spain'.[5] In the wake of Amboina, Holland might, for the moment, be considered an adversary, but the national enemy was Spain.

Sir Robert was presumably pleased by the attack on Cadiz in the autumn of 1625, though not by the result. When he thought of war against Spain, however, he did not think primarily of an invasion of the enemy's home ground. What he wanted to see was an attack on Spanish power in the New World. Primarily, he hoped that Spain's expansion might be halted and England's own empire magnified. Then the enemies of Spain might drive it from the New World. To destroy the Spanish empire, he was convinced, was to destroy the source of both Spain's wealth and power. The Caribbean was the linchpin of the Spanish empire and the main channel of the mother country's wealth, he informed Charles — who had heard the same argument many times before — in 1637: 'The West Indyes, have been for many

---

[3] SP 14/120/121. Somewhat miscalendared.
[4] YCPH, Nicholas diary (transcript), p. 149.
[5] See pp. 145 – 7.

yeers, the support of the house of Austria, & thence hath the Fewell been taken, that hath sett this part of Europe on Fire.'[6] Of course, in depriving Spain of its 'Fewell', the English also stood to enrich themselves and to add to the power of their own nation. Sir Robert held a belief, common in his day, that war with Spain would be profitable, particularly if England concentrated on despoiling Spain in the New World rather than in the Old.

Given his convictions, it is not surprising that Heath was intensely interested in colonial affairs. His interest was translated into participation in overseas projects. In 1620 he became a charter member of the Council for New England, though he appears soon to have been shunted aside by more distinguished personages.[7] That same year saw him elected a councillor of the Virginia Company, which he seems to have joined only a short time before. Perhaps more important, it saw him secure, for several partners and himself, a tract of land in Virginia. Possibly because James was hostile to the company, Heath progressively withdrew from its affairs, and apparently did nothing to settle his tract. In August 1623, his turnabout was completed when he helped Coventry prepare the report that ultimately led to the dissolution of the company. But his involvement with Virginia actually increased thereafter, and he became a prime advocate for the colony. His awareness of Virginian affairs was enhanced by his inclusion on several committees and commissions that helped to oversee the colony, 1624 – 31, and by his friendship with several important officials of the colony, notably John Harvey, governor 1630 – 5. That he was a friend of Virginia was well known to interested parties. John Smith, probably seeking to profit from that friendship, presented him with a copy of his *General History of Virginia* and dedicated a second, lesser, work to him.

Until 1629 Virginia was the southernmost English colony in North America, and as such was a bastion against Spanish expansion northward. In October 1629, however, a new colony, Carolana, was created. Extending from the thirty-first to the thirty-sixth degree north latitude, Carolana was from the first

---

[6] PRO, Colonial Office, CO 1/3/186. Considerably miscalendared.
[7] The information in this paragraph and the next is drawn from Kopperman, 'Heath', 246 – 53, and from Kopperman, 'Profile', 1 – 12.

designed as a march, at once a barrier to Spanish attempts to colonise north of the Floridian peninsula and a base from which raids and eventually, perhaps, an all-out offensive might be launched against Spanish holdings in the Caribbean. And the 'lord predominant' of this vast march was Sir Robert Heath. His success in winning the patent may to some extent be ascribed to the fact that his good services as a law officer that year, notably in the Eliot case, had won him favour. Perhaps, too, his strong background in colonial affairs was taken into account by Charles as he considered the grant. Furthermore when Heath petitioned for the patent, few courtiers competed with him, and finally, in his quest he had the backing of Carlisle, who as proprietor of the Caribbee Islands was a major colonial figure, and of several leading crown officials, notably Carleton. Whatever the basis for his success, the patent placed him in a position to enrich himself and to initiate a colonial dynasty. It also presented him with an opportunity to play a major role in the war against the Spanish empire. But he proved to be an inept proprietor, unwilling or unable to provide leadership in the business of colonisation. Worse still, he turned the job of settlement over to men who were even more inept than he. As of 1632, not a single colony had been planted in Carolana, and Heath, apparently disenchanted with the current projectors, assigned his patent to Henry, Lord Maltravers. Maltravers, however, was no more successful than his predecessors had been, despite an active colonisation campaign in 1639 – 40. In 1663 the Privy Council voided the patent, claiming that Carolana remained as yet unplanted.

Despite his failure in the primary test, Heath's interest in colonial affairs remained high during the 1630s. And he held strongly to his belief that through an aggressive programme of colonisation, particularly in the Caribbean region, England could do much to destroy the power of Spain. In 1637, several courtiers, including Maltravers, laid plans for an English West India Company, which was to cooperate with the Dutch West India Company in attacks on Spanish fleets and colonies in the Caribbean. Perhaps a minor partner in the projected company, and in any case an enthusiastic supporter of it, Heath informed the king by petition that while Spain had previously dominated the West Indies:

The hollanders of late have attempted some of thos parts: & by ther interceptions & invasions, have annoyed the kinge of

Spayne, & inriched themselves. That eather or both shold be absolute lords of the place & the trade therof, is neather profitable nor safe to your Majesty . . . Eather your Majesty must interpose your selfe, openly & avowedly, as your owne, at your pleasure; or disavowe it, as it may be best for your honor & service. The first of thes, seemeth to be less safe Both because, the times are not soe seasonable for great undertakings And a stander by, cann not well judge, howe your majestys affaires stand in conjuncture with *Spaine*; yet to doe nothing at all, in Sume, may render the worke more difficult after. The second way, may happily by attained unto If Some of experience, & quality, & well fitted for such an enterprise, *quasi aliud agentes* will eather interprise somewhat of themselves Or else, shall offer themselves to joyne with the hollanders, to joyn ther Forces & take ther fortunes with them: If it take not success, it is done of ther owne hedds, it is but the attempt of private gentelmen, the state suffers noe loss, noe disreputation; If it take success, they are your subjects, they doe it for your service, they will lay all at your Majestys feet & interess your Majesty therin: soe may you share with the hollanders your neighbores in the said Treasor & trade.[8]

Charles turned down Sir Robert's invitation to sanction an undeclared sea war, and the project collapsed. Nevertheless, Heath's petition reveals that even during the late 1630s he dreamed that England would attack Spain at the source of its wealth.

The prospect of personal profits inspired Heath's interest in colonial schemes. So did the prospects for national enrichment. But also shaping his attitude was the conviction that Spain represented a danger to England, a danger that was magnified by the Spaniards' wealth and could be quelled if the source of that wealth were removed from the Spanish orbit. Fear of Spain was an obsession in Heath's day, but still greater was the fear that England might be overthrown by traitors or by a combined

---

[8] CO 1/3/186. Proposals to found an English West India Company are CO 1/9/61–63. These proposals, along with Heath's letter, are discussed in P. E. Kopperman, 'Ambivalent Allies: Anglo-Dutch Relations and the Struggle against the Spanish Empire in the Caribbean, 1621–1641', *The Journal of Caribbean History*, 21 (1987), 59–62, 70.

assault from without and within. This concern was shared by Sir Robert.

Religion and rule

In the world as Heath perceived it, the supernatural coexisted with the temporal. All around him were Satan's servants, out to steal the souls of the unwary. Witches he saw as being a particular threat, so much the greater because some of his countrymen were coming to doubt their existence. He wrote in a meditation that dates from the Civil War period:

> I shall begin with that opinion which hath possessed verie many in thes times, and thos who pretend to religion (, I say that pretend only,) That ther are no witches at all; to such I must say as Paul did to king Agrippa, beleivest thou the Scriptures: if they doe so, who broach the opinion, I wonder why this part of the Scriptures amongst others should not deserve beleif, which saith in terminis, thou shalt not suffer a witch to live.[9]

But the danger posed by the devil and his minions could be parried by fervent devotion to God. Heath himself was intensely devout, a fact amply manifested in his surviving prayers and meditations. Ever present in his mind was the awful power of God to cast down or to save. At times, his concern for salvation was such that his meditations took on an almost predestinarian flavour: 'If we be not of the number of those which by gods grace & mercy and Godly, & soe esteemed in gods sight; we are sure to be in the number of those which are ungodly.' More often, however, he expressed confidence that God's willingness to pardon was infinite: 'The kingdome of heaven is large enough for all; & the joyes of heaven, who stand by the same grace, wherwith we are called & preserved, doe rejoyce for the conversion of a sinner.' To win God's mercy, he performed obeisance in prayer:

---

[9] Egerton 2982, f. 81. This statement helps to introduce one of Heath's most interesting meditations, 'Rebellion is as the sin of witchcraft' (ff. 81 – 4), inspired by I Samuel 15:23. In it, he compares the characteristics of witches with those of rebels (the date of composition accounts for his preoccupation) and finds the two groups to share many qualities, e.g., bloodthirstiness.

I come not Lord, resting uppon my owne righteousnes, nor puffed up with the opinion of mine owne merites: but I come as a poore Criminal to the God of mercye, as a miserable Sinner . . ., as one soiled with vices . . . as a poor begger, . . . as one having hunger & thirst of righteousnes, to him who is the bread of life, and the founteyn of living water . . . Thou Lord, . . . accept nowe of my humiliation: I am not worthy to lift up mine eyes to heaven, but be thou propitious to me which am a sinner; admitt of my pardon, seale my redemption, wash me clean from all my staines, systeyne me in my miserie, lighten my darknes, and cover my nakednes: send me not away emptie, least I faint by the waye.

Late in his life, Sir Robert felt the blissful assurance that God would guide him to heaven, for He had always guided him on earth. 'I know nothing hath happened nor cann happen unto me, but by Gods providence; and my trust in his mercye is, that as by his Grace he hath supported me heatherto, soe he will doe, til the day of my dissolution shall come; which is my hartie & daily prayer.'[10]

Heath showed his religious sense not through prayer only. He firmly believed in tithing and at one point claimed that if one wished to 'testifie his Religion' in the most elevated form possible, he should 'give the tenth to god, of all he should by gods blessing, possess'.[11] The nature of Heath's own contributions is for the most part unknown. All that can be documented is that from the late 1630s until at least 1641 he provided ten pounds per annum so that the parishioners of Otford, where he was lessee of the parsonage, could maintain an assistant curate.[12] But certainly it was not Otford alone that benefited from his generosity.

To Heath, as to thousands of his countrymen, religion had a dual role to play. There was, first of all, religion as an intensely personal experience, a channel between the individual and God. But he also saw religion as having a role that was national

---

[10] 'Anniversarium', 22; Egerton 2982, ff. 69, 85, 112.
[11] Egerton 2982, f. 78.
[12] L. B. Larking (ed.), 'Proceedings, Principally in the County of Kent, in connection with the Parliaments Called in 1640', Camden Society, *Publications*, 80 (1862), 126, 129.

in scope, as a vehicle of order and unity. And, of course, the instrument through which religion played its social function was the Church. The episcopacy played a central part in both Heath's religious and political thinking, because it could do much to unify the commonwealth. When Sir Robert saw a prelate acting in such a way as to promote contention, he did what he could to turn him toward a more irenic course. Bishop Richard Mountague, whose anti-Puritan writings had provoked attack in the parliaments of 1624, 1625, 1626 and 1628, had a taste for polemics that Heath found particularly offensive. During the early autumn of 1628 the Arminian faction, with the support of the king himself, sought to free Mountague from a charge of contempt against the Commons, and Heath found himself being ordered to prepare, and in fact to expedite, the necessary pardon. As attorney-general, he was bound to carry out the king's command, but he was able to find a technical excuse to delay completing his assignment. On 7 October 'out of private motion & affection only', he wrote to the bishop:

You are nowe a father of our church, & as a father you will I knowe tender the peace & quiet of the church, alas a little spott is seen uppon that white garment & a little fire nay a spark may inflame a great mass (& howe glad would the common adversarye be, to see us at odds amongst our selves,) we are not bound to flatter any (in their errors) but we are bound in conscience to prevent & avoyd all occasions of strife & contention, in thes things specially which are so tender as the peace of the church & the unitye of Religion . . . That if your Lordship will be pleased to review your book, to consult (first) with Almighty god the god of peace, the bond of peace, the spirit of peace (next with our most gratious & good king, & by his approbation) take away the acrimony of the stile; & explane thes things which (therein) are left doubtfull & undefined, that the orthodoxall tenets of the church of England might be justified . . . I am persuaded all scandall would be taken away, & your Lordship may be a happy instrument of reconciling (& giving a stopp to) thes unhappy differences (& indolencye) which else may trouble the quiet of our church, & may occasion the disquiet of the common wealth . . . & then the pardon would seasonably followe.

Heath could not forever postpone carrying out his assignment, and soon, apparently without having received any concessions from the bishop, he completed the pardon.[13] But he had made his stand.

Despite his rather pointed request that Mountague redefine his views in such a way 'that the orthodoxall tenets of the church of England might be justified', Heath was no doctrinaire. Within rather broad bounds, he was willing to accept as orthodox whatever the king and the episcopacy defined as being so, at least as regarded public worship. What bothered him about Mountague's opinions was that they tended to divide the nation, whereas the prelacy was supposed to unify. Like most articulate Englishmen, he believed that by using its authority wisely the Church might benefit not only itself but the State and that in fact the two great institutions were joined in a symbiotic relationship. In 1646 he linked them neatly in prayer: 'Restore peace unto this poore and distressed nation, peace in the church, and peace in the state, that soe we may sincerely serve thee who art the God of peace.'[14]

Those who resisted the authority of the Church were anathema to Sir Robert. The Catholic element of the population he looked on as being a fifth column which, if England were invaded by Spain, might assist the aggressor and which in any case sought to undermine social and political cohesion. To keep the Catholics down, he freely advocated the use of coercion. In 1625 – 6, as attorney-general, he pursued with rigour the government plan to crack down on recusants, and he complained persistently, if diplomatically, when Charles ordered that a more tolerant line be followed. In September 1641 Sir

[13] SP 16/118/33. Ironically, in view of Heath's reluctance, the Mountague pardon initiated a series of events that almost brought his ruin: see pp. 171 – 3. Heath was not the only courtier to deal with the pardon reluctantly; when the document was finally drawn, Coventry hesitated before affixing the Great Seal: J. S. Macauley, 'Richard Mountague: Caroline Bishop, 1575 – 1641', unpub. Ph.D. dissertation (Cambridge, 1964), 364. Macauley provides a good account of the Heath-Mountague episode, pp. 359 – 64; he, like most writers, believes that Heath wrote of his own volition; cf. Gardiner, VIII, 19 – 20. Heath's relationship with Mountague was often strained. In the parliament of 1625, he tended to support attacks on the bishop (Russell, *Parliaments and English Politics*, p. 233), though perhaps at the behest of the Court, he did claim privilege for him, as a crown servant (*ibid.*, p. 240). As a member of a parliamentary deputation that carried a petition on religion to Charles, he reported privately to the king on the Commons' action against Mountague, and his comments appear to reflect sympathy with the house; Gardiner, V, 372 – 3.

[14] Egerton 2982, f. 79.

Robert, riding assize as a justice of the King's Bench, ordered the execution of Edmund Barlow after the latter had freely admitted to having served the Catholics of Lancashire as their priest. Heath was by no means bloodthirsty. He openly praised Barlow for the courage and constancy that he demonstrated during his trial, but the law required him to impose the death penalty.[15] Still, he sincerely believed that the Catholics were a danger, and he was anxious to see the powers of Church and State brought to bear against them.

Heath feared the Catholics, but during the reign of Charles he came to fear the radical Protestants still more. They might claim to be hostile only to the episcopacy, but Heath, with his belief that the interests of Church and State were linked, would certainly have nodded at James's simple assertion: 'No bishop, no king'. Those who opposed the episcopal form of church government were also, therefore, to his mind a threat to the crown, to national unity, to England itself. Extreme Protestants, in fact, he saw as being little more than anarchists, a point that he made clearly in a letter he wrote to Carleton in August 1629. Noting that the citizens of Great Yarmouth had disobeyed government orders by refusing to reinstate a town official whom they had removed, he complained:

> If they submit not in thes things for the present, I conceave ther will be little hope of ther conformity for the future; ther is a great party in the town of sectaryes, averse to all government, but ther owne populer way, which must be reformed: . . . the government of the whole stands but

---

[15] On Heath's role in the anti-Catholic campaign of 1625 – 6 and his criticism of the lenient policy that followed, see above, pp. 95 – 9. The Barlow affair is discussed in Richard Challoner, *Memoirs of Missionary Priests* (London, 1742), II, 172 – 83; Challoner includes dialogue that supposedly passed between Heath and Barlow during the trial. Soon after Barlow's execution, Heath fell foul of parliament for granting a writ of habeas corpus to a prisoner who had refused to take the Oath of Allegiance: W. H. Coates, A. J. Young and V. F. Snow (eds.), *The Private Journals of the Long Parliament, 3 January to 5 March 1642* (New Haven, 1982), pp. 256, 263. Most anti-Catholicism in Heath's day was based primarily on political, rather than doctrinal, grounds — the fear that English Catholics aimed to overthrow the Protestant state, with or without outside help: C. Z. Wiener, 'The Beleaguered Isle: A Study of Elizabethan and Early Jacobean Anti-Catholicism', *Past and Present*, 51 (1971), 37 – 40; Robin Clifton, 'The Popular Fear of Catholics during the English Revolution', *Past and Present*, 52 (1971), 54 – 5.

uppon the well ordering of the parts which make up the whole.[16]

Ten months later, facing Leighton in Star Chamber, he presented a still more hostile estimate of the attitude of extreme Protestants toward Church and State:

> I shall be bold to affirme, that whosoever lives under a monarchye and would reject the discipline of the Church under the Bishops would, if they durst, reject the government of a kinge and interteyn a popular government . . . Yet this brainsick man and his complices, whose religion is never to be contented with the present times, hath indevoured . . . to defame and to destroy the whole prelacye . . . The next thing I shall observe to your Lordships is that which moves a doubt in me, whether the Jesuits or the Protestants, frayed out of ther witts, be the greatest enimys to a monarchical government.[17]

So long as the Puritans, as opposed to more radical Protestants, continued to support at least the notion of episcopacy, Heath was willing to tolerate them. However, their tendency to find fault with the bishops, even if not with the form of Church government that they represented, upset him. Although Heath had his problems with individual hierarchs, notably Mountague and Laud, he generally revered their order. In 1646, even as Church and State were tumbling down together, he prayed for the prelates: 'O Eternal god, . . . Bless the reverend and religious Bishops and fathers of the church, . . . that they may sett before ther eyes, the honor and glorie, the advancement of thy true religion, the peace & unitie of the church, and the winning of soules unto thee.'[18]

---

[16] SP 16/148/74.
[17] 'Speech on Leighton', 3 – 4, 7.
[18] Egerton 2982, f. 79. Heath was hostile to Presbyterianism and, hence, to the Scots. In May 1648, during the Second Civil War, he wrote to Nicholas: 'I despaire not of Scotland but . . . I hope well by gods *blessinge*, we shall doe our worke without them': Egerton 2533, f. 450. See also p. 298. Although religious persecution in early Stuart England was not as intense as it was in many Continental countries, the English were avid in demanding religious unity, as a buttress to social and political order; disloyalty to the Church was commonly held to be tantamount to treason: Conrad Russell, 'Arguments for Religious Unity in England, 1530 – 1650', *Journal of Ecclesiastical History*, 18 (1967), 201 – 26, *passim*.

Not for the first time, nor for the last, in that prayer he spoke longingly of 'peace & unitie of the church'. For in the well-being of the Church he saw the well-being of his England.

Crown and law

In the same prayer, having spoken of the bishops, Heath turned to an order that enjoyed no less, and perhaps more, of his reverence:

> Bless the judges and magistrates, to whom under the kings majestie, thou hast committed, or hereafter shall committ the sword of Justice, that they may wisely, justly, and with courage and without partialitie or any by-endes whatsoever, performe ther duties in ther several places, and give a good account to the kings majestie who trusteth them to the people for whom they are trusted, but especially to God Almightie, the great king and Judge of Heaven and earth.

The juxtaposition of judges and bishops in the prayer and the reference to God as the 'Judge of heaven and earth' are not merely coincidental. To Heath, the law itself was a kind of Scripture, and judges played a quasi-sacerdotal role, because it was their duty to interpret God's law for society.

To guide the judges in their exegesis there was, first of all, precedent. Not only Heath, not only common lawyers, but virtually all members of early Stuart society had profound respect for precedents, and more generally, for the voice of tradition. Heath's philosophy is apparent in a speech that he delivered to the Commons on 16 April 1624, in the course of a debate on whether to declare pretermitted wool customs to be a grievance. Sir Robert traced the customs back to their origins in the reign of Edward III, and told his fellow members that he held it 'sacred, to observe the ancient Constitutions'. In this case, his strategy failed. Bankes responded that the house should not 'wade into former times', and the members condemned pretermitted customs as a grievance.[19] In the main, however, the appeal to tradition was strong. A conference of

---

[19] *CJ*, I, 768.

both houses of parliament, 3 May 1628, saw Coke inform the delegates from the Lords 'we have a maxim in the house of commons, and written on the walls of our house, that old ways are the safest and surest ways'.[20] Such an inscription would have appealed to Coke and to Heath, to radicals and to courtiers, to Englishmen of all perspectives. But the nature of the 'old ways' was often unclear. In cases where precedents or traditions were inconsistent, ideology was left with room to manoeuvre. So it was that during the Five Knights' Case both Heath and the knights' counsel were able, with some justification, to call precedent to their defence. Sometimes the precedents cited by parties to a constitutional debate differed only in message, but often there were qualitative differences as well, and perhaps the most basic involved chronology. Few of the precedents that Sir Robert produced in court or in parliamentary debate pre-dated 1300, and most were drawn from the period after 1450. Never did he search back to the days of Ethelbert, as did Coke and his disciples. Heath does not appear to have been particularly interested in history, and this may to some extent explain the discrepancy. But more important was the fact that recent precedents tended to favour the royal prerogative. For Coke to justify his philosophy, it was helpful to have a 'Norman Yoke' theory.[21] Sir Robert needed no such appeal to antiquity, for Tudor and Stuart precedents generally boosted the cause of the crown. And when the king's interest entered a case, however remotely, it was these precedents that he hoped the judges would take to heart.

But Heath did not believe that precedent alone should determine how judges interpreted the law. Equally important was common sense. In his speech on pretermitted customs, he tried to settle the problem of analysing legislation on the subject by arguing: 'The Rule to know the Meaning of a Statute, is to know the true Use of it.' Not surprisingly, he then claimed that

[20] *ST*, III, col. 189.
[21] On Coke's appeals to ancient predecent, see Christopher Hill, *Puritanism and Revolution: Studies in Interpretation of the English Revolution of the 17th Century* (London, 1958), pp. 57 – 66; J. G. A. Pocock, *The Ancient Constitution and the Feudal Law: A Study of English Historical Thought in the Seventeenth Century* (Cambridge, 1957), ch. 2; and David Little, *Religion, Order, and Law: A Study in Pre-Revolutionary England* (New York, 1969), pp. 177 – 82. Lawyers on the Continent also used early history, often historical fictions, in support of their legal philosophies: W. J. Bouwsma, 'Lawyers and Early Modern Culture', *The American Historical Review*, 78 (1973), 325 – 7.

'the true Use' of the legislation favoured continuance of the customs. And when the knights' lawyers used the twenty-ninth chapter of Magna Carta in an effort to show that their clients had been wrongfully committed, Heath responded that officers on every level of the government were regularly committing men 'before an Indictment can be drawn, or a presentment can be made'.[22] Therefore, he implied, common sense militated against accepting the interpretation of the knights' counsel, for to rule in their favour might lead to the disruption of English law enforcement. Later that same day, he used sarcasm to belittle the arguments of those who sought to challenge the king's prerogatives: 'No doubt but the king's power is absolutely over his coins; if then he shall command his coin shall be turned into brass or leather, I confess it were inconvenient; but if the king would do it, the answer that I can make is, that he would not undo the kingdom.'[23] Again he was attempting to call common sense to his aid, by claiming that the king would not abuse his power over coinage by having leather coins stamped and implying that neither would the king exploit his other prerogatives in ways that might 'undo the kingdom'.

A final guide for the judges as they interpreted the law was, as Heath saw it, the king. If judges were close to God, monarchs were still closer, the final repositories, indeed the embodiment, of the Divine Law. So thought Heath, and his opinion was shared by most articulate members of his society, including many radicals.[24] And since the king was the repository of the law, he stood also as the ultimate lawgiver. Even Sir Thomas Richardson, a rather cynical judge, was moved to write:

> I make no Doubt but as God ordained Kings & hath given Laws to Kings themselves, So he hath authorised & given power to Kings to give Laws to their Subjects; & so Kings did first make Laws & ruld by their Laws and altered & changed their Laws from time to time as they Saw occasion for the good of themselves and of their Subjects.[25]

Naturally, encouragement for such views came from the throne. Nor were kings slow to make clear the logical extension of the

---

[22] See p. 163.
[23] *ST*, III, col. 45.
[24] On Heath's views, note Russell, *Parliaments and English Politics*, pp. 366 – 8.
[25] BL, Add. 36,856, f. 22.

belief that they were law personified — that judges could serve the law well only by serving them. In June 1616 James, in the course of an address to the judges, spoke forthrightly of the link: 'Kings are properly Judges, and Judgement properly belongs to them from God: for Kings sit in the Throne of God, and thence all Judgement is derived . . . As Kings borrow their power from God, so Judges from Kings: and as Kings are to accompt to God, so Judges unto God and Kings.'[26] James's perception of hierarchy was one that Heath would have applauded.

Of course, not all of Heath's countrymen would have joined in the applause. Many, indeed, looked to the judges to serve as bulwarks against absolutism. In particular they looked to the common law judges, for they believed the common law to be inherently anti-authoritarian. The royalists, meanwhile, boosted other legal systems. James himself claimed that equity most closely approximated God's law; many of the more fervent supporters of the royal prerogative echoed his line.[27] The civil law, too, served the cause of the crown well, and most civilians were staunch royalists.[28] Conciliar courts, feudal courts, forest courts, ecclesiastical courts, all these helped to buttress the king's position. Finally, both pro-crown and anti-crown elements called the 'fundamental law' to their defence, taking advantage of the vagueness of that concept.[29]

Heath revered the common law, and sometimes he gave indications of being biased against its competitors. On several occasions during the parliament of 1621 he denounced the Court of Wards and the 'courts of equity' in general for their alleged willingness to protect debtors, and he attacked certain court personnel, notably the masters in Chancery, for charging

---

[26] *The Political Works of James I: Reprinted from the Edition of 1616*, ed. C. H. McIlwain (Cambridge, Mass., 1918), pp. 326 – 7.

[27] G. W. Thomas, 'James I, Equity, and Lord Keeper John Williams', *The English Historical Review*, 91 (1976), 514 – 15.

[28] There were some exceptions. On the political theory of the civil lawyers, see B. P. Levack, *The Civil Lawyers in England 1603 – 1641: A Political Study* (Oxford, 1973), ch. 3.

[29] Pocock, pp. 48 – 51; James Daly, *Sir Robert Filmer and English Political Thought* (Toronto, 1979), pp. 40 – 1; S. E. Prall, *The Agitation for Law Reform during the Puritan Revolution* (The Hague, 1966), chs. 1 – 2; J.W . Gough, *Fundamental Law in English Constitutional History*, (Oxford, 1955), chs. 3 – 7.

excessive fees.[30] That the common law courts were losing business to their competitors also upset him. As a partial remedy, he introduced a bill on 4 May 1621 to limit the number of days per year when Chancery could hear cases.[31] But the bill received only a first reading, and the danger, as he saw it, continued unabated. Later, as chief justice of the Common Pleas, he again confronted the issue of competition, and in February 1633 he became party to an agreement whereby the courts at Westminster and the Admiralty agreed to observe prescribed boundaries in issuing prohibitions.[32]

But his complaints always seem to have involved the methods by which legal systems apart from the common law were administered, rather than the systems themselves. Nor did he question the utility of the courts that were not governed by common law. Instead, he saw great purpose to them. In the first place, he noted, they tended to provide, in different degrees and manners, an important source of crown income. One of the most important courts in this regard — indeed, as much a money-raising governmental department as a court — was the Court of Wards, which Heath defended in early 1649 by noting: 'The Fines, & Rents of [the] Court of Wards, & Liveryes, which is an auncient prerogative, & a very prime of the Crowne, [are] as just, & as Legall, as any he hath, & hath bin of late yeares a very considerable part of his Revenue, & may be made much greater, & yet with justice, & honour.'[33] Like most Englishmen, regardless of political philosophy, Heath believed that the courts buttressed the position of the crown by defining the prerogative in its favour and, perhaps more importantly, by bringing low its enemies. Star Chamber in particular served the crown well from Sir Robert's point of view, and in 1630 he urged that it 'be strict in punishing notorious offenders, for example & terror to others, & his majesty slowe to mitigate, the just

---

[30] CD 1621, II, 100 – 1, 154 – 5, and V, 16; Nicholas, Proceedings, I, 209, 303, and II, 12.

[31] CD 1621, IV, 304 – 5.

[32] A copy of the agreement is in Egerton 2978, f. 45. The agreement was preceded by a conference, 26 Jan., that included the two chief justices, Noy, and the judge and lords of the Admiralty. Minutes of the conference are extant (SP 16/228/15, SP 16/231/49 – 51), and they suggest that Richardson made the main statement for the common law courts.

[33] BOD, MS. Don, d. 124, p. 205. Though there is no reason to doubt Heath's sincerity, he had a vested interest in supporting the Wards, since three of his sons were officers of the court: see p. 287.

sentences of that great Court; which is the most awfull Court, & most proper to repress thos insolencyes, which shall oppose soveraigntye'.[34] He realised that the judges of that court sometimes abused their power, but the abolition of Star Chamber in mid-1641 disturbed him, and by way of private memorandum he soon thereafter wrote:

> I did willingly subscribe to that part of the act, For the regulatinge of the privye Counsell: having long been of opinion: that the privie Counsell, and that honourable board the Counsell table, should not have medled with questions of meum & Tuum. and therfore in that point, it did deserve a Regulation. But for that part which concernes the Court of Starchamber, I did wish it had been but a Regulation also, and not a totall taking away therof.[35]

Heath's memorandum reflects, certainly, a sense of loss, but it also contains criticism of the Council and, more muted, of Star Chamber. In point of fact, Heath was never blind in his support of government institutions and personnel. The government itself was far from monolithic and no sense of solidarity prevented one official from attacking another. Some cohesion was provided by the tendency of courtiers to join factions, they being of two main types. One class of factions brought together a favourite and his protégés, and in the case of the latter it often extended so as to include followers of allied patrons. The other joined officials who shared a government department or related departments. Sir Robert was a member of various factions during his time at Court. In addition, he became close to individual courtiers as a result of blood links or shared interests. But he had no special relationship with most courtiers, and those men not of his circle he scrutinised more carefully.

---

[34] SP 16/178/4.

[35] This quotation is drawn from a set of notes that Heath wrote into his copy of Staunford's *Plees del Coron*; the volume is now in the Treasure Room of the Harvard Law Library. Margaret Judson also quotes this section: *Crisis of the Constitution: An Essay in Constitutional and Political Thought in England, 1603 – 45* (New Brunswick, N.J., 1949), p. 50. The quoted portion introduces 'a Collection of thos hedds, which are Criminal and not Capital, & may legally and regulerly be punished, in & by the ordinarie courts of Justice'; in other words, a list of the sort of offences that had previously been handled by Star Chamber.

What he saw often displeased him. On 28 February 1621, in a speech to the Commons, he denounced the masters in Chancery for charging excessive fees. Other members joined him in his attack, but the masters were undaunted, and on 23 April they petitioned in favour of their new fee schedule, claiming by way of defence that the common law judges had approved it. Sir Robert quickly counter-attacked, but it was not until the afternoon that he was able to respond fully. By then, he had conferred with the judges, and he reported that according to them they had, far from approving, unanimously opposed the new fees. The Commons then condemned the schedule, and it was voided by proclamation.[36] Heath's attacks on the masters may have been inspired by factionalism, as the common law element at Court moved against equity. But it was personal as well. Sir Robert seems to have had a deeply felt hatred of rapacious officials. In denouncing the masters, he denounced greed in government. Of course, he himself was not immune from greed, and the possibility that he had a double standard cannot be discounted.

The abuse of power by government officials likewise upset him. When such abuse took place, it was proper, he believed, that the wronged parties should have recourse through the courts. In Easter term 1642 Sir Robert, as a justice of King's Bench, was confronted by a case that was to have profound implications, *Commins v. Massam*. Two problems were presented to him: whether the commissioners of sewers had overstepped their authority by requiring Commins to build a sea-wall on land that his father, now dead, had leased; and, of more general importance, whether the King's Bench in fact had jurisdiction in the case. Heath concluded that the commissioners had not abused their power, but he asserted also: 'Admitting that the Commissioners of Sewers have done anything without or against their Commission, without doubt this is reformable and examinable here.' His opinion did much to further the right of the individual to defend himself against overbearing officials.[37]

---

[36] Nicholas, *Proceedings*, I, 303; CD 1621, III, 416, n. 25; V, 16, 345; VI, 21.

[37] E. G. Henderson, *Foundations of English Administrative Law: Certiorari and Mandamus in the Seventeenth Century* (Cambridge, Mass., 1963), pp. 101 – 6, 182 – 6. Henderson further comments (p. 146), 'the germ of eighteenth-century rules [regarding judicial review of certiorari] seems to lie in Sir Robert Heath's remarkable opinion in *Commins v. Massam*'.

Though Heath was quick to denounce the abuse of power, he sympathised with the difficulties faced by conscientious officials, particularly those involved in law enforcement, the area of government that he knew best. Furthermore, since he saw the nation's legal machinery challenged at every level, he defended it at every level. The parliament of 1621 saw him particularly active in support of local law enforcement officials. On 28 May a bill was introduced that prescribed harsh penalties for any justice of the peace who was guilty of wrongful imprisonment. Heath had himself been an active justice, in several counties, before his duties at Court had tied him to London.[38] He understood the practical problems of law enforcement that the justices faced, and he therefore denounced the bill, because it penalised an official 'for doing his office necessary in discretion and not legallie'.[39] Three months earlier, in the course of the speech in which he attacked the masters in Chancery, he had accused Exchequer officials of charging exorbitant fees when passing sheriffs' accounts 'whereas they ought to have reward'.[40] A critic of some officials, he was nevertheless a supporter of most. His attitude was determined by how well they served the nation.

There was a similar complexity in his position on crown prerogatives. He did not blindly support royal power, and he accepted the limitations that were imposed by tradition. For example, at the Worcestershire assizes of 1641, which he held as a puisne justice of King's Bench, he stated: 'The kings majestie neither can nor will Remitt or Releave any fine or penalty for any offence or misdemenor unless it be to his own person.'[41] But Heath consistently defended those prerogatives that he deemed essential to the nation's wellbeing. Like many crown lawyers, among them Sir Francis Bacon, he believed that the king possessed both absolute and ordinary powers, the former being superior. He spoke of the nature of that absolute power, and its

---

[38] The best indicator of Heath's conscientiousness is that during his first few years as a J.P. for Sussex he invariably appeared at assizes: J. S. Cockburn (ed.), *Calendar of Assize Records: Sussex Indictments, James I* (London, 1975), pp. 50, 56, 61, 70, 75, 80, 84, 89. After 1619, his duties in London and at Court kept him away. As of 1622, Heath was a J.P. for five counties; as of 1637, for thirteen: PRO, Crown Office, Miscellaneous Books, C. 193/13/1, 2.

[39] *CD 1621*, VI, 172.

[40] *Ibid.*, V, 16.

[41] This quotation is drawn from the law notes of Henry Townshend: BOD, MS. Eng. Misc. e.479, f. 121.

207

source, when he addressed the bench in answer to the five knights' counsel:

> The king cannot command your lordship, or any other court of justice, to proceed otherwise than according to the laws of this kingdom . . . But, my lord, there is a great difference between those legal commands, and that *absoluta potestas* that a sovereign hath, by which a king commands; but when I call it *absoluta potestas*, I do not mean that it is such a power as that a king may do what he pleaseth, for he hath rules to govern himself by, as well as your lordships, who are subordinate judges under him. The difference is, the king is the head of the same fountain of justice, which your lordship administers to all his subjects; all justice is derived from him, and what he doth, he doth not as a private person, but as the head of the common wealth, as *justiciarius regni*, yea, the very essence of justice under God upon earth is in him.[42]

Neither in that statement nor elsewhere did Sir Robert ever attempt to define the limits of the king's absolute power. Indeed, he could not have done so, for he believed that definition resided with the king himself. At the conference on the 'Liberty of the Subject', he argued:

> the true answer for these and like cases is, this is not contrary to the laws. God has trusted the King with governing the whole. He hath therefore trusted him with ordering of the parts; and there are many cases, of infinite importance to the subject, and of undoubted trust, wherein notwithstanding it was never questioned by a subject of the King why he did thus or thus.[43]

Nor did Heath believe that the nation had any recourse if the king abused his prerogatives. When, in furthering his case against the knights, he sarcastically wondered whether the king might order the minting of leather coinage, he made it clear that prerogative would allow it. In the same vein, he soon added:

---

[42] *ST*, III, cols. 36 – 7.
[43] *LJ*, III, 757.

Now, my lord, I come to our book-cases, by which it appears what our king may do, and nothing can be said against it, but he will not do it; the king may pardon all traitors and felons, and if he should do it, may not the subjects say, If the king do this, the bad will overcome the good? But shall any say, The king cannot do this? No, we may only say, He will not do this.[44]

'He will not do this.' While Heath left the definition of prerogative to the king himself, he believed that the king would define his powers wisely and apply them with discretion. Such a conviction could have been shaken by events, had one of the Stuarts claimed that his *absoluta potestas* covered powers and policies that seemed to have little to do with the good of the commonwealth.[45] But Heath was probably never confronted by royal claims that he considered to be unreasonable. Furthermore, he knew and respected, in the case of Charles, even revered, the first two Stuart kings, and from his respect grew a trust that they would not abuse their power. Many of his countrymen did not feel the same trust.

Crown v. parliament

Not only the crown but parliament played an important part in Heath's political philosophy. To him, parliament was an

---

[44] *ST*, III, col. 45. This portion of Heath's speech particularly appealed to high-prerogative tastes, and it was later included in a compilation of pro-absolutist statements, edited by an anonymous Tory: *The Unanimous, or Consentient Opinion of the Learned . . . that . . . the King Can Do no Wrong* (London, 1703), p. 8.

[45] Judson asserts (p. 157) that Heath and other high-prerogative lawyers 'might have withdrawn their support from the king if the royalist cause meant that old traditional forms and procedures would be permanently trampled down'. This is possible, but since Heath considered the king to be the linchpin of tradition and of the legal system, it would have taken a tremendous shock to cause him to turn against him, and even then he would have to have been convinced that the king's critics had a superior conception of the law. Generally on the high-prerogative lawyers' conception of absolutism, see Judson, ch. 4; Frances Oakley, 'Jacobean Political Theology: The Absolute and Ordinary Powers of the King', *Journal of the History of Ideas*, 29 (1968), 323 – 46.

integral element of the constitution. When in late 1629 he decided to move against the purveyors of 'A Proposition for his Majesty's Service to bridle the Impertinence of Parliament', he complained to Charles that the pamphlet made it appear that 'your sacred Majesty had a purpose to alter and innovate the ancient Lawes of this kingdome, and the ancient manner and Forme of the Government thereof . . . and to make and repeale Lawes and Statutes, by your Majesties Proclamations only, without consent of Parliament'.[46] Clearly he did not then realise the irony of the situation: that the implicit charge was not altogether unfounded. But clearly, too, he saw parliament as holding a place in 'the ancient manner and Forme of the Government'. Neither the exclusion of the parliamentary element during the 1630s, nor the behaviour of the Long Parliament during the 1640s, significantly altered his opinion.

The mere existence of parliament did not satisfy Heath's constitutional scheme. He often spoke up for what he considered to be parliamentary prerogatives, and in so doing he sometimes left even the radicals behind. A stance that he took in March 1621 is a case in point. The Commons had earlier declared several patents held by Sir Giles Mompesson, a notorious monopolist, to be grievances, and, after some pause about how to proceed, the lower house had called on the Lords to try Mompesson. On 16 March the peers demanded that members of the Commons who had evidence to present against Mompesson appear before them to testify. Particularly contentious was their demand that the members should be sworn. After confused and acrimonious debate, the Commons resolved that the members who were testifying might be sworn, but only as private parties. But apparently not even this compromise was satisfactory to Heath, for during the debate he had taken one of the most inflexible positions: 'That we are all judges, as in this case so in any case, and have resolved that this is a greevance; and therefore not fitt that any of us should take an oath.'[47]

In his defence of parliamentary liberties Heath sometimes went further than the king would have wished. The debate that led to the drafting of the Protestation of 1621 found him arguing 'the liberty of the subject is the inheritance of the subject', and advising the Commons 'To make a protestation of our liberties'.

[46] *A Machavillian Plot*, 12. See pp. 183 – 4.
[47] *CD 1621*, VI, 71. On the Mompesson case, see Tite, ch. 4.

According to Chamberlain, the king was so angered by Heath's temerity that he almost deprived him of office.[48] Despite the risk of ruin, Heath continued to defend parliamentary freedoms, including the right to debate virtually any subject. On 1 April 1624, as the Commons planned a petition to James on the matter of recusancy, he even entered that most hallowed area of crown prerogative, foreign policy. Sir Robert was upset, as were many members, by the recent disclosure that the 'Spanish Match' treaty of 1623 had bound James to show leniency to English Catholics, and he called on his fellow-members: 'To make it a Piece of our Petition to his Majesty, never to entertain Treaty, that may entangle us with the like Inconvenience again.'[49] Not only did his speech deal with foreign policy, and that in a way critical of the king, but it also involved religion, another area that James insisted was his absolute preserve. For that matter, in all three of his parliaments Heath spoke out on religious issues, particularly when the debate at hand gave him an opportunity to attack the recusants. His anti-Catholic speeches, which tended to be impassioned, probably sounded sweet to most of his fellow-members, notably the Puritans, but they cannot have pleased James or, in his turn, Charles, both of whom generally tried to pursue lenient Catholic policies, and both of whom in any case condemned parliamentary intrusion into religious affairs.[50]

When Heath spoke up for parliamentary liberties, political considerations may sometimes have determined his stance. He certainly realised that members of both houses, but particularly the Commons, were becoming ever more determined to assert their rights as they saw them, and he felt that it was important for himself and for the government to be placatory. The need for diplomacy may well have inspired him when during the

---

[48] *CD 1621*, II, 526; McClure, II, 418. It was not unusual for courtier-members to take 'reformist' positions: Russell, 'Parliamentary History', 19 – 23.

[49] *CJ*, I, 752.

[50] In May 1621 Heath joined in the attack on Edward Floyd, a Catholic who was accused of having mocked Frederick and Elizabeth in the wake of their expulsion from the Palatinate: *CJ*, I, 604; Zaller, pp. 104 – 15, on the Floyd debate generally. On 24 March 1621 he insisted in debate, 'For the bill of recusants, to draw it so that the papists may not find starting holes': *CD 1621*, II, 262. On 25 June 1625 he advised the Commons to petition Charles to request a more lenient policy from the bishops in regard to their treatment of silenced preachers: 'CD 1625', 26 – 7.

summer of 1621, he forwarded to the Privy Council notes on the logwood patent:

Ther is a bill in parliament preferred by Sir Thomas Compton to establish the effect of his patent by Lawe [.] Ther is another bill in parliament by the dyers utterly to forbidd the importation for any use at all [.] The present patent is not against any Lawe. Therfore we conceave it best to leave it to the Judgement of parliament which bill they will prefer & pass.[51]

His tone was moderate, yet he made his point: in this matter, the government should not interfere, but rather let parliament decide. Aware though he was of parliamentary politics, however, Heath did not go against his conscience to placate the members. When he disagreed with them he often told them so, sometimes quite bluntly. To a house that seemed unwilling to obey the king's order to adjourn, he insisted, on 30 May 1621: 'We are a Great Council, yet never needed more counsel. We began well and so I hope shall end. Times are in God's hands and in the hearts of Kings. And the times of parliaments are absolutely in the king's hands.'[52]

Heath's reference to parliament as a 'great Council' was not off-handed. Rather, it reflected his general conception of parliament's place in the constitutional frame-work. To him, parliament existed primarily to counsel the monarch. Sir Robert did not deny that it had an important role to play in legislation, and in fact while a member of the Commons he personally proposed several bills, but they involved matters, court reform, economic issues, the regulation of society, that had long been generally taken to fall within the parliamentary province.[53] More often, and particularly if the matter in hand seemed somehow involved with crown prerogative, he called on his fellow-members to proceed by petition or by some similar device. The great debate over patents in 1621 found him making his request with regularity. For example, on 26 March he joined other

---

[51] SP 14/121/48. Coventry was technically co-author.
[52] CD 1621, II, 409.
[53] His known bills, all dating from the parliament of 1621, are noted CJ, I, 569; Nicholas, Proceedings, II, 12; CD 1621, II, 112; V, 293; VI, 239.

speakers in condemning the patent on parks and warrens, but advised the house to petition the king to recall it, rather than take a more extreme course.[54] In the end, the Commons did leave the fate of that patent, and others that it had condemned, to James, and during the following months Heath carried out the implicit wishes of the house by persuading many patentees to surrender their grants.[55] In proceeding as he did, Heath cannot have been disappointed by the behaviour of the members, because by turning the matter of patents over to James they had displayed a proper respect for the crown.

The place of parliament in Heath's constitutional scheme was enhanced by the fact that both houses, but particularly the Commons, represented the nation at large. Sir Robert believed the representative aspect to be vitally important, and he wished to see it enhanced by expanding the membership of the lower house. To widen the franchise, he generally supported moves to create new boroughs, although by so doing he occasionally came into conflict with the Court interest.[56] He also felt that since parliament represented the nation it was duty-bound to act discreetly in matters that threatened to raise contention between the king and itself, especially if the issues in question were of such moment that the course of debate might be reviewed in foreign capitals. His concern was manifest when

---

[54] CD 1621, II, 264.

[55] Heath, sometimes working with Coventry, contacted a number of the patentees and also advised the Council on how to proceed regarding the condemned patents. His activities may be inferred from sets of notes that he prepared for the Council, SP 14/121/48, 49 and SP 14/121/122, 125. Regarding Sir George Douglas's patent for hot-presses, he commented: 'He agreeth to surrender, being satisfied by us, that it is a grant of part of the penalty of a penal lawe, soe against the kings Instructions': SP 14/121/48.

[56] In May 1621 he took an equivocal stand on whether the Commons should accommodate four towns that had petitioned for the right to return members: CD 1621, IV, 360. On 6 April 1624 he reported to the Commons that James was upset over continuing petitioning for representation 'because the king had been informed of great multitudes that we meant to let in by this gap'; however, when he proposed a committee to review the records and see how many of the petitioning towns were eligible to be represented, three of the four candidates he proposed — Selden, Noy, and Cotton — were associated with the 'popular' element: YCPH, Pym's diary, transcript, p. 179. He certainly realised that the candidates he favoured would be sympathetic to most of the petitioners. In 1640, he issued a legal opinion that the franchise of Higham Ferrers should be broadened: Derek Hirst, *The Representative of the People? Voters and Voting in England under the Early Stuarts* (Cambridge, 1975), pp. 70, 235.

in late June 1625, as the Commons wrangled over the question of whether to provide Charles with a subsidy, he told the members: 'All Christendom are upon the eyes of this action, and herein do most especially observe the affection of his Majesty's subjects, which must be his strength.'[57]

Heath reacted angrily to arguments that parliament was the king's equal, perhaps even his superior. In his prosecution of Leighton, he attacked the defendant for even suggesting that parliament had the right to abolish the episcopacy. Only the king, he insisted, could change the basic nature of the Church: 'The Parliament is a great Court, a great Counsell, the great Counsell of the Kinge; but they are but his Counsell, not his governours.'[58] And when parliament itself challenged the king, Heath's sympathies were clear. Only months before his death in 1649, in a lengthy document that he despatched to the royal Court in exile, he condemned the Long Parliament for having 'assumed many exorbitant powers, & proceeded irregularly', and reiterated his position on the proper relationship between parliament and the king:

> The 2 Howses of Parliament are his highest Councell, which never had a part, or joyntly (without the Kings consent) any power to enact, or abrogate a law, but onely to remonstrate their greivances, & propose Bills, to which, itt was always in the Kings power, to give his assent, or denyall: their part is humbly to propose, & advise; the Kings onely to enact, & determine, as also to convene, & dissolve that great Councell att his pleasure.[59]

When Heath composed his political testament in 1649, the English constitution was a shambles. Such wreckage was largely the product of the 1640s, but the conflict that was ultimately responsible for civil war had been long in brewing. For almost a century, the national dedication to mixed monarchy had been breaking down, and the assertions by James I that the crown

---

[57] 'CD 1625', 8.
[58] 'Leighton', 9.
[59] BOD, MS. Don. D. 124, pp. 194 – 5. Use of the designation 'Great Council' to apply to parliament was common at the time, within both conservative and radical circles. It is Heath's interpretation of the term that is significant.

was supreme had encouraged the articulate populace to take sides on the issue of sovereignty. Prior to the 1640s few of Heath's contemporaries openly espoused the doctrine of parliamentary supremacy, though some, like Coke, claimed that while the crown might be sovereign, the king might be challenged.[60] Sir Robert would have none of this hair-splitting, and consequently he was left with a clear choice. Not surprisingly, the notion that parliament should predominate was totally alien to him. He saw but one sovereign, the king, and to him went his ultimate loyalty.

A conception of society

Heath's constitutional ordering, which found the king supreme in government, was parallelled by his conception of society, for social England, too, was to him a hierarchy, with the king at the pinnacle. In both schemes, the key was regularity. In both, the king stood as the primary source of regulation.

Since Heath's conception of society was hierarchical, and since he was, by middle age, wealthy and powerful, his social ordering naturally gave an important place to the ruling classes of England: the aristocracy, the gentry, and the men of business and trade. It was their duty to provide leadership to the nation at large. But he by no means ignored the poor, nor does he appear to have treated them with disdain. On the contrary, he was generally sympathetic to them, and often tried to relieve individual cases of poverty. For example, in November 1640 he interceded at Court on behalf of a 'poor widdowe mrs Hyde', who was in danger of being evicted from her dwelling.[61] He also acted decisively on behalf of the poor at large. In 1633, replying

---

[60] Sir James Whitelocke was one of the few to openly argue that Parliament was sovereign: R. W. K. Hinton, 'English Constitutional Theories from Sir John Fortescue to Sir John Eliot', *The English Historical Review*, 75 (1960), 425. On Coke's attitude, note W. J. Jones, 'Ellesmere and Politics, 1603–1617', *Early Stuart Studies: Essays in Honor of David Harris Willson*, ed. H. S. Reinmuth (Minneapolis, 1970), 31–2. On the decline of the doctrine of mixed monarchy, see Robert Eccleshall, *Order and Reason in Politics: Theories of Absolute and Limited Monarchy in Early Modern England* (Oxford, 1978), chs. 4–6. It has been argued that during the 1640s the mixed monarchy concept gained new impetus: C. C. Weston, 'The Theory of Mixed Monarchy under Charles I and After', *The English Historical Review*, 75 (1960), 426–43, *passim*.

[61] ITL, Miscellaneous Mss., f. 476.

in Exchequer Chamber to a series of questions put to him by Noy, he issued a series of opinions on how best local officials might interpret and implement the poor law. On the whole, his advice favoured the poor, as he regularised the collection of poor rates, defined in liberal terms the obligations of rate-payers, and argued that any poor person who had lived in a parish for one month should be considered settled there, rather than be subject to expulsion. Although his opinions were not legally binding, they quickly began to serve local officials as a guide to poor law policy, and their impact was felt well into the eighteenth century.[62] Generally speaking, where localities followed his lead, the poor were better off in consequence.

Heath was not only interested in the physical survival of the poor, however. Like almost all members of the ruling classes, he believed that the State had both a right and a duty to oversee the morals of all members of society, but especially those of the poor.[63] Possibly the area where he saw most need for reform

[62] Heath's opinions were issued under the title, 'the resolutions of the judges of assize', but his authorship is confirmed by T. G. Barnes: *Somerset 1625 – 1640*, p. 188. Barnes also comments (*ibid.*, p. 189), 'the resolutions of 1633 effected the final absorption of the Elizabethan poor laws into the routine working of the justices of the peace'. Among the judges, Heath was unusual in his willingness to define the implications of the poor laws; Anthony Fletcher writes, 'With the exception of the resourceful and brave Chief Justice Heath, who in 1633 offered some resolutions on tricky points of law which quickly became much revered, the judges seem to have ignored the cries for written guidance from JPs': *Reform in the Provinces: The Government of Stuart England* (New Haven and London, 1986), p. 57. For context (poor law enforcement during the 1630s), see Barnes, *Somerset 1625 – 1640*, 176 – 7, 196 – 8; L. M. Hill, 'County Government in Caroline England 1625 – 1640', *The Origins of the English Civil War*, ed. Conrad Russell (London, 1973), 77 – 83. Fletcher, ch. 7, is an excellent survey of poor law policy in the early Stuart period. Heath's 'resolutions' were included in the many editions of Michael Dalton, *The Country Justice* (e.g., 1705 ed., pp. 162 – 7), thereby carrying their impact through much of the eighteenth century. Even late on in that century, his opinion on who should be rated was still being cited; note Edmond Bott, *Decisions of the Court of King's Bench, upon the Laws relating to the Poor* (London, 1793), vol. I, part II, 92.

[63] Very few articulate Englishmen opposed the notion that the State had an obligation to govern morals: Joan Kent, 'Attitudes of Members of the House of Commons to the Regulation of "Personal Conduct" in Late Elizabethan and Early Stuart England', Institute of Historical Research, *Bulletin*, 46 (1973), 61 – 2. Furthermore, tradition and consensus held that an individual's body belonged to society, making, e.g., self-castration a crime, as Heath himself noted with approval: notes in Staunford's *Plees* (above, n. 35), §32.

was national policy in regard to alehouses. In July 1634, in Exchequer Chamber, he proposed a set of guidelines for corporations to use in licensing and policing alehouses, and had they been followed they would have resulted in a sharp decrease in the number of such establishments.[64] They were not, however, and May 1638 found him advising that the Committee of Trade take certain steps to regulate alehouses.[65] In yet a third statement on the subject, a memorial to the king written during the winter of 1634 – 5, Heath explained his concern: that the proliferation of alehouses was promoting idleness and drunkenness.[66] Drinking was not the only national habit that he tried to control through state action. Like James, he considered smoking to be a corrupter of youth, and during the parliament of 1621 he proposed that the import of tobacco be entirely banned.[67] Nevertheless, alehouses appear to have been his prime concern, probably because they mainly served the poor and so could be held responsible for dissipation among the lower classes. Seldom if ever did Heath denounce taverns, which served a better clientele. And smoking, vice though it might be, was not primarily a vice of the lowly.

Sir Robert's concern for the morals of the lower classes was born of the belief that the poor were naturally volatile. Particularly in his role as law officer, he regularly heard of riots and other mob actions taking place throughout the kingdom. The mob, he believed, might one day threaten the stability of the nation. By governing the morals of the poor, the government might produce in them a general sense of discipline. So thought Sir Robert, but he did not stop at moral oversight.

---

[64] W. L. Sachse (ed.), 'Minutes of the Norwich Court of Admiralty, 1632 – 1635', Norfolk Record Society, *Publications*, 36 (1967), 161 – 2.

[65] BOD, Bankes Papers, 16/58. Specific questions on policy regarding alehouses had earlier been referred to him: SP 16/389/84.

[66] Bankes Papers, 44/53. See also p. 280. Generally on the ruling-class hostility toward alehouses, see Peter Clark, 'The Alehouse and the Alternative Society', *Puritans and Revolutionaries: Essays on Seventeenth-Century History Presented to Christopher Hill*, ed. Don Pennington and Keith Thomas (Oxford, 1978), 47 – 8.

[67] *CD 1621*, V, 77. Heath's speech probably reflected his attitude toward smoking, but he came to recognise the importance of the tobacco crop to Virginia, and in 1624 he tried to gain James's approval for a compromise scheme that would protect Virginian interests: Russell, *Parliaments and English Politics*, pp. 46 – 7.

Instead, he believed that the poor had to be forced into a general social framework. The government alone could not apply sufficient pressure; rather, the cooperation of all elements of the ruling classes would be necessary. Heath for the most part supported institutions that placed members of the lower classes under the direction of their social superiors. Particularly important to him was the apprenticeship system, which served to bind children, lower-class children especially, to their masters. The very first bill that he preferred as a member of the Commons dealt with a problem in enforcing the apprenticeship laws. On 21 February 1621 he called on the house to restrict the activities of wool brokers, because they were, among other things, encouraging 'all young apprentices to run out and so to run away, for they tell them it is no felony in them'. The next day, in a committee of the whole house, for the only time in his parliamentary career, he chose to initiate an attack on a patent, claiming that Sir Henry Goldsmith had

> gotten a patent upon the statute of 5 Elizabeth, where there is a penalty put on those that exercise trade without having been bound apprentice to the same 7 years. This is a grievance, for they force them to show their indentures, or to pay, or to compound. So that every runaway, if he will compound, may have a dispensation.[68]

That Heath was anxious to have the lower classes answerable to their betters reflects the overall rigidity of society as he saw it. So does the position he took in the proposals on aliens that he prepared in 1622: that English-born sons of aliens, and likewise denizens who completed their apprenticeships, might be treated as subjects, but only if they left 'the Formes of

---

[68] *CD 1621*, II, 123. Heath's complaints seem to have accorded well with the attitude of the corporation of London, which was promoting a bill intended to curb the 'abuses and misdemeanors' of apprentices: Letter Books, HH, ff. 48 – 50. Heath's strict attitude on apprenticeship policy is reflected in his 'resolutions' of 1633. In response to the question of what should be done to poor parents who refuse to apprentice their children, although they cannot provide for them, he advises that they be committed to a house of correction: Dalton, p. 163. Heath's belief that strict enforcement of the laws on apprenticeship was necessary to buttress order was common: M. G. Davies, *The Enforcement of English Apprenticeship, 1563 – 1642* (Cambridge, Mass., 1956), pp. 2 – 9.

Straungers whereby they hold themselves in a voluntary separation from the english, both in ther congregations, aliancyes, & commerce'.[69] In other words, he wanted them to become assimilated. There was no place for pluralism in a well-ordered society.

The requirement of conformity extended to the ruling classes. In particular, Heath expected the rich and powerful to conform in their basic political philosophy. All of them were to profess loyalty to the king and to the constitution that saw him sovereign. Those who did not conform, especially if they were vocal in their dissent, were to be punished, for in arguing as they did they jeopardised the peace of the commonwealth. If they did not advocate immediate, fundamental change, or the use of force to effect change, Heath did not believe that they should be subjected to severe punishments, but he did feel that they deserved to be penalised. He was particularly partial to one means of combating the opposition: that of barring radicals from government office. It appeared to Heath, and not entirely without justice, that some men who opposed the king, especially in parliament, did so because they hoped thereby to force him to grant them preferment, as the price for keeping them quiet. The fact that they were occasionally successful, even as loyal king's men waited for place, so irritated Sir Robert that in 1630 he advised Charles 'such as are opposers of his Majestys government, [should] not be advaunced (to take them of) but they be therby rendred uncapable of favour or preferment, until ther future deserts have redeemed ther former errors[;] which els will be a mean to raise opposition, in hope to be raised therby'.[70] In the political testament that he prepared twenty years later, in the hopes of influencing Charles's son, the man whom he recognised as Charles II, he made the same point with still greater urgency:

---

[69] See pp. 116 – 18 on Heath's proposals. To balance the picture, it should be noted that he had a number of contacts in the strangers community, including Sir Cornelius Vermuyden, his partner during the 1630s. And he had some sympathy for the strangers' sense of national pride. In Dec. 1631 he issued a judicial opinion that a stranger might take the Oath of Supremacy without fear that he thereby betrayed his allegiance to the ruler of his native country: SP 16/204/39. Nevertheless, the overall thrust of his philosophy favoured assimilation.

[70] SP 16/178/4.

One thinge [the king] should take speciall care of: never to preferre, or countenance any, who have bin active agaiynst him, out of a consideration of taking such off from their engagements & obliging them to himself. For besides that he gives thereby discouragement & distast to such as have faithfully served him, & encourageth more Factious Spiritts to appeare agaynst him (when they fynde that to be the way of preferment) such men received into Service prove oftner snakes in the bosome, then faithfull Ministers.[71]

As for radicals who did not, by their words or actions, foster turbulence, Heath felt that exclusion from office was a sufficient penalty. Even his suggestion that they should be excluded, a suggestion that he is not known to have made prior to 1630, may have reflected a hardening of his attitude in reaction to the tumult of the 1620s. During his career in the Commons he often cooperated with radical members. Indeed, whether from conviction or political motives he seems to have been quite willing to work with them, even though they distrusted him, as they did all courtiers. For example, on 7 March 1621 he supported a proviso that Noy wanted tacked onto the subsidy bill, and two weeks later he applauded Noy for an attack that the latter had made on a patent.[72] In all three of his parliaments, he supported bills that had been introduced by radicals. The fact that an individual might be considered radical did not in itself make him anathema to Heath. Even when, during the last two decades of his life, he urged that such a person be barred from crown office, at least until he had made amends, there was no personal animus in his attitude.

Not surprisingly, however, he advocated much harsher treatment for those who actively challenged the political, religious, or social systems that governed England. He proposed a violent justice for revolutionaries, of a sort that would frighten away potential followers. In addressing the judges in Star Chamber, he requested that the sentence to be levied on Leighton be a harsh one, including corporal punishment, 'for the honor and peace of the kingdome [and] for a lesson to others'.[73] And when Sir Robert acted as Court avenger, he

---

[71] BOD, MS. Don, d. 124, p. 185.
[72] CD 1621, V, 60; CJ, I, 544.
[73] 'Leighton', 10.

refused to allow the advocates of revolution to justify themselves. To Leighton's insistence that he had been moved by conscience to write his tract, Sir Robert responded: 'A blind zeale and a misledd conscience are no excuse for a seditious pamphlett. All the heticall scismatikes, nay all the traytors in the world, may say the like.'[74]

Prior to the 1640s Heath, like most of his countrymen, believed that the radical element was small. Not even the closing weeks of the parliament of 1629, when member after member attacked the Court, altered his impression, and on 7 March 1629, five days after the Commons, on the point of adjournment, had acclaimed Eliot's extreme resolutions and still more extreme behaviour, he complained only of 'The untoward disposition of a fewe ill members.'[75] But while Heath thought that the opposition was smaller than it was, he did not belittle the danger that it represented. The six hundred copies of his tract that Leighton had printed were, according to Heath, 'more then enough to poyson all a whole kingdom'.[76]

Heath never took for granted the tranquillity that characterised England during most of his life. As he saw it, agitators could at any time seduce large numbers of people, particularly the lower classes, into rebellion, even revolution. Discipline would provide stability and would best protect England from the ultimate horror of civil war. And it was a strong government, led ultimately by a single govenor, that could best effect such discipline.

Particularly during his time as attorney-general, Heath played a key role in providing discipline for England, and he did so out of court as well as in. Because the government was concerned that Salisbury would return radicals to the forthcoming parliament, Sir Robert twice wrote to the mayor of the town in January 1626, asking him and the electorate to return Sir John Evelyn, a minor courtier, as one of their members. Salisbury refused him, but this affair had seen him use only diplomacy in his campaign. Later that year, when it appeared that London might refuse the king's demand to supply twenty ships for defence of the coast, he wrote to the lord mayor and aldermen to

---

[74] *Ibid.*, 9.
[75] See p. 176. Most Englishmen, including some radical MPs, shared his assessment: Kevin Sharpe, 'Parliamentary History 1603 – 1629: In or Out of Perspective?', *Faction and Parliament*, ed. Sharpe, 17 – 18.
[76] 'Leighton', 2.

advise them that the Privy Council was planning to act against the City. He added: 'Out of my Love to the Cittye, I have adventured thus farr as to lett your Lordshipps know [this news] from a frend who wished you and your Cittie all happines and should be extremely sorry that my service must be used to the hurte of any of you.' While his tone was diplomatic, the mailed fist was plainly evident, and London soon gave in, probably in part moved by the threat of legal action. The ship-money affair of 1626 was not the sort of matter to breed turbulence, and Heath's reaction to it was consequently restrained. But 18 July 1628 saw him take a very different tack, in the face of immediate danger. Conway had told him that rumours about Buckingham were circulating, rumours of the sort that would inspire hatred of the duke, perhaps even provoke an attempt on his life. To this Heath replied that he was preparing a proclamation aimed at the rumour-mongers, but he added: 'In the generall my opinion hath ever been that it is much better to restrein that itching & malitious humour by punishing the offendors; then by a verball inhibition be it never soe strict.'[77] Clearly, his action did not save Buckingham, who was assassinated just five weeks later, but Heath's reaction reflects his general attitude toward handling turbulence.

Heath's various reactions when the government was challenged were, in fact, all of a piece. When an individual or a group threatened the tranquillity of the nation, he advocated strong measures, but while he found radicalism distasteful, he would never have favoured a judicial reign of terror in an attempt to crush opposition to the crown. There was nothing vicious in his character. As a judge in Star Chamber, 1631 – 4, he consistently proposed sentences that were milder than any suggested by his colleagues.[78] Nor did he blindly oppose programmes espoused by radicals. On the contrary, during the years 1621 – 5 probably no crown official whose stature matched his more consistently supported reformist legislation, and he often worked with radicals to achieve his ends. But always the reform programme that he advocated was moderate, and never

---

[77] SP 16/110/28; Henry Hatcher, *The History of Modern Wiltshire* (London, 1843), pp. 348 – 9 (as Hatcher notes, the lord chamberlain, the earl of Pembroke, also wrote the lord mayor of Salisbury on behalf of Evelyn); M. C. Wren, 'London and the Twenty Ships, 1626 – 27', *The American Historical Review*, 55 (1950), 321 – 35; CLRO, VI, f. 71.
[78] See pp. 239 – 40.

did it challenge the basic political or social framework of the nation. Indeed, that framework itself was, to him, sacred. It might be improved — and, no less important, buttressed — through reform. It had in any case to be defended against its enemies.

While Heath's philosophy may have been of a piece, it was not unique. Indeed, it was representative of articulate Englishmen, and was in most respects as characteristic of radicals as of king's men. A key question must therefore be: what distinguished Heath from an Eliot or a Pym? There is no definite answer, of the sort that can cover all cases, but it may be said that while Heath and the radicals shared an interest in both reform and authority, they differed in emphasis. Radicals, at least prior to the 1620s, were generally willing to observe the traditional balance of authority, which saw the king supreme, provided that authority granted relief from certain grievances — specifics varied with the individual, though there was significant consistency — or in general followed policies that were to their liking. In other words, reform, rather than constitutional tradition, represented their highest priority. When it became obvious that the king would not serve as an instrument to relieve their grievances, they began to re-examine their constitutional philosophy. To Heath, preservation of the traditional framework of Church, State, and society was paramount. Reform was desirable, but not of the highest importance. It was priorities, then, rather than programmes, that most clearly set him apart from the radicals.

7

Zenith and Nadir

During Heath's years as attorney-general it was occasionally rumoured that he was soon to gain the bench. The speculation reflected normal practice, for most senior law officers eventually became either chief justice or lord keeper.[1] With Coventry ensconced as lord keeper, that line of promotion was barred, but Hyde's death, on 25 August 1631, left a chief justiceship vacant. Since the courts were not then in session there was no need for Charles to rush to fill the vacancy. It was only in late October, as Michaelmas term approached, that he decided on the new judicial order: Sir Thomas Richardson, chief justice of the Common Pleas, was to assume the most distinguished position on the bench, while Heath was to vacate his law office and take up Richardson's old place. The new attorney-general was to be Noy, formerly a prime critic of the Court, presently an architect of Thorough.[2]

The respective reactions of Richardson and Heath, as they assumed their new office on 24 October, were well reflected in their addresses to Coventry. Sir Thomas was in a belligerent mood, complaining:

> that he hoped his majesty's favour would have gone so far along with him, as to have let him have ended those few Days he had to spend in the place he was now called from.

---

[1] Of the eleven attorneys-general from 1558 to 1641, one became master of the Rolls, five became chief justices, and three became chancellor or lord keeper. The remaining two were Noy, who died in office, and Yelverton, who despite his disgrace was later appointed a justice of Common Pleas.

[2] Although some Court observers were surprised by the appointment of Noy, the Court's intention to bring him into government had apparently been long-standing, and he had been rumoured for the place of attorney of the Wards in 1629: George Gresley to Sir Thomas Puckering, 5 Nov. 1629, Birch, II, 36.

But he found, that in this World there was alteration of men's minds, Healths & places, . . . that he sought not for this place, which his Majesty had now conferred upon him, for his honour, tho some might take it for disfavour.

His apparent anger may have arisen from the fact that the income that he could expect to derive from King's Bench was less than that he had enjoyed in Common Pleas. John Rous, an astute observer of the Court scene, commented that Richardson's promotion was 'against his mind for gaine'.[3]

Richardson was something of a cynic, so it is not surprising that at the very moment when he reached the pinnacle of the legal profession he seems to have thought mainly of income. Heath, on the other hand, was ever an idealist in matters of the law, and he saw in his promotion the fulfillment of a dream. It was a proud and grateful Sir Robert who addressed Coventry:

He thought himself happy in having had the fortune to have his Majesty's favour, to follow his Lordship successively in two places . . . in both which he had the happines to have his Majesty's ear with a great deal of more favour than he could deserve . . . And therefore for a token of his thankfulness humbly desired his Lordship to present his Majesty with a ring set round with great Diamonds, being worth 1000£.

The presentation of the ring was no part of a purchase, but neither was it simply a demonstration of gratitude, thankful though Heath was for his new place. Incoming judges were expected to present expensive gifts to the king.[4] Their institution was often attended by other traditions as well, all of which were, luckily for them, far less costly. So, on the day he addressed Coventry, Heath was created a serjeant-at-law. For

---

[3] 'Diary of John Rous, Incumbent of Santon Downham, Suffolk, from 1625 to 1642', ed. M. A. E. Green, Camden Society, *Publications*, 66 (1856), 68. The summary of his speech, and Heath's, is drawn from Gresley to Puckering, 27 Oct. 1631: Birch, II, 136 – 7.

[4] W. J. Jones, *Politics and the Bench: The Judges and the Origins of the English Civil War* (London, 1971), p. 38. The king was not alone in receiving gifts. On the serjeants' giving of rings, see Baker, *Serjeants*, p. 92. Heath himself acquired at least 13 serjeants' rings: *ibid.*, 465n. On the question of whether bestowing gifts in return for preferment to office amounted to a purchase, see also Aylmer, pp. 225 – 39.

centuries the king's serjeants had held a monopoly of chief justiceships, but their hold had been steadily weakened during the sixteenth century, and by the death of Elizabeth it had become crown policy to select chief justices from among the law officers. To maintain the trappings of tradition, however, the new appointees were still required to become serjeants, and so it was that Sir Robert donned the coif.[5] The Inner Temple, too, observed tradition, by presenting him with ten pounds, neatly packaged in 'a ginger coloured leather purse with tawney silk strings', and seeing him off to Serjeants' Inn, where members of his new order normally resided. In fact, however, he kept his quarters at the Temple, by dint of a special exemption given to inmates who ascended the bench.[6]

Cowardly lions?

Those who accuse the early Stuart judges of having been a pusillanimous lot hearken back to some of Sir Robert's own contemporaries. No less a man than Selden complained:

> Wee see the Pageants in Cheapside, the Lyons & the Elephants, but wee doe not see the men that carry them; we see the Judges look big, look like lions, but we do not see who moves them . . . There could bee no mischeife done in the Comon Wealth without a Judge . . . Now the Judges they interprett the Law, & what Judges cann bee made to doe wee all knowe.[7]

To Selden, to many of his countrymen, and to countless historians since, it has appeared that the Stuart judges were only too willing to do the bidding of their royal masters. Such criticism is derived from the undoubted tendency of the bench to rule in favour of the crown when constitutional issues were at stake. Moving on from this factual basis, critics have charged that the judges, apart from a few notable exceptions like Coke,

[5] (Sir) George Croke, *The Third Part of the Reports* (London, 1676), p. 225; Edwards, pp. 30 – 1.
[6] *ITR*, II, 192, Wilde, f. 44.
[7] *The Table Talk of John Selden*, ed. (Sir) Frederick Pollack (London, 1927), pp. 60, 66.

were willing to set aside their principles, rather than stand fast against royal pressure and risk removal from the bench.

Did Heath, on October 1631, join a fraternity that was morally bankrupt? He was quick to denounce those who criticised the judges. Indeed, to his mind, it was the popular faction, rather than royal pressure, that most endangered judicial integrity. This opinion he voiced when in 1630 he appealed to Charles to stand with his men: 'If the Judges be countenaunced, who have of late been much undervalued by ther inferiors, that soe they be made harty & assured in the kings service [it] will make them reverenced, & they not to be overawed.'[8] Nor need he have contented himself with rhetoric. Had he wished to, he could have cited many cases in which the judges had taken stands that they knew would bring down upon themselves the wrath of the king. His own term as attorney-general saw him at odds with the bench on various occasions, but the judges' intransigence was yet more evidence of their integrity. When the five knights appeared to request bail, they were very nearly granted their wish, and during the proceedings several of Heath's requests were denied by the court. Eliot's Case found the judges no more cooperative. Heath could not persuade them to respond to all the questions he posed during the two interviews in April 1629, and even in the presence of Charles they refused to commit themselves on the issue of whether Eliot and his fellows had committed a treasonable offence. After the Star Chamber prosecution had failed, Hyde counselled that the cause should not be pursued, knowing that if it reached the King's Bench the judges might be forced to acquit, regardless of threats from superiors.[9] As attorney-general, Heath sometimes saw his plans, and the king's, frustrated by the courts. But seldom if ever did he see the judges make a move out of fear, rather than conscience.

That the judges were unwilling to kowtow to the Court does not mean that they were not biased in its favour. In an age when the constitution was poorly defined, they usually believed that precedent supported the crown. Whenever there was a vacancy on the bench, there were many contestants for the place, and the king could afford to be demanding when making his choice. Not surprisingly, he tended to choose individuals who he felt

8   SP 16/178/4.
9   See ch. 5.

would support his position. The judges, therefore, were typically men who had demonstrated a pro-crown bias even before they ascended the bench. It was predilection, rather than pressure, that caused them generally to rule in favour of the crown.

While the claim by some historians that the judges were craven appears unfounded, these men certainly had much to fear. They had few friends at Court — in supporting the crown they did only what was expected of them. Their very conscientiousness earned them the contempt of some courtiers, for the care that they showed in their proceedings was often mistaken for procrastination. Weston, for one, in July 1634 wrote to an impatient Wentworth that the judges were preparing answers to certain queries that Sir Thomas had put forward, but that they were proceeding only 'after their slow manner'.[10]

When the judges actively crossed the Court, as by refusing to grant it a verdict, they faced more than ridicule. The prospect of dismissal was then very real. By the time Heath ascended the bench, the tenure of common law judges had been regularised. All held their places during pleasure.[11] A decision that annoyed the Court, or even behaviour that irked some great courtier, might bring prompt dismissal. In greatest danger were the two chief justices and the chief baron of the Exchequer. The five years before Heath's appointment had seen the dismissal of Sir Ranulph Crew, chief justice of the King's Bench, for refusing to confirm the legality of the forced loan of 1626, and the suspension of Chief Baron Walter, for denying, relative to Eliot's Case, that the courts had jurisdiction over causes involving words spoken in parliament.[12] In concentrating its fire on the leaders of the various courts, the crown may have hoped to demonstrate its power. Furthermore, special responsibilities made the chief justices especially vulnerable. They were supposed not only to buttress the royal prerogative through their decisions, but to persuade their associates to follow suit. A chief justice who failed to support the crown was therefore, from the point of view of the Court, a real danger, and in

---

[10] Sheffield Central Library, Wentworth Woodhouse, Strafford Papers, 14 (123).
[11] The regularisation had come in the wake of the refusal of Sir John Walter, chief baron, to vacate his place on Charles's order: C. H. McIlwain, 'The Tenure of English Judges', *American Political Science Review*, 7 (1913), 221.
[12] Whitelocke, *Memorials*, I, 16; Aylmer, pp. 111 – 12, 352.

consequence it was he, rather than any associates who shared his bent, who was most likely to be dismissed. Nevertheless, in a crisis the entire bench might find itself in danger. Shortly after Crew had been dismissed for his stand against the forced loan, an observer reported that 'the rest of the Judges daily expect to tread the same path'.[13] As events transpired they were not removed, but certainly they recognised the threat. Nor was the prospect of dismissal reserved for crises. Indeed, it is quite possible that no Caroline judge served for more than three years without being threatened with removal.

It was the king who removed judges, just as it was he who appointed them. But sometimes the decision to dismiss was not entirely his own. Some great courtier might turn against a judge, for any of a range of reasons, and then urge the king to discipline or even dismiss him. If so, the king might well comply. Feeling their strength, courtiers occasionally browbeat judges who crossed them. In February 1631 a Court observer informed his friend that 'Judge Jones, for speaking somewhat too plainly of my Lord of Arundel's [earl marshal] court, was shrewdly shaken up by both lords chamberlain of the king's and queen's side; my lord of Pembroke calling him a saucy fellow'.[14] During the spring of 1634 Sir George Vernon, a justice of the Common Pleas, fell foul of Wentworth, apparently because he was excessively harsh in dealing with recusants in the north. At Wentworth's request, he was reprimanded by the Council and was removed from the summer circuit.[15]

Among Caroline courtiers, Laud was probably unmatched in his determination to overawe the judiciary. He believed that the bench was hostile to his policies, and he was unwilling to brook opposition. One judge who crossed him was Richardson, who in 1633 refused to comply with his demand that he rescind an order banning wakes. For his temerity Richardson was forced to appear before the Council, where Laud berated him so mercilessly that the judge, on departing, moaned that he had

[13] Edward Palmer to Edward, Lord Montagu, 14 Nov. 1626: *HMC*, Buccleuch III, 313.

[14] Joseph Mead to Sir Martin Stuteville, 27 Feb. 1631: Birch, II, 98.

[15] George Radcliffe, *The Earl of Strafforde's Letters and Dispatches, with an Essay towards His Life* (London, 1739), I, 295, 384–5; Clare Talbot (ed.), 'Miscellanea: Recusant Records', Catholic Record Society, *Publications*, 53 (1961), 387.

'almost been choked with a pair of lawn sleeves'.[16] Laud's penchant for interfering with the judiciary was well known, and when the Long Parliament brought him to trial it included as a major charge against him that he had 'by letters, messages, threats, promises, and divers others ways, to judges and other ministers of justice, interrupted and perverted . . . the course of justice in his Majesty's courts at Westminster, and other courts, to the subversion of the laws of this kingdom'.[17]

It was, therefore, a danger zone that Heath entered when he ascended the bench. Nevertheless, for some two years affairs went smoothly. No cases involving significant crown prerogatives were heard in Commons Pleas, so he could act free from the fear that his decisions might antagonise the Court. His relationship with Charles remained good, and so long as the king supported him, he was safe.

Nevertheless, early 1634 found him intensively courting Wentworth. On 27 February he sent the lord deputy a timid letter, a plea for patronage: 'I have noe busines to trouble your Lordship withall, who I knowe wants none, having soe great a weight of busines uppon you; nor have I other suite; then you will voutsafe me this favor, to esteeme me, as I shall ever be really & truly, your Lordships very ready to be commaunded.' Wentworth responded favourably, and on 7 June Sir Robert again wrote to him:

As an expression of my thankfulnes to your Lordship, that you would voutsafe to accept of mine indevours to doe your service, I am bold to interrupt your weightier affayres with thes fewe lynes; only intreatinge your Lordship to be assured that you shall not command any thing of me in the way wherein I may serve his Majesty & your Lordship, which I shall not . . . willingly performe.[18]

Both notes were rich in the rhetoric of submissiveness, but beneath this rhetoric lay genuine fear. Wentworth was in

---

[16] Peter Heylyn, *Cyprianus Anglicus* (London, 1671), p. 243; as quoted by J. S. Cockburn, *A History of English Assizes 1558 – 1714* (Cambridge, 1972), p. 233. In 1628, Richardson was reportedly in danger of being turned out of his place for 'his slow proceeding against Felton's mother, sister, and brother' in the wake of the Buckingham assassination: Mead to Stuteville, 27 Nov. 1628, Birch, I, 400.

[17] *ST*, IV, col. 326.

[18] Strafford Papers, 13 (208), 14 (91).

Ireland, many miles from the Court scene, yet Heath was seeking his patronage, in seeming anxiety. The cause of his pursuit would soon become apparent.

The dismissal

It was 13 September 1634. A shaken and frightened man begged for mercy.

> To the kings most excellent Majesty
> The humble petition of your Majestys most humble & most loyall, & nowe most distressed & disconsolate subject, Sir Robert heath knight, cheif Justice of your Majestys court of common pleas.
> In all humblenes sheweth, that to his unspeakable greif he hath very lately understood, that your majesty hath declared your Resolution to remove him from this place & from your Majestys service; The loss of the place is very extreeme unto him, his estate being weake & his charg great, but the apprehension of your Majestys heavye displeasure doth by many degrees exceed it. He therfore doth in all humilitye prostrate himself at your Majestys feet, begginge your gratious pardon for any errors past, which in soe many yeers service cann not but be many. Gods mercye is extended over his Justice, your Majesty is gods deputye on earth, & in mercye & goodnes doth imitate that great patterne. I humbly beseech your Majesty, look back with an eye of pitty, uppon the deplorable estate of him his wife & 5 sonns, who are all ruined, if your Majesty shall totally withdrawe your favor, but being supported by your gratious hand, in such measure as in your great wisdome & goodnes, you shall think fitt, (which he shall use with all duitye & moderation) he hopeth to live to doe your Majesty acceptable service: & he, his poor wife & children, shall bless god for your goodnes, & dayly & devoutly pray for your Majestys long life & happy raign.[19]

---

[19] SP 16/274/22; a copy is in Egerton 2978, f. 48. Croke, in his *Third Report* (p. 375), sets the date of the dismissal at 14 Sept., but 13 Sept. is given by Hutton, in his diary, YCPH (microfilm), f. 71.

The space of a few short hours saw the work of decades laid low. At fifty-nine, Heath was suddenly left without office, his income slashed, his honour marred.

Sir Robert's fall has won for him a most ironic notoriety. A career that knew much success is perhaps best remembered for its nadir. Historians, some prompted by the belief that the events of September 1634 provide great insight into the world of Caroline politics, others, caught by the thrill of detective work, have avidly sought to discover the cause of Heath's dismissal. Sir Robert himself provides no clues. In his memoir, he comments only: 'I was on a sudden discharged of that place of Chief Justice, noe cause being then or at any time since shewed for my removal; but I humbly acknowledged Gods hand therein, & submitted thereunto, with patience & cherefullnes.'[20] Such reticence has only heightened the sense of mystery.

Lacking hard evidence, historians have tended to explain the dismissal according to their overall view of the Caroline period. Most of them have been hostile to the Court policies of the 1630s, and they have tended to believe that Heath fell, was martyred indeed, because he refused to support some element of Thorough. Particularly popular is the notion that Charles removed him after having become convinced that Sir Robert opposed the levying of ship-money.[21] Another common assertion is that Laud engineered the dismissal because Heath had somehow antagonised him. Perhaps, it has been suggested, Sir Robert was sympathetic to Puritanism and was therefore

---

[20] 'Anniversarium', 21. It is scarcely possible that Heath has no idea why he was dismissed. When he wrote that there had been 'noe cause . . . shewed for my removal', he may have meant that the accusations that led to his dismissal had not been proven, but it is more probable that in writing as he did he hoped to put himself in a good light. He probably believed that the memoir would be read by his children, and he naturally wanted to suggest a good example for them.

[21] Among the more noteworthy historians who have espoused this view are Gardiner (VII, 361), Aylmer (p. 112), and Russell (*Parliaments and English Politics*, p. 364). The link of the dismissal to ship-money derives from Rushworth, who claims that in the wake of Heath's dismissal and the elevation of Finch: 'Great were the Discourses what the occasion should be of that sudden advancement. But Four days after the Writ for Ship-money coming forth, it was conceived by common Discourse, that he [Finch] was to be instrumental to advance that busines': *Historical Collections* (London, 1707), II, 253. Rushworth's tone suggests that the conclusion arrived at 'by common Discourse' represented a mere guess, based on coincidence.

hostile to the core of Laud's religious policies.[22] Perhaps he was too forthright in defending John Williams, bishop of Lincoln, against charges that had been brought against him by the Laudian faction.[23] Perhaps Heath fell foul of Laud in Star Chamber, owing to Sir Robert's tendency to recommend light sentences, and the archbishop sought his dismissal from the bench only as a means of removing him from the conciliar court.[24]

None of these assertions can be dismissed out of hand, and several may well be close to the mark. However, it is wise to distinguish between the occasion for the dismissal and the cause of it. The conjectural causes cited may have been causes in fact. But Heath's fall was probably not occasioned by any of them. It appears instead that Sir Robert was dismissed in the wake of revelations that he had engaged in corrupt dealings while attorney-general and that his activities had been harmful to the king's interest.

Contemporary Court observers were well aware of the rationale for Heath's removal. When on 10 October 1634 William Sheffield referred to the affair in a letter to his cousin, Lord Fairfax, his tone suggested that he feared his relative would be bored by the repetition of well-worn intelligence: 'I doubt not but your honour hath heard of the sudden displacing of my Lord Chief Justice Heath, for misdemeanours he did while he was Attorney General.'[25] A more specific account of the dismissal was included in a letter that Lord Maltravers had written to the earl of Ormonde ten days earlier. Maltravers, a major courtier and an associate of Heath's, was well situated to review the events of mid-September. He wrote:

My lord Chief justice Heath was declared a while since by his Majesty to be put out of his place and to be followed in the Star Chamber; he came presently after to the court and gave the king a petition humbly acknowledging that he had been a

---

[22] This is the opinion of J. M. Rigg, the author of the article on Heath in the *DNB*.

[23] Foss, VI, 323. Foss cites other possibilities as well. His belief that the Williams case may have been responsible for the dismissal is based on Hacket (see n. 37).

[24] Fraser, 'Heath', 161–4, 169.

[25] *The Fairfax Correspondence*, ed. G. W. Johnson (London, 1848), I, 293.

weak servant unto him, and through multiplicity of business believed he might well have incurred his Majesty's displeasure, and since it had pleased him to dispose of his place, he beseeched him to withdraw his other displeasure from him.[26]

The petition that Maltravers makes reference to is almost certainly the one that Heath submitted to the king on 13 September. Maltravers's letter also makes clear that Heath did not petition in hopes of persuading the king to allow him to remain in office, but rather as an appeal to Charles to save him from a trial in Star Chamber. The king appears to have acceded to this request, but that does not alter the fact that serious charges had been levelled against Sir Robert.

Maltravers says nothing that might provide a clue as to the nature of the charges, but two of his contemporaries do. The great antiquary Anthony Wood wrote some years after the event that Heath had been dismissed 'for bribery'.[27] Both more detailed and closer in time to the dismissal were the remarks that Thomas Crosfield included in his diary entry of 28 February 1636. Pondering 'the transmutation of some men placed in offices of Justice', Crosfield recalled, 'Sir Robert Heath put out of his office of being Lord Chiefe Justice of the Kings Bench [sic] because he made some woods of the King in Shotover & elsewhere be sold with lesse advantage to the King then was thought meet, & more to himselfe'.[28] It may be that Crosfield provides the simple answer to Heath's dismissal. As attorney-general Sir Robert had been responsible for drawing various classes of documents that involved the forests. So, for example — an important example, if one follows Crosfield — in August 1629 he had drawn, on the king's order, a grant authorising the earl of Lindsay to cut timber at Shotover.[29] During the 1630s a number of scandals centred on the royal forests, most of them

26 HMC, Ormonde I, 28.
27 Athenae Oxoniensis (London, 1721), I, col. 596. Ironically, one of the few historians to follow up Wood's claim, by asserting that Heath was dismissed for having taken bribes, is Lord Campbell, whose account of Heath's career is glaringly incorrect in many particulars: The Lives of the Chief Justices of England (New York, 1875 ed.), II, 71. Foss, a far superior scholar, indignantly denies the charge: VI, 323 – 4.
28 The Diary of Thomas Crosfield, ed. F. S. Boas (London, 1935), p. 87.
29 Fraser, 'Heath', 153; Fraser argues persuasively that Heath was probably not involved in fraudulent activities at Shotover: ibid., 153 – 4.

involving the excessive or wholly unauthorised cutting of timber, and Shotover itself was found to be the scene of much of the illegal harvest.[30] It is by no means impossible that in September 1634 Heath was found to have connived in defrauding the king of his timber. If so, these revelations may have caused his downfall.

Regardless of whether the scandal that brought down Heath was centred at Shotover, it is probable that Sir Robert was not above enriching himself at the king's expense. Sometime in 1636 John Battalion, Adam Moore, and John Mogridge informed Charles, in a petition, that James had empowered them to initiate a drainage project at King's Sedgmoor and that they had reclaimed 4,000 acres, of which the king had allowed them 400 in recompense. Some unnamed party had then offered £80,000 for the 4,000 acres, but James had not agreed to the transaction. In 1631, however, the entire moor had:

> passed in perpetuity from your Majestie by the quantity of 10,300 acres (which is worth 200000£ Fine & 100£ Rent; in which Bargainse your Majestie hath lost 68000£ in the value of your 4000 Acres . . . This bargaine seemeth to be obteyned by the corruption of Sir Robert Heath, then your Majesties Atturney generall, & Sir Cornelius Vermuyden Knight. For there is 30000£ paid out of Cash for it, which said some of money was a widowes adventure, & some of theirs; & heerof your Majestie had but 12000£ and the other 18000£ is miscarried. And your petitioners are denied their 400 Acres.[31]

Several of these claims can be corroborated. On 15 October 1631 Charles made a contract with Vermuyden to convey more than 10,000 acres of King's Sedgmoor to Heath and four other men. In return, the king was to receive £12,000, plus an annual fee-farm rent of £100. Vermuyden's principle partner in the business was Geoffrey Kirby, but he soon died, leaving his interest to his wife, Margaret. Finally, on 12 June 1635, Charles, responding to a petition by Vermuyden, directed that King's

---

[30] Mary D. Lobel (ed.), *A History of the County of Oxford*, V, *The Victoria History of the Counties of England* (London, 1957), pp. 279 – 80.
[31] SP 16/339/22. Barnes (*Somerset*, pp. 150 – 6) also discusses the King's Sedgmoor affair.

Sedgmoor be conveyed to Margaret Kirby and her assigns.[32] The documents do not reveal the role that Heath played in framing the contract of October 1631. However, it is more than possible that he had connived in securing the conveyance. Vermuyden was his main partner throughout the 1630s, and neither he nor Sir Robert had a strong sense of ethics in business.[33] In all probability, Heath acted as Vermuyden's agent in negotiating the contract.

More important, however, is the question of when, or whether, Charles came to realise that he had been cheated. While Battalion and his associates did not petition the king until 1636, they made their complaints known earlier. In May 1635 they appeared before the commissioners of the Treasury and charged Vermuyden and several others with having deprived them of their share of King's Sedgmoor. Although Vermuyden's co-defendants are not named in surviving documents that bear on the case, Heath was probably among them.[34] The plaintiffs failed to obtain satisfaction — otherwise, they would not have petitioned the king in 1636 — but their charges may well have caused the Court to reassess the transaction of October 1631. Quite possibly, Vermuyden's petition to have King's Sedgmoor conveyed actually came in response to a crown directive, an angry one. But no matter how the Court responded in May 1635, the King's Sedgmoor business cannot have contributed to Heath's downfall unless his role in the earlier 'corruption' was known by September 1634, and there is no reason to imagine that it was. Regardless of whether it prompted the dismissal, however, the conveyance of King's Sedgmoor in 1631 exemplifies the sort of activity that provided the king with a reason to remove Heath from the bench.

Nevertheless, the question remains: Was corruption the cause of Heath's dismissal or merely the rationale for it? It may have been the cause. Regardless of which specific scandal brought him down, Sir Robert, while attorney-general, had probably through sharp dealings cost the king thousands of pounds — this, while serving in an office that was charged with enhancing

---

[32] C. 66/2688. This document provides details on the earlier contact as well.
[33] See ch. 8.
[34] CSPD, Charles I, VIII, 80. The plaintiffs' replication to Vermuyden's answer is in BL Stowe 326, f. 25. Battalion sued Vermuyden over several issues, 1630 – 6, and some of the cases may have involved Heath: Stowe 326, ff. 1 – 31.

royal income — and the revelation that he had cheated the crown in a major transaction may well have prompted Charles to dismiss him. The evidence suggests, however, that corruption was not the true cause of Heath's dismissal, or at most was only part of it.

As has been claimed, the possibility exists that Charles dismissed Heath not because the latter had engaged in corrupt practices while attorney-general — though that was the reason given out — but because he was opposed, or was thought to be opposed, to some important crown policy. But what about specific hypotheses? Was, for example, Sir Robert ousted for standing against ship-money, as many have suggested? The answer in this case is, probably not. Heath was himself involved in ship-money schemes in 1626 and perhaps in 1628, and as king's serjeant he was in 1640 given the responsibility of prosecuting a ship-money case, hardly the sort of assignment that was likely to go to one who was opposed to the tax.[35] Furthermore, there is the question of timing. The ship-money writs of 1634 were entirely in accordance with precedent, and in fact the imposition was little opposed that year. Even if the Court had anticipated trouble, it would not have expected any ship-money case to be heard by Heath for at least a year. So it appears that Sir Robert's dismissal had nothing to do with ship-money. Nor is it likely that, as some writers have maintained, Heath was removed because he sympathised with the Puritan cause. He was never a Puritan, and indeed the evidence suggests that during the 1630s he came to associate Puritanism, at least in its more extreme forms, with anti-statism, which he of course abhorred.[36] If the Court imagined that he was a Puritan sympathiser it sadly misjudged him, though it was not immune from such misjudgement.

While some interpretations of Heath's fall seem not to accord well with the evidence, others do. It is possible, in fact probable, that as a number of historians have claimed the dismissal was

---

[35] Heath's delaying tactics when the case was heard brought him the censure of the judges: Edmund Rossingham to Edward Viscount Conway, 23 June 1640, SP 16/457/104. On 11 July 1639 Heath, Bankes, and Littleton, responding to an enquiry by the Council, advised on ways in which sheriffs who refused to levy ship-money were punishable: Bankes Papers, 5/40. On Heath's involvement with the ship-money schemes of 1626 and 1628, see pp. 107, 221 – 2.

[36] See pp. 198 – 9.

engineered by Laud. Two arguments that have been put forward to explain his motivation are particularly worth reviewing. Either may be valid, and both help to throw light on his character.

It has been argued that Laud cast Heath down because the latter took the side of Williams, Laud's enemy, during his trial in Star Chamber. The source for this allegation is John Hacket, Williams's biographer. Laud, according to Hacket, turned the case over to Richard Kilvert, an unscrupulous lawyer, who in his prosecution:

> left not one Rule or Practice of the Court unbroken, menacing, and intimidating Witnesses, Clerks, Registers, Examiners, Judges, and the Lord keeper himself . . . Sir *Robert Heath*, Lord Chief Justice of the *Common Pleas*, was but one of the Lords Assessors, yet as just and sufficient as any of his order; and the indignity done to him, was as if done to all: Who made his own Complaint, *That* Kilvert *threatned to procure him to be turn'd out of his place for his forwardness* . . . Beshrew the Varlet, that kept his word, (which he was not wont to do) for Sir *Robert Heath* was displaced, and for no Misdemeanour proved. But it was to bring in a Successor, who was more forward to undo *Lincoln*, than ever the Lord *Heath* was to preserve him.[37]

Hacket is not without his faults, either as a reporter or as an analyst. His comment that Heath was dismissed 'for no Misdemeanour proved' suggests that he was not as privy to Court news as were Maltravers, Sheffield, and even Crosfield though it might be noted that he does not claim that no misdemeanour was alleged. His lurid picture of Kilvert's behaviour in court was probably drawn for him by Williams, not the most dispassionate of sources. One might also wonder why, if Heath was dismissed for his stand on Williams, the dismissal came in 1634, a year that saw virtually no action on the case against the bishop. Still, it is entirely possible that Sir Robert did favour Williams's position and thereby antagonised Laud.[38]

---

[37] *Scrinia Reserata*, II, 116, 118.
[38] There is no evidence to corroborate Hacket's claim that Heath supported Williams in Star Chamber. However, Sir Robert had defended the bishop against critics in the Commons in 1624: Willson, *Privy Councillors*, p. 251.

If in fact the Williams trial brought Laud and Heath into conflict, it was not the only case that did so. It may have been their overall relationship as Star Chamber judges that resulted in Heath's dismissal. The two often clashed in Star Chamber, most dramatically over sentences, for Heath tended to propose the lightest fines of any judge, Laud, the heaviest. When in February 1633 Henry Sherfield, recorder of Salsibury, was tried in Star Chamber for having broken a stained-glass church window that he considered idolatrous, Laud demanded that the fine be fixed at £1,000, while Heath suggested that 500 marks was a more appropriate penalty. October 1633 found Laud recommending a £2,000 fine, Heath £1,000, for a man who had been convicted of exporting forty tons of fuller's earth, and they repeated their respective suggestions the following January, this time in reference to a builder who was responsible for unlicenced construction. February 1634 brought William Prynne's first trial. Heath suggested a £4,000 fine for Prynne, certainly not a negligible amount, but Laud demanded that the figure be set at £10,000. During Heath's last few months as a judge in Star Chamber his recommendations for fines seemed to fall ever further from Laud's. Shortly after the court passed sentence on Prynne, Peter Apsley was brought before it, charged with having had the temerity to challenge the duke of Northumberland to a duel. Laud recommended a £10,000 fine, but Heath advised £1,000, a suggestion that had no backers. Sir Robert stood alone again in June, when at the trial of two petty officials who were accused of having charged excessive fees, he claimed that the prosecution had not even proven its case. The other judges not only disagreed with him, but set the fine at £3,000, the highest figure recommended, and Laud stated that if anyone had asked for a higher fine he would have supported him.[39]

While Laud and Heath tended to be at opposite extremes in the sentences they recommended, the final judgement tended

[39] *ST*, III, cols. 541 – 3; SP 16/248/7, SP 16/259/36, SP 16/259/71, SP 16/270/39; S. R. Gardiner (ed.), 'Documents relating to the Proceedings against William Prynne, in 1634 and 1637', Camden Society, *Publications*, new series, 18 (1877), 17 – 20, 26 – 8. Heath and Laud had also differed in at least two cases in 1632: S. R. Gardiner (ed.), 'Reports of Cases in the Courts of Star Chamber and High Commission', Camden Society, *Publications*, new series, 39 (1886), 151 – 2, 169 – 70, 172 – 3.

to be closer to the archbishop's position than to Sir Robert's.[40] Given this fact, and given that Laud did not have in most cases the personal stake that he had in Williams's, one might wonder whether he was much concerned by Heath's proposals for sentences. In all probability, he was. Laud consistently called for harsh penalties because he had a tendency to see every offence in the gravest light possible. His logic was on display in February 1634, when John Goodenough appeared in Star Chamber, charged with suborning witnesses at an earlier trial. Moreover, the judges were told, Goodenough had used Scripture in an attempt to demonstrate to prospective witnesses that perjury was no sin. This revelation brought Laud to his feet. He demanded that a £10,000 fine be levied, and he fumed: 'Goodenoughe would overthrowe all foundation of lawe justice and Religion, For Choak and smoother the truth and farewell all religion and Justice.'[41] By his progression of logic, subornation came to approximate treason. Such a connection was not out of character for Laud, since he saw traitors everywhere, chipping away at the foundations of Church and State. Meanwhile, in Star Chamber he saw Heath, making light of treason.

Laud was particularly sensitive to any challenges to Church authority, and often he perceived the judges as being challengers. So he did in a noteworthy case in early 1631. Sir Giles Alington was called before High Commission for having married his niece. Seeking refuge, he obtained a prohibition out of Common Pleas. High Commission ignored this writ and proceeded with the trial, eventually fining Alington £10,000, but Laud was nevertheless incensed that Common Pleas had interfered. Before the Council, he burst out: 'If this prohibition had taken place, I hope my Lord's Grace of Canterbury would have excommunicated throughout his province all the judges

---

[40] Generally speaking, the Star Chamber judges who knew the law as a vocation (i.e., the two chief justices and the lord keeper) were more lenient than the rest. The clerics, notably Laud, tended to be harsh in proposing fines, though usually they did not support corporal punishment. Among the lay privy councillors during the early 1630s, Sir Francis Cottington was probably the most consistently severe in the sentences he proposed.

[41] BL, Add. 11,764, f. 7. In this case, no other judge proposed even half the fine that Laud did for Goodenough; indeed, most of the judges concentrated their fire on Goodenough's three co-defendants, who were charged with having illegally sold saltpetre: *ibid.*, ff. 5 – 7.

who should have had a hand therein.'[42] Laud's reaction to the decision by Common Pleas to issue a prohibition in the Alington case reflected his general sense that the judges were a danger to the Church.

Heath played no part in that affair but while a judge he angered Laud by opposing a campaign that was directed by the latter, to regain lands that had been taken from the Church during the Reformation. Heath's attitude towards this campaign was amply evident in his response to attempts by the see of Chichester to reclaim the manor of Selsey, a Church property until it had been seized by the crown early in the reign of Elizabeth. Mountague, who as bishop of Chichester had launched a suit to recover the manor, also reported the outcome to Laud. Heath, he complained, had been instrumental in causing Common Pleas to reject the suit. Worse still, the chief justice had judged not only the case at hand, but like initiatives that the Church might take in the future: 'Justice Heath openly answered that if way should be given in this case (his Conscience I thinke telling him, it was but right) they should be troubled with hundreds of Cases in like nature. And better a mischeife, it seems then an inconvenience, better God the Church, Justice should suffer, then injust actions be reversed.'[43] Mountague wrote on Friday, 12 September 1634. Heath was dismissed the following day. Laud spent the weekend of 13 – 14 September with the king.[44] Is it possible that Mountague's report so angered the archbishop that he demanded Heath's dismissal? It certainly is, assuming that the letter was delivered early enough to influence Laud's thinking. Even if it was not, Laud may well have known about Heath's statement on Selsey. In any case, he probably knew that Heath opposed the initiative to reclaim Church lands, and he was not one to tolerate opposition to the Church's, or his, policies.

It is quite possible, however, that Laud had additional reasons for seeking Heath's dismissal. Sensitive as he was to criticism of his policies, he was even more concerned when his own place seemed endangered. All around him he saw conspirators, bent on his destruction. He had real enemies, notably Weston, but

---

[42] Pory quotes Laud in a letter to Stuteville, 20 May 1631: Birch, II, 120. Laud added that, had the archbishop not acted, he would have excommunicated the judges within his diocese.

[43] SP 16/274/18.

[44] *Works of Laud*, VII, 88; SP 16/274/17.

any courtier whom he did not know to be a friend he distrusted, and Heath was not his friend.

The summer of 1634 was critical for Laud. In early August, after weeks of languishing, Noy died. As attorney-general, he had generally supported Laud and his policies, and the archbishop, a man not given to grief, lamented in his diary: 'I have lost a dear friend of him, and the Church the greatest she had of his condition, since she needed any such.'[45] To make matters worse, Weston and his clique mounted a formidable challenge to Laud's hold over the attorney-generalship by putting forward their own candidate, Sir John Bankes, the prince's attorney. Bankes had no friends in Laud's camp, and Wentworth responded sourly when Sir Francis Cottingham praised him: 'You say well, Sir *John Banks* will make an Attorney for once; take my Warrant for it, he will have something of the indifferent in him, betwixt the Sow's Ear and the Silken Purse.'[46] Anxious to prevent Weston's man from obtaining the attorney's place, Laud joined Henrietta Maria in supporting the candidacy of Sir John Finch, the queen's attorney. Contention grew; on 11 September a Court observer reported, 'some clasheings have beene betwixt Sir John Bankes and S. John Finche, about the atturnyship. which his majestie hath appointed to heare'.[47] Charles soon resolved the issue, by

---

[45] *Works of Laud*, III, 221.

[46] Radcliffe, I, 294. Significantly, Cottington was in Weston's camp: Alexander, 193 – 5; M. J. Havran, *Caroline Courtier: The Life of Lord Cottington* (London, 1973), chs. 10 – 11.

[47] Reginald Burdin to Sir John Lambe, SP 16/274/17. On 2 Aug. 1634 'Hombre Fiel' reported to Sir Robert Phelips that: 'The Queen and her officers (L. of Holland, and Dorset, &.c.) be verie earnest for her atturney, by whom the archbishop hath also bin courted lately': *HMC, Third Report*, 283. Certainly, Laud was not Finch's only backer. In particular, one wonders if Henrietta Maria, anxious to find a place for Finch, may have played a part in Heath's dismissal. Little is known about her relationship with Sir Robert. He seems to have felt lukewarm toward her, perhaps because of her religion. In a prayer that he wrote in 1646 he asked God to bless her and 'make her to be truly a helper' to Charles (Egerton 2982, f. 79), implying thereby that she had not been a true helper in the past. He may have served as the queen's solicitor during the late 1630s: Hirst, pp. 70, 82. If so, his office may reflect her favour, but possibly she felt differently in Sept. 1634. In any case, although she engaged in Court intrigue, she was not nearly so interventionist as Laud, so it is unlikely that she helped to engineer Heath's removal.

making Bankes his attorney. The Laudian faction was not set down entirely, however, for the man who replaced Heath as chief justice was Finch.

While Laud may not have been satisfied with the trade-off that Charles had engineered, viewed in a larger context the victory was clearly his. Earlier that summer Richardson, long his antagonist, had been suspended, though not removed, from the bench.[48] At about the time Heath was dismissed, Shelton was forced to surrender his patent, probably not because, as Clarendon would have it, he was 'an old, useless illiterate person' — though this characterisation may be fair enough — but rather to make way for Sir Edward Littleton, recorder of London and counsel for Oxford, Laud's preserve.[49] With Littleton as solicitor-general, Laud was less fearful of the man who occupied the senior law office. Weston, the archbishop's great enemy, had been out-flanked.

Reviewing the evidence, it is possible to deduce the main factors in Heath's dismissal. Laud, who may not have been warm to him even before he became a judge, was probably antagonised by some of Heath's stands in Common Pleas, especially those that seemed to reflect hostility to his schemes for increasing the power and wealth of the Church. That Heath often stood against him in Star Chamber, notably in the Williams case, may have antagonised him further. The death of Noy and the prospect that the next attorney-general might be of Weston's retinue made him fear that the legal machinery of the nation would soon be in the hands of his enemy, and to forestall such an eventuality he determined to oust Heath. On 12 or 13 September he presented to the king evidence that Heath, while

---

[48] Cockburn, *Assizes*, p. 233. Richardson apparently feared that even worse was to come, and he and his patrons tried to make peace with the Laudian faction. On 3 Oct. 1634 Arundel wrote to Wentworth 'for your Lordships most humble servant of the Kings Bench he holdes his owne & was with me even nowe, and is the olde man': Strafford Papers, 14 (174).

[49] Clarendon, II, 110; Foss, VI, 346. According to Hutton (diary, YCPH microfilm, f. 71), Littleton was also involved, with Bankes and Finch, in the contest for tha attorney-generalship. Since Shelton had committed no offence of the sort that might justify his displacement, and since law officers held their offices during good behaviour, he was able to bargain for the solicitor's patent, and he opted to become a king's counsellor at large, with his former status and profits, rather than be appointed a king's serjeant or puisne justice: George Gerrard to Wentworth, 10 Nov. 1634, Strafford Letters, 14 (211); Croke, *Third Report*, 375 – 76; Hutton diary, f. 72.

attorney-general, had cheated the crown. The particular case, or cases, of corruption that he exposed must have been grave, for Charles's reaction was bitter. At first Heath faced the frightening possibility of being tried in Star Chamber. Only his abject plea saved him from a fate that might have been far worse than dismissal. Even as Heath begged for mercy, Laud was moving to solidify his hold over the legal apparatus of England. In all probability it was he who persuaded Charles to force Shelton out and to replace him with Littleton. By the close of summer he had turned back Weston's challenge, and his position was stronger than ever. But the real loser was Heath.

Post-mortem

While Laud engineered Heath's dismissal and Charles effected it, Sir Robert himself was ultimately responsible. There were two rules that a courtier was wise to observe. Firstly, he was not to enrich himself at the expense of his superiors. Secondly, he was to maintain friends who were more powerful than his enemies. There rules were known to every courtier who was even moderately perceptive. Heath undoubtedly knew them. Nevertheless, he violated both, and this error cost him his place.

The opportunities for an important crown officer to acquire wealth were many, and in fact the Court expected him to profit from his position. However, he was also expected to look after the best interests of his superiors, particularly the king. Almost any misuse of power would be forgiven at Court if it appeared that by his action he had sought the king's advantage. In February 1637 it was revealed that Bankes had regularly permitted exporters of coin to pay a heavy fine, rather than undergo a trial in Star Chamber, as prescribed by proclamation. When his policy was exposed the outcry was so intense that many observers expected him to be removed from office. But Charles was apparently impressed by the fact that the scheme, illegal though it was, had helped to fill the royal coffers, so he stood by Bankes: 'He also acknowledged the faithful and good service of his attorney, telling his attorney that he was his friend, and although he had many enemies, yet, so long as he was his friend, they could do him no harm.'[50] During his time as

---

[50] Rossingham to Puckering, 14 Feb. 1637: Birch, II, 277. Weston's death had by then deprived Bankes of his main patron.

attorney-general, Heath, like Bankes, helped to design and to execute policies that were intended to boost the king's income. But he was clearly not above seeking profit at the expense of the crown, and he pursued his enrichment fully aware of the consequences that lay in store if his activities were exposed. Why he took the risk, and why he violated the trust of a king whom he genuinely revered, cannot be known. But his desire for gain was always intense.

Heath also violated the second rule of survival, for he failed to secure himself in the world of patronage. Although he won Carlisle as a patron in the wake of Buckingham's death, he did not seek an alternative, even when it became clear that the earl was too indolent and too indifferent to Court intrigue to be of much use to him. He retained his friends at Court, but the closest of them, Conway, was not powerful enough to protect him, and in any case he died in 1631. Perhaps he thought that the king was his friend and that, as Charles himself told Bankes, 'although he had many enemies, yet, so long as he was his friend, they could do him no harm'. But the king, although favourably inclined toward Heath, never had a deep affection for him. Heath needed to look elsewhere, to a high-ranking courtier who needed his support and would and could provide protection in return. The obvious choices were Weston and Laud. For too long, however, Heath held back.[51] Perhaps he hoped that, by courting neither, he would antagonise neither. If so, he miscalculated, at least in Laud's case. Perhaps the fact that he occupied high office may have caused him to think that he no longer needed a patron, particularly after his elevation to the bench fulfilled his ultimate ambition. Whatever his reasoning, he unwisely remained aloof from the world of the client, and his mistake cost him dearly. It is possible that by 1633 he had come to realise his error and was attempting to ingratiate himself with Laud, but that the prelate, by then decidedly hostile, rebuffed him. Now recognising the precariousness of his position, he appealed to Wentworth for patronage, hoping

---

[51] It is possible that Heath was close to Weston. The lord treasurer did come to his assistance during his crisis of February 1629 (above, pp. 172 – 3). Also, Weston (along with Coventry) served as Heath's patron at his creation as a serjeant: Baker, *Serjeants*, 439. However, the lack of evidence of an alliance between the two, or of a master-man relationship, in a period when Heath's life is fairly well documented, suggests that if there was a link, it was tenuous.

to win his way into the Laudian faction through the good graces of the lord deputy. Wentworth was, however, too far from the Court to be able to serve him well in a crisis, such as the dismissal, and their relationship was still tenuous in September 1634, so it is unlikely that he would have intervened in any case. When Heath decided to seek a new patron, he did well to look toward Laud. His mistake lay in waiting too long before making his move.

The rules for survival at Court were deceptively simple. If a courtier did not cheat his superiors, and if he maintained a strong position in the hierarchy of patronage, he would probably thrive. However, in an environment where officials were left free to enrich themselves at the expense of private parties and where supervision was weak, reducing the chances of detection, neither the moral atmosphere not the prospect of exposure was likely to discourage the sort of activities that brought down Heath.[52] Furthermore, winning a great patron was never easy. To be successful, a pursuer of patronage had to be dedicated, as well as skilful. And a courtier who thought his place secure was likely to be inspired by pride to give up his role of protégé. Heath was not alone in ignoring the rules, for human nature made them hard to follow. But the fact that many behaved as did he did not reduce the penalty for transgression, nor did it reduce his pain.

---

[52] Heath, for that matter, displayed a fair degree of resistance to temptation — otherwise, he would have earned even more while a law officer than he actually did — though sometimes he clearly gave in; see pp. 103 – 5.

8

Pound Foolish

In the petition that he presented to Charles on hearing of his dismissal, Heath begged the king to 'look back with an eye of pitty uppon the deplorable estate of him, his wife & five sonns, who are all ruined, if your Majesty shall totally withdrawe your favour'. The circumstances dictated that an emotive appeal was in order, but Heath was not, in fact, exaggerating the precariousness of his financial condition. He was then deeply in debt, and while his lucrative offices had previously served to secure credit, he knew that once word of his fall spread, the duns would swoop.

It was his own miscalculations that had brought him to this state. During his years in public service he had also enjoyed a private career as a speculator, in colonisation, in land improvement, in business projects of many kinds. His ventures had been as varied as they had been unsuccessful. Because of them, he had lost a fortune, for his years in high office alone, 1621 – 34, had seen him earn perhaps £200,000, this at a time when a typical Kentish gentleman could expect an annual income of perhaps £270.[1]

Income

In Heath's England, the legal profession was a high road to wealth. Even as a fledgling utter barrister John Heath earned

---

[1] Everitt, pp. 41, 328 – 9 (a table of the numbers and wealth of the ruling classes). A typical knight earned £873 p.a.: *ibid*. The Kentish landowners were comparatively wealthy, because their property lay near the London markets: Gordon Batho, 'Land-owners in England', *The Agrarian History of England and Wales*, IV, ed. Joan Thirsk (Cambridge, 1967), 292.

£500 annually, and there is no reason to imagine that his father, at a comparable stage in his career, had made much less.[2] Legal studies also provided entrance to a vast range of offices, many of which were highly remunerative, if not prestigious. Sir Robert's place as trustee of the King's Bench clerkship, for example, brought him £500 – £800 each year, and he retained that post even while a law officer, surrendering it only in 1629.[3]

As recorder of London, Heath's annual salary was only £80, but fees raised his total income to several times that figure. Shortly before Fleetwood left office in December 1591, he reported to Lord Burghley that his income as recorder amounted to:

> cc£ p Anno viz lxxx£ for the Fee of the office vi£ xiiis iiiid for the presentinge of the Sherifes at the Eschetor barr . . . And the knowledginge of Statutes of the Staple, knowledginge of deades, takinge of Recoveries, & Lastly, the takeinge of recognizances with diverse other casualties the which doe amount layinge all together to the yerely valewe of fower hundreth markes.[4]

In calculating his income Fleetwood did not include the fees that he received as a private lawyer, even though the prestige and influence associated with his office undoubtedly helped to boost his practice. Nor, wisely, did he include in his estimate any gifts that he received for favours. By the time Heath took office, the average yearly income of the recorder, counting his practice, probably approached £1,000, and the gifts that were bestowed

---

[2] John mentioned his pre-war income in the course of a petition to Clarendon, c. 1660: Egerton 2979, f. 32. W. R. Prest examines the nature of lawyers' fees and concludes that in c. 1600 a lawyer could expect an annual income of £400 from his practice: 'Counsellors' Fees and Earnings in the Age of Sir Edward Coke', *Legal Records and the Historian*, ed. Baker, 165 – 84.

[3] Aylmer, pp. 305 – 6; the surrender is enrolled in C. 54/2813. The value of the clerkship is discussed by Chamberlain in two letters to Carleton, 7 Nov. 1618 and 3 Feb. 1621: McClure, II, 181, 337 – 8. During the 1620s, Heath probably executed the office by deputy. Lawyers believed that their profession might serve to promote not only themselves but their families. Manningham claims: 'The posterity of Lawyers hath more flourished then that either of the Clergy or Citisens': *The Diary of John Manningham of the Middle Temple 1602 – 1603*, ed. R. P. Sorlien (Hanover, N.H., 1976), p. 78.

[4] Lansdowne 67, no. 91.

on Heath by the corporation and the companies in 1619 – 20, because of his efforts to reach an accommodation in the concealments business, undoubtedly added hundreds of pounds to the total.[5]

The only hard statistic available in assessing the income of the law officers is their basic annual salary, £51 for the solicitor-general, £81 for the attorney. But beyond that, Bacon, who occupied both offices, provides important estimates of income. In 1608, he estimated that his place as solicitor was worth £1,000 per annum, his practice £1,200.[6] Heath presumably profited at least as much while solicitor, especially since the favours that were his to provide were of great consequence and therefore worth much to his clients. In all probability, Sir Robert's public service and private practice during his term as solicitor-general provided him with a total annual income, including salary, fees, and gifts, of £2,000-£4,000.

In February 1616 Bacon, who was then attorney-general, informed the king that he considered his office to be 'honestly worth 6000£ *per annum*'.[7] But he appears to have had in mind only the sum, mainly based on fees, that he received for performing his official duties. Not included were the fees that he received from his burgeoning law practice, so much more lucrative because of his office, and the gifts that were presented to him in return for favours.[8] Contemporaries did not ignore these sources in judging the income that attached to his office. Moreover, many believed the attorneys-general to be a rapacious breed, clever enough and unscrupulous enough to take advantage of every opportunity to make money, honestly or

---

[5] See pp. 33 – 4.

[6] Spedding, IV, 86. According to patent, Shelton (and presumably Heath) was to receive £20 p.a. out of the Exchequer and £70 6s 8d p.a. from the Inner Temple and the Middle Temple; in addition, the Temple was to provide him with use of a mansion house: Wilde, f. 5. That the solicitor got some regular salary from non-government institutions was not exceptional, for the attorney-general received £10 p.a. from London: Lincoln's Inn Library, Ms. 582, p. 6. The base salaries of law officers are noted in *Copy of a Ms. Entitled 'A True Collection . . . of all . . . Offices and Fees* (London, 1606), pp. 4 – 5.

[7] Spedding, V, 242. A schedule of the attorney's fees, as they stood in 1693, is included among Sir Edward Ward's papers: Lincoln's Inn Library, Ms. 582, pp. 5 – 6.

[8] See pp. 100 – 2.

dishonestly. During his time in office Coke acquired a reputation for being exceptionally avaricious and exceptionally successful in using his office as a source of wealth. According to John Aubrey 'Old John Tussell (that was my attorney) has told me that [Coke] gott a hundred thousand pounds in one yeare, viz. 1° Jacobi, being then Attorney-Generall. His advice was that every man of Estate (right or wrong) should sue-out his Pardon, which cost 5 punds which belonged to him'.[9] The figure of £100,000 is undoubtedly inflated, but Coke did profit greatly from the attorney-generalship. Writing in 1600, Wilson commented 'the Queen's atturney . . . within this 10 yeeres in my knowlege was not able to dispend above 100£ a yeare and now by his owne lands, his coyne, and his office he may dispend betwixt 12 and 14 thousand'.[10] Wilson's estimate rings true, and it is possible that in exceptional years like 1603 Coke earned, hence was able to 'dispend', considerably more than £12,000 – £14,000. As for Heath, a fairly conservative estimate of his income while attorney, including the sums that he received for favours and for private legal services, would be £10,000 – £12,000 per annum.

Elevation to the bench enriched him still further. According to Wilson 'the 12 cheefe judges and the multitude of sergents . . . are most of them counted men of 20,000 or 30,000£ yearly'.[11] By 'sergents' Wilson probably meant king's serjeants only, but even so his estimate of income is far too high. Nor did the puisne judges receive an amount even close to £20,000. But it is possible that the chief justices did earn £20,000 – £30,000 annually. Their huge income was derived primarily from fees, for neither chief justice enjoyed a base yearly salary of more than £150. Besides fees, they could depend on a steady stream of gifts, in cash or in kind, usually small but sometimes substantial. With these gifts, litigants hoped to persuade the judges to move their cases up or down on the dockets, as their needs dictated, or to grant them some advantage in pleading.

[9] *Brief Lives*, p. 67.
[10] 'The State of England', 25.
[11] *Ibid*.

Only rulings were not for sale.[12] All judges profited from gifts and fees, but it was the chief justices who received the most. It was a truly remarkable source of wealth that Heath lost on 13 September 1634.

Apart from his offices, Heath's main source of income was his land. One can only guess how valuable his property was to him, for of the more than twenty manors that he held at some time, particulars exist for only a few, and even less is known of his other properties, such as tenements. It may be said, however, that during the 1630s he was annually drawing about £300 apiece from two of his manors, Broadway and Soham, rents accounting for more than ninety per cent of the total and timber sales, fees from manorial courts, and other incidentals accounting for the balance.[13] Broadway and Soham were both large, but they were marshy, so it is not likely that they were his two most profitable properties. Taking this into account, it seems altogether probable that during the time when Heath's landholdings were greatest, roughly, 1625 – 37, the annual income that he derived from his properties amounted to £2,000 – £3,000. In addition to that, the same period saw him deriving significant income from various business ventures, as well as from lesser sources, like patents.

The evidence suggests that during his lifetime Heath earned in the vicinity of £250,000. But however much he earned, he spent more.

Associates

There were, of course, those who were anxious to help him spend his money. While material on Heath's business associa-

---

12 Jones, *Politics and the Bench*, p. 37; Cockburn, *Assizes*, pp. 54 – 7. Several schedules of judges fees — including fees that were seldom levied, involving rare actions — are extant, including, notably, Coventry's *A Perfect and Exact Direction to All Those that Desire to Know the True and Just Fees of . . . the Court of Common Pleas* (London, 1641), pp. 90 – 5. The giving of gifts to judges, as well as to other officials, was usually accepted as being a fair price for favours. On 4 Dec. 1638 Edward Heath wrote to John, relative to a suit in Chancery: 'I would have mony offered for I beleive it will not bee donne without it': U. of I., Heath Papers. Nevertheless, a body of Englishmen opposed the trade in gifts for favours, especially to judges, and the Long Parliament forbade the taking of gifts by judges, limiting them instead to a fixed income of £1,000 p.a.: Cockburn, *Assizes*, p. 56.

13 The most precise account of income from Soham is Egerton 2987, f. 67; on Broadway, Egerton 3007, f. 24.

tions prior to 1610 is sparse, a sizeable number of bonds dating from the 1610s identify his principal partners in that decade. Many names appear with Heath's on the bonds, but the eight occurring most often, in decending order of frequency, are Simon Chamber, George Sheirs, Sir Thomas Watson, Sir Edward More, George Cole, Robert Seliard, Robert Titchbourne, and Thomas Warr.[14]

At least seven of Heath's primary associates were gentlemen, Warr's status being unknown. Most were born in Kent, or at least were generally associated with some Kentish community during the 1610s, Watson with Halsted, Cole with Sutton, Seliard with Brasted and Edenbridge, Titchbourne with Edenbridge, and Warr with Hestercombe. Sheirs lived for many years in Sleyfield, Surrey, a Heath family stronghold and for long the principal residence of Sir Robert's father. More, while mainly associated with Odiham, Hampshire, during the early seventeenth century maintained a residence at Crabbet, in the parish of Worth, Sussex. Sir Robert and his father also had close links with Crabbet, and in fact most of Heath's children were born there. Of Heath's main partners, only Chamber had no known link with Kent, Sussex, or Surrey, being instead from Exton, Rutland, but not even he was much removed from the centre of Heath's domain, for he maintained a residence in London.[15]

By training, most of Heath's associates were lawyers, although ironically none of them was a member of the Inner Temple. Chamber and Seliard were associated with Clifford's Inn, and they may have been there when Heath was a student at the inn. Cole studied there as well, but long before Heath arrived he had moved on to the Middle Temple. More was also a Middle Templar, as were Watson and Warr. Sheirs may have had some legal training, but the offices that he is known to have held do not suggest that he made a career of the law, and Titchbourne certainly did not, for he was at an early age apprenticed to a Skinner, gaining the freedom of the company in 1594.[16]

---

[14] Most of the bonds are in SG, Top. Mss., under eight heads, esp. 'Rutland, Exton' and 'Hampshire, Odiham'. The rest are in Unbd. Mss., 'Heath', or the Close Rolls.

[15] All information on the social status and geographical associations of Heath's partners is drawn from the extant bonds.

[16] J. F. Wadmore, *Some Account of the Worshipful Company of Skinners* (London, 1902), p. 174; H. A. C. Sturgess (comp.), *Register of Admissions to the Honourable Society of the Middle Temple* (London, 1949), I, 34, 46, 49, 66.

Several of Heath's business associates at some time sought success through the Court. As a servant of the earl of Bedford, Chamber oversaw several of his lord's enterprises, notably the stamping of farthing tokens. His only crown office, a minor one, he gained in 1626, possibly on Heath's recommendation, and held until his death in 1637. Sheirs was slightly more successful. In June 1599 he gained a reversion as yeoman apothecary. In October 1603 James appointed him perfumer to the king, queen, and prince, and less than two months later Sheirs became apothecary to the king's household. His progress ended there, but he retained his two offices at least until the mid-1620s. Warr seems not to have held any appointment until 1632, when, probably at the instance of Heath, he received a share in a minor Common Pleas office. Although Chamber, Sheirs, and Warr all profited from their places, Sheirs especially, the most successful courtier among Heath's major partners was undoubtedly Watson. In about 1590 he entered the service of Sir George Carey, and he soon found other prominent patrons as well, notably Cecil. On being appointed treasurer of the wars in Ireland in 1602, Carey departed for Ireland, taking Watson with him as his deputy. His death in 1603 induced Watson to return to Court, where in 1605 he gained, probably with Cecil's aid, the coveted office of teller of the Exchequer. The post of teller, which he retained for the rest of his life, was highly remunerative, and he became an avid speculator, particularly in land, numbering among his partners not only Heath but such notable courtiers and businessmen as Cranfield and Sir Arthur Ingram. Watson also became a minor favourite, and in June 1618 he hosted a feast for the king, an honour, although an expensive one.[17]

In 1610 most of Heath's partners were, like himself, in their thirties. Cole and Watson were approaching fifty, however, and More was nearly sixty. A few, at least, were long-standing acquaintances. Seliard and Titchbourne, relatives by marriage, had quite possibly been his childhood playmates. More was Cobham's brother-in-law, and Heath may well have made his acquaintance when he and his father were members of the lord

---

[17] On Chamber, CD 1621, VII, 358, 414, 430; C. 66/2748. On Sheirs, Calendar of State Papers, Domestic Series, of the Reign of Elizabeth, 1598 – 1601, p. 219; CSPD, James I, 1603 – 1610, 38, 48; L. G. Matthews, The Royal Apothecaries (London, 1967), pp. 78, 84 – 6, 91, 177. On Warr, HMC, Fourth Report, 22. On Watson, HMC, Laing I, 93, and Sackville [Knole], 144; SP 14/36/46; John Nichols, The Progresses . . . of James the First (London, 1828), III, 482.

lieutenant's retinue. Cole and Warr he had probably met at the Middle Temple. Heath may first have encountered Watson at Court, but it is more likely that he had met him through Cole, Watson's relative by marriage.[18] Sheirs he had perhaps come to know at Sleyfield; Chamber, at Clifford's Inn.

However he met them, Heath followed a pattern of choosing his business associates. He had a clear preference for men from his own region, western Kent in particular. Titchbourne and Seliard were natural partners, being relatives by marriage. No blood relation belonged to Heath's circle of associates, at least during the 1610s, but perhaps no family member who had money for speculation shared his particular interests. In seeking out partners, Heath seems, naturally enough, to have looked to wealthy men, men like Sheirs and, even more, Watson. Heath may also have valued business experience in his partners, and Watson, at least, had a fair background. With more certainly it may be said that he looked to the legal profession as a source of associates. In part, the preponderance of lawyers among his principal partners undoubtedly reflects the fact that during the 1610s the Temple was the centre of his life in London, so his early contacts were most likely to be lawyers. Furthermore, he felt an affinity for men who shared his vocation. Finally, however, he was quite possibly moved to associate with lawyers because he recognised what the law could do. The world of business and of land speculation was dominated by legal instruments, such as contracts, and lawyers knew how to manipulate these instruments to the advantage of themselves and of their partners.

During the 1620s Heath's associations changed. Watson died in 1622, More in 1623, Cole in 1624.[19] Sir Robert remained close to the others throughout the decade, and in fact even into the 1640s he counted Sheirs, Seliard, and Warr among his friends.[20] However, as the 1620s wore on he associated with them less and less in business ventures. His large income now enabled him to venture into many enterprises alone. Furthermore, by about 1626 he had become involved with another partner, one who

---

[18] J. B. Burke (comp.), 'The Genealogie or Pedegree of . . . Sir William Cole', *Miscellanea Genealogica et Heraldica*, 2 (1876), 240 – 2; K. W. Murray (ed.), 'Extracts from a Seventeenth-Century Note-Book', *The Genealogist*, new series, 33 (1917), 63.

[19] PCC wills: 3 Savile, 53 Swann, 75 Byrde.

[20] As reflected in the Heath family correspondence. In his will, drawn up on May 1637, Sheirs named Heath an overseer: Surrey Record Office, 65/1/525.

was to be his principal associate until the late 1630s. This was Sir Cornelius Vermuyden, the noted Dutch engineer. Vermuyden's apparent attraction for Heath was his unparallelled expertise in land drainage. He arrived on the Court scene in the mid-1620s, to find in Sir Robert a man who was dreaming of the profits that might be won through the drainage of inundated lands and mines. Both Heath's dream and his association with Vermuyden were to cost him dear.[21]

An improving landlord

During his adulthood, Heath maintained several residences. Apparently the first home that he and Margaret knew as man and wife was Crabbet House, which may have made them neighbours of More. The next centre of their life together was Mitcham, Surrey, where they lived until about 1633.[22] When they decided to leave Mitcham, Sir Robert may at first have considered moving the family to his great manor of Colliweston, in Northamptonshire.[23] Instead, however, he established his principal residence at Brasted Place, which he had purchased from William Crow in May 1619 for £497, in a transaction that also cleared a debt Crow owed him.[24]

Besides his principal residence, Heath maintained several other households. When business kept him in London he had his quarters at the Inner Temple, but more luxurious living was usually close at hand, particularly during his years of wealth and power. During his time as attorney-general, for example, he rented a mansion house and eighteen acres of surrounding land

---

[21] On the partnership, L. E. Harris, Vermuyden's best biographer, comments 'Heath undoubtedly was a useful friend to Vermuyden [and] his friendship had a very definite value . . . And yet, . . . Vermuyden was prepared to jettison any loyalty to that friendship in his own interests': *Vermuyden and the Fens: A Study of Sir Cornelius Vermuyden and the Great Level* (London, 1953), p. 58.

[22] 'Liber E. H.', 158, 163; *Visitations of Sussex 1633–4*, p. 134. See also p. 62.

[23] In Feb. 1633 Guy Palmer, Heath's agent, wrote him that he was glad to hear that he was building a new house at Colliweston and was 'hopinge you intend to settell there': Kent Archives Office, U55 E100. However, the house was probably intended for Edward; see p. 66.

[24] Kent Archives Office, U55 T38.

in Clapham.[25] Even during the late 1630s, when the state of his finances counselled thrift, he was to be found paying the considerable annual rent of £45 for a residence in St Martin Ludgate.[26] Outside London, and virtually throughout England, there were numerous properties, especially manor houses, that he had to keep up.

The cost of maintaining his various properties must have been huge. In Heath's mansion at Brasted Place, the dining hall alone contained in 1647 'a large table, two square tables, a couch, two great armed chayres, twelve high backt Chayres, two low backt Chayres, Fowre high stooles All of Redd cloath trimmed with yellow silke fringh with yellow bayes covers to them, a pair of Iron doggs [and] A weather glass in a wooden case'.[27] Presumably the residence also housed Heath's collection of plate and jewels, which in January 1633 was worth well in excess of £1,000.[28] Manor houses on Heath's other properties would not have been nearly so well-appointed, but they had to be maintained and the upkeep was considerable.

Brasted Place served Heath principally as a place of residence, as had the properties at Mitcham and at Crabbet. Extant accounts, which are especially full for Brasted, suggest that on the manors where he maintained his domicile, he was apparently content to accept the modest rents that had been traditionally paid. By not challenging the status quo he helped to maintain a tranquil environment for his family, as his choice left the tenants reasonably content. But serenity had its price, quite literally. With inflation cutting sharply into the value of rents, and with much land still in copyhold and therefore not normally subject to rent increases, Heath and his fellow-landlords looked desperately for a way to boost their income. The most obvious course was to charge higher rents, even on unimproved lands, although they then ran the risk of so angering the tenantry that violence might result. With regard to most of his manors, Heath was ready to take that risk. Reviewing the records of Broadway, he noted in September 1638: 'There are Demesnes 640 acres in lease for 17 yeares yet to come at the rent of 180£ p annum . . . The revertion of the

25 Minet Library, London, Surrey Deeds, 9521.
26 T. C. Dale (ed.), *The Inhabitants of London in 1638* (London, 1931), I, 127.
27 Drawn from an inventory: Egerton 2983, f. 85.
28 Assessment based on a schedule drawn by Heath, two copies of which survive: Kent Archives Office, U55 E104; SBT, DR 98/1289.

demesnes after the expiration of the lease is worth at least 50£ p annum above the present rent.'[29] Since Heath purchased most of his large manors, including Broadway, after he was fifty, since many of the leases that had been negotiated by previous landlords were years away from expiration, and since the civil war intervened, he was almost certainly not able to bring his rentals policy into effect on a broad scale. Still, he laid plans.[30]

Landlords might improve their financial situation through the simple expedient of rack-renting, but the real path to profit was improvement. Enclosure was, of course, the standard method of improving land, loudly though it might be denounced by social reformers, violently though it might be resisted by peasants.[31] Heath was a strong proponent of the policy, and in fact usually moved so quickly to enclose after purchasing a new property

[29] Egerton 3007, f. 20. The practice of rack-renting was widespread: Cliffe, pp. 33–4. However, it was probably more common for landlords to sharply increase the entry fee: A. B. Appleby, *Famine in Tudor and Stuart England* (Stanford, 1978), pp. 71–83; Cliffe, pp. 38–41. Heath may well have done this, but no proof exists.

[30] In the case of North Inglesby, Lincolnshire, however, he had time to work. In 1609, shortly after having leased the 800-acre manor from the king, Heath completed a survey — the earliest extant document entirely in his hand — in which he calculated the total rents to be £294 3s 6d p.a. Shortly after reclaiming the manor, in the wake of the Restoration (see ch. 9, n 59), Edward prepared a survey that showed the total annual rent to be £556 6s 8d. Both surveys are included in Lincolnshire Archives Office, Lind. Dep. 15/6. It is fair to assume that Sir Robert was responsible for much of the increase.

[31] Of course, enclosure came in several forms, and often the tenants were amenable to it: Cliffe, pp. 35–8. During the early Stuart period, there was still widespread fear that enclosure caused depopulation, and the attitude was sometimes reflected in parliament: J. R. Kent, 'Social Attitudes of Members of Parliament 1590–1624', unpub. Ph.D. dissertation (London, 1971), 223–4, 253–4. During the 1630s, particularly 1635–40, the Privy Council directed a vigorous campaign against landowners whose enclosures were thought to cause depopulation, and many of the landlords were fined: E. C. K. Gonner, 'The Progress of Enclosure during the Seventeenth Century', *The English Historical Review*, 23 (1908), 486–7. Among the landlords investigated was Edward Heath, who in Oct. and Dec. 1639 begged John to help him get further details on a case that saw him charged with causing depopulation through enclosure: U. of I., Heath Papers; SG, Top. Mss., under 'Rutland, Cottesmore'. Quite possibly, the Council's campaign reflected 'a familiar mixture of paternalism and pickpocketry': Maurice Beresford, 'Habitation versus Improvement: The Debate on Enclosure by Agreement', *Essays in the Economic and Social History of Tudor and Stuart England*, ed. F. J. Fisher (Cambridge, 1961), 50. For a general review of enclosure, 1500–1640, see Joan Thirsk, 'Enclosing and Engrossing', *The Agrarian History of England and Wales*, IV, ed. Thirsk, 200–55.

that he may in part have decided which manors to buy on the basis of how much of their land might yet be enclosed for profit. He apparently felt that the profits were right at Soham, for within a year of purchasing that Cambridgeshire manor, in 1628, he had obtained an Exchequer decree granting him 5,000 acres of wasteland and common. Broadway, Somerset, he acquired in 1628, and the winter of 1628 – 9 found him involved in litigation with a tenant who opposed his attempts to enclose the common. He purchased a portion of Malvern Chase in early 1632, and by May had launched an ambitious enclosure project.[32]

Heath did not, however, improve through enclosure only. He also made considerable use of a second, less common, improvement technique: land drainage. Drainage was expensive and frequently unsuccessful. But it could lead to phenomenal profits, and the dream of wealth made Heath ignore the danger.

In pursuit of his dream, Sir Robert made himself party to the most ambitious drainage scheme of the early Stuart period, the so-called 'Bedford Project'. In September 1630 the earl of Bedford contracted with Charles to drain 95,000 acres of the Great Level. On completing the project, Bedford was to retain 83,000 acres, the remainder reverting to the crown. Bedford was at that time presumably already acting in partnership with a number of fellow-projectors, but it was only in December 1631 that a second document identified thirteen partners and revealed their obligations and their recompense. Among the partners was Heath. For £500 and a pledge to bear at least one-twentieth of the entire cost of drainage, Sir Robert received 4,000 acres of fenland. Vermuyden was to oversee the drainage. The project was extremely ambitious. In 1634 a traveller related that at Wisbech he had 'spent best part of an houre in viewing a little Army of Artificers, venting, contriving, and acting out-landish devises'. To that time, the work was generally a failure, and the same writer noted that it was 'not soe fitt to passe the Washes, being neither firme nor safe for Travellers, especially now of late, by reason of the new made Sluces and Devises for turning of the naturall course of the waters neere adjoyning'. In 1637 Vermuyden pronounced the project completed, and he

---

[32] On Soham, PRO, Exchequer Decrees and Orders, E. 125, ff. 482 – 3. On Broadway, Heath document (probably a draft of a petition), 14 Jan. 1629, SG, Top. Mss., under 'Somerset, Broadway'. On Malvern, Heath to Sir John Coke, 9 May 1632, *HMC*, Cowper I, 457.

claimed qualified success, but to most observers the work constituted an unqualified failure. Charles in July 1638 reclaimed the 'Bedford Level', and although Bedford and his partners did receive 40,000 acres to divide among themselves, the land was almost worthless. According to Vermuyden, the project had cost over £100,000, meaning that if Heath fulfilled his obligations he spent more than £5,000 doing so, in return for a few thousand acres of sodden soil.[33]

The failure of the Bedford Project appears to have done little to shake Sir Robert's belief that land drainage was likely to result in huge profits. On his own properties, he sought to drain inundated sections, and, indeed, just as he tended to purchase property that could be improved by enclosure so was he apparently attracted to manors that were water-logged. Fenny farmland was cheap to buy; drained, it could be sold or rented for a sizeable profit. As he moved through middle age, Heath seems to have become progressively more excited by the potential for improvement through drainage, and his bias is neatly reflected in the record of his land purchases. Prior to 1615 he usually bought property located in the traditional centre of Heath family life, the Kent-Middlesex-Surrey-Sussex area. Among the properties that he inherited on his father's death, however, were several in the Lincolnshire fenland. In 1618 he leased crown lands in the 'Marshland' area of Norfolk, near the Ouse, and thereafter most of his purchases included sizeable stretches of fen.[34]

Where his lands were marshy, Heath sought to improve them through drainage. Perhaps his most ambitious drainage efforts were at Soham, the huge manor that was located in the Great Level. By June 1633 a drainage project had already been attempted and had failed, as Isaac Barrow, a local justice of the peace, reported to him that month: 'The fenns are so miserably

---

[33] The quotations are drawn from H. C. Darby, *The Draining of the Fens*, second ed. (Cambridge, 1956), p. 46; Darby discusses the project generally, pp. 38 – 48. F. A. Bates details the division of land: *Graves Memoirs of the Civil War* (London, 1927), pp. 246 – 8. Vermuyden's estimate of cost, which is self-serving but also reasonable, is included in his pamphlet, *A Discourse touching the Drayning the Great Fennes* (London, 1642), p. 2.

[34] Heath's lease of the Marshland property is noted in a Privy Council order of 25 Nov. 1618: *APC*, 1618 – 1619, 313. He purchased additional property in the area later that year: C. 54/2419. Heath's main properties are all referred to in the text or notes of this chapter; a complete list of his known holdings is in Kopperman, 'Heath', 360 – 3.

drained that noe proffit could have been made of moste of the grounds though they had been enclosed.[35] Still, Heath was not discouraged. In March 1638 he noted in a manorial particular:

The meer of Soham containeing 1500 acres or thereabouts, whereof yet noe benefitt is made but by the fishing, let [at four years' purchase] the valew is not above 30£ p annum, if the drayneing succeed and with a very smale charge may the greatest part of it be made firme and good land, and that which remaineth a better commodity both for fish and fowle; the improvement of this worth — 1000-00-00.

A year later he was apparently no closer to success, but was if anything more optimistic, for in a second particular he wrote: 'The meere containeing 1400 acres of ground whereof the one halfe may easily be made firme ground, the improvement therby, worth — 1000-00-00.'[36] It is unlikely that he succeeded in any of his major drainage projects, at Soham or elsewhere, but he was nothing if not persistent.

When he acted to improve his property, whether by drainage or by enclosure, Sir Robert usually faced determined opposition from his tenants. Their anger was heightened by the fact that he tended to provide minimum recompense. Occasionally even his own agents encouraged him to be more generous. In April 1638 John Symms wrote to Sir Robert from Broadway, to report to him on the activities of William Broome. Broome, a tenant, had consistently opposed Heath's efforts to enclose the Broadway common, and as early as 1628 Sir Robert had sued him in an effort to force him to stop grazing his cattle there. He refused, however, to compensate him in any way for the loss of grazing right, for Broome possessed no copyhold. The case was still hanging fire in April 1638, when Symms sought to make peace:

I acquaynted Broome with what you wrote me, & his answer was that he would never betray his honer though he lost his whole common. but that if he might have but a reasonable proposition (suche as I should thinke fytt) of acres to be annexed to his tenament he would be contented to give way

[35] U. of I., Heath Papers.
[36] Egerton 2987, ff. 67, 74.

to the enclosure . . . I am of opinion that wilbe somethinge hard to exclude him, [given] his . . . usage of his common above 200 years . . . I knowe out of your owne noble disposition you will not doe aniethinge that shall have the least shew of unjustice.

Heath, however, seems to have remained obdurate and Broome continued to graze his cattle on the common.[37]

Heath's drainage policies also met with opposition. Sir Robert might consider the marsh at Soham to be entirely a wasteland, useless 'but by the fishing', yet precisely that fishing, combined with such other activities as reed-gathering, undoubtedly helped some of his poorer tenants to survive. Furthermore, when he wrote cheerfully of raising the rental on the moor thirtyfold after the drainage project was completed, he was applauding the same prospect that terrified the existing renters.[38] Many of those who fought his improvement policies, both the drainage and enclosure, believed that they were fighting for their survival.

Their fight was bitter. During 1630 a series of enclosure riots broke out at Soham. Similar violence swept Malvern in 1632 and Broadway in 1643. In each case, Heath responded by calling to his defence the legal machinery that he knew so well. In 1630 he persuaded Hyde to order two local justices, one of them Barrow, to arrest several individuals who recently, at Soham, had allegedly 'in a most tumultuous & ryotous manner disturbed the possession of the said Sir Robert Heath in such parte of the said wast or Common as have bene sett out & bounded by the surveyor'. Heath not only procured the directive, but helped to

---

[37] The Symms letter is in U. of I., Heath Papers. On 28 May 1638 Richard Knight and John Russell reported to Heath from Broadway that Broome was still 'oppressing our comon'; on 21 Oct. 1639 Edward Heath complained to John that the enclosure project at Broadway could not be completed until the suit against Broome proved successful: both letters in SG, Top. Mss., under 'Somerset, Broadway'.

[38] Joan Thirsk, 'The Farming Regions of England', *The Agrarian History of England and Wales*, IV, ed. Thirsk, 38 – 9; Darby, pp. 50 – 5.

draft it.[39] The justices may have carried out their orders, and 1631 appears to have been a quiet year at Soham, but several of the same men whom Hyde designated as being rioters seem also to have been active in riots that broke out in the spring of 1632.

The riots of 1632 were aimed not only at preventing enclosure but at intimidating the labourers who were working on Heath's drainage project, and Sir Robert conceded that the turbulence was disrupting work. Responding to the new danger, he petitioned the Council, and it ordered a number of tenants of Soham to apprehend the alleged ringleaders, only to see some of them join the rioters. Several of Heath's own agents were beaten by the mob, and although a few were arrested, Barrow and his colleagues were generally slow to act, fearing for their safety. Still more violence, perhaps the worst yet, came in 1633. Again many of the alleged ringleaders were the same, but Barrow was too frightened to move against them. Hoping to justify his hesitancy, he wrote to Heath in June: 'It is impossible to take them at Soham without much bloodshed which I know your Lordship disireth not[;] the course must be to weed them out by one & one.' Barrow appears not to have done much weeding, and he must have been relieved when, for some reason, quiet returned to Soham. For several years the relationship between Heath and his tenants at Soham was, though probably cool, not so bitter as to inspire violence, and Sir Robert proceeded with his enclosure and drainage schemes. In 1641, however, came new riots, and the enclosures were torn down. In response, an angry Heath petitioned the Lords to affirm that he had a right to manage Soham as he saw fit, free from intimidation, and the house complied. There was, however, little that Sir Robert, or even parliament, could do. At that time, on the eve of the civil war, public authority was weakening and egalitarian notions were beginning to radicalise

---

[39] An early draft, with annotations by Heath, is in Egerton 2987, ff. 29 – 30. Although landlords usually had an advantage over their tenants in court (Heath's stature and connections helped him still further), the courts, particularly the equity courts, showed some sympathy for tenants and occasionally supported their position in lawsuits against landlords: Appleby, *Famine*, pp. 73 – 4. References to riots at Malvern are included in three letters from Heath to Coke, 9 May, 23 June, and 25 Aug. 1632: *HMC*, Cowper I, 457, 461, 472. The riots at Broadway are discussed in a letter from Richard Knight, William Handerwicke, and Matthew Paul to Edward Heath, 23 Jan. 1643, SG, Top. Mss., mistakenly filed under 'Worcestershire, Broadwas'.

the peasantry. Soham was not alone the scene of riots, for
violence was spreading rapidly in Cambridgeshire and the
adjoining counties. This much was noted by William Barnes, a
justice from the vicinity of Soham, in a letter that he wrote to
Heath in June 1641, and he also advised Sir Robert not to
attempt to rebuild the enclosures. The cost would be too high,
he pointed out, but beyond that was the simple fact that the
tenants would not allow the hedges and fences to cut them off
again from their grazing lands, for they had 'a resolve to dye in
the busines, rather then they should be reinclosed'.[40]

In pursuing his programme of drainage and enclosures, Heath
cannot have imagined that only a few stood against him or that
improvement, followed as it would be by huge increases in
rents, would benefit the mass of his tenants. That he pushed on,
knowing many tenants would suffer if his policies were realised,
suggests a callous nature, suggests that even when he expressed
sympathy for the poor, as he did often and to good effect, he
was just being hypocritical.[41] However, Heath believed not that
he was taking advantage of his tenantry, but quite the reverse.
To his mind, the peasant was of a low nature, devious,
rebellious, quick to take advantage of a kind-hearted lord. A
typical peasant also, he believed, hostile to authority, and he
could call on personal experience to support his contention, for
in the summer of 1625, prior to buying the huge manor of
Rochdale, in Lancashire, he 'dyd summon a Court of Survey
. . . they denyed to appear, but at the kings Court, & would
neither shewe there leases nor acquaynt me with theier
partyculer rents: requyring time to consider'.[42] Heath was
convinced that his tenants would cheat him if he were too soft.
In a survey of Broadway he noted sarcastically: 'The Coppihold
tenements have been valued by the tenants themselves, who

---

[40] Barnes's letter is in SBT, DR 98/1652; Barrow's, U. of I., Heath Papers.
   Other materials relevant to Soham riots: Henry Payne et al., petition to
   Council, 12 June 1632, SP 16/218/40; order of Council, 22 June 1632, SP 16/
   219/1; PC 2/42, ff. 11, 20, 43, HMC, Fourth Report, 94; LJ, IV, 343. On the
   extent of rioting in England, particularly as the Civil War approached, see
   Brian Manning, The English People and the English Revolution 1640 – 1649
   (London, 1976), pp. 122 – 37. The Soham riots are placed in the context of
   general violence in the area in Keith Lindley, Fenland Riots and the English
   Revolution (London, 1982), pp. 83 – 6, 130. There was also rioting at Soham
   during the 1650s: Lindley, p. 184.
[41] On Heath's attitudes toward the poor, see pp. 215 – 17.
[42] Quoted from Heath's notes on his tour of four manors during the summer
   of 1625; only a copy, not in his hand, exists: Kent Archives Office, U55 E104.

will never over value them.'[43] And when in 1638 he decided to pay to have his demesne lands at Broadway disafforested, in order to secure himself against fines that might be levied under the forest laws, he refused to do the same for his tenants, instead insisting that if they wanted their lands disafforested they would have to bear the cost. As he explained to Edward that September: 'I wish them well in other things yet when it comes to payment of mony & freeing ther lands from such a servitude, I were much to blame, & have not thanks for my mony, but they may rather laugh at me for my labour.'[44]

The mutual sense of dislike and distrust that poisoned the relationship between Heath and his tenants destroyed all chance that they would cooperate in matters of land usage. Sir Robert, fearing that his tenants would take advantage of him, sought to push through his improvement schemes, not by providing adequate compensation to the families that stood to lose much, but by bringing the power of government to bear on the tenantry. If he had the law on his side, however, those who opposed improvement had the numbers, and they used them to wreck his plans, by tearing out his hedges and destroying his sluices. Heath's improvement programmes were costly, and so was their failure. In the end, Sir Robert had little to show for his pains, except debt.

Other ventures

Land improvement was one means by which Heath sought to augment his wealth, and instead found ruin. But still more dramatic were the failures he met in other enterprises. His business interests stretched as far as the New World, where he became involved in various projects, the most important of which were centred on his own proprietary, Carolana. Certainly he believed that the successful planting of Carolana would be in the best interests of crown and country, particularly as it might result in the weakening of Spain. It is equally certain, however, that he hoped to profit from the colony. Since neither the Carolana project nor his other colonial ventures bore fruit, these

---

[43] Egerton 3007, f. 15.
[44] Northamptonshire Record Office, NPL 1344.

hopes came to naught. Still, Heath could find solace in the thought that if he gained little through colonial enterprises neither did he lose much, for his own financial commitments seem to have been small.[45] The same could not be said of several projects that he became involved in closer to home.

In 1628 Sir Robert, acting at the behest of a kinsman from the Kepier line, leased a strip of land on the bank of the Tyne, at South Shields, and soon afterwards ordered that a ballast shore be built there. Thus he entered a major salting enterprise, for with a group of co-adventurers he sought to involve himself in the rising salt-production industry of South Shields. The shore itself was apparently intended to provide a platform for a saltern, and it may also have been designed to serve as a base for wharves. If one accepts a claim that Heath made several years later, in the beginning Newcastle was amenable to the salting scheme. However, the city soon turned against Heath and his partners, apparently because it feared the project threatened its hegemony on the Tyne. Shortly after work began on Sir Robert's shore, the city insisted that construction cease, claiming that ballast was leaking and might soon choke the river. It appears that Heath sought to demonstrate that the shore posed no danger, for in February 1629 he obtained the opinion of Trinity House that local trade and the river were in no way threatened by his project. But the city remained obdurate, and during the period 1630 – 40, particularly 1632 – 4, the Council received numerous petitions from both camps, as Newcastle, which was reluctant to state its real concern, argued that the shore represented a threat to the Tyne, while Heath called on the Council to order that the city be barred from interfering further with construction. The same years saw Heath active in supporting his partners. In February 1635 he appeared before the Committee of Trade to present their petition to be incorporated, and it may largely have been his efforts that led to a charter being granted, in December 1635, to the South and North Shields Saltmakers' Society. Not surprisingly, he also worked against their competitors, as when in January 1636 he again visited the Committee of Trade, this time to oppose a petition for incorporation that had been submitted by London salters. On the whole, he was successful in his efforts on behalf of his partners and himself, and his crowning success came in

---

[45] The extent of his involvement is dealt with in Kopperman, 'Profile', esp. 11, 17, 21.

May 1640, when the Council ordered Newcastle to cease interfering with the construction of his shore. But the decision came too late to be of much use to him, for Heath's project was soon lost in the turmoil of the 1640s. Furthermore, Newcastle remained opposed to the salting venture, and in 1658 the city purchased, for £610, what was left of Heath's shore. In all probability, the purchase price fell far short of Sir Robert's investment.[46]

Yet more costly was Heath's involvement with the Dovegang lead mine of Wirksworth, Derbyshire. The Dovegang was a huge complex, containing more than three hundred shafts, but it was largely inundated, and the king, its owner, sought vainly for a lessee who could successfully work it. In 1615 James leased the mine to George Sayers, who was, or was soon to be, in partnership with the earl of Dover, among others. But despite all efforts by the new associates the mine remained flooded, and in 1629 Heath, arguing that Sayers and his partners could not provide a profit for the crown while he could, persuaded Charles to lease the Dovegang to him. Probably Heath was from the beginning associated with Vermuyden in the venture, but they did not finalise the terms of their partnership until October 1631, when Sir Robert agreed to fund totally all drainage work at the mine, as well as several related projects; in return,

---

[46] Roger Howell, Jr., *Newcastle upon Tyne and the Puritan Revolution* (Oxford, 1967), pp. 32 – 3, 312, provides coverage of the general controversy. The Council orders regarding Heath's shore are in PC 2/42, ff. 66, 257; PC 2/44, f. 24; PC 2/49, f. 548; PC 2/51, ff. 508, 584, 595 – 6; SP 16/232/115; SP 16/455/22. Two petitions submitted by the master and society of Trinity House, opposing the construction, are extant (22 May 1633 and 11 March 1634): SP 16/239/23; SP 16/262/50. In Feb. 1629, however, Trinity House had approved the Heath project: *HMC*, Eighth Report, I, 244. The corporation of Newcastle's petitions are recorded in PC 2/42, f. 224 (27 Feb. 1633), and 2/44, f. 4 (1 June 1634). Heath's petitions regarding the ballast shore are SP 16/167/ 29 (26 May 1630), PC 2/42, f. 66 (Council order follows; 13 July 1632). His petitions regarding the Newcastle salters and their opponents are SP 16/283/ 113, SP 16/312/47; relevant material SP 16/283/46 – 7. Several of Heath's letters relate to the issue: to the mayor of Newcastle, 22 May 1631, SP 16/ 216/68; to Sir William Becher, 3 April 1633, SP 16/236/9; to Coke, 23 May 1633, SP 16/239/40; to Nicholas, 20 May 1640, SP 16/454/35. How much Heath invested in his project is unknown, but it should be noted that the extraction of salt at the Tyneside sites was involved, and setting up and maintaining the necessary apparatus, as well as providing fuel, must have been costly; note Joyce Ellis, 'The Decline and Fall of the Tyneside Salt Industry, 1660 – 1790: A Re-examination', *The Economic History Review*, second series, 33 (1980), 46 – 7.

Vermuyden promised only his expertise in drainage. As though the agreement were not unbalanced enough, the partners also decided that Heath was to receive only one-third of whatever profits remained after the king had taken his share, the balance going to Vermuyden. For his part, Charles could expect a cut of the profits, plus £1,000 annual rent, which may have been shared by the partners. Even after the lease had been drawn, however, Heath and Vermuyden still faced legal challenges. Time and again, the earl of Dover challenged their lease, claiming that he and his partners had invested £3,000 in draining the mine and had been on the verge of success when they had been ousted. He lost his case at every level, including, finally, the Long Parliament, but the threat posed by him may have caused Heath and Vermuyden to hold back, fearing that otherwise they might lose their investment. It seems to have been only in 1635, after the Privy Council had confirmed their lease, that they began to work with determination. By 1637 the Dovegang was turning a profit, and the partners were laying plans to dredge the Derwent, which passed near Wirksworth, so as to make it navigable as far as the Trent. After 1638, however, activity at the mine decreased, and soon the civil war turned Heath's attention elsewhere. Vermuyden used the turbulence of the 1640s to his advantage by seizing Sir Robert's share in the mine. It was not until 1673 that John Heath, after much litigation, was able to reclaim it.[47]

Responding to the last of Dover's many petitions against him, Heath informed parliament that since 1635 he and Vermuyden had 'expended many thousand pounds But Sir Robert Heath for his share hath never yett in any one yeere gained 300£ cleere'.[38]

---

[47] On the background to the Heath-Dover controversy, see F. N. Fisher, 'Sir Cornelius Vermuyden and the Dovegang Lead Mine', Derbyshire Archaeological and Natural History Society, Journal, 72 (1952), 92 – 4; Nellie Kirkham, 'The Tumultuous Course of Dovegang', Derbyshire Archaeological and Natural History Society, Journal, 73 (1953), 8 – 11. On the dispute between Vermuyden and Edward Heath (later, John), over the mine, see Fisher, 114 – 16; Calendar of the Proceedings of the Committee for Compounding, III, 2776 – 7. The Dovegang lease is described in PRO, Signet Office, Docket Books, IND/6809. The litigation with Dover may be traced through Essex Record Office, D/DL L59, pp. 8 – 11; Lincoln's Inn Library, Ms. 77 (82), no. 3; Bankes Papers, 50/23 and 65/54; HMC, Fourth Report, 114. The dredging of the Derwent is the subject of two of Heath's letters: to Coke, 6 Feb, 1637, HMC, Cowper II, 153 – 4; to Bankes, 14 Aug. 1638, Bankes Papers, 65/26.

[48] Essex Record Office, D/DL L59, p. 8. The mine seems not to have been worked, 1638 – 51, except briefly during 1643 – 4: Fisher, 114.

Given the nature of his agreement with Vermuyden, Heath probably bore a far larger share of the expenses than his partner, and it is quite possible — almost certain, in fact, if the dredging of the Derwent was seriously undertaken — that Sir Robert's involvement in the Dovegang cost him more than £10,000. His salting venture, too, was undoubtedly expensive, but the Dovegang project was probably the most costly failure in a business career that saw few successes.

Creditors

Heath's penchant for speculation made him a constant borrower, and although he also lent money on occasion he was primarily a debtor during his adult life. Just as the 1610s saw him involved with a number of partners, so did it see him borrowing on every hand, usually small sums. During the 1620s, however, the loans became larger, the number of creditors smaller. Shortly after he was dismissed from the bench, Sir Robert prepared a schedule of his debts, pursuant to an indenture that bound him and Edward to make good the sums 'by the sale of lands'. Included in the list were twenty-five individuals and the respective debts owed them, to a total of £16,411.[49]

The identity of Heath's major creditors in late 1634 is revealing. Few of them were professional moneylenders. Of the three individuals who were his creditors to the amount of £500, one was, indeed, a scrivener, but the others were Christiana Cavendish, dowager-countess of Devonshire, and Sir Matthew Mennes, a man who was very remotely related to Heath, and by marriage only, but who was, ironically, the father of a girl whom John Heath was to marry some thirty years later. Only one blood-relative of Sir Robert's was included on the list, that being Thomas Heath, of the Tamworth line, who was owed £672. That Sir Robert did not borrow more from within the family was probably because few of his relatives had much money to lend. Thomas Heath showed himself to be a good cousin, first in lending Sir Robert cash, then in not suing to regain it. Perhaps

---

[49]   U. of I., Heath Papers.

because he did not force the issue, he was apparently never repaid in full, although Heath covered part of the debt, in 1637, by conveying a small manor to him.[50]

Thomas Heath was probably an amateur in the world of finance, but Sir Robert's leading creditors were for the most part quite experienced. The only exceptions were John and Henry King, both of whom were important Churchmen, the latter being a noted poet as well. Like most wealthy men they lent money, and Heath's schedule showed him to be in debt to them for £2,250.[51] Heath's other major creditors were all somehow involved in the business world of London. Giles Vandeputt, a wealthy merchant of Dutch extraction, was owed £1,185. Heath also owed £2,394 to the heir of Paul, Lord Bayning. Bayning had been a professional moneylender, and his relationship with Sir Robert had begun at least as early as June 1612, when Heath and four partners had bound themselves to him for slightly more than £1,000.[52] In the wake of Bayning's death, in 1629, his widow had married Sir Dudley Carleton, now Viscount Dorchester, Heath's friend, but she had been widowed again in 1632. Beyond Bayning, Heath's schedule included one other major creditor, Nathaniel Wright, a Skinner. A second Skinner, Philip Holman, held Heath's largest credit, though for some reason he was not named in the schedule. Titchbourne, Heath's partner and relative by marriage, was also a Skinner, and he may have introduced Sir Robert to Wright and Holman, but in all probability no introduction was necessary, for money-lending was a sideline of many liverymen.

Desperate for cash after 1634, Heath turned to new creditors, the most important of whom, in terms of the amount borrowed, was Anne Hutton, a wealthy widow. By the close of 1636 Sir Robert was bound to Holman for £5,500, to the widow for

---

[50] C. 54/3118. Thomas Heath became a master in Chancery in 1640, and there is some possibility that Sir Robert helped him gain the post. In May 1643 Edward and Francis Heath were bound to pay him £52: SG, Unbd. Mss., under 'Heath'. On Cavendish, see *DNB*. The Mennes family was closely linked to the Boys', a family that Heath's aunt, Joan, had married into: Hasted, IV, 266.

[51] On the King brothers, see *DNB*. They were not the only clerics Heath borrowed from. In Feb. 1634 he sent a letter to the bishop of Worcester, thanking him for his 'Love & patience in forbearing the 300£ which by promise & agreement is a debt due to you from me', excusing his tardiness, and promising prompt repayment: SG, Unbd. Mss., under 'Heath'.

[52] SG, Top. Mss., under 'Rutland, Exton'. On Bayning, see Ashton, *Money Market, passim*, esp. pp. 73 – 4; on Vandeputt, *ibid.*, p. 72.

£3,000, both figures denoting principle and interest, plus penalty.[53] For most of the debts that Heath acquired during the 1630s, including these, Edward and John were bound with him. The elder sons, Edward especially, were to suffer with their father. In fact it appears that Edward made greater sacrifices to clear the debts than his father did. In 1639 he and Lucy sold East Hanny. Three years later he purchased Broadway and North Inglesby from Holman, whom Sir Robert had satisfied by selling him the manors at low prices, so that their re-sale might bring a large profit. But Edward did not enjoy the new properties for long. They were sequestered during the civil war, and although he was eventually able to reclaim them, the legacy of his father's debts forced him to sell Broadway — as well as Colliweston, which he had just inherited — in 1649. Ten years before, his father had agreed never again to bind him for debt.[54] But Edward already stood bound for earlier debts, and that situation seems to have embittered his relationship with Sir Robert. After the mid-1630s he became progressively less willing to heed his father's commands and even went so far as to feud with his mother. At the same time, he began to complain that Lucy's estate was less than he had hoped for.[55] There had been tensions in the Heath family prior to 1634, but they were exacerbated by the money problems caused by Sir Robert's fall.

With Edward's cooperation, however reluctantly given, Sir Robert was able to clear most of his debts by the close of 1642. In the main, he did so by mortgaging or selling land. Even as he strove to repay his debts, however, his creditors pursued him in the courts. Viscountess Dorchester had, in fact, not waited for his dismissal before entering into litigation, and already by December 1633 she had forced him to acknowledge a recognizance of £3,800, an amount that was based on principal, interest, and penalty. The later 1630s found her launching still more suits and demanding that Heath repay the debt entire, the money to go to her son. Holman, too, was successful in court, and in 1638 he forced Heath to acknowledge his full debt of

[53] C. 54/3106; Kent Archives Office, U55 E104. Two of Heath's bonds with Holman, 2 July 1627 (apparently the start of their relationship) and 6 Jan. 1631, are in SG, Top. Mss., under 'London, St. Benet Fink'.

[54] Kent Archives Office, U55 E102. Edward notes his land sales in an account of his debts, c. 1650, Kent Archives Office, U55 E104, and in Edward's undated answer to a deposition in Chancery, U. of I., Heath Papers.

[55] Edward to John, 21 Oct. 1639: SG, Top. Mss., under 'Rutland, Cottesmore'; see also p. 71.

£5,500, principal, interest and penalty. He, too, could have demanded the entire amount, but in keeping with standard practice he accepted an accommodation, one that left him with a tidy profit. After Viscountess Dorchester died in 1638 her executors kept up the pressure on Heath, in 1646 persuading the Committee for Sequestrations to extend Edward's lands for the Bayning debt, which was now fixed at £3,000, all of it penalty, Sir Robert having repaid the basic debt of £1,975 shortly before the death of the viscountess. Nevertheless, grasping though the executors were, they, too, reached an accommodation with Edward. So did the executor of Anne Hutton's estate, who in 1648 agreed that if Edward and John paid him roughly £2,000, rather than the £3,000 principal, interest and penalty that was legally due to him, he would consider the debt satisfied.[56]

His relationship with creditors shows Sir Robert to have been a poor risk. He personally was hard on men who were slow to repay their debts, and while a member of the Commons he on several occasions spoke out against the protection of debtors.[57] In this regard, however, he was apparently slow to condemn in himself the sins that he saw in others. Instead, he moved slowly to satisfy his creditors, and in some cases he entirely failed to act until they threatened suit. Edward, for one, recognised his indifference, and in October 1639 he complained to John:

> I am sure I live at stake for the money for the Lord Banning, and have many times an ague fit to think how neer danger I am in for it. I pray put my father in minde of those businesses, as from me: I knowe he is too regardless of them,

---

[56] Information on the status of the Bayning debt is in C. 54/2996 (which also shows that Vandeputt had been repaid) and Egerton 2978, f. 189; on Holman (and Henry King — John died in 1637 — their debts being settled together), the key documents are C. 54/3276, 3305 and an indenture between King and Heath (et al.), 22 July 1641, SG, Top. Mss., under 'Somerset, Broadway'; on Hutton, Essex Record Office, D/DGn/329 – 32. Wright was also repaid — a note on the schedule of Heath's debts (1634) confirms this — but it is uncertain how or when this was done. During the turbulent 1640s, creditors often negotiated a settlement for their debts, rather than hold out for all they were legally entitled to; note John Broad, 'Gentry Finances and the Civil War: The Case of the Buckinghamshire Verneys', *The Economic History Review*, second series, 32 (1979), 191 – 4.

[57] CD 1621, IV, 67, and V, 16.

but your safety and mine depends upon it.[58]

The tone was bitter. Edward's store of patience, never large, had long since evaporated. As months passed and the debts remained, he appears to have felt ever more betrayed by his father.

Heath as a businessman

Edward should never have faced the danger that he did in 1639, nor, indeed, should his father. Sir Robert could have been a very wealthy individual. That he never amassed a fortune, despite his great income, was due to one fact in particular: He was an extremely poor businessman. As a landlord and in every other form of business enterprise that he sampled, he fell victim to an array of shortcomings. The business world of the time, which forgave many forms of misbehaviour, would not forgive him his ineptitude.

Heath's weaknesses as a businessman were many, but four were perhaps most glaring. Firstly, he continually under-estimated the obstacles that faced him in his various ventures. He appears to have been genuinely surprised that Newcastle challenged his right to build a ballast shore on the Tyne, and the ferocity and determination of his tenants, as they attacked his improvements, shocked him. That he was so often caught unawares can be traced to a second weakness. Heath often failed to adequately examine the nature of an enterprise before he undertook it. Had he reviewed the nature of Newcastle's politics in the 1620s, particularly in relation to the Tyne, he might not have committed himself to the controversial salting venture at South Shields. Had he realised how hostile to improvement his tenants were, he might have divided them by mollifying the more amenable, or he might have introduced his programme more gradually. As it was Heath not only pushed ahead with projects before adequately reviewing the situation, but he failed to make himself familiar with important details even after he was involved. In 1638, ten full years after he had purchased Colliweston, he mentioned in a letter to Edward that

---

[58] SG, Top. Mss., under 'Rutland, Cottesmore'.

he was uncertain whether the tenantry on the manor included any freeholders.[59] Sir Robert's failure to study his enterprises adequately also led to his third main shortcoming as a businessman: a tendency to overestimate the value of his possessions, particularly his lands. He consistently believed that his properties were undervalued. He therefore believed that he might justly raise rents, even on unimproved land, and when he sold properties he often held out for prices that were unrealistic. During his period, a landlord could normally expect about a five per cent annual return on his property.[60] Heath looked for several times that amount, largely because he thought his properties were worth more than they in fact were. A final weakness of Heath's was that he tended to put his faith in untrustworthy partners and servants. Most of his eight major partners from the 1610s seem to have played him fairly, though he had a violent quarrel with Chamber in 1633, apparently because he believed that his long-time associate had appropriated rent-money from Broadway.[61] But if Chamber misbehaved towards Heath, his chicanery was as nothing compared to Vermuyden's. Time and again Vermuyden gulled his partner, even as Heath laboured at Court to help advance his projects. Although many times burned by the relationship, Heath did not break with Vermuyden until the late 1630s, if then.[62] He could scarcely have chosen a partner who was less deserving of trust, yet he trusted him. Not only partners but

[59] Northamptonshire Record Office, NPL 1344. In Heath's defence, the arrangement of tenures on a manor could be highly complex: Batho, 293. Heath composed many particulars of his manors, and a fair number survive. They reflect the complexities of managing a manor. At Rochdale, his largest manor (containing almost 43,000 acres), the tenants included c. 300 leaseholders and 240 copyholders; the unmanageability of the manor may explain why Heath quickly mortgaged it and why he seems not to have involved himself much in Rochdale affairs: 'The Survey of the Manor of Rochdale in the County of Lancaster . . . Made in 1626', ed. Henry Fishwick, Chetham Society, *Publications*, new series, 71 (1913).

[60] H. J. Habakkuk, 'The Long-Term Rate of Interest and the Price of Land in the Seventeenth Century', *Economic History Review*, second series, 5 (1952), 33.

[61] In two letters to Heath, 25 March and 4 May 1633, Chamber tried to vindicate himself; he also pleaded for mercy, since Heath was planning a lawsuit: SG, Top. Mss., under 'Worcestershire, Castlemorton'; U. of I., Heath Papers (this letter is quoted at length in Kopperman, 'Heath', 284).

[62] Hine claims (p. 92) that Heath, toward the end of his life, denounced Vermuyden, and while he does not substantiate his assertion, he may well be correct.

agents often served him poorly, either by deliberately giving him bad advice, by mistake, or by cheating him. Since his landholdings and his business ventures were not centred in any one area of England, he naturally had to rely on others to look after his interests.[63] But too often his reliance seems to have verged on blind trust. Had he paid more attention to his business affairs, he might not have been so trusting.

Heath's weaknesses are clearly manifest in his venture at Great Malvern. Anxious for cash, Charles in 1631 – 2 had Malvern Chase disafforested, and he then conveyed his share to Vermuyden. The new owner soon became disenchanted with his property, however, possibly because a clause in his agreement with Charles required him to plant madder at Malvern, perhaps because the tenantry appeared restive. Whatever his reservations, he found a willing dupe to assume responsibility — Sir Robert, who purchased the manor in early 1632. True to form, Heath immediately launched an ambitious enclosure scheme on his new property, and, as usual, suffered, seeing Great Malvern torn by riots from May to August 1632. The violence may have discouraged him, for on 25 February 1633 he wrote to his 'good friends and commissioners' at Malvern, Chamber — their break had not yet come — and George Duncomb, and ordered them to sell between one-third and one-half of the property, mainly the 'worser' sort. For the better land, he wrote, 'reserving unto my selfe so much as you conceave will yeald 1500£ per annum, which I think 1500 acres will doe, I give you power to sell any or all of the rest to such as are willing to buy them'. That Heath believed one half of the land at Malvern to be worth one pound per acre per annum reflects how weak his sense of value in fact was, for the property was worth far less. After Heath fell out with Chamber, he relied increasingly on Duncomb, a man who for some reason was loath to see his master sell Malvern. In May 1632 Duncomb had written to him: 'I doe not thinke your Lordship hath cause to like the worse of your land at Malvern or to dowpt the rent or sale full out aswell and much better and beyond your expectation and better and better still the longer you forbear.' Under Sir Robert's orders he did attempt to sell the land, but the process moved so slowly that it suggests that he was incom-

---

[63] Absentee landlords became progressively more common during the Stuart period: F. T. Melton, 'Absentee Land Management in Seventeenth-Century England', *Agricultural History*, 52 (1978), 147 – 8.

petent or half-hearted. Duncomb first attempted to explain the slowness by suggesting to Heath the possibility that potential purchasers had formed a 'Combynacion' in an attempt to keep prices down. Later, however, he seems to have claimed that would-be buyers were concerned by the requirement that madder was to be planted at Malvern. In May 1637, after two petitions, Heath was finally able to persuade the king to void the madder clause, and by the close of the year he had disposed of the troublesome manor, in its entirety, but for only a fraction of the price that he had originally anticipated. Since he had first become interested in the manor five years before, Sir Robert had been poorly served by his agent, but he had also served himself poorly, by not studying the relevant issues deeply enough.[64]

In selling Malvern to Heath in early 1632, as in projects at the Dovegang and elsewhere, Vermuyden took advantage of his partner. Betrayal of trust was not unusual, particularly if business associations were not reinforced by blood ties. Indeed, the early Stuart business scene was geared to amorality. For his part, Heath was not above taking advantage of others for his own profit. In 1629 he persuaded William Rowlands — 'an unskilful young man', in Rowlands' own characterisation — to aid him in overthrowing the Sayers lease on the Dovegang and also to contract for £600 of lead ore, all in return for an office. Rowlands seems to have kept his side of the bargain, but Sir Robert did not produce the promised place, and 1636 found an embittered Rowlands denouncing him in a petition to the king.[65]

If Rowlands suffered at Heath's hands, his loss was slight compared to that of Thomas Phelips. Phelips, lord of the great manor of Kirby Misperton, in Yorkshire, fell into debt to the crown during Elizabeth's reign, and James, soon after his accession, took control of the manor. In 1609 James agreed to return Kirby Misperton at such time as Phelips fulfilled various obligations, chief among them being the payment of £1,500 of

---

[64] B. S. Smith, *A History of Malvern* (Leicester, 1964), pp. 154–5; G. M. Rushforth, 'A Sketch of the History of Malvern and Its Owners', Bristol and Gloucestershire Archaeological Society, *Transactions*, 42 (1920), 51–3. The original of Heath's letter of 25 Feb. 1633 is in the U. of I., Heath Papers; a copy is in the Kent Archives Office, U55 E104. Heath's petitions are discussed in a note from Cottington to Bankes, 22 May 1637, Bankes Papers, 9/15. Duncomb's letter is in the Kent Archives Office, U55 E100/1–139.

[65] SP 16/310/11; *HMC*, Ninth Report, II, 389. With his petition, Rowlands submitted a letter, dated Aug. 1629, in which Heath had promised him an office, in return for lead ore.

his debt, and pending such fulfilment the king leased the manor to one of his Scottish favourites, Sir James Creighton. Creighton and Heath had earlier joined in serving Balmerino, and by 1609 they were partners. Several of Heath's other partners, too, particularly Sheirs, became involved in managing Kirby Misperton, while Phelips, whose position had been desperate for some time, saw his hopes of reclaiming the manor further weakened when he was imprisoned for debt. During his time in prison, Phelips received legal advice — from Heath, whose involvement in the ring of partners was unknown to him. Heath had by then broken with Creighton, and he advised Phelips to mortgage his manor to Sheirs. The prisoner agreed, but the document that Heath drew up for him was a conveyance, rather than a mortgage, and Phelips by signing it unwittingly sold Kirby Misperton to Sheirs. Heath, for his part, assumed a moiety in the manor, and when Phelips was released from prison he could only cry out to his 'attorney', in rage and pain, 'I was drawen to engaging my self so desperately as I did from the confidence I reposed in you'.[66] Later, in a vain attempt to reclaim Kirby Misperton, Phelips affirmed that he had lost his manor 'all by the corrupt dealing of heath who taking the advantage of Phelips trust & necessityes himselfe underhand a partner in the bargayne & from the beginning hovering like a bird of pray [seized] this inheritance'. The experiences of Phelips and Rowlands clearly demonstrate that, while Heath was often victimised by the dishonesty of others, he was scarcely a lamb in a world of wolves.

Sir Robert's best-documented business ventures reveal a person who was sometimes dishonest, often mean, and consistently grasping. As a crown official Heath showed his willingness to go to great lengths for profit, but in his private enterprises he seems to have been still more covetous and still less fettered by ethics. Yet, his drive for profit may not have been directed primarily towards selfish ends. He lived well, but it cannot be said that he squandered his income in pursuit of personal comfort. Instead of engaging in conspicuous consumption, he usually invested his earnings and profits in land or in other enterprises.

---

66 Phelips to Heath, 20 June 1620, SP 15/41/79. Otherwise, all of the material contained in this paragraph is drawn from a deposition that Phelips prepared relative to a lawsuit that he brought, in vain, against Heath and Sheirs in May 1620: SP 14/115/43. Other documents — SP 14/48/80, 82; SP 14/115/45 – 7 — tend to corroborate Phelips's claims.

That he invested, rather than squandered, suggests strongly that Sir Robert did not seek profit primarily for himself. So does the fact that most of his major investments, on and off the land, were made after he was fifty, and many came after he was past sixty. True, his income was highest during his sixth decade, so it was then that he could best afford to become involved in major enterprises, but nevertheless in view of his age it is doubtful that he expected to live long enough to reap the bulk of the profits that his ventures might produce. In reality, his efforts in the business world, at least from middle age on, seem not to have been intended mainly to benefit him, but rather his family, particularly his elder sons. Several of his investments were openly made in his sons' names. His share in the South Shields salting enterprise was purchased for John, and indeed the fact that Heath was fighting for his son's interest, rather than for his own, may help to explain his tenacity in the battle with Newcastle over the ballast shore.[67] Certainly he could have given up and sold out, as he did in the case of Malvern. He could similarly have left Soham to be handled by others, for after February 1631 it technically belonged to Edward and Lucy, but instead he continued to manage the manor throughout the 1630s, investing much time and money in an attempt to make it a profitable enterprise.[68] Heath the businessman was born of Heath the family man. It was a tragic irony that his enterprises brought the family ruin and contention.

---

[67] That his share in the venture was in fact John's is noted by Heath in a letter to Coke, 23 May 1633, SP 16/239/40. One 'John Heath', probably Sir Robert's son, was included among the members of the South and North Shields Saltmakers' Society when the company was chartered in Dec. 1635; however, he was not included in the second charter, March 1639: 'Select Charters of Trading Companies A. D. 1530 – 1707', ed. C. T. Carr, Selden Society, *Publications*, 28 (1913), 142 – 8, 167 – 72.

[68] On the ownership of Soham, see p. 66.

9

Coda

His dismissal from the bench left Heath without office, but probably not without hope. Many a career in early Stuart England followed an irregular course, and an experienced courtier like Sir Robert would have known that a fall from power did not preclude a second rise. Just as he had witnessed Yelverton's disgrace in 1620, so had he seen him become a judge in 1625. Such examples may have buoyed up Heath's spirits, though he probably could not have imagined how far in fact he would climb.

Charles, even as he removed Heath, showed some compassion, for he gave him leave to practise in Common Pleas. Appearing before his erstwhile associates, in the rank of puisne serjeant, Heath quite possibly felt humiliated.[1] The treatment accorded him by some clients may also have rankled. As late as April 1640 he had the experience of being brushed aside by one Mr Blunt, who was party to a case that involved a legacy. On Blunt's urging, Heath set up a meeting between him and James Kinge, another party. Blunt not only failed to appear, but when next he encountered Sir Robert he told him to stop interfering in the case.[2] Such treatment may well have been galling to one who ten years before had been the king's own lawyer. On the

---

[1] 'Anniversarium', 21. Heath was apparently in fact given leave to practise in all courts at Westminster, Star Chamber alone excepted: Croke, *Third Report*, 375; anonymous note, Sept. 1634, SP 16/274/69. However, it may be that he chose to concentrate on Common Pleas. According to Croke, on the first day of Michaelmas term 1634 Heath 'appeared at the Common Bench Barre . . . and, being in his place of junior Sergeant at Law, pleaded for his Clyents': *Third Report*, 375.

[2] Berkshire Record Office, Trumbull Add. Mss. 49/27.

278

other hand, at a time when his financial situation was desperate, Heath drew a sizeable income, probably more than £1,000 per annum, from his private practice. His clientele appears to have included few significant courtiers, but it did include men who possessed some social standing and, probably more important from his point of view, some wealth.[3] Perhaps a fair proportion of clients valued his counsel because of his great experience, but it may well be that most were more impressed by the fact that he still had important friends at Court and was quite willing to use them in furthering suits. Reflecting that willingness, he wrote in February 1635 to his 'worthy friend', Sir Nicholas Carewe, chamberlain of the Exchequer, relative to a case in which Carewe had been assigned to mediate. The litigants were brothers, contesting a legacy. Heath wrote: 'My client John Atwood will attend you . . . & I intreate you to appointe some convenient time . . . to setle a peace & final ende betwene them, The plaintiff is a Citizen of London & followeth his trade well & carefully & is very unfitt for suites, & I think mr. Harman Atwood doth not delight in suits neather.'[4]

In dealing with clients, however, Heath observed some boundaries. Charles, he knew, was angry with him and might be further antagonised if he handled a suit that the Court opposed, so he avoided cases that might place him at odds with the king. But he also knew that his policy would do him little good if he followed it secretly, whereas if the Court were made aware of it Charles might be impressed by the loyalty of his former servant. On 12 November 1634, two months almost to the day after his dismissal, Heath notified Finch that, although he had recently taken a certain case, he had done so without realising that the king had an interest in the matter which ran contrary to that of Sir Robert's client. Being now informed of the conflict, he went on, he was dropping the case, for he was resolved never to serve as counsel in a cause that might prove harmful to the crown.[5] By such communications did Sir Robert signal to the Court that he was a loyal king's man still.

---

[3] One of his more important clients was Sir Thomas Holland, who retained him as counsel in Feb. 1635: *HMC*, Fifth Report, 418.

[4] Berkshire Record Office, D/ELC C1/168.

[5] SP 16/277/37.

Meanwhile, Heath's friends at Court were seeking some means to restore him to office.[6] Laud and his other enemies were, for their part, apparently convinced that he was no longer in a position to do them harm, so they did not attempt to keep him from Court. And most important, Charles himself appears to have believed that the dismissal was adequate punishment for Heath's past misconduct. So there was some support for Sir Robert in his attempts to reclaim favour, while there was little if any opposition. It is not surprising, therefore, that he was soon welcomed back into the king's service.

By 3 December 1634 Heath was already back in government, for on that date an unnamed crown official ordered him to advise on how the number of alehouses, as well as the brewing trade generally, might best be regulated.[7] He quickly took up the assignment, and within a few weeks put forward a proposal that the central government, rather than the justices of the peace, should thereafter supervise the alehouses. Not surprisingly, Heath claimed that if his scheme were carried through it would greatly profit the crown.[8] January 1635 found him submitting, apparently on his own initiative, a memorandum on customs, in which he advised the king, 'for the supplye of any suddeyn & pressing occasion, [how] to raise any sum of mony, out of marchandise'.[9] Neither of the schemes that Heath put forward during the winter of 1634 – 5 appears to have been acted upon by the Court, but he probably believed that, in view of the king's dire financial condition, he could help his position by suggesting how the crown might profit.

During 1635 and 1636 Heath often carried out assignments from the Court, drafting documents, giving legal counsel.[10] His official status during these months is unclear, but on 12 October

---

6 The identity of Heath's benefactors is unknown. Coventry was probably among them, however, for in 1638 he was responsible for winning Heath, by then a king's serjeant, a place as justice of assize: Coventry to Coke, 24 Feb. 1638, SP 16/383/1.

7 The order is referred to in a letter from Heath to its author, an unnamed 'lord', 4 Dec. 1634: BOD, Bankes Papers, 64/9.

8 BOD, Bankes Papers, 44/53. Note also p. 217.

9 The memorandum, SP 16/282/16, is printed entire by Fraser: 'Heath', 204 – 5.

10 On 17 Feb. 1635 he noted the entry of a decree, indicating that he had played some role in drafting it: SP 46/82/122. On 18 June he and several members of the king's counsel advised the Court on the validity of a will: SP 16/290/112.

1637 he suddenly gained an important place, king's serjeant.[11] One week after his elevation a Court observer noted, 'Sir Robert Heath . . . is again in the way to gain the King's favor'.[12]

The cleavage

The late 1630s were, on the whole, kind to Heath personally. His new place as king's serjeant was prestigious, a quality that he undoubtedly found attractive, but perhaps even more attractive to him, in view of his financial problems, was the fact that the serjeanty was highly lucrative.[13] He still had hopes of success at Wirksworth and South Shields, and he continued to produce schemes for improving his lands — and profits — at Soham and elsewhere. The family scene was clouded, for Lucy and Margaret had begun to feud, while Edward's relationship with his mother was generally civil at best.[14] On the other hand, Lucy and Edward were probably on the best terms they were ever to know, and their daughter Margaret — 'my Pegg', as Sir Robert called her — had become the object of her grandfather's love. Though Heath's younger sons were still caught up in their studies, Edward and John were beginning to take their place in English government. It was undoubtedly a proud Sir Robert who informed his heir in July 1639: 'You are put into the Commission of peace by Mr Justice Berklys motion to the Lord Keep.'[15] Heath had apparently always hoped that his sons would follow him into crown service. As early as August 1635 he had assured Edward: 'I will take care of finding your office.'[16] Now his elder sons were coming of age, at a time when, being restored to high office, he could do much to advance them.

While Heath's estate was on the rise, that of his king was falling. Sir Robert saw the plight of the crown neatly reflected when in 1639 Charles, facing war with Scotland, required 'gifts'

---

[11] His patent is enrolled in C. 66/2789.
[12] William Hawkins to the earl of Leicester, *HMC*, De L'Isle VI, 126.
[13] In 1628, two years after his dismissal as chief justice, Crew complained, 'Well was it with me when I was King's Serjeant, I found profitt by it'; quoted by Cooper, 'Promotion and Politics', 15.
[14] See p. 71.
[15] U. of I., Heath Papers.
[16] SG. Unbd. Mss., Heath Papers.

from his judges and his learned counsel. Heath donated fifty pounds, the recommended amount, and in all probability he was quite willing to contribute, but he may also have wondered if the situation was at such a pass that the king could sustain himself only by mulcting his servants.[17] Even then, however, he seems to have had no sense of foreboding. The late 1630s found him somehow insulated from the factors that would soon destroy his England. He played no role in the events that provoked the crisis, including such triggers as the second trial of Prynne and Hampden's Case. Heath, canny politician that he was, undoubtedly realised that some crown policies had aroused widespread opposition. But like most of his countrymen, he probably had no visions of the deluge.

Since Heath had never shared the king's antipathy to parliament and did not consider it to be inherently anti-Court, he may have been relieved when Charles, in March 1640, reluctantly issued writs of election. But soon after the writs had been sealed, he witnessed a vivid demonstration of the popular anger that so concerned his king. The Court, hoping to see its own men returned and radical candidates defeated, encouraged courtiers to stand in boroughs that it deemed crucial. Heath himself stood at Reading. Since he had never had much contact with the borough and does not appear to have had any reason to stand there, it is likely that the Court put him up, in the hope that he might be returned in place of one of the Francis Knollys. On the day of the election, however, the Knollys, father and son, radicals both, were returned overwhelmingly, Sir Robert receiving not a single vote. The results might have been different — though only slightly so, in all probability — had not any potential supporters of Heath's been cowed by a mob that, at the hour of election, demonstrated near the polling place, chanting loudly its demand that the Knollys be returned.[18]

The behaviour of the Short Parliament can have encouraged neither the king nor Heath. After the parliament's dissolution came a brief return to Personal Rule, as the government sought desperately to resolve the varied crises that threatened to engulf king and nation. But in October, Charles, as a last resort, again

---

[17] SP 16/538/84. Fraser provides a complete list of contributors: 'Heath', xxii – iv.

[18] J. H. Guilding (ed.), *Records of the Borough of Reading* (London, 1894), III, 493; J. K. Gruenfelder, 'The Election to the Short Parliament, 1640', *Early Stuart Studies*, ed. Reinmuth, 220.

issued writs of election, this time bringing into being the most famous, and probably the most important, parliament in English history.

Heath apparently did not stand for the Long Parliament, and if he did he was not returned. However, a political twist soon provided him with a role, albeit a marginal one, in parliamentary activities. On 9 December 1640 Sir William Jones died, and on 23 January 1641 Heath was accorded his place in the King's Bench.[19] As a judge, Sir Robert was bound to attend the Lords, and for more than a year he carried out the orders of the house, investigating petitioners' claims, bearing messages to the Commons.[20] During that time he witnessed the start of a revolution. It is entirely possible that he sympathised with the reformist aims of the less radical parliamentary factions. At least it may be said that he approved of initiatives to limit the judicial powers of the Council. Yet, when these initiatives resulted in, among other things, the abolition of Star Chamber, he expressed concern that parliament had gone too far.[21] In essence, he remained what he had been, a moderate. But the centre was becoming increasing irrelevant as the political world of England spun towards opposite extremes. By February 1642 the king had left London, and Heath was aware of crisis. 'I am not well', he wrote to Edward, '& I fear the commonwealth is more sicke than I, God put it into a true temper again.'[22]

Undoubtedly painful for Heath to watch was parliament's attack on the English judiciary. The members, along with many of their countrymen, were outraged by the staunch royalism of the judges, particularly when they saw that royalism translated into rulings that buttressed the king's prerogative. The decision

---

[19] Heath's patent is printed in Rymer, XX, 448. In an unexplained sequence of events, he was in May 1641 made master of the Wards (*ibid.*, 517), only to be removed within a few days: Sir John Coke to his father, 18 May 1641, *HMC, Cowper II,* 283.

[20] *HMC, Fourth Report,* 72, 79, 82; *The Journal of Sir Simonds D'Ewes from the First Recess of the Long Parliament to the Withdrawal of King Charles from London,* ed. W. H. Coates (New Haven, 1942), 22, 25, 221.

[21] See p. 205.

[22] U. of I., Compton-Verney Book, no. 54. In the same letter, he expressed fears of invasion, but also hope that the warlike preparations in England would discourage enemy action.

that members found most galling was the one that had favoured Charles over Hampden in the great ship-money case of 1637, and parliament quickly moved against the judges who had ruled for the king. First to feel the members' wrath was Finch, who on 21 December 1640 heard himself denounced for furthering tyranny through various judicial decisions, notably that on Hampden. At length a member called for his impeachment and, alluding to him and his fellow-judges, asked bitterly, 'shall not some of them be hanged that have robbed us of all our propriety?' Fearing for his life, Finch fled to Holland that very evening. The next day the Lords bound over six other judges, each in £10,000, to answer charges that the Commons was then drawing against them. The charges were long in coming, and in fact only two of the six were actually tried.[23] However, parliament had made its point: Judges who failed to support the right — in other words, the popular — causes could expect retribution. And when Charles in January 1641 agreed to a parliamentary demand that judges in the future hold their places during good behaviour, the Court lost its ability to impose countervailing pressure.[24] As the nation lurched towards war, parliament redoubled its efforts to secure a docile judiciary. Sir Thomas Malet, perhaps the most ardent supporter of crown prerogative still on the bench, was imprisoned during the spring of 1642, for opposing the Militia Ordinance. On being released he resumed his judicial function, but when he continued to rule in favour of the crown parliament had him dragged from court by a troop of horse and cast into the Tower, where he remained for more than two years. The treatment of Malet undoubtedly shocked the legal and judicial establishment.[25] Still, parliament failed to make the judges its loyal servants. Charles had stocked the bench with men whose philosophy of government was akin to his own. Despite the danger, most judges remained staunch royalists.

[23] Jones, *Politics and the Bench*, pp. 139 – 43, 197.
[24] McIlwain, 222 – 3.
[25] Clarendon, II, 247. Excellent background, not only on Malet but on the general struggle for control of the judiciary is provided in T. P. S. Woods, *Prelude to Civil War 1642: Mr. Justice Malet and the Kentish Petitions* (Wilton, Salisbury, 1980).

While parliament was unable to force the judges to render decisions that were not in keeping with conscience, it did succeed in binding most of them to London. In May 1642 Charles called on the judges to come to him at York, but most failed to obey, partly because the royal order had not been sealed, partly — perhaps mainly — because they feared parliamentary retaliation. Of the six judges who stood bound to answer the Commons' charges, not one joined the king. The remaining judges had never been bound, owing to the fact that they had been translated to the bench in 1639 or thereafter and therefore had not been involved in the more controversial rulings of the 1630s. Parliament did not, therefore, have a hold over them comparable to the one it enjoyed with regard to their six colleagues, and they were somewhat freer to move, though not entirely without fear of reprisal. Three of these judges decided to join Charles. Theirs was apparently a fairly casual departure, for they appear to have realised that parliament would do nothing to bar their way. One of them, Bankes, who was by now chief justice of the Common Pleas, even requested, and received, the Lords' permission to leave.[26] The others did not seek permission, but at least one of them made no secret of his plans, for shortly after he left London, on 2 June 1642, an observer commented, 'his going was known'.[27] Sir Robert Heath was riding north to join his sovereign.

Remaining behind as Heath left was Bramston, who was now chief justice of the King's Bench. Indeed, none of the men who served with Sir Robert in King's Bench joined him in following the king to York and, later that year, to Oxford. On 10 October Charles, perhaps tiring of his chief justice's excuses for non-attendance and in any case realising that he had to reorder the bench, removed Bramston, and on 18 October he replaced him with Heath. Sir Robert, not wishing to appear an opportunist and not, it would appear, having been one in fact, promptly wrote to Bramston, 'when you shall truely understand the passage of things you will know that I have binn farr from supplantinge you, whome I did truely love and honour, and

[26] S. F. Black, 'The Judges of Westminster Hall during the Great Rebellion 1640 – 1660', unpub. B.Litt. thesis (Oxford, 1970), 30 – 9.
[27] William Montagu to Edward, Lord Montagu, 2 June 1642: *HMC*, Buccleuch I, 304.

that I have binn and will be your servant'.[28] Still, he probably saw in his elevation the fulfilment of a dream, for the office he now held was the highest on the English bench. Eight years before, his career had lain in ruins. Today, he stood at the peak of that profession which he adored above all others. He presumably realised that his latest translation was due primarily to bizarre circumstances. But he could not be grateful for the national crisis that by tortuous paths had brought him his place. So he thanked God, and God alone, for his success:

> For my publicke callinge, wherein of thy great mercye thou hast placed me; who didst first sett me in a great place of Judicature, above my brethren and from thence didst in thy wisdome take me downe (that I might knowe that my standing was & must be in & by thee) who didst againe sett me on the Judgment seat, and hast nowe given me a higher preferment then before; for [that] it is just thou shouldst expect a greater increase of thankfulnes.[29]

Heath was happy not only for himself but for his sons. Now, more than ever before, he was in a position to launch them on their careers. One by one they followed him to Oxford, Edward bringing with him Lucy, who, after one last pregnancy, her twelfth, died in May 1645.[30] By the close of 1642 all five of Heath's sons had joined him. Probably the last to arrive was George, who spent the first months of the war at West Grinsted,

---

[28] 'Autobiography of Sir John Bramston', 87, provides the text. Bramston's son claims the Heath was made chief justice because the king needed an active and available chief coroner — the chief justice of the King's Bench held the chief coronership as a collateral office — to attaint dead rebels, so that the crown might seize their property; he also implies that Heath used unscrupulous means in taking Bramston's place: *ibid.*, 84 - 7. The assertion that Charles displaced Bramston mainly because he needed a chief coroner is disputed by Clarendon (II, 349 - 50), who claims rather that the king needed Heath to attaint living rebels, notably the Earl of Essex. Whatever Charles's motive, he needed to rebuild his judiciary, and he had waited long enough for Bramston. There is no reason to believe that Heath did anything underhanded to win the chief justiceship.

[29] Egerton 2982, f. 66.

[30] 'Liber E. H.', 160. Francis and John Heath both served as colonels in the king's army: P. R. Newman (comp.), *Royalist Officers in England and Wales, 1642 - 1660: A Biographical Dictionary* (New York, 1981), pp. 183 - 4.

where he was rector, but left for Oxford in December 1642, perhaps fearing for his safety — as the son of a leading royalist — if he remained in his parish. Sir Robert had only limited access to the avenues of clerical preferment, so he could help his third son but slightly. Nevertheless, in 1640 he had purchased the advowson of Westbourne, Sussex, and in 1644 he sought, probably in vain, to have George installed there.[31] For his other sons he could do much more. In June 1643 he had John and Robert made auditors of the Court of Wards, and he later bestowed on them the office of prothonotary and clerk for the crown. In February 1644 he assigned to Edward and Robert jointly the lucrative office of custos brevium of the King's Bench and the related post of clerk of the nisi prius. For Francis, the youngest, he was able to secure a place as usher of the Court of Wards.[32] Such nepotism was not out of place in Heath's England; indeed, a father was supposed to help his sons find preferment. Sir Robert was, at this juncture, well positioned to secure places for his sons, because his own high office gave him a significant store of patronage and because 1643 – 4 found the Court with many vacant posts to fill, since large numbers of civil servants had chosen not to accompany the king to Oxford and had thus forfeited their places.[33] In taking advantage of the opportunity, Heath did only what most fathers would have done, given the chance.

While serving his family, Heath did not ignore his office. Despite his years he remained active on assize — as active as the deteriorating military situation permitted. In December 1642 and again in March and June 1643 he rode circuits in Oxfordshire and in at least one case ventured as far as Lincoln. Even as the noose tightened around Oxford, he continued to ride out. As late as December 1644 he could be found riding

---

[31] West Sussex Record Office, Add. Mss. 4412, 4416. Heath had earlier held land at Westbourne (Kopperman, 'Heath', 363), and he may have retained property there. On George Heath's removal from West Grinsted, see John Walker, *Walker Revised: Being a Revision of John Walker's Sufferings of the Clergy during the Great Rebellion, 1642 – 60*, ed. A. G. Matthews (Oxford, 1948), 357.

[32] SBT, DR 98/1290; Egerton 2978, f. 139; Egerton 2979, ff. 26, 30. In 1661 Francis presented several petitions to Parliament, arguing for the restitution of the Court of Wards: Egerton 2979, ff. 45 – 58.

[33] Aylmer, pp. 409 – 11. A list of officers of the Wards who refused to obey Charles's order to come to Oxford is in Egerton 2978, f. 76.

circuit in Devon, more than 150 miles from the safety of Oxford.[34]

Part of his judicial function was to act as crown advisor, a familiar role to him. The evidence is sparse, but it appears that, as in the past, Sir Robert served as referee on a wide range of petitions. Furthermore, as judge he was naturally also expected to handle thorny legal problems, particularly those pertaining to the government. Sometimes the questions he was faced with reflected the peculiar state of the time. There was, for example, the problem put to Heath in March 1644: Who had jurisdiction over tithes when the bishop who was normally responsible was detained, in exile, or otherwise unavailable? Sir Robert responded that the archbishop, the Court of Arches, or any common law court could assume jurisdiction. By such opinions did he seek to buttress the superstructure of society.[35]

During Heath's lengthy stay at Oxford, various roles linked him to the royalist centre. Each role he appears to have executed conscientiously and with the best interests of the townspeople in mind. In his judicial aspect, he in April 1644 ruled, probably to the chagrin of many royalist officers, that the army policy of appropriating carts from merchants was illegal.[36] He and other courtiers also played a role in governing the university, and in November 1643 he participated in the election of the new Savilian Professor of astronomy.[37] For their part, the faculty, inspired perhaps by a sense of what was expedient, had eight months earlier honoured Heath and several other judges by making them doctors of civil law.[38] With professors being appointed and degrees conferred, there was some sense of normality at Oxford, especially early in the war. But danger was never far off, and Oxford was in reality less a university town than an armed camp. Close cooperation between the crown and local government was essential, and Sir Robert served both as

---

[34] *Calendar of Proceedings of the Committee for Compounding*, II, 1517; 'The Life and Times of Anthony Wood', ed. Andrew Clark, *Oxfordshire Record Series*, 19 (1891), 72, 90; *HMC* Buccleuch I, 530. The decrease in the size of the circuits of Royalist judges, and of consequent income, is dealt with by Black, 70 – 2; he also provides tables (p. 83) that show the decline in the caseload at Westminster, 1640 – 6.

[35] SP 16/501/39.

[36] Herbert Barnett (ed.), 'Glympton: The History of an Oxfordshire Manor', Oxfordshire Historical Society, *Publications*, 5 (1923), 12.

[37] SP 16/498/47.

[38] Black, 47.

messenger.[39] In a more assertive role, he and Edward were commissioners in charge of fortifying the city, and in January 1644 they and their colleagues ordered each college to pay a fixed amount to maintain the fortifications.[40] Also in his role as commissioner, Heath prepared two lengthy sets of proposals on how the city should prepare for investment. His detailed suggestions dealt with matters as various as, on the one hand, how women, children, and old men should be evacuated if the need arose and, on the other, how the supply of beer and ale might be kept up in the face of siege.[41] Quite possibly he suffered from the strain of war, but his proposals show him to have been as incisive and as thorough as ever.

Heath's dedication was scarcely likely to win him admirers in parliament. An early manifestation of parliamentary sentiment came on 10 June 1642, when, only eight days after he had left London, the Lords received from him a petition, in which he apologised for his absence, explained that he had gone only because the king had demanded his presence, and expressed the hope that Charles would soon allow him to return. The Lords were unimpressed by his defence, however, and denounced him for violating his oath to attend the house.[42] Feeling against him intensified in December, when he presided at the trial of captured Roundhead soldiers and officers, among them John Lilburne. Heath's behaviour toward the prisoners certainly did not suggest that he was vindictive or bloodthirsty — Lilburne himself later recalled that during his trial Sir Robert 'prest me to save my self' — but parliament believed, probably with reason, that if the proceedings were followed to their conclusion, several of the defendants would be condemned to hang. It therefore threatened to order the execution of two Roundhead prisoners for every Roundhead executed by the crown, and the Court, intimidated, ordered a halt to the trial.[43] The first days of 1643 saw both king and

[39] 'Life and Times of Anthony Wood', 92.
[40] G. C. Richards and H. E. Salter (eds.), 'The Dean's Register of Oriel', Oxfordshire Record Office, Oxfordshire Record Series, 84 (1926), 299. The work of the Heaths as commissioners, particularly Edward, is dealt with by Toynbee and Young, pp. 3 – 4, 6 – 8.
[41] BOD, Add. Ms. D.114, ff. 12 – 13, 99. I wish to thank Miss Margaret Toynbee for having directed me to these documents.
[42] LJ, V, 113.
[43] John Lilburne, A Whip for the Present House of Lords (London, 1648), pp. 4 – 5, 93; The Memoirs of Edmund Ludlow, ed. C. H. Firth (Oxford, 1894), I, 35.

parliament step up their respective campaigns to seize control of the judiciary, as Charles directed that during Hilary term all judges were to sit at Oxford, and parliament retaliated by banning any sittings in term outside Westminster.[44] By the autumn, parliament, which had never had much patience with the Oxford judges, retained hardly any, and when it heard that Heath and three of his colleagues had sought to persuade a grand jury at Salisbury to indict for high treason several Roundhead leaders, it moved swiftly against them. Even though the jury refused to find the bill, the Commons ordered a committee to consider grounds for impeaching the judges who had been involved.[45] The matter then seems to have been dropped, but Heath was spared only for the moment.

Also at Salisbury, in that same autumn assize of 1643, Heath and his colleagues condemned to death Captain Robert Turpin, a Roundhead officer. Turpin was not executed immediately, and indeed he was offered for exchange, but the earl of Essex rejected the terms, considering them unfavourable. Then, early in July 1644, Turpin was hanged, in retaliation for the recent execution by the Roundheads of a royalist soldier who had earlier deserted their ranks. In reporting the news to parliament, Essex fumed: 'I am informed it was by Prince Maurices Comand, but if it please God I may have time to make them repent it.[46] It was not on Maurice, however, but on the judges that parliament vented its wrath. Actually, even before Turpin was executed the members had begun to move against Heath, for on 12 June the Committee for Advance of Money had fined him £1,000. News of the execution provided parliament with an excuse, if it felt it needed one, for still stronger measures, and on 22 July the committee increased Heath's fine to £2,000.[47] That same day the Commons resolved: 'Sir *Robt. Heath* Knight, shall be forthwith impeached of High Treason, by this House, in the Name of all the Commons of *England*, for adhering to the Enemies of the King, Parliament, and Kingdom, now in Arms against the Parliament.'[48] Impeached with Heath were the two judges who had joined him in sentencing Turpin. The outcome

---

[44] Black, 36 – 9. The battle for the judges continued into 1645: *ibid.*, 51 – 83.
[45] Hatcher, 397. Whitelocke, *Memorials*, I, 230 – 1.
[46] SP 21/16/123.
[47] *Calendar of the Proceedings of the Committee for Advance of Money*, I, 400.
[48] *CJ*, III, 567. Whitelocke links the impeachment to Turpin's death: *Memorials*, I, 282.

of the proceedings against them is unknown, but in late 1644 their estates were sequestered, and in September 1645 and December 1646 parliament granted Turpin's daughters awards from those estates.[49] The impeachments and the sequestrations were merely two highlights of the final campaign against the royalist judges. That parliament did not move faster than it did may reflect the fact that during 1644 – 5 it faced a host of problems and could not afford to rivet its attention on any one. Besides, by 1645, and particularly after the New Model Army's decisive victory at Naseby, the king's legal machinery lay in ruins, so there was no need for parliament to move quickly against Heath and his colleagues. When time allowed, however, it acted decisively. On 24 November 1645, both houses declared Heath and four other royalist judges to be legally dead and vacated their offices on the grounds that they had 'deserted their Places, and, by their Councils and Actions, . . . advised and assisted the War against the Parlaiment'.[50]

Sir Robert may have hoped that parliament would be less vindictive once it had reached a final accommodation with the king, but the articles of peace that were agreed on in July 1646 specifically excepted him from pardon.[51] By that time, Heath was an open target, for Oxford had fallen in June. But parliament was more concerned with affairs of state than with the capture of an old man. Indeed, it appears that during 1646 Heath was told by parliamentary agents that he would be free to live out his life in England. However, they apparently also told him that he would be considered a delinquent and would be dealt with harshly if he ever in the future offended parliament. Two years later he recalled that he 'had his liberty, either to exile myself into a forreyn country, or to runn the hazzard of further daunger'.[52] Exile was his choice, though in a letter he wrote to Edward in May 1647 he himself rejected the word: 'I doe not call it an exile, because I made choice to desire it, rather than to live

[49] Calendar of Proceedings of the Committee for Compounding, I, 25, 51.
[50] C. H. Firth and R. S. Rait (eds.), Acts and Ordinances of the Interregnum, 1642 – 1660 (London, 1911), I, 805.
[51] A Collection of the State Papers of John Thurloe, ed. Thomas Birch (London, 1742), I, 80. While treating with Charles at the Isle of Wight, in Oct. 1648, parliament repeated the exception: SP 16/516/100. In March 1649 the ban was yet again recorded: Calendar of Proceedings of the Committee for Compounding, I, 139.
[52] 'Anniversarium', 22.

suspected.'[53] So it was that at the age of seventy-one he ventured abroad, probably for the first time. He was never again to see England.

'This our Perigrination'

As he prepared to depart, Sir Robert penned one of his most touching prayers: 'O Eternal God . . . who knowest our necessities, before we aske, and our ignorance & infirmities in asking: bless and protect us in this our perigrination into these forreyn parts, occasioned . . . for our preservation, against the present powre and violence of our adversaries, turne their hartes, as thou dist the hart of Esau, to his brother jacob.'[54] The prayer completed, he sailed for Calais. With him went John. Margaret and Edward would, he hoped, soon follow.

The crossing at least was easy. On 22 November John wrote to Edward: 'wee came safe to Calis [yesterday] morning, almost without being sick in passage, wee ly yett at the silver Lyon, butt shall remove shortly to private Lodgeings'. One week later Sir Robert, obviously relieved and anticipating a reunion with his eldest son, wrote to Edward: 'I receaved your letter, at the ende of this week, I shall be glad to see you, at least to hear of you; . . . we are in health, god be praised at Calais.'[55]

Apparently, at first the main problem that Sir Robert and John faced was financial. By the close of December they were in Paris, 'well in health, and reasonable well accommodated with lodgeings and dyett, butt at deare rates', as John informed his older brother. The following 1 February he complained to him: 'Wee find the charge at Paris for dyett and lodgeing to bee 20 Crownes a month besydes fyre and washing and other extraordinarys . . . if you think of comeing make use of some freind experienced in Exchange to watch for you when Exchange goes highest from London to Paris and in the nick take bills.'[56] Sir Robert decided soon after that the cost of living in Paris was such as to necessitate yet another move for himself

---

[53] U. of I., Compton-Verney Book, no. 65.
[54] Egerton 2982, f. 79.
[55] U. of I., Heath Papers, include both letters.
[56] U. of I., Heath Papers.

and John. 'My Helth', he wrote to Edward, 'I praise god continues very well; & that I may continue that, & my purse hold out the better, I think within a week or tenn days to remove to St Germane: a place of much better ayre & pleasure & not soe percing into the perse by a third part at least.'[57] For over two years Saint-Germain was his home.

During 1647 the Heath family moved from sorrow to sorrow. In January Sir Robert heard from Edward that Mary had recently come to him at Halnaker and had told him that for some time her husband had been given to beating her. Prior to then she had dissembled, so well in fact that the Heaths had considered her marriage a beautiful one. Now, with the truth out, their love of Sir William Morley turned immediately to hatred, and John was quick to applaud when Edward moved against Mary's tormentor:

> I understand with much trouble the baseness of my brother Morleys behaviour; I am very glad you have so well handled him, and they that thinke to keepe him from mischiefe, must keepe him in awe, for love of goodness will never prevayle upon him. The best course to secure my sisters quiett, is to make her promise, to give you notice where you are of any future ill usage, and lett him knowe she so promises.[58]

The crisis passed. But in France an old man grieved for his daughter across the Channel.

Edward's situation, too, brought grief to Sir Robert. During the civil war, he, like his father, had seen his property sequestrated. Early in 1647, however, he compounded with parliament. He was then allowed to reclaim the lands that he had held earlier, and he also inherited much of the property of his father, who was legally dead. Accompanying both kinds of estates were records that, owing to wartime conditions and the indifference of parliamentary commissioners, were in disarray, and Edward spent much of the year attempting to bring them to order. Where the records were of properties that had once belonged to Sir Robert, he did not hesitate to besiege his father with queries about business transacted long before. Considering that Edward generally called for detailed information, some of

---

[57] U. of I., Heath Papers. While in France, John kept an account of the expenses of the Heath party: Egerton 2982, ff. 66–73.

[58] U. of I., Heath Papers.

Sir Robert's responses were impressive, but as he explained to his son, he had left his own records behind — he thought they might be with Mary — and in consequence his answers often lacked detail.[59]

It was not only chaotic property records that aggravated Edward during 1647, but also creditors, who had been pursuing him for years, claiming that he was responsible for paying off the debts his father owed them. Edward believed that many of their claims were bogus and looked to his father for confirmation, but again Heath was not always able to furnish particulars. Sir Robert was upset by his inability to help. For him, the chief end of existence had been to serve his family. Now, in sad irony, he was leaving his children a legacy of debt. All he could do was express his sorrow. 'For our private businesses', he wrote to Edward on 30 October, 'I cann say but little, as the case stands with me I am not a little troubled, that my children or frends should suffer for my sake.' Still more pained were the words he wrote six days later: 'I am heartily sorry that I put you to these troubles, and have not any means at present to relieve you or help you. God direct you and god blesse us all in these sad times.'[60]

While Edward's problems bore heavily on his father, Sir Robert at first did not have to bear them alone, for there was John to comfort him, but during the autumn of 1647 Heath's second son departed for England, to look after business there. Knowing that parliament looked askance at him because of his long stay in France, in early 1648 he informed the Committee for Compounding with Delinquents that he had left England only on doctor's orders, after a fever had caused him to become 'very crazy and infirme'. The committee, probably less impressed by his account than by his cash, permitted him to compound, and he settled at Brasted.[61] He had probably left France with his father's blessing, but his departure cannot but have saddened

---

[59] The sequestration and subsequent mismanagement of Edward's lands is discussed in Egerton 2983, f. 32, a petition by Edward. In 1650 parliamentary commissioners sold Sir Richard Ingoldesby the manor of North Inglesby, Lincolnshire, a former crown property that had been held by Edward, George, and Robert; after petitioning Clarendon, Edward was able to reclaim it: Lincolnshire Archives Office, Lind. Dep. 15/6.

[60] SG, Unbd. Mss., under 'Heath' (both letters).

[61] Egerton 2978, f. 228; *Calendar of Proceedings for the Committee for Compounding*, II, 1471. Other relevant documents are Egerton 2978, ff. 232, 234, 267.

the old man. Now Heath apparently had but one constant companion, David Powell, a servant.

Without any family to comfort him, Sir Robert was forced to endure the greatest sadness of a sad year. In early December, he learned that Margaret had recently died at Brasted. The year of his exile had seen them share a hope that they would soon be reunited. Of their last moments together, Heath recalled 'my dear and lovynge wife and I were then inforced with heavie harts and mutual teares to take our leave of one another; at that time not without hope of a comfortable meeting againe'.[62] But Margaret, whose health had long been poor, was not equal to the demands of the trip, while Heath was in no position to return, and during 1647 Sir Robert had several 'preadmonitions' that she would soon die.[63] However presaged, Margaret's death was hard on her family, hardest of all on her husband. Soon after it, a cousin wrote to Edward: 'I have lost a worthy friend, you a tender Mother, and my lord a deer & loving wife, whose greefe must needs be surpassinge, and I doubte will be laid by him too much to harte.'[64]

Having no family at hand, Heath looked to friends for consolation. He had already won the friendship of a number of his new neighbours and he also remained close to many courtiers who shared his exile. Perhaps his dearest friend was Nicholas, his last link with the Buckingham years, and an intimate during his time at Oxford. Nicholas visited him occasionally in Saint-Germain, and his visits, as well as those of other friends, helped to revive Heath's spirits. By 1 May 1648 Sir Robert had, for the moment, overcome his grief. 'As you say, you are glad to find me soe cheerefull', he wrote to Nicholas, 'as in truth I praise god I am.'[65]

But events that year tested him further. News from across the Channel continued to be gloomy. Of national importance was the second civil war, which ended, from Heath's point of view, as badly as the first, with Charles defeated and imprisoned.

---

[62] 'Anniversarium', 9.

[63] *Ibid*. Margaret's health had for some years been a subject of concern. On 11 July 1639 Sir Robert had written to Edward that, while the family had hoped that Margaret would be able to travel to Colliweston that summer 'your Mother is soe full of payne, that I doubt She will not be fitt for soe long a journey': U. of I., Heath Papers.

[64] Comment of Robert Heath, probably Edward's second cousin, of Dartford: SBT, DR 98/1652.

[65] Egerton 2433, f. 450.

Family news also gave Sir Robert cause for anxiety. In May Edward was arrested for having allegedly criticised the army, and although he denied the charge he remained in custody throughout the summer.[66] Finally, physical problems heightened Sir Robert's misery. He had always enjoyed excellent health, except for the gout that had afflicted him occasionally since the mid-1630s. At some point during 1648, however, he became paralysed on one side, perhaps from a stroke.[67]

The news from England depressed him, as did his failing health. Less and less did he esteem his world. Always devout, he withdrew progressively into religious meditation. Death he knew was near, but his thoughts centred on life after death, and the prospect, far from frightening, cheered him. In paradise, he was certain, Margaret awaited him. The anniversary of her death found him longing to be reunited with her, in 'the like state of bliss, wheather I am confident by Gods mercy she is gone before me'. But not even the joyous prospect of reunion could blot out the misery that he knew in his current life:

And nowe being left behind, in this vale of miserie, my humble & harty and dailie prayers to God must be, that I may be always prepared for that houre, which although I may not hasten, but . . . I am sure cannot be long; yet I may pray for it, and say Come Lord Jesus, come quickly. The joyes of this life are soe allayed with the miseries which accompany it, that we have little cause to desire the protraction thereof.'[68]

---

[66] Egerton 2978, f. 238 (the order for Edward's arrest and his petition for release).

[67] 'Anniversarium', 16. In a letter to Edward, 21 Oct. 1639, John had expressed a hope that Sir Robert was recovering from the gout: SG, Top. Mss., under 'Rutland, Cottesmore'.

[68] 'Anniversarium', 8, 16 – 17. He also wrote (ibid., 16) 'our souls are . . . divided for the present, hers in the absolute possession of heaven, mine truly militant upon earth, until it shall please God that we may meet againe in that kingdom where we shall live for ever, not in those qualities of husband & wife, but in much more unspeakable comfort & happines as coheirs of that inheritance in the highest heavens which shall never faile'. Obviously Heath was preparing for death and was concentrating on matters of personal religion. Quite possibly, most of his prayers and meditations (Egerton 2982, ff. 66 – 119) date from the time of his exile. But he also devoted time, at least early in the exile, to writing jeux d'esprit, such as his comments on different types of tongues, hands, and eyes (Egerton 2982, ff. 120 – 2; transcription in Fraser, 'Heath', 202 – 4), and his 'Collar of SS' (see ch. 2, n 107).

Then, suddenly, he was again caught up in temporal affairs. The execution of Charles, on 30 January 1649, sent shock waves throughout Europe. Sir Robert Heath himself was stunned, as were his intimates. He had, up to this point, been surprisingly reserved in his comments on the radicals who controlled England. Undoubtedly he had hoped that Charles would be able to win back his throne, but pending such a restoration he had urged cooperation with the de facto government, as for example when he approved of Edward's plan to compound.[69] Despite his exile he had remained free of animosity. In February 1647 he had written to Edward 'I am not confident of any great crymes, worthy of soe much displeasure, even from my enemys', but he had quickly added 'I thank god I doe not particulerly know nor inquire after [them], & cann forgive freely', and three months later he had commented: 'Thank god I can pray for them who esteem me as an enimye, which to their persons I am not, & to their cause I meddle not but live retired & I hope think the better of my long journey & my last.'[70] The shock of Charles's execution, however, caused him temporarily to shift his attention from the next world to his own. He might, and did, denounce the 'most horrid, & unheard of Murther' of the king, but he knew that hand-wringing would solve none of England's problems.[71] Instead of dwelling on the past, even on the killing of his beloved sovereign, he looked to the future especially to the enthronement of the man whom he now recognised as Charles II. Once restored, Charles would have to govern a nation that had just endured a period of unparalleled disruption. He would have to rebuild a governmental structure that had been reduced to ashes. He would have to win the confidence of a sharply divided populace. All of this would be asked of a man who was not yet nineteen and who had little experience in practical affairs of government. Recognising the problems that the young king faced and would face, Heath sensed an obligation to help. Quickly he offered his services to

---

[69] His approval is noted in a letter from John to Edward, 25 Jan. 1647, U. of I., Heath Papers.

[70] U. of I., Compton-Verney Book, no. 65; U. of I., Heath Papers. In his memoir, Heath wrote that he had been exiled 'for noe other crime objected against me (for anything I ever yet herd), but for my fidelitie to my gracious master and soveraigne': 'Anniversarium', 8. But even here, the tone is one of resignation.

[71] Quotation drawn from BOD, Ms. Don. D.124, p. 181.

the government in exile, and the next few months found him drafting, advising, travelling the same paths that he had known for decades.

During the early months of 1649 Charles II and his court anticipated that he would soon return to the throne, so it is not surprising that one of the first assignments Heath carried out was the drawing up of a commission that was to be used after Charles had been restored. The lengthy instrument, directed to various unnamed officials, detailed the procedure for settling war claims.[72] But Heath had his own ideas of how the new king should govern after the restoration and indeed how he could speed the day of his return to England, and he detailed them in a treatise that he presented to Charles during the late winter or early spring of 1649.[73] This document, prepared so late in his career, was probably Heath's lengthiest piece of writing, but he had much to say. He wished, first of all, to counsel Charles on how to win back the throne. Heath advised against a direct invasion of England. Rather, he believed, Charles should join forces with the Irish. The Scots, too, might be willing to act as allies, but in return they would probably demand that Charles should make Presbyterianism the established religion in England, while the Irish could be won over by a mere promise that their Catholicism would thereafter be tolerated. Cromwell's campaign in Ireland soon destroyed the possibility that the Irish might help Charles to victory, but Heath in any case never imagined that Irish help was essential if the Stuarts were to be restored. He was convinced that the parliamentary regime was profoundly unpopular and that most Englishmen would support Charles in his efforts to claim the throne. However, he also believed, and so advised the new king, that Charles could boost his popular support still further by issuing, at the appropriate time, a declaration in which he promised to restore the traditional mode of government to England. Once in power, he was to carry out his promise: Heath went into great detail in describing the steps by which this could be accomplished. A vexing problem was how former Roundheads should be dealt with, once the monarchy was restored. Heath had every reason to detest the radicals, and certainly he did not entirely forgive

---

[72] A complete transcription of this document is included in Fraser, 'Heath', 233 – 45.

[73] 'Memorialls for the Kings Service': BOD, Ms. Don. d.124, pp. 181 – 217. This copy is not in Heath's hand, but it is ascribed to him in a marginal notation.

them. In his treatise he complained 'writing will never restore the king to his Crownes, & perhaps in his fathers tyme too much use was made of the penknife, when the Sword should have been employed'. Nevertheless, he did not demand vengeance. Quite the contrary, he advised Charles that after he had secured power he should follow a moderate course in dealing with those who had rebelled against his father. Only regicides were to be considered 'not capable of mercy'. Other notorious rebels were to forfeit their estates, the property being used to enhance the king's wealth and to recompense royalists who had suffered at the hands of parliament. Heath, not a cruel man himself, was repelled by the prospect of massive retaliation. Always fearful of contention, he was convinced that vindictive policies would not promote domestic tranquillity.

Not long after submitting his treatise, Heath returned to Calais, possibly so that his children could reach him more easily, when the time came. His health continued to deteriorate, and in early August Powell sent word into England that a dying man wished to see his sons once more. Within a few days John set out; however, the ship he sailed on landed far from Calais, forced off course by bad weather and by pursuing pirates.[74] Meanwhile, Sir Robert lay in agony, hoping not for recovery, but only for time enough to see his son. One foot became gangrenous and had to be amputated, a move that merely postponed the inevitable for a few days. On 17 August Powell wrote to his friend Thomas Tuxwell, in London:

> My lord grows every day weaker & weaker, & I feare wee shall not enjoy him longe. I pray god prepare him for a better world, for in his condition he is now in his Lordshipp indures a great deale of misery . . . I well hoped some one of his sonnes would have come to him out of England before this.

Before despatching his letter the next morning, Powell added a postscript: 'John came not this post as wee expected rather writ . . . My lord had rayther seene one of his sonnes. the dockter & Sorgans says hee hath but a short time to live. I desier you & the rest of his frinds to pray for him.'[75]

---

[74] Noted in a letter from John to Edward, 3 Sept. 1649: U. of I., Compton-Verney Book, no. 70.
[75] U. of I., Compton-Verney Book, no. 68.

On 18 August, Sir Robert dictated his will. It was a strange document, in format more of a letter to John. 'Sonn John', he began, 'if God pleas to take me in his mercy unto himselfe, by this long and scharp sickness, I shall humbly submitt thereunto. Some things I have thought uppon which I commend to the especiall care of your brother Edward and your selfe in trust that you will continue as Fathers unto your younger Brothers, as hether you have done.' He then went on to list his bequests, which were few and small, owing in part to the assaults on his estate by creditors and by Roundheads, in part to the fact that, since he had been legally dead since 1645, most of his property had already been distributed among his sons. He asked John to keep his books on common law, while those on civil law went to Francis and those on religion to George, the balance being divided between Edward and Robert. Most of the other bequests also went to his children, but Heath left most of his wardrobe to Powell and asked John to find his servant 'some fitt Imployment'. Closing, he named as overseers two friends of recent vintage, Sir Cornelius de Glarges, a Walloon, and Henry Booth. Witnessing were Rowland Jenkes and William Bennett, both distant kinsmen, and Peirce le Say, another new friend.[76]

The sad but inevitable news went out two days later. Powell wrote to Tuxwell:

> I have in my former letters given you notice of my Lords weake condition, & now this afternoon betwene 3 & foure o'clock yt hath pleased God to take him out of this miserable world, & place him in a better, after hee had borne with admirable patience & constancy the affliction he underwent which would have bene heavye uppon another man, but to him seemed small, God had indued him with such a measure of courage, that amid'st the sorrow his friends suffered for him, they were yet comforted.[77]

A few days later John arrived, to be consoled and, on 24 August, to attempt to comfort his older brother. The courage that their father had by all accounts exhibited, he wrote to Edward, was such as attested to:

[76] SBT, DR 98/1652. A transcription appears in Fraser, 'Heath', 197 – 8.
[77] This letter is appended to 'Anniversarium', 23 – 4; a transcription from the original is in the U. of I., Compton-Verney Book, no. 69.

his much greater fitness for heaven then this world . . . I found by those that were about him that though he was willing to have lived longer if it had pleased God, more for others sakes then his own, yett when he perceived which way his fancy tended, he not only embraced it with willing cheerfulness, but almost outrunne it with longing desyres & earnest ejaculations, full of fayth & piety for a dissolution. Hee much wished to have seene some of us before his death, but it was not gods will it should bee; and he perceiving submitted in that also with contentedness & thus we must do so too by his example.

When near death, Sir Robert had told Powell that he wished to be buried beside Margaret. Now John, to effect his father's request, asked Edward to secure a pass and come to Calais, so that he might escort the body home. He further suggested that Edward bring enough mourning cloth for Heath's friends, both English exiles and continentals. Anticipating that his brother might fear the wrath of the current regime, John added, with more than a hint of anger: 'They will not I hope grudge to grant his buriall there hee being now incapable of doeing them any more misheif (as they call it).' Nevertheless, he advised Edward to arrange that the funeral be held furtively, at night, because the governing powers were opposed to 'Christian' funerals.[78] Ironically, it appears that these bitter words were soon read by the very men whom they were directed against, for as Powell sailed back towards England, carrying with him a number of John's letters, including the one to Edward, the ship was intercepted and the correspondence confiscated. Soon the Council of State, acting on the information included in one of the letters, was moving to impound a cabinet of Heath family papers, and John, still at Calais, could only moan to Edward: 'I feare I am undone by it for in the cabinett are not only all my father's warrants & papers of that nature but all my own evidence & among them diverse deeds of secret trust.'[79]

In seeking out the cabinet, the Council of State was probably actuated in part by a desire to secure Sir Robert's papers.

---

[78] U. of I., Compton-Verney Book, no. 70.
[79] U. of I., Compton-Verney Book, no. 73. The order of the Council of State is SP 18/6/52.

Although dead, he had died out of grace with parliament. But the council may also have wished to review the papers that John had left behind, for he, too, was now considered an enemy. The reason why he had not brought his father's body home was that he had decided not to return to England until he could do so with Charles II. Prior to leaving England he had kept his own counsel, but as he wrote to Edward from Calais: 'I knewe before I went that I must not thinke of lookeinge back.'[80] Soon he was to enter the service of the crown, there to remain throughout the Restoration and for more than thirty years beyond, until his death.[81] Another Heath was to serve the Stuarts and serve them well.

Meanwhile, on 7 September Sir Robert was laid to rest beside Margaret in the Heath Chapel at Brasted Church. Some months later the sarcophagus in which they lay was adorned with alabaster carvings of their recumbent figures. Sir Robert himself was represented in his SS collar and judicial robes.[82] It was as he would have wished to be remembered.

Heath's death came at an entirely appropriate time. A window on his own age, he would have been largely irrelevant to the

[80] U. of I., Compton-Verney Book, no. 70.

[81] John already seems to have been involved in at least one attempt, in 1648, to stage a Royalist coup: David Underdown, *Royalist Conspiracy in England 1649 – 1660* (New Haven, 1960), p. 37. On his later career, see above, ch. 2, n 103.

[82] 'Liber E. H.', 164, provides the date of Heath's burial. A description of the sarcophagus and of the Heath Chapel generally, as well as a transcription of Heath's epitaph, is included in Cave-Browne, pp. 36 – 7. Sir Robert's funeral was apparently a costly affair, for a list of Edward's debts, prepared in about 1650, shows as still owing a debt of £229 5s, to cover funeral expenses; Kent Archives Office, U55 E104. Besides the recumbent effigy and the Hollar etching that serves as the frontispiece of this volume, seven portraits of Heath, not including copies, are known to exist: a bust profile on the medal engraved by Thomas Rawlins in 1645, which is the frontispiece to Fraser, 'Heath' (Fraser has reservations about its authenticity); a painting, in the Public Library, Nassau, The Bahamas, reproduced in Michael Craton, *A History of the Bahamas* (London, 1962), facing p. 60; a painting, property of St John's College, Cambridge, printed in Kopperman, 'Profile', 4; a painting, formerly the property of Lord Willoughby de Broke, and located in Woodley House, but present whereabouts uncertain; a bust and a painting, both property of the Inner Temple; a painting, formerly in Lord Clarendon's collection, but now untraceable. In most, perhaps all, of these portraits, Heath appears in judicial dress. I am grateful to J. H. Baker for having informed me of the existence and status of several of the portraits mentioned in this note, and for having shown me photographs of them.

next. January 1649 had seen the execution of the king whom Sir Robert had regarded as 'the best of men'. Within weeks of Charles's death, the work of his reign, the work in fact of centuries, had been undone. England as Sir Robert left it had no king, no House of Lords. The common law had been pushed aside, and the constitution that it reflected was no more. Church, as well as State, lay in ruins, and society was in an uproar — the sad but natural consequence, Heath would have explained, of the removal of both great national unifiers. The world turned upside down was to be to some extent righted in 1660, but the equilibrium upon which Restoration England was founded was very different from that which Heath would have known. Sir Robert had been born, reached manhood, found success in his dual professions of lawyer and courtier, and grown old, in an England that, while not changeless, was largely of a piece. Only the years of civil war and of exile had disrupted the world of his acquaintance. But the chaos and extremism that was 1649 bore witness to the fact that his world was no more. For a man so much at home in his age, the close of that age marked a fitting time to depart.

Bibliography

Manuscript collections

(* indicates that the class is, except in the first reference, cited in footnotes without the archive being designated.)

All Souls College, Oxford
  Ms. Vol. 204

Berkshire Record Office, Reading
  DEHy; D/ELC; Trumbull Additional

Bodleian Library, Oxford
  Additional D.; Ashmolean; Bankes Papers*; Don. D.; Eng. Misc.; Tanner

British Library, London
  Additional; Cottonian; Egerton*; Hargrave; Harleian*; Lansdowne*; Stowe

Cambridge University Library
  Additional; Dd.; Mm

Corporation of London Records Office
  City Cash; 'The Elizabethan Book of Oaths' (Ms.); Letter Books*; 'Liber Fleetwood' (Ms.); Odd Membranes from Missing Files, 1616 – 1622; Remembrancia; Repertories*; Sessions Records

Drapers Hall, London
  Wardens' Accounts

Essex Record Office, Chelmsford
  A/SR; D/DGn; D/DL; D/DPZ; Q/SR

Foreign and Commonwealth Office, London
  India Office Records, Court Minute Books (CMB) of the East India Company

Gloucestershire Record Office, Gloucester
D185

Goldsmiths Hall, London
Goldsmiths Company, Wardens' Accounts and Court
Minutes

Grays Inn Library, London
Additional

Guildhall Library, London
Livery Company Court Minute Books (CMB): Armourers;
Brewers; Grocers; Haberdashers; Ironmongers; Plaister-
ers; Weavers

Harvard University Library, Cambridge, Massachusetts
Law School Library, Treasure Room: Heath's notes in
Staunford's *Plees del Coron*

Inner Temple Library, London
Miscellanea; Miscellaneous Mss.

Kent Archives Office, Maidstone
U55

Lincolnshire Archives Office, Lincoln
Lind. Dep.

Lincoln's Inn Library, London
Ms. Vols. 77 (82), 582

Mercers Hall, London
Acts of Court

Minet Library, London
Surrey Deeds

Northamptonshire Record Office, Northampton
NPL

Public Record Office, London (Chancery Lane, Kew)
Close Rolls (C. 54)*; Crown Office, Miscellaneous Books (C.
193); Exchequer (E. 215); Patent Rolls (C. 66)*; Prerogative
Court of Canterbury wills (PCC)*; Privy Council Registers
(PC 2)*; Star Chamber (St. Ch. 8); State Papers, Colonial
(CO 1)*; State Papers, Domestic (SP 14, 15, 16, 18, 20)*;
Signet Office, Docket Books

Shakespeare's Birthplace Trust, Stratford upon Avon
Willoughby de Broke Papers (DR 98)

Sheffield Central Library, Archives Division
Wentworth Woodhouse Muniments, Strafford Letters*

Skinners Hall, London
Court Books

Society of Genealogists, London
Topographical Manuscripts: 'Hampshire, Odiham'; 'London, St. Benet Fink'; 'Rutland, Cottesmore'; 'Rutland, Exton'; 'Somerset, Broadway'; 'Worcestershire, Broadwas'
Unbound Manuscripts: 'Croke'; 'Heath'

Surrey Record Office, Kingston upon Thames
18/31; 65/1; 78/10

University of Illinois Library (Urbana), Rare Book Room
Compton-Verney Book; Heath Papers

West Sussex Record Office, Chichester
Additional

Yale Center for Parliamentary History, New Haven
Transcripts of parliamentary diaries; microfilm of diary of Sir Richard Hutton

Printed primary sources

Acts of the Privy Council of England, vols. for 1618 – 19, 1619 – 21, 1621 – 3, 1623 – 5, 1625 – 6, 1626, 1627 – 8, 1629 – 30, 1630 – 1
Aubrey, John, *Brief Lives*, ed. O. L. Dick (Ann Arbor, 1957)
Bannerman, W. B. (ed.), *The Visitations of the County of Surrey Made and Taken in the Years 1530 . . . and 1633 – 4*, Harleian Society, *Publications*, 53 (1905)
Barnett, Herbert (ed.), 'Glympton: The History of an Oxfordshire Manor', Oxfordshire Historical Society, *Publications*, 5 (1923)
Birch, Thomas (ed.), *The Court and Times of Charles the First*, vol. I (London, 1849)
Bloom, J. H. (ed.), 'Wedding Trousseau of a Lady c. 1630', *Notes and Queries*, twelfth series, 4 (1918), 291 – 2
Bowyer, Robert, and Henry Elsing, 'Notes of the Debates in the House of Lords officially Taken by Robert Bowyer and Henry Elsing, Clerks of the Parliaments, A.D. 1621, 1625, 1628', ed.

F. H. Relf, Camden Society, *Publications*, third series, 52 (1929)

Boyle, (Sir) Richard, earl of Cork, *The Lismore Papers of Sir Richard Boyle, First and 'Great' Earl of Cork*, ed. A. B. Grosart (London, 1886), vol. II

Bramston, (Sir) John, 'The Autobiography of Sir John Bramston, K.B.', ed. Charles, Lord Braybrooke, Camden Society, *Publications*, 32 (1845)

Burke, J. B. (comp.), 'The Genealogie or Pedegree of . . . Sir William Cole', *Miscellanea Genealogica et Heraldica*, 2 (1876), 234 – 50

Calendar of Proceedings of the Committee for the Advance of Money, vol. I

Calendar of Proceedings of the Committee for Compounding, vols. I – II

Calendar of State Papers, Colonial Series, vols. for East Indies, 1625 – 9, 1630 – 4

Calendar of State Papers, Domestic Series, of the Reign of Charles I, vols. I, II, VII

Calendar of State Papers, Domestic Series, of the Reign of Elizabeth, vol. for 1598 – 1601

Calendar of State Papers, Domestic Series, of the Reign of James I, vols. for 1603 – 10, 1611 – 18, 1619 – 23

Calendar of State Papers relating to English Affairs, Existing in the Archives and Collections of Venice, vol. XIX

Calendar of the State Papers relating to Ireland, of the Reign of Charles I, series IV, vol. I

Calthrop, Henry, *The Liberties, Usages, and Customes of the City of London* (London, 1642)

Carr, C. T. (ed.), 'Select Charters of Trading Companies A.D. 1530 – 1707'. Selden Society, *Publications*, 28 (1913)

Challoner, Richard (ed.), *Memoirs of Missionary Priests* (London, 1742), vol. II

Chamberlain, John, *The Letters of John Chamberlain*, ed. N. E. McClure, American Philosophical Society, *Memoirs*, 12 (1939), vol. II

Clarendon, Edward Hyde, earl of, *The History of the Rebellion and Civil Wars in England*, ed. W. D. Macray (Oxford, 1888), vols. I – II

Clutterbuck, H. H. (ed.), 'State Papers relating to the Cloth Trade, 1622', Bristol and Gloucestershire Archaeological Society, *Transactions*, 5 (1880 – 1), 154 – 62

Cockburn, J. S. (ed.), *Calendar of Assize Records: Sussex Indict-*

ments, James I (London, 1975)

Coke, (Sir) Edward, *The Fourth Part of the Institutes of the Lawes of England* (London, 1644)

Coke, Roger, *Detection of the Court and State of England during the Last Four Reigns* (London, 1696)

Cooper, W. D. (ed.), 'Lists of Foreign Protestants, and Aliens, Resident in England 1618 – 1688', Camden Society, *Publications*, 82 (1862)

Copy, A, of a Ms. Entitled 'A True Collection . . . of All the Kinges Majesties Offices and Fees . . .' (London, 1606)

Coventry, (Sir) Thomas, *A Perfect and Exact Direction to All Those that Desire to Know the True and Just Fees of . . . the Court of Common Pleas* (London, 1641)

Cozens-Hardy, B. (ed.), 'Presents to the Sheriff of Norfolk, 1600 – 1603', *Norfolk Archaeology*, 26 (1936), 52 – 8

Croke, (Sir) George, *The Third Part of the Reports* (London, 1676)

Croke, P. A., 'Paulus Ambrosius Croke: A Seventeenth Century Account Book, *Notes and Queries*, twelfth series, 4 (1918), 5 – 7, 36 – 8

Crosfield, Thomas, *The Diary of Thomas Crosfield*, ed. F. S. Boas (London, 1935)

Dale, T. C. (ed.), *The Inhabitants of London, 1638* (London, 1931)

Dalton, Michael (ed.), *The Country Justice* (London, 1705)

D'Ewes, (Sir) Simonds, *The Autobiography and Correspondence of Sir Simonds D'Ewes, During the Reigns of James I and Charles I*, ed. J. O. Halliwell (London, 1845), vol. I

—— *The Journal of Sir Simonds D'Ewes. From the Beginning of the Long Parliament to the Trial of the Earl of Strafford*, ed. Wallace Notestein (New Haven, 1923)

—— *The Journal of Sir Simonds D'Ewes. From the First Recess of the Long Parliament to the Withdrawal of King Charles from London*, ed. W. H. Coates (New Haven, 1942)

Dugdale, (Sir) William, *Origines Juridiciales* (London, 1666)

Eliot, (Sir) John, *De Jure Maiestates or Political Treatise of Government (1628 – 30) and the Letter Book of Sir John Eliot (1625 – 32)*, ed. A. B. Grosart (London, 1882), Vol. II

W. S. Ellis, ed. 'Genealogical Memoranda relating to the family of Seyliard', *Miscellanea Genealogica et Heraldica*, second series, I (1886), 9 – 20, 117 – 20

Fairfax, Thomas Fairfax (Lord), *The Fairfax Correspondence*, ed. G. W. Johnson (London, 1848), vol. I

Fanshawe, (Sir) Thomas, *The Practice of the Exchequer Court* (London, 1658)

Firth, C. H., and R. S. Rait (eds.), *Acts and Ordinances of the Interregnum, 1642 – 1660* (London, 1911), vol. I

Fishwick, Henry (ed.), 'The Survey of the Manor of Rochdale in the County of Lancaster . . . Made in 1626', Chetham Society, *Publications*, new series, 71 (1913)

Foster, Joseph (comp.), *Alumni Oxonienses: The Members of the University of Oxford, 1500 – 1714* (Oxford, 1891), vol. II

—— (comp.), *The Register of Admissions to Gray's Inn* (London, 1889)

Gardiner, S. R. (ed.), 'Debates in the House of Commons in 1625', Camden Society, *Publications*, new series, 6 (1873)

—— (ed.), 'Documents relating to the Proceedings against William Prynne, in 1634 and 1637', Camden Society, *Publications*, new series, 18 (1877)

—— (ed.), 'The Fortescue Papers', Camden Society, *Publications*, new series, 1 (1871)

—— (ed.), 'Reports of Cases in the Courts of Star Chamber and High Commission', Camden Society, *Publications*, new series, 39 (1886)

Goodman, Godfrey, and J. S. Brewer (eds.), *The Court of King James the First* (London, 1839), vol. II

Guilding, J. M. (ed.), *The Records of the Borough of Reading* (London, 1894), vol. III

Hacket, John, *Scrinia Reserata: A Memorial Offered to the Great Deservings of John Williams, D.D.* (London, 1693), vol. II

Hakewill, William, *Modus Tenendi Parliamentum: or, The Old Manner of Holding Parliaments in England* (London, 1671)

Hart, W. G. (comp.), *The Register of Tonbridge School from 1553 to 1820* (London, 1935)

Heath, Edward, 'Liber Edwardi Heath', ed. J. H. Bloom, *Miscellanea Genealogica et Heraldica*, fifth series, 4 (1925), 158 – 64

Heath, (Sir) Robert, 'Anniversarium', ed. E. P. Shirley, Philobiblon Society, *Publications*, 1 (1854), separately paginated

—— 'Collar of SS', ed. E. P. Shirley, *Notes and Queries*, 10 (1854), 357 – 8

—— *A Machavillian Plot* (London, 1642)

—— *Maxims and Rules of Pleading* (London, 1694)

—— *Praxis almae curiae cancellariae* (London, 1694)

—— 'Speech of Sir Robert Heath, Attorney-General, in the Case of Alexander Leighton, in the Star Chamber, June 4, 1630', ed. John Bruce and S. R. Gardiner, Camden Society, *Miscellany*, 7 (1875)

Heath, Robert, *Clarastella, Together with Poems, Occasional, Elegies, Epigrams, Satyrs (1650)*, ed. F. H. Candelaria (Gainesville, Fla., 1970)

Hovenden, Robert (ed.), 'The Visitation of Kent, Taken in the Years 1619 – 1621', Harleian Society, *Publications*, 42 (1898)

Howell, T. B. (ed.), *A Complete Collection of State Trials and Proceedings for High Treason and Other Crimes and Misdemeanors from the Earliest Period to the Year 1783* (London, 1816), vols. II, III, IV

Hudson, William, 'A Treatise on the Court of Star Chamber', *Collectanea Juridica*, ed. Francis Hargrave (London, 1792), II, 1 – 240

Hughes, Edward (ed.), 'A Durham Manuscript of the Commons Debates of 1629', *The English Historical Review*, 74 (1959), 672 – 9

Inderwick, F. A. (ed.), *A Calendar of the Inner Temple Records* (London, 1898), vols. II – III

James I, *The Political Works of James I: Reprinted from the Edition of 1616*, ed. C. H. McIlwain (Cambridge, Mass., 1918)

R. C. Johnson et al. (eds.), *Commons Debates 1628* (New Haven, 1977), vols. II – III

Journals of the House of Commons, vols. I, III

Journals of the House of Lords, vols. III, V

Larkin, J. F., and P. L. Hughes (eds.), *Stuart Royal Proclamations* (Oxford, 1973), vol. I

Larking, L. B. (ed.), 'Proceedings, Principally in the County of Kent, in connection with the Parliaments Called in 1640', Camden Society, *Publications*, 80 (1862)

Laud, William, *The Works of . . . William Laud . . . Archbishop of Canterbury*, ed. James Bliss and William Scott, *Library of Anglo-Catholic Theology*, 58 – 64 (1847 – 60), vols. III, VII

'Lay Subsidy Assessments for the County of Surrey in 1593 or 1594', *Surrey Archaeological Collections*, 19 (1906)

Leighton, Alexander, *An Epotime or Briefe Discoverie . . . of the Many and Great Troubles that Dr. Leighton Suffered* (London, 1646)

Le Neve, John, *Le Neve's Pedigrees of the Knights Made by King Charles II, King James II, King William III and Queen Mary, King William alone, and Queen Anne*, ed. G. W. Marshall, Harleian Society, *Publications*, 8 (1873)

Lilburne, John, *A Whip for the Present House of Lords* (London, 1648)

List, A, of the By-Laws of the City of London, Unrepealed (London,

1769)

Ludlow, Edmund, *The Memoirs of Edmund Ludlow*, ed. C. H. First (Oxford, 1894), vol. I

Malcolm, J. L. (ed.), 'Charles I on Innovation: a Confidential Directive on an Explosive Issue', Institute of Historical Research, *Bulletin*, 53 (1980), 252 – 5

Malynes, (Sir) Gerrard de, *Consuetudo vel Lex Mercatoria* (London, 1604)

Manningham, John, *The Diary of John Manningham of the Middle Temple 1602 – 1603*, ed. R. P. Sorlien (Hanover, N.H., 1976)

Mun, Thomas, 'England's Treasure by Forraign Trade, or the Ballance of Our Forraign Trade is the Rule of Our Treasure', *A Select Collection of Early English Tracts on Commerce*, ed. J. R. McCulloch (London, 1859), pp. 115 – 209

Murray, K. W. (ed.), 'Extracts from a Seventeenth-Century Note-Book', *The Genealogist*, new series, 33 (1917), 59 – 64

Nicholas, (Sir) Edward, 'Correspondence of Sir Edward Nicholas, Secretary of State', ed. G. F. Warner, Camden Society, *Publications*, new series, 50 (1892)

—— *Proceedings and Debates in the House of Commons in 1620 and 1621* (London, 1766), 2 vols

North, Roger, *The Lives of . . . Francis, North, Baron Guilford, . . . Sir Dudley North . . . and . . . Rev. Dr. John North*, ed. Augustus Jessopp (London, 1890), vol. II

Notestein, Wallace, and F. H. Relf (eds.), *Commons Debates for 1629* (Minneapolis, 1921)

—— —— and Hartley Simpson (eds.), *Commons Debates 1621* (New Haven, 1935), 7 vols

Oglander, (Sir) John, *The Oglander Memoirs*, ed. W. H. Lond (London, 1888)

Radcliffe, George, *The Earl of Strafford's Letters and Despatches with an Essay towards His Life* (London, 1739), vol. I

Richards, G. C., and H. E. Salter (eds.), 'The Dean's Register of Oriel', *Oxfordshire Record Series*, 84 (1926)

Riley, H. T. (trans.), *Liber Albus: The White Book of the City of London* (London, 1862)

Rous, John, 'Diary of John Rous, Incumbent of Santon Downham, Suffolk, from 1625 to 1642', ed. M. A. E. Green, Camden Society, *Publications*, 66 (1856)

Royal Commission on Historical Manuscripts, *Reports*, Reports I, III – IX: Buccleuch I, III; Cowper I – II; De L'Isle and Dudley, V – VI; Exeter; Gawdy; Gurney II; Hastings IV; Laing I; Ormonde I; Sackville [Knole]; Salisbury XI; Various

Collections I

Rushworth, John (ed.), *Historical Collections* (London, 1707), vol. II

Rymer, Thomas (ed.), *Foedera, conventiones, literae, et cujuscunque generis acta publica* (London, 1704–32), vols. XVII, XIX, XX

Sachse, W. L. (ed.), 'Minutes of the Norwich Court of Admiralty', Norfolk Record Society, *Publications*, 36 (1967)

Selden, John, *The Table Talk of John Selden*, ed. (Sir) Frederick Pollack (London, 1927)

Shaw, W. C. (comp.), *The Knights of England* (London, 1906), vol. I

Steele, Robert (ed.), *Tudor and Stuart Proclamations 1485–1714* (Oxford, 1910), vol. I

Stockwood, John, *Disputatiuncularum* (London, 1619)

Stow, John, *A Survey of the Cities of London and Westminster*, ed. John Strype (London, 1720), vol. I

Sturgess, H. A. C. (comp.), *Register of Admissions to the Honourable Society of the Middle Temple* (London, 1949), vol. I

Talbot, Clare (ed.), 'Miscellanea: Recusant Records', Catholic Record Society, *Publications*, 53 (1961)

Thurloe, John, *A Collection of the State Papers of John Thurloe*, ed. Thomas Birch (London, 1742), vol. I

Unanimous, The, or Consentient Opinion of the Learned . . . that . . . the King Can Do no Wrong (London, 1703)

Venn, John and J. A. (comps.), *Alumni Cantabrigienses* (Cambridge, 1922), part I, vol. II

Vermuyden, (Sir) Cornelius, *A Discourse touching the Drayning the Great Fennes* (London, 1642)

Walker, John, *Walker Revised: Being a Revision of John Walker's Sufferings of the Clergy during the Great Rebellion 1642–60*, ed. A. G. Matthews (Oxford, 1948)

Weldon, (Sir) Anthony, 'The Court and Character of King James', *Secret History of the Court of James the First*, ed. (Sir) Walter Scott (Edinburgh, 1811), I, 313–482

—— 'The Court of King Charles', *Ibid.*, II, 19–68

Whitelocke, Bulstrode, *Memorials of the English Affairs* (Oxford, 1853), vol. I

Whitelocke, (Sir) James, 'Liber Famelicus of Sir James Whitelocke', ed. John Bruce, Camden Society, *Publications*, 70 (1858)

Whitmore, J. B., and A. W. H. Clarke (eds.), *London Visitation Pedigrees, 1664*, Harleian Society, *Publications*, 92 (1940)

Whythorne, Thomas, *The Autobiography of Thomas Whythorne*,

ed. J. M. Osborn (Oxford, 1961)

Wilson, (Sir) Thomas, 'The State of England Anno Dom. 1600', ed. F. J. Fisher, Camden Society, *Miscellany*, 16 (1936), 1 – 47

Winthrop, John, 'The Winthrop Papers', vol. I, ed. R. C. Winthrop et al., Massachusetts Historical Society, *Collections*, fourth series, 6 (1863)

Wood, A. C. (comp.), 'List of Escheators for England, with the Dates of Appointment', Typescript, Public Record Office, 1932

Wood, Anthony, *Athenae Oxoniensis* (London, 1721), vol. I

—— 'The Life and Times of Anthony Wood', vol. I, ed. Andrew Clark, *Oxfordshire Record Series*, 19 (1891)

Woodhouse, R. I. (ed.), *Registers of Merstham* (London, 1902)

Wright, Thomas (ed.), *Queen Elizabeth and Her Times: A Series of Original Letters* (London, 1838), vol. II

Secondary works

Adair, E. R., 'The Petition of Right', *History*, new series, 5 (1920), 99 – 103

Alexander, M. V. C., *Charles I's Lord Treasurer: Sir Richard Weston, Earl of Portland (1577 – 1636)* (Chapel Hill, 1975)

Anderson, C. B., 'Ministerial Responsibility in the 1620's', *Journal of Modern History*, 34 (1962), 381 – 9

Appleby, A. B., *Famine in Tudor and Stuart England* (Stanford, 1978)

Appleby, J. O., *Economic Thought and Ideology in Seventeenth-Century England* (Princeton, 1978)

Ashton, Robert, *The City and the Court 1603 – 1643* (Cambridge, 1979)

—— *The Crown and the Money Market 1603 – 1640* (Oxford, 1960)

—— 'The Parliamentary Agitation for Free Trade in the Opening Years of the Reign of James I', *Past and Present*, 38 (1967), 40 – 55

Aylmer, G. E., *The King's Servants: The Civil Service of Charles I, 1625 – 1642* (London, 1961)

Baker, J. H., 'The Law Merchant and the Common Law before 1700', *Cambridge Law Journal*, 38 (1979), 295 – 332

—— *The Order of Serjeants at Law*, Selden Society, *Publications*, supplementary series, 5 (1984)

Baker, Thomas, *History of the College of St. John the Evangelist, Cambridge* (Cambridge, 1869)

Ball, J. N., 'Sir John Eliot and Parliament, 1624 – 1629', in Kevin Sharpe (ed.), *Faction and Parliament: Essays on Early Stuart History* (Oxford, 1978), pp. 173 – 207

Barnes, T. G., 'Due Process and Slow Process in the Late Elizabethan-Early Stuart Star Chamber', *The American Journal of Legal History*, 6 (1962), 221 – 49, 315 – 46

—— *Somerset 1625 – 1640: A County Government during the 'Personal Rule'* (Cambridge, Mass., 1961)

—— 'Star Chamber Litigants and Their Counsel, 1596 – 1641', in J. H. Baker (ed.), *Legal Records and the Historian*, Royal Historial Society, *Studies in History*, 7 (London, 1978), pp. 7 – 28

Bates, F. A., *Graves Memoirs of the Civil War* (London, 1927)

Batho, Gordon, 'Landowners in England', *The Agrarian History of England and Wales*, IV, ed. Joan Thirsk (Cambridge, 1967), pp. 256 – 356

Beaven, A. B., *The Aldermen of the City of London* (London, 1908), vol. I

Bereford, Maurice, 'Habitation versus Improvement: The Debate on Enclosure by Agreement', in *Essays in the Economic and Society History of Tudor and Stuart England*, ed. F. J. Fisher (Cambridge, 1961), pp. 40 – 69

Bisschop, W. R., *The Rise of the London Money Market 1640 – 1826* (London, 1910)

Black, S. F., 'The Judges at Westminster Hall during the Great Rebellion 1640 – 1660', unpub. B.Litt. thesis (Oxford, 1970)

Bland, D. S., 'Learning Exercises and Readers at the Inns of Chancery in the Fifteenth and Sixteenth Centuries', *Law Quarterly Review*, 95 (1979), 244 – 52

Blomefield, Francis, *An Essay, Towards a Topographical History of the County of Norfolk* (London, 1851), vol. VI

Bonner, R. E., 'Administration and Public Service under the Early Stuarts: Edward Viscount Conway as Secretary of State, 1623 – 1628', unpub. Ph.D. dissertation (Univ. of Minnesota, 1968)

Bott, Edmond, *Decisions of the Court of King's Bench, upon the Laws relating to the Poor* (London, 1793), vol. I, part II

Bouwsma, W. J., 'Lawyers and Early Modern Culture', *The American Historical Review*, 78 (1973), 305 – 28

Broad, John, 'Gentry Finances and the Civil War; The Case of the Buckinghamshire Verneys,' *The Economic History Review*, second series, 32 (1979), 183 – 200

Brooks, C. W., 'Litigants and Attorneys in the King's Bench and

Common Pleas, 1560 – 1640', *Legal Records and the Historian*, ed. Baker, pp. 41 – 59

Campbell, John (Lord), *The Lives of the Chief Justices of England* (New York, 1875), vol. II

Campbell, Mildred, *The English Yeoman under Elizabeth and the Early Stuarts* (New Haven, 1942)

Cave-Browne, John, *The History of Brasted, Its Manor, Parish, and Church* (Westerham, Kent, 1874)

Challis, C. E., *The Tudor Coinage* (Manchester, 1978)

Chitty, C. W., 'Aliens in England in the Sixteenth Century', *Race*, 8 (1966), 129 – 45

Clark, Peter, 'The Alehouse and the Alternative Society', *Puritans and Revolutionaries: Essays on Seventeenth-Century History Presented to Christopher Hill*, ed. Don Pennington and Keith Thomas (Oxford, 1978), pp. 47 – 72

―――― *English Provincial Society from the Reformation to the Revolution: Religion, Politics, and Society in Kent 1500 – 1640* (Hassocks, Sussex, 1977)

Cliffe, J. T., *The Yorkshire Gentry: From the Reformation to the Civil War* (Oxford, 1974)

Clifton, Robin, 'The Popular Fear of Catholics during the English Revolution', *Past and Present*, 52 (1971), 23 – 55

Cockburn, J. S., *A History of English Assizes 1558 – 1714* (Cambridge, 1972)

Collinson, Patrick, 'The Elizabeth Puritans and the Foreign Reformed Churches in London', *Huguenot Society of London, Proceedings*, 20 (1964), 528 – 55

Cooper, H. H. A., 'Promotion and Politics amongst the Common Law Judges of the Reigns of James I and Charles I', unpub. M.A. thesis (Liverpool, 1964)

Cooper, J. P., 'Economic Regulation and the Cloth Industry in Seventeenth-Century England', *Royal Historical Society, Transactions*, fifth series, 20 (1970), 73 – 99

Copinger, W. A., *The Manors of Suffolk* (London, 1905), vol. III

Craig, John, *The Mint* (Cambridge, 1953)

Craton, Michael, *A History of the Bahamas* (London, 1962)

Cunningham, William, *The Growth of English Industry and Commerce*, fifth ed. (Cambridge, 1912)

Curtis, M. H., 'The Alienated Intellectuals of Early Stuart England', *Past and Present*, 23 (1962), 25 – 41

Daly, James, *Sir Robert Filmer and English Political Thought* (Toronto, 1979)

Darby, H. C., *The Draining of the Fens* (Cambridge, 1956)

315

Davies, M. G., *The Enforcement of English Apprenticeship, 1563 – 1642* (Cambridge, Mass., 1956)

Dictionary of National Biography

Eccleshall, Robert, *Order and Reason in Politics: Theories of Absolute and Limited Monarchy in Early Modern England* (Oxford, 1978)

Edwards, J. L. J., *The Law Officers of the Crown* (London, 1964)

Ellis, Joyce, 'The Decline and Fall of the Tyneside Salt Industry, 1660 – 1790: A Re-examination', *The Economic History Review*, second series, 33 (1980), 45 – 58

Evans, F. M. G., *The Principal Secretary of State: A Survey of the Office from 1558 to 1680* (Manchester, 1923)

Everitt, Alan, *The Community of Kent and the Great Rebellion 1640 – 60* (Leicester, 1966)

Fisher, F. N., 'Sir Cornelius Vermuyden and the Dovegang Lead Mine', Derbyshire Archaeological and Natural History Society, *Journal*, 72 (1952), 74 – 118

Flemion, J. A., 'The Dissolution of Parliament in 1626: A Revaluation', *The English Historical Review*, 87 (1972), 784 – 90

Fletcher, Anthony, *Reform in the Provinces: The Government of Stuart England* (New Haven and London, 1986)

Forster, John, *Sir John Eliot: A Biography 1590 – 1632* (London, 1864)

Foss, Edward, *The Judges of England* (London, 1857), vol. VI

Foster, F. F., *The Politics of Stability: A Portrait of the Rulers in Elizabethan London*, The Royal Historical Society, *Studies in History*, 1 (London, 1977)

Foster, Stephen, *Notes from the Caroline Underground: Alexander Leighton, the Puritan Triumvirate, and the Laudian Reaction to Nonconformity*. [*Studies in British History and Culture*, 6] (Hamden, Conn., 1978)

Fraser, I. H. C., 'The Agitation in the Commons, 2 March 1629', Institute of Historical Research, *Bulletin*, 30 (1957), 86 – 95

—— 'Sir Robert Heath: Some Consideration of His Work and Life', unpub. M.A. thesis (Bristol, 1954)

Fraser, William, *Elphinstone Family Book* (Edinburgh, 1897), vol. II

Gardiner, S. R., *History of England from the Accession of James I to the Outbreak of the Civil War, 1603 – 42* (London, 1883 – 4), vols. III, V, VII

Girton, Tom, *The Triple Crowns: A Narrative History of the Drapers' Company 1364 – 1964* (London, 1964)

Godwin, G. N., *The Civil War in Hampshire (1632 – 45)* (Southampton, 1904)

Gonner, E. C. K., 'The Progress of Enclosure during the Seventeenth Century', *The English Historical Review*, 23 (1908), 477 – 501

Gough, J. W., *Fundamental Law in English Constitutional History* (Oxford, 1955)

Gould, J. D., 'The Royal Mint in the Early Seventeenth Century', *The Economic History Review*, second series, 5 (1952), 240 – 8

Gruenfelder, J. D., 'The Election to the Short Parliament, 1640', *Early Stuart Studies: Essays in Honor of David Harris Willson*, ed. H. S. Reinmuth (Minneapolis, 1970), 180 – 230

Guy, J. A., 'The Origins of the Petition of Right Reconsidered', *The Historical Journal*, 25 (1982), 289 – 312

Habakkuk, H. J., 'The Long-Term Rate of Interest and the Price of Land in the Seventeenth Century', *The Economic History Review*, second series, 5 (1952), 26 – 45

Hair, P. E. H., 'Bridal Pregnancy in Rural England in Earlier Centuries', *Population Studies*, 20 (1966), 233 – 43

Hammersley, George, 'The Revival of the Forest Laws under Charles I', *History*, new series, 45 (1960), 85 – 102

Harris, L. E., *Vermuyden and the Fens: A Study of Sir Cornelius Vermuyden and the Great Level* (London, 1953)

Harris, P. R., 'William Fleetwood, Recorder of the City, and Catholicism in Elizabethan London', *Recusant History*, 18 (1963), 106 – 22

Harrison, W. J., *Life in Clare Hall, Cambridge, 1658 – 1713* (Cambridge, 1958)

Hasted, Edward, *The History and Topographical Survey of the County of Kent* (Canterbury, 1778 – 99), vols. I, IV

Hatcher, Henry, *Salisbury* [*The History of Modern Wiltshire*, by R. C. Hoare et al., VI.] (London, 1843)

Havran, M. J., *Caroline Courtier: The Life of Lord Cottingham* (London, 1973)

—— *The Catholics in Caroline England* (Stanford, 1962)

Henderson, E. G., *Foundations of English Administrative Law: Certiorari and Mandamus in the Seventeenth Century* (Cambridge, Mass., 1963)

Hill, Christopher, *Puritanism and Revolution: Studies in Interpretation of the English Revolution of the 17th Century* (London, 1958)

Hill, L. M., 'County Government in Caroline England 1625 – 1640', *The Origins of the English Civil War*, ed. Conrad Russell (London, 1973), 66 – 90

Hine, Reginald, *The Cream of Curiosity* (London, 1920)

Hinton, R. W. K., 'English Constitutional Theories from Sir John Fortescue to Sir John Eliot', *The English Historical Review*, 75 (1960), 410 – 25

—— 'The Mercantile System in the Time of Thomas Mun', *The Economic History Review*, second series, 7 (1955), 277 – 90

Hirst, Derek, *The Representative of the People? Voters and Voting in England under the Early Stuarts* (Cambridge, 1975)

Houghton, W. E., Jr., 'The English Virtuoso in the Seventeenth Century', *Journal of the History of Ideas*, 3 (1942), 51 – 73, 190 – 219

Howell, Roger, Jr., *Newcastle upon Tyne and the Puritan Revolution* (Oxford, 1967)

Hulme, Harold, *The Life of Sir John Eliot 1592 to 1632: Struggle for Parliamentary Freedom* (London, 1957)

—— 'The Sheriff in the House of Commons', *Journal of Modern History*, 1 (1929), 361 – 77

Johnson, E. A. J., *Predecessors of Adam Smith: The Growth of British Economic Thought* (New York, 1937)

Jones, W. J., *The Elizabethan Court of Chancery* (Oxford, 1967)

—— 'Ellesmere and Politics, 1603 – 1617', *Early Stuart Studies*, ed. Reinmuth, 17 – 45

—— *Politics and the Bench: The Judges and the Origins of the English Civil War* (London, 1971)

Jordan, W. K., *Social Institutions in Kent 1480 – 1660: A Study of the Changing Pattern of Social Aspirations, Archaeologia Cantiana*, 75 (1961)

Judges, A. V., 'The Origins of English Banking', *History*, 16 (1931), 138 – 45

Judson, M. A., *Crisis of the Constitution: An Essay in Constitutional and Political Thought in England, 1630 – 45* (New Brunswick, N.J., 1949)

Kent, J. R., 'Attitudes of Members of the House of Commons to the Regulation of "Personal Conduct" in Late Elizabethan and Early Stuart England', *Institute of Historical Research, Bulletin*, 46 (1973), 41 – 71

—— 'Social Attitudes of Members of Parliament 1590 – 1624', unpub. Ph.D. dissertation (London, 1971)

Kirkham, Nellie, 'The Tumultuous Course of Dovegang', *Derbyshire Archaeological and Natural History Society, Journal*, 73 (1953), 1 – 35

Knafla, L. A., *Law and Politics in Jacobean England: The Tracts of Lord Ellesmere* (Cambridge, 1977)

Kopperman, P. E., 'Ambivalent Allies: Anglo-Dutch Relations and the Struggle against the Spanish Empire in the Caribbean, 1621 – 1641', *The Journal of Caribbean History*, 21 (1987), 55 – 77

—— 'Profile in Failure: The Carolana Project, 1629 – 1640', *The North Carolina Historical Review*, 59 (1982), 1 – 23

—— 'Sir Robert Heath (1575 – 1649): A Biography', unpub. Ph.D. dissertation (Univ. of Illinois, 1972)

Lang, R. G., 'The Greater Merchants of London in the Early Seventeenth Century', unpub. D.Phil. dissertation (Oxford, 1963)

Langbein, J. H., *Torture and the Law of Proof: Europe and England in the Ancien Régime* (Chicago, 1976)

Laslett, Peter, *The World We have Lost: England before the Industrial Age*, second ed. (New York, 1973)

Levack, B. P., *The Civil Lawyers in England 1603 – 1641: A Political Study* (Oxford, 1973)

Lewis, A. H., *A Study of Elizabeth Ship Money* (London, 1928)

Lindley, Keith, *Fenland Riots and the English Revolution* (London, 1982)

Little, David, *Religion, Order, and Law: A Study in Pre-Revolutionary England* (New York, 1969)

Lobel, Mary D. (ed.), *A History of the County of Oxford*, V, *The Victoria History of the Counties of England* (London, 1957)

Lockyer, Roger, *Buckingham: The Life and Political Career of George Villiers, First Duke of Buckingham, 1592 – 1628* (London, 1981)

Macauley, J. A., 'Richard Montague: Caroline Bishop, 1575 – 1641', unpub. Ph.D. dissertation (Cambridge, 1964)

MacFarlane, Alan, *The Family Life of Ralph Josselin, a Seventeenth-Century Clergyman* (Cambridge, 1970)

McIlwain, C. H., 'The Tenure of English Judges', *American Political Science Review*, 7 (1913), 207 – 30

Mander, C. H. W., *A Descriptive and Historical Account of the Guild of Cordwainers of the City of London*, (London 1931)

Manning, Brian, *The English People and the English Revolution 1640 – 1649* (London, 1976)

Manning, Owen, and William Bray, *The History and Antiquities of the County of Surrey* (London, 1814), vol. III

Matthews, L. G., *The Royal Apothecaries* (London, 1967)

Melton, F. T., 'Absentee Land Management in Seventeenth-Century England', *Agricultural History*, 52 (1978), 147 – 59

Mitchell, W. H., *The Rise of the Revolutionary Party in the English House of Commons, 1603 – 1629* (New York, 1957)

Moir, T. L., *The Addled Parliament of 1614* (Oxford, 1958)

Morrill, J. S., *Cheshire 1630 – 1660* (Oxford, 1974)

Mullinger, J. B., *Cambridge Characteristics in the Seventeenth Century* (Cambridge, 1867)

Munden, R. C., 'James I and "the Growth of Mutual Distrust": King, Commons, and Reform, 1603 – 1604', *Faction and Parliament*, ed. Sharpe, 43 – 72.

Newman, P. R. (comp.), *Royalist Officers in England and Wales, 1642 – 1660: A Biographical Dictionary* (New York, 1981)

Nicholas, Donald, *Mr. Secretary Nicholas (1593 – 1669): His Life and Letters* (London, 1955)

Nicholl, John, *Some Account of the Worshipful Company of Ironmongers* (London, 1851)

Nichols, John, *The Progresses . . . of King James the First* (London, 1828), vol. III

Norsworthy, Laura, *The Lady of Bleeding-Heart Yard: Lady Elizabeth Hatton, 1578 – 1646* (London, 1935)

Norton-Kyshe, J. W., *The Law and Privileges relating to the Attorney-General and Solicitor-General of England* (London, 1897)

Notestein, Wallace, *The House of Commons 1604 – 1610* (New York, 1971)

—— *The Winning of the Initiative by the House of Commons* (London, 1926)

Oakley, Frances, 'Jacobean Political Theology: The Absolute and Ordinary Powers of the King', *Journal of the History of Ideas*, 29 (1968), 323 – 46

Pearl, Valerie, *London and the Outbreak of the Puritan Revolution: City Government and National Politics, 1625 – 1643* (Oxford, 1961)

Pocock, J. G. A., *The Ancient Constitution and the Feudal Law: A Study of English Historical Thought in the Seventeenth Century* (Cambridge, 1957)

Porter, H. C., *Reformation and Reaction in Tudor Cambridge* (Cambridge, 1958)

Prall, S. E., *The Agitation for Law Reform during the Puritan Revolution* (The Hague, 1966)

Prest, W. R., 'Counsellors' Fees and Earnings in the Age of Sir Edward Coke', *Legal Records and the Historian*, ed. Baker, pp. 165 – 84

—— *The Inns of Court under Elizabeth I and the Early Stuarts 1590 – 1640* (Totowa, N.J., 1972)

—— 'Legal Education of the Gentry at the Inns of Court,

1560 – 1640', *Past and Present*, 38 (1967), 20 – 39

Price, F. G. H., *A Handbook of London Bankers: With Some Account of Their Predecessors, the Early Goldsmiths* (London, 1876)

Prideaux, W. S., *Memorials of the Goldsmiths' Company: Being Gleanings from Their Records Between the Years 1335 and 1815* (London, 1896), vol. I

Pulling, Alexander, *The Laws and Customs of the City of London* (London, 1854)

Rabb, T. K., 'Free Trade and the Gentry in the Parliament of 1604', *Past and Present*, 40 (1968), 165 – 73

Ramsay, G. D., *The Wiltshire Woollen Industry in the Sixteenth and Seventeenth Centuries* (Oxford, 1943)

Relf, F. H., *The Petition of Right* (Minneapolis, 1917)

Richards, R. D., *The Early History of Banking in England* (London, 1929)

Richardson, W. C., *A History of the Inns of Court: With Special Reference to the Period of the Renaissance* (Baton Rouge, 1975)

Rivington, Septimus, *The History of Tonbridge School from Its Foundation in 1553 to the Present Day* (London, 1925)

Ruding, Rogers, *Annals of the Coinage of Great Britain and Its Dependencies* (London, 1840), vol. I

Ruigh, R. E., *The Parliament of 1624: Politics and Foreign Policy* (Cambridge, Mass., 1971)

Rushforth, G. M., 'A Sketch of the History of Malvern and Its Owners', *Bristol and Gloucestershire Archaeological Society, Transactions*, 42 (1920), 41 – 57

Russell, Conrad, 'Arguments for Religious Unity in England, 1530 – 1650', *Journal of Ecclesiastical History*, 18 (1967), 201 – 26

—— 'Parliamentary History in Perspective, 1604 – 1629', *History*, 61 (1976), 1 – 17

—— *Parliaments and English Politics 1621 – 1629* (Oxford, 1979)

Schwartz, Hillel, 'Arminianism and the English Parliament, 1624 – 1629', *The Journal of British Studies*, 12 (1973), 41 – 68

Scouloudi, Irene, 'Alien Immigration into and Alien Communities in London, 1558 – 1640', unpub. M.Sc. thesis (London, 1936)

Seddon, P. R., 'Robert Carr, Earl of Somerset', *Renaissance and Modern Studies*, 15 (1970), 48 – 68

Sharpe, Kevin, 'The Earl of Arundel, His Circle and the Opposition to the Duke of Buckingham, 1618 – 1628', *Faction and Parliament*, ed. Sharpe, 209 – 44

—— 'Parliamentary History 1603 – 1629: In or Out of Perspective?', *Faction and Parliament*, ed. Sharpe, 1 – 42

—— Sir Robert Cotton 1586 – 1631: History and Politics in Early Modern England (Oxford, 1979)

Sharpe, R. R., London and the Kingdom (London, 1894), 2 vols

Simon, Joan, Education and Society in Tudor England (Cambridge, 1966)

Simpson, A. W. B., 'The Early Constitution of the Inns of Court', Cambridge Law Journal, 28 (1970), 241 – 56

Slater, Miriam, 'The Weightiest Business: Marriage in an Upper-Gentry Family in Seventeenth-Century England', Past and Present, 72 (1976), 25 – 54

Smith, A. G. R., Servant of the Cecils: The Life of Sir Michael Hickes, 1543 – 1612 (London, 1977)

Smith, B. S., A History of Malvern (Leicester, 1964)

Smith, L. P., The Life and Letters of Sir Henry Wotton (Oxford, 1907), vol. II

Smith, T. S., 'The Persecution of Staffordshire Roman Catholic Recusants: 1625 – 1660', Journal of Ecclesiastical Studies, 30 (1979), 327 – 51

Snow, V. F., 'The Arundel Case, 1626', The Historian, 26 (1964), 323 – 49

Somerville, (Sir) Robert, History of the Duchy of Lancaster (privately printed, London, 1970), vol. II

Spedding, James, The Letters and Life of Francis Bacon (Oxford, 1907), vols. IV, VII

Stone, Lawrence, 'The Size and Composition of the Oxford Student Body 1580 – 1909', The University in Society, ed. Stone (Princeton, 1974), vol. I, 3 – 110

—— 'The Educational Revolution in England, 1560 – 1640', Past and Present, 28 (1964), 41 – 80

—— The Family, Sex and Marriage in England 1500 – 1800 (London, 1977)

Supple, B. E., Commercial Crisis and Change in England, 1600 – 1642 (Cambridge, 1959)

Surtees, Robert, The History and Antiquities of the County Palatine of Durham (Durham, 1816), vol. I

Sutherland, L. S., 'The Law Merchant in England in the Seventeenth and Eighteenth Centuries', The Royal Historical Society, Transactions, fourth series, 17 (1934), 149 – 76

Swales, R. J. W., 'The Ship Money Levy of 1628', Institute of Historical Research, Bulletin, 50 (1977), 164 – 76

Swanson, R. A., 'The Office of Attorney-General in England, 1558 – 1641', unpub. Ph.D. dissertation (Univ. of Virginia, 1976)

Thirsk, Joan, 'Enclosing and Engrossing', *The Agrarian History of England and Wales*, IV, ed. Thirsk, 200 – 55
—— 'The Farming Regions of England', *ibid.*, 1 – 112
Thomas, G. W., 'James I, Equity, and Lord Keeper John Williams', *The English Historical Review*, 91 (1976), 506 – 28
Tite, C. G. C., *Impeachment and Parliamentary Judicature in Early Stuart England* (London, 1974)
Toynbee, Margaret, and Peter Young, *Strangers in Oxford: A Side Light on the First Civil War 1642 – 1646* (London, 1973)
Trevor-Roper, H. R., *Archbishop of Laud 1573 – 1645* (London, 1963)
Underdown, David, *Royalist Conspiracy in England 1649 – 1660* (New Haven, 1960)
Wadmore, J. F., *Some Account of the Worshipful Company of Skinners* (London, 1902)
Weston, C. C., 'The Theory of Mixed Monarchy under Charles I and After', *The English Historical Review*, 75 (1960), 426 – 43
White, S. D., *Sir Edward Coke and "The Grievances of the Commonwealth", 1621 – 1628* (Chapel Hill, 1979)
Wiener, C. Z., 'The Beleaguered Isle: A Study of Elizabethan and Early Jacobean Anti-Catholicism', *Past and Present*, 51 (1971), 27 – 62
Willson, D. H., *King James VI and I* (New York, 1956)
—— *The Privy Councillors in the House of Commons 1604 – 1629* (Minneapolis, 1940)
Woods, T. P. S., *Prelude to Civil War 1642: Mr. Justice Malet and the Kentish Petitions* (Wilton, Salisbury, 1980)
Wren, M. C., 'London and the Twenty Ships, 1626 – 27', *The American Historical Review*, 55 (1950), 321 – 35
Zaller, Robert, *The Parliament of 1621: A Study in Constitutional Conflict* (Berkeley, 1971)

Index

65, 65n; marriage, 71; career and offices, 72, 247 – 8, 287, 302; business affairs, 267, 277, 277n; with father in exile, 292, 293; returns to England, 294; attempts to rejoin Sir Robert, reacts to death, 299, 300 – 1

Heath, Lucy, 66 – 71, 67n, 270, 277, 281; death of, 286

Heath, Margaret (wife of Sir Robert), 67, 255, 292, 296, 296n, 301, 302; relationship with husband, 61 – 2; with children, 62, 64, 71, 281; death of, 295

Heath, Margaret (grand-daughter of Sir Robert), 70, 72n, 281

Heath, Mary, 62, 65, 293

Heath, Matthias, 7n

Heath, Nicholas, 4

Heath, Sir Richard, 4n, 5n

Heath, Robert (father of Sir Robert), 5n, 6, 11 – 2, 12n, 41, 61, 61n

Heath, Robert (d. 1615; son of Sir Robert), 73

Heath, Robert (son of Sir Robert), 62, 63, 65n, 72, 72n, 294n, 300

Heath, Sir Robert

chronology: birth and childhood, 6 – 7; education, 7 – 9; married, 61; made an utter barrister, 10; elected recorder of London, 19; knighted, 38, 38n; appointed solicitor-general, 38; attorney-general, 50, 77; chief justice of Common Pleas, 224; dismissed as chief justice of Common Pleas, 1, 231 – 2; returns to private practice, 278, 278n; resumes government service, 280, 280n; appointed king's serjeant, 280 – 1; circumstances in late 1630s, 281; appointed justice of King's Bench, 283; joins Charles at York, 285; appointed chief justice of King's Bench, 285 – 6, 286n; impeached, 290, 291; excepted from pardon, 291, 291n; goes into exile, 291 – 2; failing health, 296; draws will, 300; death of, 300 – 1; burial, 302, 302n

family relationships: family background, 4; relationship with cousins, 5n, 7n, 60; with parents, 6, 11, 12, 61n; with wife, 61 – 2, 71; with children, 62 – 73; gains special treatment, appointments for sons, other relatives, 29, 65, 114 – 15, 117, 281, 286 – 7; relationship with grandchild, 281; with in-laws, 66 – 71; concerns for children, during exile, 293 – 4; impact of wife's death, 295, 296

residences, 255 – 6; Inner Temple, 42, 77, 159, 226. *See also* Brasted, Broadway, Crabbet, Mitcham

offices, government, pattern of promotion, 50n, 86, 224, 224n; Heath's career in and nature of: escheator of Kent and Middlesex, 11 – 12; clerk for enrolling the pleas in the King's Bench, 13, 14, 15 – 16, 16n, 38n, 51, 55, 58, 248; recorder of Guildford, 14, 14n; recorder of London, 2, 19 – 39, 20n, 21n, 24n, 29n, 31n, 50, 137, 248 – 9; solicitor-general, 19, 38, 40, 50, 78, 80, 81, 84, 85 – 6, 108; attorney-general, 19, 50, 77, 78 – 105, 106 – 7, 108, 154 – 87, 224; master of Rolls (reversion), 50 – 1, 54n; justice of the peace, 21, 99 – 100, 207n; chief justice of Common Pleas (and serjeant-at-law), 94, 94n, 224 – 5, 230; queen's solicitor, 242n; king's serjeant, 89, 237, 281; justice of King's Bench, 198, 206, 207, 283; collateral offices, 24, 100n; briefly master of Wards, 283n; chief justice of King's Bench, 285 – 91, 286n

career in parliament: elections to, 140; not returned from Reading, 282; advisor to Lords, 141; service on committees in Commons, 143 – 4; chairs committee of whole, 153, 153n; in debate, 143, 144 – 7; ability as debater, 1, 141n, 145n, 147n; exerts influence, 148, 150; failure to influence, 148 – 50,

attitude toward judges: defines the
ideal judge, 74, 74n; a high
calling, 200; guidance of,
through precedent, 200 – 1;
through common sense, 201 – 2;
through the king, 202 – 3;
defends, 227
political philosophy: proximity of
king to God, 202 – 3; proper
extent of royal power, 202,
208 – 9; trust in king, 209; King
as unifier, 215; defends
reputation of Charles I, 183,
184n; plans to promote crown
income, power, 106 – 7, 118,
280; ship-money, attitude
toward, 237, 237n; concern for
national security, 189 – 90;
bellicosity, 190 – 1; anti-Spanish
attitude, 190 – 3; interest in
empire, 190 – 3, 264 – 5;
assessment of just powers of
parliament, 209 – 15, 214n;
attitude toward Long
Parliament, 283; attitude toward
radical regime, 297; reacts to
execution of Charles I, 297;
advice to Charles II, 298 – 9
part in government factions, 205;
stands against government
rapacity, interference, 206, 206n;
general support for officials, 207
radicals, attitude toward, 43, 43n,
219 – 23; disparages power of,
176, 221; fears potential, 221;
wants them barred from
government, 219 – 20;
cooperates with, 220
social philosophy: emphasis on
national unity, order, 137 – 8,
185, 189; attitude toward poor,
215 – 16, 216n, 217, 218, 218n;
desire for conformity, 218 – 19;
apprenticeship, 218, 218n; State
governs morals, 216 – 17, 216n;
attitudes on tobacco, 217, 217n;
alehouses, 216 – 7, 280
economic philosophy and proposals:
the cloth trade, 111 – 13, 121,
134, 135; coinage, 112, 123 – 8,
133, 134, 135 – 6, 138; banking,
129 – 33, 134, 135 – 6, 138; free
trade, commerce, 137 – 8;

influences on, 135 – 6, 135n;
attitude toward innovation,
138 – 9
aliens, proposals and attitudes
regarding, 114 – 18, 120 – 1, 137,
218 – 19, 219n
religious attitudes: religion a support
in adversity, 73, 295, 296,
300 – 1; belief in witches, 194,
194n; devoutness and prayer,
194 – 5; tithing and charity, 195;
Church as buttress to State,
unity, 196 – 7, 199 – 200; attitude
toward Presbyterianism, Scots,
199n, 298; toward Irish, 298;
toward Catholics, 97 – 8, 197 – 8,
211, 211n; toward radical
Protestants, 198 – 9; toward
Puritanism, 237; supports
Puritan positions, 211n
assessments of, by contemporaries,
74 – 5, 89n, 168; by historians,
141, 141n, 145n, 147n, 206n,
216n; interpretations of the
dismissal, 232 – 3, 232n
Heath, Roger, 4n, 5n
Heath, Thomas, 268 – 9, 269n
Heath families: of Kepier, 4, 5n,
265; of Tamworth, 4, 4n, 268
Henrietta Maria, 28, 242, 242n
Herrick, Robert, 72n
Hestercombe (Kent), 252
Heveningham, Sir John, 166
Heydon, Sir John, 102 – 3, 103n
Hickes, Sir Michael, 11
Higham Ferrers, 213n
High Commission, 89, 240
Hobart, Sir Henry, 28n
Hobart, Sir Miles, 175, 183
Holland (Henry Rich), earl of, 242n
Holland, Sir Thomas, 279n
Holles, Denzil, 141, 175, 177, 182,
183
Holman, Philip, 269, 270 – 1
Howard, Thomas, earl of Arundel,
97, 154 – 5, 243n
Hudson, William, 92 – 3, 93n
Hurst, John, 61
Hutton, Anne, 269 – 70, 271
Hutton, Sir Richard, 69, 74 – 5, 75n
Hyde, Sir Nicholas, 28n, 161, 162,
164, 181 – 2, 185, 186 – 7, 224,
227, 261

London, 2, 5, 114, 130, 137, 137n, 138, 188, 249n, 252, 265, 283, 285; petitions Privy Council, 114n, 120n; nature of government, 19 – 27; relations with Court, 16 – 19, 26 – 36, 38 – 9, 38n, 140n, 221 – 2; opposes aliens commission, 119 – 20, 120n
Long, George, 173, 174
Long, Walter, 175, 181n, 182, 183
Lords, House of, 141, 142, 169, 262; in Arundel and Bristol cases, 154 – 7, 155n; in Long Parliament, 283, 284, 285, 289; abolished, 303

Magna Carta, 162, 163, 202
Malet, Sir Thomas, 284
Maltravers, Henry, Lord, 192, 233 – 4, 238
Malvern Chase, 258, 261, 274 – 5, 277
Malynes, Gerard de, 121, 122, 127, 136, 136n
Manwaring, Roger, 171
Martin, Richard, 16, 19
Mary I, 4
Maurice, Prince, 290
Mennes, Sir Matthew, 268, 269n
Micklethwaite, Dr Paul, 45, 45n, 47
Middle Temple, 43n, 45, 47n, 249n, 252, 254
Middleton, Sir Hugh, 54
Miller, John, 61
Mint, Mint officials, 123 – 4, 125, 127, 131, 135, 136, 136n
Misselden, Edward, 122n
Mitcham (Surrey), 62, 188, 255, 256
Mixed monarchy, 215n
Mogridge, John, 235
Mompesson, Sir Giles, 210
Montagu, Sir Henry, earl of Manchester, 16, 16n, 27 – 8, 28n, 181
Moore, Adam, 235
More, Sir Edward, 252, 253, 254
Morley, Sir John, 65n
Morley, Sir William, 65, 293
Moss, Clement, 35, 37
Moundeford, Sir Edward, 74
Mountague, Richard, bishop of Chichester, 171, 196 – 7, 197n, 199, 241

Mun, Thomas, 121, 122n, 124n, 126
Murray, John, 30 – 1, 34

Naseby, battle of, 291
Neile, Richard, 171
Neroche Forest, 102
Netherlands, Holland, Dutch, 189 – 90, 192, 193, 284
Nethersole, Sir Francis, 175n
Newcastle-upon-Tyne, 265 – 6, 272, 277
Newdigate, John, 96
Nicholas, Sir Edward, 10, 51, 59, 75, 295
Norfolk, 259
Norman Yoke, 201
Northampton (William Compton), earl of, 55
North Inglesby, 257n, 270, 294n
North, Sir John, 49 – 50
North, Roger, 86n, 100
Northumberland (Algernon Percy), duke of, 239
Norwich, 117
Norwich (Edward Denny) earl of, 75
Noy, William, 38n, 204n, 216; in parliament, 213n, 220; five knights' counsel, 162, 164; appointed attorney-general, 100n, 224, 224n; and 'fiscal feudalism', 106, 107, 107n; death of, 106, 224n, 242, 243

Odiham (Hants.), 252
Oglander, Sir John, 56
Onslow, Richard, 142n
Ormonde (James Butler), earl of, 233
Otford (Kent), 195
Ouse, 259
Overbury, Sir Thomas, 15
Oxford, Oxford University, 4, 64n, 243, 286, 286n, 287 – 8, 290, 291, 295

Palmer, Guy, 255n
pardons, 22n, 57, 80 – 1, 81n, 82, 92n, 171, 196 – 7, 197n
Paris, 292
Parker, John, 18
parliament, 1, 2, 130; favours courtiers, 151 – 2; increasing

hostility to Court, courtiers,
145, 147 – 8, 151 – 3, 152n;
privilege, 177, 178, 179,
209 – 15; particular parliaments:
of 1614, 140, 142 – 3; of 1621,
109, 112n, 114, 137 – 8, 148 – 50,
151 – 3, 206, 207, 210 – 11, 212 –
13, 217, 218, 220; of 1624, 112n,
137, 138, 150, 151, 211, 238n; of
1625, 95, 145 – 7, 150 – 1; of 1626,
154 – 9; of 1628 – 9, 98, 165 – 75,
221; Short Parliament, 282; Long
Parliament, 210, 230, 251n, 267,
283 – 5, 289 – 91
patronage system, 11 – 12, 48 – 60,
244 – 6
Pembroke (and Montgomery)
(Philip Herbert), earl of, 117,
119, 222n, 229
Perkins, John, 10
Petition of Right, 1, 165, 169 – 70
Petre, William, Lord, 97
Phelips, Sir Edward, 142n
Phelips, Sir Robert, 171, 172, 242n
Phelips, Thomas, 275 – 6
Plowden, Edmund, 10
Polonius, 63
Popham, Sir John (d. 1607), 142n
Popham, Sir John, 153
Porter, Endymion, 57n
Pory, John, 51, 107n
Powell, David, 295, 299, 300 – 1
precedent, importance of, 128,
138 – 9, 200 – 1. See also
innovation
pretermitted customs, 200, 201 – 2
Privy Council, councillors, 13, 45,
80n, 83, 100, 100n, 113, 114n,
116, 124, 129, 135, 137, 142,
147n, 153n, 159n, 205, 283;
directs government business,
10n, 21, 34, 81 – 2, 99, 108 – 10,
118, 122, 123, 192, 212, 229,
237n, 257n, 265, 266, 267; gives
vague or confusing orders, 80,
110 – 11; overwhelmed by
business, 84 – 5; abolishes aliens
commission, 119, 120, 120n;
slow to act, 109, 133 – 4, 237n,
257n, 265, 266, 267, 283
proclamations, 54, 77 – 8, 80, 81 – 2,
81n, 122, 126, 222; particular,
102, 109n, 112, 124

Protestation of 1621, 149, 210 – 11
Prynne, William, 239, 282
Purbeck (Frances Coke), Lady, 52,
54
Puritans, 42, 196, 199, 211, 237
Pym, John, 148, 159 – 60, 223

rack-renting, 257n
radicals, suspicious of courtiers,
153. See also Heath, Sir Robert,
radicals, attitude toward
Raleigh, Sir Walter, 76, 76n, 92
Read, Thomas, 80
Reading, 282
reafforestation, 107, 107n
Richardson, Sir Thomas, 74n, 94,
94n, 142n, 202, 204n, 224 – 5,
229 – 30, 230n, 243, 243n
Rochdale (Lancs.), 263, 273n
Roper, Sir John, 13, 14, 15, 16, 51
Rosso, Andrea, 157n
Rous, John, 225
Rowlands, William, 275, 275n
Rushworth, John, 232n
Russell, John, 261n

Saint-Germain, 293, 295
St John, Oliver, 183
St Martin Ludgate, 256
Salisbury, 221, 222n, 290
salting, 265 – 6, 266n
Sandwich, 117
Savage, Robert, 88, 88n
Sayers, George, 266, 275
Scotland, Scots, 199n, 281, 298
Selden, John, 43, 43n; in the
Commons, 162, 165 – 6, 167n,
170, 172, 213n; association with
Eliot case, 141, 175, 177 – 8,
177n, 180, 181, 182 – 4, 185, 186,
criticizes judges, 226
Seliard, Robert, 60, 114, 117, 252,
253, 254; Seliard family, 6, 61
Selsey, 241
Selwood Forest, 102
Serjeants' Inn, 226
Seymour, Sir Frances, 174 – 5
Sheffield, William, 233, 238
Sheirs, George, 252, 253, 254, 276
Shelton, Sir Richard, 143, 165 – 6,
165n, 166n, 167n, 243, 243n,
249n
Sherfield, Henry, 239

333

ship-money, 107, 107n, 232, 237, 237n
Shotover, 234 – 5, 234n
Shrewsbury Drapers, 137, 137n
Shute, Robert, 16, 16n, 17, 24n, 38, 38n, 45, 52, 54
Sibthorpe, Robert, 171
Sleyfield (Surrey), 252, 254
Sligo, Donough O'Connor, 83n
Smith, John, 191
Soham (Lincs.), 66, 251, 258, 259 – 60, 261 – 3, 277
solicitor-general, position relative to attorney-general, 85 – 6, 86n; duties in Commons, 142 – 3. *See also* Heath, Sir Robert, offices, government
Somerset, earl of, *see* Carr, Sir Robert
South Shields, 265, 272, 277, 281
Spain, Spaniards, 55, 119, 123, 124, 135, 145, 146, 150, 155n, 190 – 3, 264
Speaker of Commons, 142, 142n, 175, 176, 177
Stacy, Richard, 64
Staffordshire, 4
Star Chamber, 222, 233, 234, 243, 244, 278n; powers of attorney-general in, 86, 87, 88n, 91 – 2, 92n; buttress to crown, 204 – 5; difficulties for crown causes in, 92 – 3, 93n, 180, 187; purview, 204 – 5, 205n; trials in, 35, 37, 38, 141, 160, 179 – 80, 182, 183 – 4, 186, 187, 199, 220, 238 – 40, 240n; abolished, 205, 283
Staunford, Sir William, *Plees del Coron*, 10, 205n
Stockwood, John, 8, 8n, 42
Stow, John, 9
Strode, William, 175, 182 – 3
Surrey, 4
Sutton (Kent), 252
Symms, John, 260 – 1

Tanfield, Sir Lawrence, 29n
tenants, chances in court, 262n; *see also* Heath, Sir Robert: as a businessman, atttitude toward tenants
Three Cranes, 177 – 8, 177n

Titchbourne, Robert, 60, 114, 117, 252, 253, 269; Titchbourne family, 6
Tonbridge, 61; Tonbridge School, 7, 8, 41
Tooker, Robert, 101
torture, 88 – 9, 89n
trade, commission of, 112, 113, 113n, 123; Board of Trade, 113n; Committee of Trade, 265
tunnage and poundage, 169
Turpin, Robert, 290 – 1
Tussell, John, 250
Tuxwell, Thomas, 299, 300

Valentine, Benjamin, 175, 176, 177, 179, 182, 183
Vandeputt, Giles, 269
Vermuyden, Sir Cornelius, 219n, 235 – 6, 236n, 255, 255n, 258 – 9, 266 – 8, 273, 273n, 274
Vernon, Sir George, 229
Vicars, John, 74
Villiers, George, duke of Buckingham, 27n, 75, 82, 123, 124, 152n, 245, 295; as a patron, 45, 49 – 59, 52n, 54n, 56n; association with King's Bench office, 15 – 16, 16n; with aliens commission, 117, 119, 135n; puts forward candidates for offices, 17, 18, 38n, 50n, 52, 53; pursues vendettas, 35n, 52; attacked in parliament, 154 – 60, 155n, 157n, 159n; assassination of, 57 – 8, 59, 87, 222, 230n
Virginia, Virginia Company, 191, 217n
'Virtuoso', 189, 189n

Wallis, John, 93
Walter, John, 18, 228, 228n
Waltham Forest, 107
Ward, Sir Edward, 78n, 79n
Wards and Liveries, court of, 204n, 287, 287n
Warr, Thomas, 252, 253, 254
Watson, Sir Thomas, 51, 252, 253, 254
Weldon, Sir Anthony, 54, 56n
Welsh cloth, 109n, 137, 137n
Wentworth, Sir Thomas, 165, 228, 229, 230 – 1, 242, 243n, 245 – 6

334

Westbourne (Sussex), 287, 287n
West Grinsted (Sussex), 286, 287n
West Indies, 190 – 1, 192 – 3;
  projected West India Company,
  192 – 3
Weston, Sir Richard, 56, 56n,
  172 – 3, 228, 241, 242, 242n, 243,
  244, 244n, 245, 245n
Whitaker, William, 42
Whitelocke, Bulstrode, 74, 178n
Whitelocke, Sir James, 12, 13, 15,
  15n, 16n, 17, 18, 28n, 167, 178n,
  215n
Wigmore, Richard, 79
Williams, John, 233, 238, 238n, 239

Wilson, Sir Thomas, 44, 250
Wisbech (Cambs.), 258
witches, 194, 194n
Wood, Anthony, 234
wool brokers, 137 – 8, 218
Worcester (John Thornborough),
  bishop of, 269n
Worth (Sussex), 188
Wotton, Sir Henry, 50
Wright, Nathaniel, 269, 271n

Yelverton, Sir Henry, 17, 26, 30,
  30n, 31, 31n, 34 – 5, 35n, 36 – 7,
  86, 97n, 142 – 3, 224n, 278
York, 285